The History of Canadian Business 1867-1914

Volume Two

The History of Canadian Business 1867-1914

Volume Two
Industrial Development

R. T. Naylor

James Lorimer & Company, Publishers
Toronto 1975

0-88862-093-4 paper
0-88862-095-0 cloth

Cover design: Robert MacDonald
Design: Lynn Campbell

James Lorimer & Company, Publishers
Egerton Ryerson Memorial Building
35 Britain Street
Toronto

Printed and bound in Canada

Published with the assistance of the Social Science Research Council, using funds provided by the Canada Council.

Canadian Shared Cataloguing in Publication Data

Naylor, R. T.
 The history of Canadian business, 1867-1914.

 2 v.

Bibliography:
Contents: v.1. The banks and financial capital. —
v.2. Industrial development.
ISBN 0-88862-094-2 (v.1) ISBN 0-88862-092-6 (v.1) pbk.
ISBN 0-88862-095-0 (v.2) ISBN 0-88862-093-4 (v.2) pbk.

1. Canada - Commerce - History. 2. Canada - Industries
- History. 3. Canada - Economic conditions. I. Title.

HF5349.C2N39 1975   380'.0971   69541

CONTENTS

The Canadian Pacific Company should be taken over by the Canadian Government, and when that happy time arrives there will be an end to undue competition, and the Grand Trunk proprietors will be glad to help the Government in any way they can in making as little loss as possible in working the Canadian Pacific Railway.

Sir Henry Tyler, 1885

CHAPTER IX
Staple Production and the Canadian Railway System

Western Expansion, 1870-1896

Immediately after Colonel Garnet Wolsely had made Manitoba safe for democracy, civilization, and Donald A. Smith, there came a second army of invasion, composed of land speculators and dealers in Métis scrip. Land grants of 160 acres each were distributed to the troops with the option of selling it, and the land speculators secured the bulk of these lands as well. The effect was that even by 1870 bona fide settlers were being pushed away from the Winnipeg area to more inaccessible areas.[1]

The transfer of Rupert's Land to the Dominion from the Hudson's Bay Company was followed by the Manitoba Act, which marked a watershed point in Canadian political development. Under the terms of the Act, all public lands and natural resources were annexed to the federal government for distribution as railroad subsidies or political patronage. From that event the Macdonald coalition that had created Confederation out of land-hungry Liberals and capital-seeking Tories, already weakened by defections, began to crumble. The Liberal wing of the coalition was increasingly alienated from the policies of land monopolization and favouritism towards Montreal commerce. In 1869, Macdonald was desperate enough in his efforts to maintain some semblance of a coalition that Francis Hincks was brought into the Cabinet as nominal head of the Ontario Liberal wing. By the time of the 1872 election, Hincks was so closely identified with the Tory camp that his presence was a liability, helping to produce the serious losses of the Macdonald government in Ontario and Quebec. The Pacific Scandal and the subsequent

Liberal administration under Alexander Mackenzie restored the traditional party structure — commercial Toryism versus agrarian Liberalism. It was the need for a new class coalition to revive the Tory cause, a coalition based on an amalgam of Montreal commercial capital with a rising Ontario protectionist industrial capital, that led directly to the National Policy and the restoration of the railroad magnates to power, hence determining the pattern of western development to be followed.

During the decade that followed the crushing of the first Riel rebellion, growth of Manitoba and the Northwest was slow. The Homestead Act of 1872, while containing provision for free grants of up to 160 acres, did not include any pre-emption provisions, placing the potential settler, who could not make such a small farm commercially viable, at the mercy of whichever land or railway company owned the adjoining sections. Land speculators, and the high prices demanded for lands near to transportation facilities, drove many potential settlers to the U.S.[2] The largest of the private landlords was the Hudson's Bay Company, which had been left in control of the areas around the fur trading posts plus one-twentieth of the total land to be chosen from the fertile areas. The contentious problem of the claims of the wintering partner to a share of the proceeds of the transfer and of the land had been settled. Donald Smith had gone to London to fight for their cause, had secured a payment for their share of the fur trade, had done nothing for their much more important claim to a part of the lands, and had been made land commissioner of the HBC in 1874 by a grateful London council.

By 1880, conditions were ripe for another effort to settle the West with white farmers. Enormous blocks of land were ceded to the CPR, and other smaller lines promoted by eminent Tories, most of which were eventually absorbed into the CPR, received land grants as well. One of the largest of these was the Alberta Railway and Coal Company headed by Sir Alexander Galt with a group of British capitalists, a resource road built to tap the coal lands Galt was given by his confrères in the federal Parliament. In the final analysis, ten western "colonization" railways received land grants, generally from a different province (or part of the North West Territory before 1905) from that through which the roads' mileage ran. Manitoba, fortunate in having been bequeathed responsible government by Louis Riel, got 1,287 miles of railroads for three-and-one-half million acres; Alberta 805 miles for thirteen million acres; Saskatchewan 885 miles for over fifteen million acres. All ten of the railways selected Saskatchewan lands, while only three had mileage there. And of the three an enormous percentage of their grants were in

Saskatchewan, 99%, 89%, and 72%, while their respective Saskatchewan mileages were but 43%, 19%, and 22% of the total.
Land companies, too, began early. In 1880 John Schultz (one of
the instigators of the Riel rebellion and one of Winnipeg's
leading speculators — subsequently rewarded with a knighthood
and the Lieutenant Governorship of the province) formed a land
speculating company called the British and North West
Colonization Co.[3] In 1881 Sir John A. Macdonald announced
that government land, apart from the Homestead areas, would
be sold, not given away,[4] the reverse of his policy in 1873 just
before his defeat. Macdonald had learned from experience that if
he had to choose between the support of Ontario farmers and the
support of Donald Smith, Smith was the better political proposition.

The result of the new policy was to open the way for an enormous wave of speculation. The land boom began to develop
around Portage la Prairie following Tupper's announcement that
a colonization road would pass through the town,[5] and it spread
to Winnipeg and further to the west. With it came renewed pressure to force the Indians into reserves, and expropriate the
existing Métis holdings. New land companies were formed, the
largest of which was the British North West Land Company
established by the CPR syndicate. It received from its parent a
five million acre concession along with half interest in each
townsite west of Brandon to the eastern border of B.C. along the
main line.[6] Another company, the British Canadian Colonization
Co., floated with an authorized capital of one million dollars; the
Honourable Alexander Mackenzie, its president, with George
Cox and Robert Jaffray on its board, acquired 100,000 acres in
Qu'Appelle.[7] Most of the so-called colonization companies
wound up in a few years, relieved of their responsibilities by the
federal government, the sole beneficiaries of their activities being
the company directors.

The peak of the land boom coincided with the 1882 election
campaign, in which the National Policy, the CPR contract, and
the alienation of the West were all dangerously under siege in
Ontario. Part of the problem was alleviated by the Great Gerrymander of 1882, whereby one-sixth of Ontario was effectively
deprived of representation. Under the pretense of adding four
more seats to Ontario's representation, the borders of 54 constituencies were changed so that although the Liberal Party had
almost exactly divided the vote in 1882 and 1887, and had a
majority in 1891, it had a sizeable minority of seats each year.[8] In
addition, in the Northwest by the end of 1882, some 2,295 townships had been applied for by leading Tories, most subsequently

granted, and the effect on the elections was quite pronounced.

While such tactics sufficed for the federal level of politics, the tendency for the opposition to become entrenched in the provincial houses proved a distinct problem for the Tory machine. Ontario in particular remained stubbornly Liberal. In 1885, in a desperate attempt to break Oliver Mowat's administration, the Conservatives under William Meredith and with the collaboration of the federal party undertook to bribe certain members of the Liberal ranks with offers of cash or government office to cross the floor. Unfortunately for the architects of the scheme, one recipient took the cash, presented it to the Speaker of the Assembly, and unveiled the entire conspiracy.[9]

The West, including the disputed territory in northwestern Ontario, was a huge patronage-generating machine. After the disputed territory was allocated to Ontario, Macdonald decreed that not a stick of timber would accrue to the province, and the area was parcelled out to Conservative favourites. In the disputed territory of 115 timber limit applications, 110 were Tories, five Liberal; all were granted permission to cut in the area. In addition, vast areas of land were given out.

In the West, the traffic in land was lucrative. One Tory M.P. got an area for $250 that he sold immediately for $100,000. Another received $650,000 for a parcel that cost $7,500. Grazing lands were another eagerly sought prize. By early 1886 some two-and-one-half million acres were leased to party favourites at one cent an acre, yielding $66,255.50 to the federal government in revenue. Coal was another prize, most of the coal lands being ceded to A. T. Galt to supplement the townships he had already received.[10]

The completion of the CPR to the Pacific coincided with a second outbreak by the Métis under Louis Riel. The Métis, pushed even further west by the eastern land grabbers, and having lost their traditional livelihood by the disappearance of the fur trade, the buffalo hunt, and their monopoly of prairie transportation by virtue of the rise of the railways, rose in rebellion. They were accompanied by several Indian nations left starving on arid reservations as Ottawa, in the face of the collapse of revenues from the tariff in the 1884-5 recession, cut back allocations to minor priorities like the fulfilment of its treaty obligations in favour of maintaining the flow of public money to the CPR. As a result of the hanging of the Métis leader, the Métis assumed a role in Canadian history that few contemporary Métis would have conceived possible. The Métis regarded themselves as a "new nation," a nationality totally distinct from British North Americans of either anglophone or francophone nationalities. Yet the Métis were pushed firmly into Canadian historical folklore as representative of the treason of the anglophone towards the francophone. Two political forces were responsible for this transmogrification. In Quebec, Honoré Mercier came to power in 1886 on a program of hysterical nationalism so designed as to give him the political leverage to extract a larger share of the public purse from Ottawa to give away to his friends, who were busy promoting local railways, especially for colonization within Quebec. In Ontario the Clear-Grit-Liberal administration used the crisis to whip up an equal xenophobia in an attempt to strengthen the province by embarrassing Ottawa and therefore acquire more freedom from the actions of the Montreal commercial capitalists who controlled the Macdonald administration.

Others too got their share of the spoils of the West. After the actions of speculators and the government had goaded the Indians and Métis into rebellion, the volunteers in the expeditionary force got 320 acres each plus $80 in scrip which could be applied to the purchase of Dominion land or the rent of grazing land, with the option of transferring the rights to someone else. Americans, too, registered an interest and in 1884 a plan was hatched by S.J. Ritchie, Senator Payne (an iron and nickel promoter who was linked to Standard Oil), and Erastus Wiman to try to secure part of the Northwest for the U.S. Wiman, however, revealed the plan to Macdonald.[11]

This was not Wiman's only foray into the Canadian Northwest. He had begun his career as the Canadian agent of the American mercantile agency, Dun, Barlow and Co., and on Charles Barlow's death joined the U.S. firm which thus became Dun, Wiman and Co. By 1880 he had begun a series of promotions of railways and land in Staten Island,[12] and in 1886, in conjunction with these, he penned the following request to John A. Macdonald after the suppression of the second Riel rebellion and the seizure of the Indian and Métis leaders.

Would you like to get rid of Poundmaker, the Indian who, I understand, is a prisoner?. . . Sitting Bull, when he was a prisoner of the United States Government was rendered innoxious by being taken out by "Buffalo Bill" as a curiosity and exhibited through the country in his great show "The Wild West." This show intends to exhibit on Staten Island during the summer months. I have a very large interest, as you perhaps know in the traffic between Staten Island and New York and this is one of the attractions we are going to use. Buffalo Bill (who is a member of the Nebraska Legislature) and Mr. Saulsbury are the owners of the show, and are anxious to get hold of Poundmaker.[13]

Getting control of western land was a relatively easy matter, but selling it was much more difficult. Both the CPR and the Bay initially tried to market land in large amounts during the early years of the new rush of settlement. The CPR worked through Sir A.T. Galt, at that time Canadian High Commissioner in London, to propagate news of its holdings among prospective immigrants, and Sir John Rose, George Stephen, and the Canadian Department of Agriculture helped the promotional campaign. The Department of Agriculture took the liberty of adding twelve degrees to the data on the June mean temperature in the Northwest, and 24.5 degrees to the February temperature. Professor John Macoun, the Dominion Field Naturalist and Botanist, published a book containing this and similar misleading information, and the CPR used Macoun's figures in its advertisements to try to sell its stock and its lands. Numerous deaths through freezing occurred among new arrivals who had no idea of the real climatic conditions,[14] and Henry Hind's denunciation of the fraud went unheeded.

TABLE IX (1)

Homestead Entries

Year	Entries	Cancellations
1875	499	303
1876	845	153
1877	845	457
1878	1,788	1,377
1879	4,068	2,045
1880	2,074	679
1881	2,753	937
1882	7,483	3,845
1883	6,063	1,818
1884	3,753	1,330
1885	1,858	597

Source: *CYB*, 1926, p. 923.

Lands sold freely until 1883; then the collapse came. With the end of the boom, over 60% of the lands sold by the Hudson's Bay Company largely to speculators, went into default.[15] The London governors, with a body of stockholders greedy for dividends to placate, were forced to try to continue to sell lands and fed the downward spiral in land values, until near the end of 1883 when Donald Smith seized control of the company and effected a virtual merger of its policy with that of the CPR.[16] Thereafter, the HBC withheld from selling land until conditions improved. The CPR, too, adopted the strategy of not selling until all government free lands had been ceded, after which a higher price could be obtained.[17] In 1880, Sir Richard Cartwright had predicted that alienation of much of the land into the hands of a few big companies would seriously impede settlement,[18] and this turned out to be an accurate forecast. Under Laurier, the land grant system was virtually abolished, partly through shortage of land left for giveaway, partly because of the blockages to settlement that had resulted from the earlier policy.[19]

Manitoba as early as 1878 had begun to fight the absentee land ownership system imposed upon it. That year, it levied a school tax of one cent an acre on resident-owned lands and five cents on non-resident, but this tax was invalidated in court.[20] In 1884, a tax was imposed on unpatented lands, denounced as unconstitutional, and abandoned.[21] With the ending of the boom, Manitoba moved to protect bona fide settlers against the speculators by exempting from seizure any real estate under occupation up to the value of $2,500 and furniture worth up to $500, and abolished other techniques used to uproot settlers.[22] The result was a howl of outrage from the creditor class in Canada, from the wholesaler dealers and banks in particular. These were all branches of eastern, especially Montreal institutions, and with their allies in the financial press they began a campaign for disallowance.[23] However, the Act stood. Some conciliation may have been provided eastern interests by the fact that, at George Stephen's request, the law was repealed which had prohibited settlers on government land from having mortgages in excess of $500, or at an interest rate greater than six per cent.[24]

While the flow of European immigration continued to move unabated to the U.S., efforts to stop the outflow of population from Quebec to New England proved equally in vain. Industrial underdevelopment and the resulting chronic unemployment were the problem, while the solutions proposed went little beyond efforts to force a return to the land. Such was the rationale behind the spate of colonization railroad projects undertaken by the province at the request of the Church.[25] In 1884, to supplement the provincial colonization road project — then in difficulty because of Mercier's inability to find more funds — Father Antoine Labelle (known as "the Apostle of Colonization" to his followers — namely the big railway magnates like Hugh Allan) organized a lottery to raise $100,000 for such a project, but it was disallowed by the Quebec upper house.[26]

A return to the land project was self-defeating in any event, for much of the exodus from Quebec was attributable to the mortgage companies who drove many off the farms. Land hoarding, together with the Church's encouragement of population growth, led to the subdivision of farms beyond the limits of subsistence, and rapid soil exhaustion resulted. While the bulk of the emigrants went into factory work some took up abandoned farms in New England,[27] or free land in the American West.[28] In addition to the permanent labouring or agricultural émigrés, a very large temporary group migrated to the brick works or hired on as seasonal agricultural labour during harvest seasons to try to pay off mortgages on their farms. By 1891, it was estimated that there were a total of 400,000 Québécois employed as wage workers in the eastern U.S., especially in the cotton and shoe factories.[29]

A large exodus from the Maritimes and Ontario occurred as well. By 1890, the bulk of the mining, lumbering, and farming population of Michigan was reckoned to be émigré Canadian.[30] The safety-valve of emigration to the U.S., which helped keep the lid on discontent with the government in Canada, met with considerable opposition in the U.S. In 1889 Calais, Maine, began enforcing the Alien Labor Laws to keep Canadian workmen out, and some unemployment in border New Brunswick areas resulted.[31] The complaints of Canadian workers being used in violation of these laws became more general during the critical 1889-1890 period.[32] In 1893, too, there was an instance, probably one of many, of the use of unemployed Canadian workers as strikebreakers in U.S. lumber yards, which led to the strikebreakers being driven off the work yard physically.[33] During industrial recessions in the U.S. the émigrés tended to return home.[34]

With the National Policy in ruins, the tariff failing to generate sufficient employment, the West empty, Ontario in revolt, and discontent rife in Manitoba and Nova Scotia, the Old Chieftain rose to the occasion. A time of grave national crisis required strong, imaginative leadership. The Macdonald government responded by falsifying the 1890-1 census returns, bribing the statistician to exaggerate the number of factories and hands employed.[35] In one riding, the census takers were given instructions to include in the list of factories all blacksmiths, shoemakers, and artisans engaged in handicraft production. In another, 72 new industries were reported as having begun since 1881 — in fact not a single one existed.[36] To increase the apparent population, the names of people who had moved to the U.S. were carefully reported as still present in Canada.[37] The Macdonald government was saved that year only by the gerrymander and by working the loyalty cry to a maximum, a strategy which included rewarding Erastus Wiman for his information regarding S.J. Ritchie's northwest ambitions by campaigning on the issue that a Wiman-Cartwright plot for annexation existed.[38]

The "Laurier Boom"

While homestead entries troughed in 1896 along with wheat prices and thereafter began to trend upward, it was not until 1902-1903 that a major burst of settlement occurred, with wheat output tending to lag settlement by about three years, the average gestation period of wheat.[39] With it came the return of the land companies. The CPR's reorganized Canada North West Land Company directed by Van Horne, R.B. Angus, Thomas Shaughnessy, E.B. Osler, with the grain dealer W.D. Matthews and the miller Robert Meighen new additions,[40] was the largest of the companies. But there were several others of note. The Minneapolis, Duluth and Western Canada was a joint venture of American and Canadian capital which purchased 1,100,000 acres in Saskatchewan to settle families from the American northwest states.[41] Another was the Saskatchewan Valley Land Co., organized by a syndicate of Toronto financiers including Edmund Walker and well represented in Parliament in the Liberal Party ranks. Under Sir Clifford Sifton's tenure in the Ministry of the Interior some 250,000 acres of choice lands were sold to the company at $1.00 per acre, lands which were easily worth $8.00.[42]

By about 1905, European capital was anxious to join the great prairie land barbeque. French, Belgian, German, and Dutch money flowed in, either in the form of mortgage companies whose shareholders as well as debenture holders were European or in the form of land companies directly owning large tracts of farm and urban land. Their activities centred in Winnipeg, in which submetropolis their Canadian head offices were usually located, managing their domains throughout the prairies and B.C. Winnipeg boasted as well the headquarters of the Hudson's Bay Company and a horde of independent land brokers and speculators.[43]

Both the HBC and the CPR began marketing land again. The alternate-blocks method of land grant proved a boon to the companies, for the improvements put into his block by the settler automatically raised the value of the railway block adjacent.[44] The HBC similarly adopted the policy of selling only parts of its holdings in a section, and waiting for the settlers' efforts to raise the value of the residual.[45] Under the CPR's system of sales, no more than two sections totalling 1,280 acres could be sold to one

individual. One-twentieth was to be paid in cash, the rest in
nineteen annual instalments at six per cent, and the entire debt
could not be settled in less than five years.[46] The CP lands rose
rapidly in price after 1902. That year they averaged $3.26 an
acre, by 1908 $9.54, and by 1911 $14.69. Canadian Northern's
lands, small by comparison with the CPR's, sold for somewhat
less because it had acquired inferior land by its takeovers of local
roads with provincial land grants. In 1908, its lands averaged
$8.32, and by 1911 $12.00.[47] The HBC's lands sold for a little
more than railroad tracts. At just the moment when the price of
lands began to trend sharply upward, the federal government
again obliged the railways and land companies by cancelling in
1905 the pre-emption rights that had been introduced into the
Homestead regulations in 1890.

TABLE IX (2)

Railway and Hudson's Bay Company Land Sales

Year	Acres Sold	Average Price Per Acre
1893	120,211	$2.93
1894	68,668	3.02
1895	114,713	1.94
1896	108,016	3.34
1897	222,225	3.23
1898	448,623	3.18
1899	462,494	3.28
1900	648,379	3.27
1901	621,027	3.36
1902	2,201,795	3.56
1903	4,229,011	3.46
1904	1,267,187	4.39
1905	990,005	5.09
1906	1,642,684	6.01
1907	1,237,759	6.02
1908	346,693	8.00
1909	109,373	11.08
1910	1,184,790	13.36
1911	1,406,651	13.59
1912	1,329,390	13.70
1913	707,149	13.95

The numerous little land companies naturally had more difficulty marketing their lands than the CPR and the HBC, who
had had first choice of the best. They had to resort to tricks like
blanketing adjoining homesteads by fictitious entries, enabling

them to hold these free lands vacant until there was a prospect of selling their own land. Then the settlers would be sold their quarter-section on the promise that the company would then cancel its claim to the adjoining quarter in favour of the settler.[48]

To find a settler population for the land, an inflow was encouraged from the Maritimes and rural Ontario, which had undergone relative declines in population; a great influx of European immigrants was encouraged as well, many of them nominally via the agency of the North Atlantic Trading Company. Prior to its formation, individual booking agents were paid bonuses for the immigrants they diverted to Canada.[49] But in 1899 W. T. R. Preston, the Immigration Commissioner, and Donald Smith, the High Commissioner, organized the booking agents in London into a combine incorporated in Amsterdam, since the Netherlands was the only European country where there were no laws prohibiting the solicitation of emigration to other countries. (These laws proved rather sticky on occasion: at one point Lord Strathcona was persona non grata in Imperial Germany, with a warrant out for his arrest for flagrantly violating them.)[50]

Under the terms of the arrangement between the Interior Department and the North Atlantic Trading Company, the company had to do nothing at all to earn its bonus of $5.00 per head of family, $2.00 for all other members. Its bonus was paid not according to numbers of emigrants sent, but according to those arriving at certain ports of entry from certain countries. By 1906 the unearned payments reached $300,000, payments which were sent to Strathcona for administration.[51] Although the immigrants selected were supposed to be agricultural only, in fact Preston's habit of encouraging an influx of skilled and unskilled labour led to the unions calling for his dismissal.[52]

And once again western land was used as a cheap sort of pension fund for soldiers. For the veterans of the South African War a scrip system for up to 320 acres was established in 1908. Predictably, speculators were among the chief beneficiaries, with scrip sold to them by the veterans at $200-$500 — rising to $1,200 in 1910 immediately after the Ministry of the Interior granted an extension to the time limit for selection. As the new limit approached, the scrip fell in value, and by the beginning of 1912 "unlocated scrip was just as worthless as Confederate notes." However, the location time was extended again, and the scrip shot up in value.[53]

The Agricultural Frontier

The western wheat farmer was the foundation of the "national policy." Piled on top of him were the exactions of the railroads, elevator companies, tariff-coddled manufacturers, and the banks and mortgage loan companies. All of these concerns contributed to the creation and maintenance of a single cash-crop frontier in the West. The five-year mortgage schemes which almost always had to be renewed, the banks' three-month notes, reliance on advances from implement dealers, and debts to grain moving firms locked the economy into the staple trap. Farmers' problems with the implement dealers had a long history. In the 1870's and 1880's, when Ontario was the centre of the wheat staple, independent or quasi-independent dealers would roam the countryside conning farmers into the purchase of useless machinery or swindling them on promissory notes, or both.[54]

In the West, before the National Policy, the implement business was largely in the hands of American firms operating through dealers in St. Paul and other border cities. But after the tariff, Ontario manufacturers, led by the Harris firm, began to set up distributing agencies there. By late 1882, John Watson had a distribution branch in Winnipeg, the largest in the city, and his agents were active all over Manitoba.[55] That year, too, exports of implements from the Gurney foundry reached B.C.[56] While one of the Macdonald government's multitude of select committees with a keen eye for political advantage and a blind one for the truth where the two conflicted, claimed that the effect of the tariff was to give Canadian firms virtually the whole of the northwest trade,[57] in fact American dealerships established in Winnipeg had little difficulty maintaining the American hold. In 1883, the agricultural implements tariff was raised again to try to force the American firms to establish manufacturing branch plants in Canada.[58] No branch plants followed the tariff, except one short-lived venture, and for some time the American hold in the West was strong.[59] But gradually, with the considerable aid of American patents, the Canadian firms won the West.

With their victory the problems of the wheat farmer multiplied. Under the system of competition among implement firms, retail prices were maintained and competition took the form of a proliferation of dealers extending credit facilities. The farmer purchased implements from the dealers on time, paying from seven to ten per cent on the notes before they fell due, and ten to twelve after, during the period of the wheat boom. And, in fact, if a sale was made on time, prices were raised five to ten per cent above cash prices even before the interest was added on. Credit that cost the implement firms six per cent to obtain in central Canada was thus extended to western farmers at a minimum of twelve. Moreover, notes were generally scheduled to fall due in November, forcing farmers to throw their produce on the market as soon as threshed to meet the note.[60] And these exactions occurred over and above the fact that spot cash prices in Canada were higher not only than American but even than the foreign export prices of Canadian-made agricultural machinery. In 1895, after a cut in the tariff, prices in neighbouring Canadian and American farm communities were about equal. But by 1907, after mergers in the industry and after the tariff revision, a spread of about fifteen per cent between the higher Canadian and the American prices was recorded.[61] At the same time, the export prices of Canadian-made implements were as much as 20% below domestic, despite the fact that both domestic and export sales received the same rebates on duty paid on imported inputs. The effect was equivalent to a subsidy to the Argentinian or Australian wheat farmer to assist him in competition with the Canadian wheat farmer on world markets.[62]

In addition, the old problems of phony advertising and derelict merchandise remained acute. In 1913, Alberta had to pass special legislation to protect farmers from the dealers. Under the terms of the Farm Machinery Act, any contract that a judge deemed "unreasonable" was not binding. And the vendor had to stand behind all representations of his agents during negotiations for sale and to guarantee the quality of first-hand machinery.[63] The passage of the law led to the predictable cries of protest from the implement dealers and the financial press.

With the shift in the locus of wheat farming to the West had come an initial restructuring of eastern agriculture towards mixed and dairy farming. Even in 1890, well before the main surge of western wheat production, a bishop in Quebec put the tithe on hay as well as grain because of the switch from grain to pasturage.[64] After 1896 came the disruption and stagnation of Ontario mixed farming, and a drain of population out of the rural areas. Part of the loss of population was to the new wheat areas of the West, part of it went to feed the demand of the new industrial growth of Ontario for labour. Farm labour became increasingly difficult to obtain in the face of the lure of higher wages in the cities or of independent farms in the West.[65] Large areas of Ontario's farmland in Bruce, Huron, Kent, Grey, Lambton, and Middlesex counties ceased producing food.[66]

As mixed farming stagnated while industrialism grew, the need for imports of food increased substantially. For the West itself was a net importer of food of all sorts. Even flour for consumption was imported into the prairies,[67] because of the peculiarities of the commercial patterns that evolved under the auspices of the National Policy. At the same time that food costs in Canada, including flour prices, were escalating rapidly, Canadian wheat flour was selling in England considerably cheaper than in Canada despite the enormous difference in physical distance to market. Frank and Robert Meighen's Lake of the Woods Milling Company reported the following price structure in 1913. The difference in price was imputed to the fact that the costs of distribution in Canada exceeded the cost of transportation to the U.K. By 1900, Ontario grain was cheaper to produce than American, but Ontario grain ceased to be marketable abroad because of the discrimination of the railroad companies in favour of American, and subsequently western Canadian grain.[68]

TABLE IX (3)

Domestic and British Prices of Canadian Flour, 1913

Grade	Domestic Price	English Price
First Patent	$5.50	$ —
Second Patent	5.00	4.10
Mixed	4.80	4.00
First Class	4.95	3.70
Second Class	3.30	3.27

Source: *CLR I*, pp. 756 - 7.

The Grain Trade

The grain trade of the western provinces made its first hesitant step in 1876, when a shipment of 807 bushels was sold for export at 85c per bushel.[69] The same year, T. E. Kenny's wholesale export and import firm in Halifax made its first export shipment of grain,[70] the origin of which was probably local.

Progress was slow. Winnipeg's rail connections to the outside world were not completed until the St. Paul, Minneapolis, and Manitoba Railway reached the city in 1878. In 1880, A. W. Ogilvie and Co. began selling wheat from Manitoba to Minnesota for milling[71] and the following year it opened a mill in Winnipeg.[72] The Ogilvie mill was somewhat of an exception; most mills in fact located in central Canada, with the prairies functioning as a raw material hinterland. There were also efforts in Halifax from as early as 1883 to get a share of the grain trade,

when Halifax merchants established a flour mill there to compete with western mills and to try to develop a grain export trade
with Newfoundland and the West Indies.[73] A grain elevator was
built too on the Intercolonial, was destroyed by fire and replaced
at great expense, and then remained idle until 1903 when Manitoba grain began to flow through Halifax for the first time.[74]

The movement of grain was tightly cartelized, if not in the
hands of outright monopolies. In 1884, the CPR magnates
formed a wheat syndicate to move grain to the Lakehead and
hold it for export. Grading of wheat at Port Arthur was conducted by a company official, and from the start complaints over
the grading from farmers were heard.[75] And that year the Manitoba and North West Farmers' Union began calling for a
number of reforms: the right of the province to charter railways
and control natural resources, building of the Hudson's Bay
Railway, repeal of the tariff on agricultural implements, and
amendment of the provincial municipal act to permit municipalities to build elevators, grain warehouses, and mills and to issue
debentures to defray their cost.[76] During the second Riel rebellion Ottawa had fears of white settlers joining the Métis and
Indians.[77]

Until the second round of transcontinentals, the CPR had a
monopoly of movement of grain, and while it built an elevator in
Fort William in 1888,[78] this was not competition for the Ogilvie
Company, for the CPR and Ogilvie's worked hand in glove. A.
W. Ogilvie too had joined George Stephen and the Gaults of
Montreal in promoting the Sun Life Assurance Company in
1885.[79] And when Ogilvie's was reorganized in 1902, the Bank of
Montreal underwrote a bond issue for the new syndicate, both
the Bank of Montreal and the Royal Bank underwrote a prefer-
ence issue,[80] while Sir Edward Clouston of the Bank of Montreal,
Sir Hugh Allan of the Merchants, and Sir Herbert Holt of the
Royal all sat on the new firm's board of directors.

The CPR enforced monopoly in provision of elevators by
refusing to deal with any but elevators built to CPR standards,
and would not allow the loading of grain from flat warehouses
or direct from farmers' vehicles. The result was to drive out of
business many of the smaller grain buyers. Moreover, the monopoly given particular elevators in certain localities made it easy
to cheat farmers in grades, weight and prices.[81] Many of the elevators continued to be under the control of eastern milling companies; Ogilvie, for example, as early as 1894 had a system of 42
elevators across the prairies and into Ontario. Its largest milling
operations were concentrated in southern Ontario and Montreal.[82]

While the ushering-in of the new prosperity after 1896 saw the creation of a great deal of new elevator capacity and new firms organized, farmers by 1898 were already complaining of being fleeced by a combine of grain buyers in control of storage facilities.[83] Almost, it seems, to prove the point, within a few months of the farmers' complaints an effort was launched to merge all the leading elevator systems. Though the merger was not effected, a cartel of the elevator companies was formed and operated openly.[84] A few minor companies existed in the grain movement business. Erastus Wiman with the American flour milling industrialist C. A. Pillsbury established a system of canal and lake shipping to move flour.[85] But until the entry of the new railroads competition was negligible. And after their arrival it was restricted to the prolifcration of "plant," not rate reductions. Periods of chronic car shortage, real or contrived, still emerged during crop moving season, and railway employees used to demand bribes from farmers to ensure priority to their harvest.[86]

The same considerations were true with the grain buyers. Attempts to organize grain dealing in Winnipeg began in 1883, though not until 1887 was the Winnipeg Grain and Produce Exchange opened, and incorporation was not secured until 1891.[87] Initially, seats sold for only fifteen dollars, but with the advent of the wheat boom prices shot up until the last seat was occupied in 1906 for $4,000.[88] Commissions were fixed at one cent a bushel on all grains, and cartelization was enforced by a system of fines, or by the expulsion of members not conforming to the fixed price system. Any effort by buyers to try to deal independently was checked by the organized dealers' bringing their collective power to control prices to bear, and wrecking the independents. The exchange embraced most of the elevator owners and grain buyers of the West, and the rest could generally be expected to conform to the rules.[89]

Until 1901 there was no futures market in Winnipeg. All hedges were made through Chicago. Then a movement headed by Sir Rodmond Roblin to establish a futures system and a clearing house for options resulted in its organization.[90] Rather predictably, the establishment of the futures market was followed almost immediately by a campaign against the "bucket shops" at the request of the exchange. The Premier of the province — Sir Rodmond Roblin — ordered the police into action. The largest of the independents, the Canadian Stock and Grain Co., was raided and its president and officers arrested, but they began operations again as soon as they were out of jail, the police having neglected to confiscate their books. A second raid was more successful, and that seemed to be the end of the independent futures dealers.

The bucket shop operations were simply added to the repertoire of the established brokerage firms. One of them, Richardson and Sons Ltd., engaged in some speculation on behalf of a farmer in 1911 on which losses occurred. The farmer was sued for recovery of the losses, and the Manitoba Supreme Court dismissed the farmer's defence that the deal was illegal and therefore unenforceable. The Supreme Court of Canada reversed the decision, however, and brought forward the old doctrine that if no delivery was intended the contract was simple gaming and therefore illegal. A few years later Richardson and Sons fought and lost another bucket shop case on the same grounds.[91]

In 1906 the Grain Growers' Grain Co., the farmers' co-operative, secured membership on the grain exchange, and was expelled the next year. A suit was brought against the exchange by the Grain Growers' Co. as being a combination in restraint of trade on the grounds that through the North West Grain Dealers Association it controlled the elevator system as well, and because the high fees charged for membership blocked participation.[92] But the case was dismissed. The Grain Growers' Association was reinstated to the exchange after it was made an issue in the 1907 Manitoba elections, and restrictions were placed on the exchange leading to its dissolution and reorganization on a voluntary, non-incorporated basis as the Winnipeg Grain Exchange in 1908. While the format of operations had changed, the character had not, nor had the farmers' antagonism to the organized dealers and speculators. A series of royal commissions deliberated on the complaints of the farmers. Typically, all farmers called as witnesses claimed that futures trading by the speculators hurt the farmer, all grain dealers called as witnesses claimed it was good for the farmer, and the Commissioners concurred with the grain dealers.

Railway Competition and Cartels

In the 1870's the northwest trade of Canada was nonexistent, and the major railways concentrated their attention on the grain-exporting states of the American midwest. The Great Western and the Grand Trunk extended to the southwest in competition for the trade — the Grand Trunk gradually outdistancing its weaker rival, which was cramped by the lack of access to sufficient long-term financing to sustain an extended traffic war. In

1871 the Grand Trunk built the International Bridge at Buffalo from funds raised by a bond issue in Britain, and this yielded it a connection to the New York Central, the Erie, and other U.S. routes, giving Ontario easy access to New York and New England.[93] It was estimated at the time that an extra £100,000 per annum worth of traffic was diverted to the GTR by the bridge.[94] By 1880, the Grand Trunk had pushed its own line to Chicago, and the only thing saving the Great Western from bankruptcy was the American traffic.[95]

The American traffic was critical to other roads as well. Both of the companies organized in 1871 to compete for the CPR contract stressed the need for American connections in their charters.[96] And when in 1888 a quarrel broke out between the Allan Line of steamships and the Grand Trunk, the Allan Line diverted its ships to Halifax away from Portland and caused a boom in Halifax.[97]

As the West opened up, the lure of traffic there attracted more of the railroads' attentions. In 1879 the GTR sold its unprofitable Rivière du Loup section to the Dominion government and used the funds to acquire a western outlet to Chicago, giving it access to the western American railways, and via them to Manitoba and the Northwest.[98] The new CPR syndicate of 1880 too was born from an American-based road extending into Manitoba. And the American lines themselves began extending north as the Manitoba government initiated a series of efforts to fight the CPR's western monopoly. In 1881, Jay Cooke's Northern Pacific bought a controlling interest in the Manitoba South Western, a line promoted by the future Lieutenant Governor of the province, Dr. Schultz. At George Stephen's request, Macdonald refused it a land grant,[99] and it was soon absorbed by the CPR, Donald Smith assuming the presidency.[100] That began a long series of conflicts between Manitoba and the CPR, culminating in the granting of a guarantee of $6,500 per mile to the Northern Pacific in 1888 after the CPR's monopoly clause was revoked.[101] The same year an arrangement was made between the St. Paul, Minnesota, and Manitoba, now under control of J.J. Hill who had left the CP syndicate, to permit the GTR to enter Winnipeg on St. Paul tracks.[102] Later that year the GTR took over the Northwestern railroad to begin to establish its own system in the Canadian West.[103]

In the East, the war between the GTR and the Great Western produced a great deal of apprehension over the value of their holdings by the British investors of both lines. In 1879, the Manchester shareholders of the Great Western met and urged union with the Grand Trunk.[104] By 1881, the fears for the returns

on investment from the continuing rate war[105] pushed the GTR
closer to agreement, and early in 1882 the war was secretly
ended,[106] followed by the absorption of the weaker line into the
Grand Trunk.[107] The critical factor precipitating final agreement
was the threat newly posed in the East from the CPR. And with
the merger the GTR secured every rail approach to the Canadian Northwest through the United States except for J.J. Hill's
St. Paul line. The CPR also attempted to secure the Great
Western, and its absorption would have involved no doubling of
lines, for the CP had no lines in the area served by the Great
Western, whereas the GTR and its smaller rival had duplicated
facilities. When the CP bid failed, the syndicate had to lay down
its own track, with the result that three lines existed to service
enough traffic to sustain one[108] at a time when the GTR was
unable to meet its fixed interest charges.

But the intrusion of the CP into this territory did not lead to
rate competition. Freight rates remained fixed while competition
took the form of a proliferation of feeder and branch lines and
systematic efforts to wreck each others' credit ratings. Early in
1883, the CP secured Duncan McIntyre's Canada Central and
made a move towards leasing the Credit Valley.[109] In response,
the GTR secured the North Shore Railroad for $5 million from
a syndicate of members of the Quebec Legislative Assembly who
had just bought it from the Quebec government for four million.[110] An arrangement between the two lines was almost
achieved on the basis of the CPR's being left in control of the
Northwest while the GTR was to keep a monopoly of the
western Ontario-Montreal traffic.[111] But the peace was broken.
Henry Tyler denounced the CPR's intent to hook up with Cor-
nelius Vanderbilt and intrude into the Montreal-western Ontario
trade. The CPR secured the Credit Valley line with exactly this
in mind.

That the space was open for it to do so was in part the result
of the fact that the GTR had promised the Government of
Canada that it would use the proceeds of the sale of the Rivière
du Loup section to lay double tracking between Toronto and
Montreal. Instead, it diverted the funds to its extensions into the
American Midwest grain trade. In 1884, a new effort was made
to divide up traffic; while it was unsuccessful, the tacit freight
rate fixing agreement was nonetheless maintained. Later that
year, a more successful arrangement was made by which the
GTR gave the CPR running rights over its North Shore line
while the CPR gave the GTR rights on a line from the North
Shore to the GTR main line.[112] These arrangements were
regarded with some alarm among those who used the railways,

and the 1884 CPR loan contained a clause forbidding the CPR to merge with the GTR.[113]

The arrangements broke down in short order, but the tacit price fixing lasted even during peak moments of hostility[114] partly no doubt due to the pressure of British bondholders. In 1891 a formal agreement was concluded. While outright merger was prohibited, to expedite the agreement Duncan McIntyre was elected to join the GTR board. The intention of the arrangement was then baldly announced by Sir Henry Tyler:

> We are thoroughly agreed that we will, so far as these two companies are concerned, maintain rates, and that we will get all we can out of the Canadian people.[115]

At the same time the companies were fixing rates, CPR rates were impervious to government regulation. Under the terms of the charter the rates could not be reduced until the profit on capital invested reached ten per cent, "in other words, never."[116] This stipulation may well have favoured the issue of common stock for financing, as opposed to bonds, for by suitably watering the stock the rate of profit could always be kept below ten per cent.

Competition during the period, and indeed the next as well, took the form of extending feeders or absorbing other short lines to develop traffic, especially in resources, the burden of which fell on the taxpayer through government subsidy and guarantee programs. After its main line was complete, the CPR pushed feeders into phosphate mines in Quebec, copper in Sudbury, coal in Lethbridge,[117] and in 1892 absorbed the Montreal and Western, a resource road controlled by a syndicate headed by Sir Adolphe Chapleau.[118]

The Grand Trunk's position continued to be precarious. By 1894 its fixed charges exceeded revenue by £224,000. Having nothing to lose, it commenced an energetic expansion program against the CPR, which began to embrace the West, hitherto a CP preserve, after the great expansion began. When the Canadian Northern system was in its infancy, an attempt to buy it failed, for the GTR could not meet the price, and the stage was set for a replication on a grand scale in western Canada of the absurdities already achieved in southern Ontario, with three complete railway lines each eager to generate long-distance traffic. Yet even then it was not until 1898 that bitterness over the Klondike traffic led to a rate war between the CPR and the GTR, lasting only three months.[119] And at that, it was restricted to passenger traffic. Nonetheless British investors were decidedly uneasy and fearful of depreciation of their securities,[120] a restlessness that came to the surface again with each new manifestation of serious railway hostility that might lead to rate cutting.[121]

During the opening years of the new expansion, rate competition took new forms. In 1897, while the railway lines kept to their fixed schedules, their express company subsidiaries and electric railway affiliates waged bitter rate struggles. As early as 1887, American Express had agreed to withdraw from Canada in deference to the CPR's Dominion Express Co.[122] Shortly afterward the GTR promoted a rival Canadian Express Co. and rate war broke out. But in 1897 the war stopped and collusion began.[123] These express companies were the source of fabulous returns to the parents under the new arrangements. While their actual assets in 1911 were only $800,000, they were capitalized at five million, all held by the parents, and were paying dividends on that sum.[124] Dominion Express had cost only $5,800 to build, the CPR invested another $24,500 in its operations, and by 1916 its assets reached $2,834,000 and it had returned $13,500,000 in dividends. The express companies of both major lines for many years had blocked the establishment of a federal parcel post which would compete with their traffic.

Also in 1897 there was an outbreak among electric railways in southwestern Ontario, behind which stood the two railway companies. The Galt Electric Railway ran freight for the CPR to Galt, Hespeler, and other nearby towns that the CPR did not service. The Grand Trunk covered part of the area with its Harrisburg-Guelph line, but asked the Galt electric line for a similar arrangement to that of the CPR. When this was refused, the GTR put freight wagons on the electric railway route and began delivering goods free of charge. In retaliation, the CPR and the Galt electric line arranged for free delivery by wagon at points reached by the GTR line but not formerly by the Galt or the CPR.[125]

Towards the end of the century, in the West the CPR was faced with a challenge from the American roads before the two new trans-Canada lines were under construction. J. J. Hill began a series of forays into the B.C. mining districts, followed by a move into Manitoba. This last was countered by an arrangement between the two lines whereby Hill would extend west with the aid of the Manitoba government, then withdraw, selling the lines constructed from public funds to the CPR in return for concessions on the West Coast.[126] This arrangement was stopped by the fall of the Greenway government which was promoting it, and the coming to power of Rodmond Roblin with his "nationalization" plans. Within a year, Mackenzie and Mann had running rights over nearby U.S. lines to use as an outlet for Manitoba wheat,[127] and the Canadian Northern system was on its way to glory.

The traffic arrangement with the American lines was not a new phenomenon, for international pools and cartels, as well as price fixing arrangements, were frequent adjoints to domestic cartels from at least as early as 1871, when the Great Western entered into a 21-year earnings pool with the Michigan Central, both roads bonding themselves not to interchange traffic with any new line across Canada and Michigan.[128] In 1880, the Grand Trunk made serious efforts to come to terms with the American trunk lines over the Chicago trade, an agreement delayed by quarrels over the division of the market and finally settled by Vanderbilt, who acceded to the GTR's demands for a larger share.[129]

In the West, arrangements with American lines were essential to the early entrants. In 1879, the St. Paul and Pacific (St. Paul, Minneapolis and Manitoba) reached a uniform tariff agreement on freight with the Northern Pacific in flagrant and open violation of the agreement between the Stephen-Smith-Hill syndicate and the Canadian government which gave them control of the Northwest trade.[130] By 1883 J. J. Hill had broken with his CPR confrères and the St. Paul line became an object of the Grand Trunk's attentions.

The CPR, because of J. J. Hill's hostility and because the Grand Trunk had a long, fruitful working relationship with the American lines, was seldom involved for long in the major American pools and cartels. In 1895 it tried to join the Union or Joint Traffic Association, a huge pool of nine trunk lines including the GTR, but negotiations failed. This trunk pool was formed to control the Chicago to Atlantic coast traffic. It was not only the CPR that was a problem. The Grand Trunk itself broke ranks shortly after the pool was formed, and began cutting rates. Under J. P. Morgan's auspices a new agreement was eventually worked out, but now the CPR refused to abide by it.

There followed a rate war mainly in the U.S. from New York to Winnipeg, with CP rates falling to half those of the pool, forcing the Northern Pacific and Great Northern to come to terms.[131] While the U.S government prosecuted the cartel, this seemed a minor deterrent, for the CPR joined a few months later.[132]

At the same time the freight pool was being organized, efforts were made to organize passenger traffic. The Transcontinental Passenger Association was formed by all the U.S. and Canadian lines in 1897, but this broke down with the Klondike rush and the outbreak of rate cutting there.[133] And in 1898 the CP was expelled from the immigration clearing house by the American trunk lines, shutting it out of immigration traffic at Boston and New York,[134] though it seems that Van Horne and Hill did achieve a consensus on rates in 1898 before their efforts at a Manitoba arrangement.[135]

By 1900, J. J. Hill had begun another concerted drive against the CPR in B.C., including taking control of a series of valuable collieries.[136] His line had also made forays into Ontario and Quebec, establishing itself as a new grain outlet. In Quebec it was given free use of the government docks, and all steamships run in connection with the road were exempt from harbour, port, and other dues for five years.[137] The Laurier policy of favouring rivals brought the fury of the CPR upon the federal government. After the Intercolonial was completed to Montreal, almost all of the domestic traffic originating along it was turned over to the Grand Trunk. When the federal government in 1900 refused the CPR an interchange arrangement with the Intercolonial that would have monopolized the eastern end of the trans-Canada traffic, the CPR threw its weight behind the Tories in the general elections. It gave particularly heavy backing to Sir George Foster against the Minister of Railways in St. John, New Brunswick,[138] but had to wait until after 1911 to collect its reward.

It was in the West that the bitterest battles were fought and the resulting damage the greatest. Competition in the West took the form of building feeder lines to tap resource traffic and the grain trade and divert it along the trunk line. Wherever resources were found, the railways were quick to enter. This was due in part to the heavy burden of fixed interest charges on the new lines, which forced them to develop long-distance traffic in raw materials as quickly as possible. Rapid exploitation of mines and timber lands resulted, with the output being exported from the resource-producing area rather than processed locally. In addition, the heavy peak-load character of grain traffic, which was the *sine qua non* of success, forced double tracking to capture the return flows of merchandise — and double tracking by all three transcontinental lines. In part, too, the wasteful process of building competitive feeder lines was built into the logic of railway competition. Since rate wars were disastrous, especially for lines with heavy fixed debt charges to meet, competition by quantity of facilities was the sole recourse — over and above their shenanigans in the London capital market.

Because of this structure, the West was reinforced in its position as a staple-producing hinterland dominated by eastern commerce and finance. With the boom in the mining districts in

British Columbia and Yukon near the end of the nineteenth century, for example, pressure mounted for the building of the Crow's Nest Pass Railway. The Dominion government gave the CPR a guarantee of up to $11,000 a mile to build the line, which not only served as an access route to the Kootenay Mining District and permitted eastern Canadian mercantile interests to replace the Americans in controlling the area's trade,[139] but secured the company's position in southern B.C. as well. In the process a series of feeder lines were acquired in 1897 with access to mines and smelters, along with the B.C. Southern Railway, which brought with it 3,350,000 acres of land and six square miles of coal fields.[140] In 1898, the CP went on to acquire the Colonization and Western Railroad of B.C., adding another 1,600,000 acres to its holdings.[141] In 1901, it established a fleet of coastal steamers to tap the developing Pacific coast trade.[142]

By 1903, the Canadian Northern system was becoming a serious threat to the CPR's western hegemony, for by that date it had 1,276 miles of track, 857 in Manitoba, and had added grain elevators and docks at Port Arthur to establish its share of the west-east grain flow. In addition, the CN telegraph system duplicating existing CP facilities was in operation.[143] The CP was alarmed, and began to consolidate its holdings, taking over a number of lines including the Calgary and Edmonton which it had formerly leased.[144] In 1905 it solidified its hold in B.C. by acquiring the Esquimault and Nanaimo Railroad, and with it 1,600,000 acres on Vancouver Island.[145] The next year it secured the Alberta Railway and Immigration Company and with it coal supplies.[146] And in 1910 it entered Shawinigan Falls, tapping the trade associated with the rapid growth of pulp and paper and other industries that collected about the large power developments there.[147]

The Canadian Northern kept pace with its older rival. 1906 saw a substantial increase in its grain, cattle, and coal traffic. In addition, it began shipping large amounts of iron from Port Arthur to the U.S. for processing, and began a series of takeovers of Ontario and Quebec railroads, giving it access to Ottawa, Montreal, and many urban Quebec centres. Its mileage reached 2,482. The importance of developing the raw material trade to offset fixed charges and to keep up with the CPR's rate of expansion was fully recognized by the directors. Grain traffic by itself was inadequate and risky, for one poor crop meant trouble for the railroad. But other raw materials did not entail the same climatic hazards, and the iron ore exports, the directors reported, "will enable your company to face years of bad crops, whenever they come, with equanimity."[148]

Some processing of the ore into pig iron under the federal iron bounty program began in 1907 at Port Arthur in the refineries of the Atikokan Mining Company, wholly owned by Mackenzie and Mann.[149] In 1908, the CN acquired a series of small railroads. In one coup it got the Qu'Appelle, Long Lake and Saskatchewan, giving it access to an enormous grain-growing area in central Saskatchewan.[150] In 1910 it followed the CP into coal lands in B.C. and Alberta;[151] in 1911 it was tapping the huge timber limits near Prince Albert and expanded its Alberta coal contacts. That year it established its own steamship line, and began extensive connections with, and direct lines to, American pulp and paper and timber producing areas.[152] By 1912 its coal traffic was growing at a rate of 120%; it carried 32% of the total grain traffic; and its mileage reached 4,400.[153]

Freight Rate Discrimination

Although the rate structure tended usually to be fixed between companies, a great deal of discrimination between various users was built into the common tariffs. This discrimination took four forms: favouring American over Canadian traffic, favouring the East over the West in Canada, discriminating in favour of raw materials one way and finished goods the other, and encouraging long-distance (especially international) trade as opposed to local traffic.

In 1871, the Dominion Board of Trade objected to the Grand Trunk's granting of better terms to American than Canadian freight over equivalent distances, a discrimination regarded as particularly galling in light of the amount of public assistance given the line. Instances had arisen whereby instructions were issued to leave all local freight untouched and send all the available cars to Sarnia to secure the American through trade.[154]

Montreal in particular was under the complete control of the GTR at a time when Toronto was connected via the Great Western to the New York railways and Toronto freight rates were only half of these paid by Montreal shippers over equivalent distances. In addition, the GTR tended to divert Montreal's export trade to Portland while its local produce accumulated without transportation facilities. By December of 1873, the accumulated stock of grain in Montreal due to lack of railway service reached over a million bushels of wheat and 90,000 of flour. Furthermore, the through rates from Chicago to Liverpool were 80c per 100 lb., while the through rate from Montreal to

Liverpool was 93c per 100 lb. for wheat; at the same time Chicago was 1,145 miles from the sea and Montreal 297.[155] The milling interests of Canada were particularly vehement in their objections to the GTR's discrimination.[156]

The CPR charter was supposed to put an end to these problems. Instead, the new railway was immediately faced with charges of discrimination of its own. In 1880, the Winnipeg business community began to fret about the possibility that traffic would be diverted along the syndicate's Pembina branch and the St. Paul, Minneapolis and Manitoba to Chicago, completely bypassing Winnipeg.[157]

The CPR, once operational, discriminated in favour of American grain as effectively as had the GTR. In 1890 it was carrying wheat from Winnipeg to Halifax for 63.5¢ per 100 lb., while it carried it from Minneapolis to Portland and Boston for 42.5¢, and to New York for 37.5¢. General merchandise flowing back showed a similar pattern. The first class rate from St. John to Winnipeg was $2.64 per 100 lb., and from Montreal to Winnipeg $2.08; while from Portland and Boston to Minneapolis the company charged only $1.05 per 100 lb.[158] The CPR thus exploited to the full its monopoly within Canada while its rates were kept down to a lower level in the U.S. by the cartel agreements or the intermittent rate wars. The effect on wheat shipment was especially harmful, as it raised the costs of shipping from Winnipeg to Liverpool one-third above the rate from Minneapolis to Liverpool,[159] a factor that must have contributed to the retardation of development of the Canadian West.

After 1900, the CP began to undercut the rates of the Great Northern and the Northern Pacific in contiguous U.S. territory, and the differential between Canadian and U.S. rates grew.[160] In addition, the CP schedules listed higher charges on transcontinental rates to B.C. towns than to nearby American ones, which favoured American over Canadian merchants wherever they came into competition; it gave U.S. cattle exporters an advantage over Canadian; and it augmented its discrimination with a system of secret rebates to favoured shippers, reducing the real charges below the nominal.[161]

The rate structure prevailing at the turn of the century not only favoured American routes over Canadian but also trans-Atlantic trade over intra-Canadian, Vancouver-Liverpool costs for some items being less than Vancouver-Toronto. The result was to undermine substantially the protective incidence of the tariff, contributing in no small measure to the manufacturers' ever-escalating demands for higher protection on certain commodities, such as cotton and woollens.

TABLE IX (4)

Freight Rates Per 100 lb., 1901

Route	Class	Mileage	Trade	Local
Chicago-St. Paul	1	410	$ .60	$ —
Winnipeg-Moose Jaw	1	398	1.20	1.26
Chicago-St. Paul	2	410	.20	—
Winnipeg-Moose Jaw	2	398	.49	.58
Montreal-Halifax	1	746	.56	—
Winnipeg-Calgary	1	840	1.82	2.08
Montreal-Halifax	2	746	.28	—
Winnipeg-Calgary	2	840	.77	.94

Source: Royal Commission on Railway Grievances, *Report*, p. 47.

Item	Liverpool-Winnipeg	Liverpool-Vancouver	Toronto-Winnipeg	Toronto-Vancouver
calicoes	$1.52	$1.74	$1.38	$1.73
cotton cloth	1.96	2.29	1.82	2.25
misc. dry goods	1.96	2.60	1.82	2.25
carpets	1.96	2.60	1.82	2.75
wool clothing	1.96	2.40	1.82	2.85
hemp carpet	1.09	2.20	1.82	2.75
oil cloth	1.58	1.58	1.24	1.70
kid gloves	1.96	3.26	1.82	2.85

Source: *IC*, July 1901, p. 303.

Within Canada, discrimination in favour of through traffic over local prevailed. And the rates in Canada were higher in the West than in the East for equivalent mileages and identical merchandise.[162] Nor could this be justified in terms of cost differentials, for the prairie sections of the railroads were much cheaper to build and operate than those in central Canada. Agitation against the discrimination began early, and by 1887 Van Horne had denounced Manitoba businessmen who complained of it as "annexationists."[163]

Rate fixing and rate discrimination led to serious enough opposition that the government was forced to that tried-and-tested, time-wasting, and dissent-deflating tactic, the establishment of a royal commission. This commission was enpowered to investigate whether or not freight rates should be regulated. Just to ensure that it was objective, Sir Alexander Galt was appointed as its one-man commissioner. Much to everyone's surprise, he reported that, in his considered opinion and with due regard to all the evidence, no regulation of railway rates was necessary. As a result, until 1903, the only body to whom appeal could be made against the rates charged by railways was a House of Commons committee — staffed of course by the same M.P.s who so often relied on railway largesse to win their seats, if not their extra-parliamentary daily bread.

The parliamentary railway committee was openly a tool of the railways, and pressure mounted for the creation of an independent regulatory agency.[164] But this was of little consequence. Despite the building of the new transcontinentals and the promises of Van Horne and others that expanded volume would lead to lower rates, no changes were made. Volume doubled in ten years after the turn of the century, but the discrimination remained.[165]

The Commission took the position that east-west discrimination was justified on the grounds that in the East there was competition from waterways and U.S. lines, and that rate cutting by the big lines would bankrupt the weaker and leave the CPR with a monopoly.[166] It was bizarre logic. The West was to bear the burden of the East's competition. As to the bankruptcy of the weaker lines, it would make little difference to rate charge, and happened in any event. The argument about water competition in the East was ludicrous, for very few points were linked by water routes except the Great Lakes area.[167]

The rate structure served to reinforce the West's staple-extracting role. Even the only significant case of rate reduction helped to confirm the division of labour. Under the Crow's Nest Pass agreement negotiated between the two sovereign bodies, the CPR and the Dominion Government, freight rates on wheat and flour from any point in the prairies to Fort William were reduced three cents per 100 lb., while rates on some items of merchandise consumed on the prairies were reduced on the east-west run. There is a critical theoretical point involved here. Just as reducing the rate of tariff on imported inputs holding constant the nominal rate on finished products serves to heighten the effective degree of protection inhering in any nominal tariff structure, so too will railway rate discrimination. If the freight rate one way is lower than the other on raw materials, with the opposite relation holding for finished products, the amount of protection afforded for manufacturing at one end against the possibility of competition from the other is increased significantly. And rate reductions on raw materials and finished products that are restricted to one-way flows in opposite directions increase the effective protection inhering in the rate structure.

Such discrimination could clearly work to the advantage of one locality over another, as well as affect the east-west balance. Within the West before the Canadian Northern became important, the CP controlled the competition of local merchants by giving them special distributive rates. Winnipeg was granted special rates which made it the distribution centre of the West. When this was threatened under the Crow's Nest Pass agreement with its east-west reductions, the CPR re-established the differential in the city's favour.[168] Calgary merchants in 1902 could ship along the Calgary-Edmonton branch into Edmonton territory while Edmonton merchants could not ship back.[169] The result was to make one centre, in this case Calgary, more attractive to eastern business as a distribution centre, and a large number of wholesale branches of eastern business moved into that town.[170] Complaints over this were rampant throughout the West, for which town got the special distributive (traders') rate was entirely the decision of the company. In addition, the secret rebate system could be used to hide the differential.

In the East, rates favoured Montreal over Toronto. From Toronto to Montreal in 1904 general merchandise moved first class for 50c per 100 lb., fifth class for 25c; while from Montreal to Toronto the equivalent rates were 44c and 22c. In addition, raw material rates from Toronto to Montreal were lower than from Montreal to Toronto.[171]

Manufacturers Versus Railroads

The manufacturers saw in the railroad companies the greatest threat to their profit position. As early as 1882 it came to light that grist and saw mills manufactured in Brantford at the Waterous plant and shipped to Brandon had a markup due to freight one-third more than when they were sent to Australia via New York.[172] Fears over the proposed Great-Western-Grand-Trunk merger were rife, for much of Ontario would then be in the grips of one great railroad, and the rest in the hands of another, with no price competition.[173] That the railways could offset the effect of a tariff by appropriating the revenue themselves, and could dictate the location of manufacturing, was recognized early.[174] And complaints of favouritism given to American producers, and to international over local trade, were constant grievances until well after the turn of the century.[175]

There were many instances where rates on the export of raw materials were more favourable than on exports of finished or semi-finished products made from that raw material. Until 1900, the Grand Trunk gave special low rates on the export of sawn logs to American pulp mills. Not until the CPR agreed to alter its special system of rates for the export of lead ore was it possible for smelting to get underway at Rossland, B.C.[176] Needless to say there was a price attached to its concession — namely that the federal government institute a system of bounties to lead smelters. And the CPR's Consolidated Mining and Smelting Company operation at Trail monopolized almost all of the smelting of lead, and hence received virtually all of the cash bounties. It was the Intercolonial and Grand Trunk discrimination in favour of the long distance over the local traffic in coal that came close to wrecking the Londonderry iron and steel works in their early years. From the milling industry the long-standing complaint that it cost more to ship flour to Liverpool than wheat was heard time after time.[177] And during the wheat boom the spread between the export rates on flour and wheat widened sharply from 1.5¢ per 100 lb. in 1900 to 12¢ per 100 lb. by 1913. Canadian millers were thus hindered in their competition against British millers.[178] Such a rate structure helped, no doubt, to impede the development of grain milling in Canada at a time when food costs were skyrocketing.

For the farmers too, of course, the railways were a constant source of monopoly exaction. Not only did the railways help the destruction of wheat farming in Ontario by their discrimination in favour of American grain, but once the West was opened up to large-scale production the wheat farmer there was forced to pay tribute in many forms. The spread between export and domestic prices of farm implements made in Canada, and the Canada-U.S. differential, were due in part at least to the system of rate discrimination. To move implements from Toronto or Montreal to the Pacific Coast of Canada in 1904 cost $1.38 per cwt., while to ship them from Boston, Portland, or New York to the coast over the CPR cost $1.30. The general machinery rate in Canada was $1.53, for the U.S., $1.45. From Chicago to the sea, cattle cost 28¢ per cwt. to move on Canadian lines, while from Toronto it cost 23¢ — the difference in distance was 500 miles. From Buffalo to Boston cattle cost 15¢ per cwt; from Toronto to Boston, 25¢ — making a difference of up to $1.50 per head. The spread was just as bad over longer hauls. From St. Paul to the sea over the CPR the cattle rate was 40¢, while from Winnipeg it was 62.5¢.[179] These patterns certainly helped ensure that Canadian cattle were shipped south to the American export centres, at the same time ensuring higher meat prices in Canada than in the U.S.

The CMA underwent a substantial reorganization in 1900, and while many changes resulted, its antagonism to the railway companies did not alter, especially vis-à-vis the tariff issue:

The railway companies truly control economic destinies in this country; they are absolute monarchs . . . .The railway

companies do not hesitate to say that in arranging for their
rates they consider the protective tariff, and rather than our
manufacturers should obtain that protection which has been
granted them, the railways come and reach out their hands
and take it themselves.[180]

Baron Shaughnessy of the CPR was reputed to have explained
the American-Canadian rate differential to Canadian manufacturers by saying, "you have the tariff." While protection in
Canada led to high commodity prices, no small part of this represented protection to inflated railway rates, and thus to the
British security holders.

The individual manufacturers were helpless before the power
of the railroads, but manufacturers as a whole, organized into
bodies like the CMA, were conscious of their collective bargaining strength against the railroads, representing as they did
many major customers. The railroads were also aware of it, and
refused to deal with firms except on an individual basis.[181]

Efforts were also made, to no avail, by manufacturers to form
alliances with organized farm groups as a united front of the
"productive" class against commercial capital in general, and the
railways in particular. But the tariff was the critical wedge. The
CMA rhetoric emphasized the increased demand for farm products that would result from higher protection to industry.

If the request of the Canadian manufacturers for increased
protection is granted, instead of the money of our farmers
going over to the United States to pay American workingmen,
it will remain in Canada and will be paid out in wages to the
Canadian farmer in payment for food.[182]

This argument about harmony of interests among the productive sectors of society against the parasitical ones ignored one
crucial point, that the farm community whose organized support
the CMA attempted to secure was not oriented towards production for home consumption in a balanced self-sufficient
economy. The growing part of the farm sector was geared to producing staples for export markets. Its sales were effected on
unprotected markets, while its purchases were within the protected sphere, resulting in a deterioration of its terms of trade.
The resultant asymmetry doomed all efforts to bring the greater
part of the farm sector within a protectionist frame of reference.
Some farm groups did in fact seek protection, but these were
groups like B.C. fruit growers, whose markets were mainly Canadian and who faced direct competition within Canada from
American producers. Such groups were exceptional.

Notes to Chapter IX

1. R.C. Bellan, *The Development of Winnipeg*, pp. 18-19.
2. *FA,* Aug. 1879, p. 171.
3. *MT,* May 7, 1880, p. 1316.
4. *MT,* Nov. 25, 1881, p. 639.
5. R. C. Bellan, *The Development of Winnipeg,* p. 46.
6. *CFC,* June 10, 1882, p. 662.
7. *MT,* June 23, 1882, p. 1571.
8. Sir Richard Cartwright, *Reminiscences,* p. 226.
9. Ontario, Commission of Enquiry . . . Conspiracy to Corrupt and Attempt to Bribe Certain Members of the Legislature, *Evidence,* Ontario Sessional Papers, 1885.
10. *HCD,* May 4, 1886, pp. 1033-1060.
11. E. Wiman to John A. Macdonald, Sept. 6, 1884, *Macdonald Papers.*
12. *MT,* April 30, 1880, p. 1286; Aug. 13, 1880, p. 176.
13. E. Wiman to John A. Macdonald, Feb. 10, 1886, *Macdonald Papers.*
14. H. Y. Hind, "Manitoba and the North West Frauds," pp. 4, 10-11, 28.
15. J.S. Galbraith "The Land Policy of the Hudson's Bay Company 1870-1913," p. 11.
16. *MT,* Dec. 14, 1883, p. 657.
17. W. Vaughn, *Van Horne,* p. 155.
18. *HCD,* Dec. 17, 1880, p. 146.
19. J. W. Dafoe, *Sir Clifford Sifton in Relation to His Time,* p. 132.
20. J. S. Galbraith, "Land Policies. . ." p. 6.
21. *MT,* May 22, 1885, p. 1312.
22. *MT,* March 23, 1885, p. 1030.
23. *MT,* May 22, 1885, p. 1312.
24. *MT,* Aug. 28, 1885, p. 235.
25. *MT,* Aug. 25, 1882, p. 207.
26. *MT,* June 20, 1884, p. 1427.
27. *Globe,* Dec. 19, 1890.
28. *JC,* Nov. 2, 1883, p. 342.
29. E. Hamon, *Les Canadiens Français de la Nouvelle Angleterre,* pp. 9-13.
30. *Globe,* Dec. 26, 1890.
31. *MT,* Oct. 4, 1889, p. 400.
32. *MT,* April 25, 1890, p. 1321.
33. *MT,* Aug. 25, 1893, p. 225.
34. *MT,* Aug. 4, 1893, p. 190.
35. *HCD,* June 12, 1894, p. 4126.
36. *HCD,* June 12, 1894, pp. 4130-1.
37. *HCD,* June 12, 1894, p. 4153.
38. John A. Macdonald to George Stephen, March 31, 1891, *Macdonald Papers.*
39. *CBC,* 1913, p. 455.
40. *MT,* April 11, 1902, p. 1318.
41. *MT,* May 23, 1902, p. 1523.
42. *CAR,* 1906, p. 573; *MT,* June 27, 1902, p. 1679; *CAR,* 1907.
43. A. G. Brown and P. H. Morres, *Twentieth Century Impressions,* p. 605.
44. E. B. Biggar, *The Canadian Railway Problem,* p. 108.
45. J. S. Galbraith, "Land Policies. . .", p. 7.
46. *CLR I,* pp. 68-9.
47. CPR, *Annual Reports,* 1902, p. 5; 1908, p. 6; 1911, p. 7; *CNR, Annual Reports,* 1908, p. 9; 1911, p. 6.

48. C. Martin, *"Dominion Lands" Policy,* p. 328.
49. Public Accounts Committee, House of Commons Journals 1906, Appendix 3, p. 56.
50. Public Accounts Committee, 1906, p. 43.
51. *CAR,* 1906, p. 574.
52. Public Accounts Committee, 1906, p. 145.
53. *GGG,* Jan. 1, 1913; Jan. 29, 1913.
54. *MT,* July 11, 1879, p. 65; March 5, 1880, p. 1047; March 14, 1884, p. 1030; Nov. 18, 1887, p. 644.
55. *MT,* April 21, 1881, p. 1232; *MT,* Dec. 15, 1882, p. 659.
56. *CM,* March 31, 1882, p. 119.
57. *SCTA,* p. 14.
58. *HCD,* March 30, 1882, pp. 342-3; April 19, 1883, p. 714; *MT,* Aug. 20, 1883, p. 175; *CM,* May 2, 1882.
59. *RCRLC,* Ontario Evidence, pp. 389, 610, 674, 837.
60. *CBC,* pp. 369, 386, 407.
61. O. J. McDiarmid, pp. 199-250.
62. E.C. Porritt, *The Revolt,* p. 81.
63. *Statutes of Alberta,* 1913, Chap. 15; *GGG,* April 19, 1913.
64. *MT,* Oct. 17, 1890, p. 465.
65. *Canadian Countryman,* Jan. 10, 1914, p. 5.
66. *FA,* June 11, 1912, p. 43; Feb. 27, 1913, p. 369; *Farm and Dairy,* Jan. 25, 1912, p. 4.
67. *CLRII,* p. 995; *CLRI,* p. 11.
68. *MT,* Dec. 21, 1900, p. 792.
69. Royal Grain Inquiry Commission, *Report 1938,* p. 17.
70. *MT,* Oct. 13, 1876, p. 418.
71. *MT,* March 19, 1880, p. 1106.
72. D.A. MacGibbon, *The Canadian Grain Trade,* p. 404.
73. *MT,* Sept. 21, 1883, p. 316.
74. *MT,* Nov. 6, 1903, p. 577.
75. *MT,* Jan. 16, 1885, p. 801.
76. A.S. Morton, *History of Prairie Settlement,* p. 94.
77. D. Creighton, *John A. Macdonald,* II, pp. 384-5.
78. H.A. Innis, *History of the CPR,* p. 139.
79. *CAR,* 1910, Historical Supplement, p. 52.
80. *MT,* April 4, 1902, p. 1291.
81. Royal Commission on the Shipment and Transportation of Grain, *Report* 1899, pp. 7-9.
82. H.W. Wadsworth, *The Dominion Commercial Travellers Association,* p. 143.
83. *MT,* Dec. 9, 1898, p. 767.
84. MT, July 7, 1899, p. 8; *MT,* Aug. 25, 1899, p. 231.
85. *MT,* Feb. 5, 1897, p. 1048.
86. *GGG,* Dec. 10, 1913.
87. Royal Grain Enquiry Commission, *Report* 1925, p. 121.
88. *MT,* Oct. 27, 1906, p. 605; Nov. 3, 1906, p. 64.
89. Royal Commission on the Grain Trade, *Report* 1906, pp. 14-16.
90. Commission to Inquire into Trading in Grain Futures, *Evidence* 1931, pp. 163-173; *MT,* April 26, 1901, p. 1146.
91. *MT,* March 16, 1902, p. 1443; April 20, 1902, p. 1652; Jan. 3, 1919, p. 83.
92. D.A. MacGibbon, *The Canadian Grain Trade,* p. 51; *CAR,* 1907, p. 475.
93. *Ec,* March 18, 1871, p. 313.
94. *CFC,* April 8, 1871, p. 427.
95. *Ec,* March 27, 1880, p. 353.
96. H.A. Innis, *History of the Canadian Pacific Railway,* p. 78.

97. *MT,* Jan. 6, 1888, p. 847.
98. Anon., *Canada Under the National Policy,* p. 56.
99. H. Gilbert, *Awakening Continent,* p. 88.
100. *MT,* June 13, 1884, p. 1396.
101. *MT,* Aug. 3, 1888, p. 123.
102. *MT,* April 20, 1888, p. 1302.
103. *MT,* Dec. 2, 1888, p. 1097.
104. *MT,* Aug. 1, 1879, p. 149.
105. *MT,* Aug. 19, 1881, p. 211.
106. *CM,* July 28, 1882, p. 377.
107. *MT,* May 5, 1882, p. 1357.
108. H. Lovett, *Canada and the Grand Trunk,* pp. 107-8.
109. *MT,* April 13, 1883, p. 1147.
110. *MT,* April 27, 1883, p. 1203.
111. *MT,* April 20, 1883, p. 1177.
112. *MT,* Feb. 22, 1884, pp. 941-2; June 13, 1884, p. 1396.
113. *MT,* March 7, 1884, p. 1008.
114. *MT,* Feb. 1, 1889, p. 877.
115. *MT,* Nov. 20, 1891, p. 606.
116. Royal Commision Upon Railway Grievances Etc., *Report,* p. 36.
117. W. Vaughn, *Sir William Van Horne,* p. 144.
118. *MT,* Sept. 2, 1892, p. 239.
119. *MT,* March 4, 1898, p. 1157; March 18, 1898, p. 1227; April 29, 1898, p. 1410; June 3, 1898, p. 1575.
120. *MT,* Dec. 16, 1898, p. 799.
121. *Ec,* Feb. 28, 1903, p. 385.
122. *MT,* April 8, 1887, p. 1180.
123. *MT,* May 28, 1897, p. 1562.
124. *FA,* March 30, 1911n pp. 542-3; *MT,* July 9, 1897, p. 40. E.B. Biggar, *The Canadian Railway Problem,* p. 143.
125. *MT,* Nov. 25, 1898, p. 694.
126. *MT,* May 19, 1899, p. 1513.
127. *MT,* Jan. 12, 1900, p. 935.
128. *CFC,* April 29, 1871, p. 529.
129. *CFC,* June 12, 1880, p. 624; *MT,* July 2, 1880, p. 11; Aug. 20, 1880, p. 211.
130. *MT,* May 9, 1879, p. 1384.
131. *Brad.* April 6, 1895, p. 211; April 13, 1895, p. 227; July 27, 1895, p. 466; Oct. 12, 1895, p. 642; Oct. 26, 1895, p. 678; *MT,* Sept. 13, 1895, p. 338; Oct. 18, 1895, p. 498; Dec. 20, 1895, p. 785.
132. *MT,* Jan. 17, 1896, p. 913; July 10, 1896, p. 42.
133. *Brad.,* Feb. 26, 1898, p. 130; March 5, 1898, pp. 147-8.
134. *MT,* Feb. 25, 1898, p. 1117.
135. *Brad.* July 30, 1898, p. 480.
136. *MT,* Feb. 15, 1901, p. 1046; May 3, 1901, p. 1478.
137. *MT,* Feb. 10, 1900, p. 280; May 12, 1900, p. 945.
138. *Ec,* Aug. 11, 1900, p. 1149; MT, Nov. 2, 1900, p. 563.
139. Toronto Board of Trade *Annual Report,* 1897, p. 12, *Annual Report,* 1902, p. 46.
140. *CP, Annual Report,* 1897, p. 8.
141. *CP, Annual Report,* 1898, p. 6.
142. *CP, Annual Report,* 1901, p. 7.
143. *CN, Annual Report,* 1903, p. 15.
144. *CP, Annual Report,* 1903, pp. 6-7.
145. *CP, Annual Report,* 1905, p. 7.
146. *CP, Annual Report,* 1906, p. 7.

147. *CP, Annual Report,* 1910, p. 9.
148. *CN, Annual Report,* 1906, p. 8.
149. *CN, Annual Report,* 1907, p. 10.
150. *CN, Annual Report,* 1908, p. 9.
151. *CN, Annual Report,* 1909, pp. 7-8.
152. *CN; Annual Report,* 1910, pp. 6-7, 10.
153. *CN, Annual Report,* 1912, p. 5.
154. Dominion Board of Trade, *First Annual Meeting,* 1871, pp. 62-3.
155. Montreal Board of Trade, *Semi-Centennial Report,* 1892, p. 65.
156. *SCCD,* 1876, p. 74.
157. *MT,* Dec. 31, 1880, p. 752.
158. Goldwyn Smith, *Canada and the Canadian Question,* p. 60.
159. *MT,* Dec. 13, 1889, pp. 706-7.
160. Royal Commission on Railway Grievances, *Report,* pp. 48-55.
161. *Ibid.,* p. 64.
162. *Ibid.,* p. 47.
163. *MT,* Sept. 9, 1887, p. 335.
164. Royal Commission . . . Grievances, *Report,* p. 38.
165. *CF,* May 17, 1911, p. 449.
166. *CF,* April 15, 1914, p. 373.
167. *IC,* Aug. 1906, p. 17.
168. R.C. Bellan, The Development of Winnipeg, p. 93; *MT,* June 4, 1897, p. 1597.
169. Royal Commision. . . Grievances, *Report,* p. 43.
170. Calgary Board of Trade, *Annual Report,* 1903, p. 8.
171. *IC,* Nov. 1904, p. 202.
172. *CM,* April 28, 1882, p. 153; *MT,* March 10, 1882, p. 1104.
173. *CM,* May 26, 1882, p. 194; July 28, 1882, p. 377.
174. *CM,* April 14, 1882, pp. 134-5; *Globe,* March 3, 1910.
175. *CM,* March 15, 1895, p. 244; *IC,* July 1901, p. 301; *IC,* Oct. 1904, pp. 165-7; *Globe,* April 14, 1910.
176. *MT,* July 20, 1897, p. 146.
177. *MT,* Aug. 5, 1892; p. 128.
178. *CLRI,* p. 759.
179. *Farming World,* March 1, 1904, p. 174.
180. *IC,* Sept. 1900, p. 52.
181. *IC,* Nov. 1909, p. 110.
182. *IC,* Aug. 1903, p. 10.

The people of the United States would be glad to join with the people of Canada in developing this great area.

H. N. Whitney, 1910

CHAPTER X
Patents, Foreign Technology, And Industrial Development

Invention and Industrial Growth

The use of imported technology had a role in the development history of most advanced industrial economies. Theft of technology and skilled workers, even the murdering of artisans to preserve secrets from potential or real competitors, and similar policies — all played their role in European mercantilist strategy. The preservation, or attempted preservation of industrial secrets as an objective of national policy was also in evidence even well into the nineteenth century. Britain, for example, tried to maintain industrial hegemony through the prohibition of the export of machinery and the blocking of the emigration of skilled labour. At the same time, other countries were earnestly stealing and bribing away British technique and workers, with the result that in France and Germany, much of the textile industry (to name but one of major importance) grew up under the tuition of British émigré workers.[1]

A policy of preserving industrial secrets externally really required strict preservation internally as well. International monopoly required national monopoly, for the obvious reason that a system of small competitive firms could not possibly be closely controlled in terms of the secrecy of industrial technique. And in the late eighteenth and early nineteenth centuries it was common opinion that industrial growth was best secured by widespread diffusion of industrial techniques among domestic firms. Thus, in Britain in 1754 the state sponsored the Society For The Encouragement of Arts, Manufactures and Commerce, which offered premiums to inventors who were willing to put their devices at the free disposal of all industrialists, and many of the leading industrialists did refuse to take out patents. The implication of this was that the patent system could be a hindrance to innovation in a highly competitive system of small firms.[2] But by the end of the nineteenth century, the presumption was strong that technological advance came fastest in established, wealthy oligopolies, though in Canada in 1913 a government commission recommended that the revocation of patent privileges be used to force competition in the event of combination in restraint of trade.[3] An examination of the operation of the Canadian patent system suggests that it both fostered and hindered innovation at the same time. It helped to create, as was its intent, the rapid replication of American techniques in Canada, while it hindered the development of indigenous innovative capacity.[4]

Historically, there have been four distinct ways in which Canadian dependence on American technology and industrial capital has manifested itself. First was the theft of U.S. techniques, processes, and patterns; second, the immigration into Canada of American industrial entrepreneurs: both of these seem to have been standard until 1872, but much less in evidence thereafter — with the spectacular exception of the primary iron and steel industry. Following the Patent Act of 1872 and the National Policy of 1878-9, two other means became dominant — licensing of American patents in Canada and/or joint ventures with Canadian capital, and direct investment in branch plants.[5] While from a purely technological point of view it was simply a matter of degree, from an economic and a political perspective there was an important distinction in that theft of patents and immigration of entrepreneurs implied domesticating American technology to Canadian requirements, while licensing and branch plants implied domesticating the Canadian economy to U.S. technology. And the second two, unlike the first two, implied a measure of extraterritorial control, for licensing was as much a means of integration of the productive apparatus of the two countries as was direct investment. While the ownership relations differed, the control relationship did not. Furthermore, industries could and often did change as regards the pattern of control exercised by parent over subsidiary. In Canada over short periods of time there were instances of direct investment preceding licensing, licensing preceding direct investment, and direct investment remaining direct investment. Over the long run the level of foreign ownership of virtually every industry, and especially the most modern, capital-intensive, and technologically advanced, increased fairly steadily.

Pre-Confederation Patterns

Prior to Confederation, American technology entered Canada in the form of stolen patents, often copied from imports, and in large migrations of American skilled workers and entrepreneurs, who brought with them their savings, their technical knowledge, and often their machinery as well. For example, saw milling, the first industry to be established on any scale on capitalist, as opposed to handicraft lines, and the leading industry in Canada for the most of the nineteenth century in terms of employment and capital invested, was introduced by Americans who imported with them the capital, the machinery, and the skilled labour.[6]

American entrepreneurs in fact formed the industrial leadership of Ontario and the Eastern Townships before, and even well after, Confederation. Among the more prominent were Wall and Jackson, who built the first paper mill in 1804; E. W. Hymen's tannery in 1835; the Gurney iron foundry of 1842; J. William's carriage works in 1845; Cossitt, Massey, Frost and Harris in agricultural implements; Goldie, the leading Ontario flour miller; Raymond in sewing machines; Hiram Walker, Gooderham and Worts in distilling; to name but a few. [7] To a considerable extent, the migration of American entrepreneurs and capital coincided with the shift in Canadian consumption patterns with American goods largely replacing British in woollens and cottons, iron tools, axes and scythes, and similar products. It is impossible to completely unscramble the direction of causation, but the fact that American goods were cheaper than British, and were more suitable to Canadian agricultural conditions,[8] lends support to the view that demand was the initiating factor: the migration of American farmers and artisans to Canada led to the Americanizing of tastes and preferences.

In 1844, the first cotton factory in Canada was founded at Sherbrooke by A. T. Galt on a pattern to be repeated many times subsequently. Galt, a British born financier and land speculator, joined two Massachusetts capitalists who put up much of the venture capital and provided the management ability. The corporate form facilitated the division of function implicit in the venture, Galt providing commercial connections and the Americans the industrial capacity. The machinery was all imported.

In the capital goods industry, the first important Canadian ventures were very short-lived. Several engine works appeared rather suddenly in the boom of the early 1830's and disappeared just as quickly in the crash of 1836-7 — in one case with the help of the Bank of Upper Canada. Even earlier, two engine works to service steamships appeared in Montreal in the 1820's, one arising from the efforts of imported American engineers, the other from British.[9]

Two other industries that merit special attention because they represent fairly advanced technology for the period are agricultural implements and sewing machines. Sewing machines are especially interesting because Singer was the first American multinational firm in the modern sense, and was an early entrant into Canada, establishing its Montreal branch plant in 1885. But unlike many of the early American branches in relatively new industries, Singer never dominated the Canadian market. In 1857 Charles Raymond, an American from Massachusetts, received the patents on a machine competitive with Singer's and migrated to Canada, establishing an unsuccessful factory in Montreal in 1860, and a successful one in Guelph, Ontario, in 1862.[10] In 1869 the Raymond Sewing Machine Company produced an offspring when two of its foremen left to establish, with two local craftsmen, a new sewing machine company in Guelph. The venture was very profitable until 1874. It was then reorganized as the Guelph Sewing Machine Co. and persisted until the last of the original four partners went into assignment in 1882, possibly a victim of the National Policy which had provoked adverse criticism from some members of the sewing machine industry.[11]

Equally successful was another American émigré, R. W. Wanzer, who arrived in Hamilton from Buffalo in 1855. With the backing of Edmund Gurney, Wanzer's "Canadian" sewing machines found their market all over the world.[12] The distinction at the time between the American émigrés in the 1850s and the Singer branch plant two decades later was marginal to the business community in Canada, and to its politicians. Both represented the eagerly cultivated movement of American industrial capital and technique. The long-run consequences were, of course, vastly different.

The agricultural implements industry, as opposed to simply making tools on a handicraft basis, began when an American émigré, Daniel Massey, imported a thresher into Ontario and copied it. In 1851, his son returned to Canada from a visit to New York with the Canadian patent rights and patterns for the Ketchum mower and Burrell reaper;[13] in 1855 they acquired the rights to the patents on the Manny combine.[14] Similarly, F. T. Frost of Frost and Wood, another American immigrant, imported most of his parts from the U.S. and made his implements according to American patents he had acquired in 1861

and used without paying any royalties.[15] The American firms
supposedly gave him the patents out of friendship, but in all like-
lihood, the fact that non-residents could not secure patent rights
in Canada had something to do with it as well. The Harris
family, too, were American émigrés who had acquired the
patents from the American inventor of the Kirby machines. [16]

In 1853, the government of Canada itself got into the act of
trying to facilitate the influx of U.S. technique in the agricultural
implements industry. William McDougall was sent to the U.S. to
examine patented machinery and report on the possibility of its
introduction into Canada. The Department of Agriculture published his report along with detailed descriptions of certain
coveted machines. In 1857, the matter of technological transfers
was again in the fore with the reorganization of the administration of the patent law. The fact that the Department of Agriculture was empowered to administer patent matters demonstrated
clearly the type of American technology that was most desired in
the overwhelmingly agrarian province. That year two Boards of
Arts and Manufactures were established in both parts of the
united province on which academics, agricultural experts, and
representatives of the boards of trade and of the Mechanics Insti-
tutes of the two regions would sit and promote the diffusion of
technical knowledge in general, and the establishment of exhibitions of models of foreign agricultural implements in particular.

It was largely through Canadian interest in promoting the
influx of American technology in the agricultural implement
industry that the pattern of Canadian patent legislation took
shape. In 1849, the first general Patent Act of the Province
extended the validity of Upper Canada or Lower Canada patents
to both parts of the united province of Canada. And it stipulated
that machinery from the U.S. or other parts of British North
America could continue to be imported freely. Thus no Canadian patent could interfere with the influx of U.S. technology. In
1857 the Act was extended further. Any Canadian was free to
pirate technology from abroad and patent it, *except from the
U.S. and the Empire.* Canadian patents could not be issued that
would interfere with the free diffusion of American technique.
American patents could be freely copied, but the pirating could
not become the legal prerogative of any one person. It was generally felt that by leaving the whole field of U.S. manufacturing
open to Canadian mechanics and manufacturers they would
quickly appropriate everything valuable for reproduction at
home, especially for agricultural implements. In fact this failed
to occur on the desired scale. Canadian capitalists often could
not shoulder the heavy fixed costs necessary to produce under

American patterns. And the fact that anyone else resident in Canada could also pirate the patent and compete against the initial pirate deterred them. Moreover, American inventors took whatever defensive strategy they could to block the pirating. In those cases where pirating led to manufacture in Canada for re-export to the U.S., the remedy lay in the banning of such imports; and certain Canadian industries' products were put on New York's contraband list in 1857.

Agitation by American industry mounted through the 1850's. Under the existing laws, Canadians could get patent rights in the U.S. on the same terms, albeit at a slightly higher fee than Americans while foreign patents were still prohibited in Canada; American manufacturers began pressuring for the Canadian government to grant them patent protection *as a precondition of their introducing American technology freely into Canada.* McDougall declared in favour of the change in his 1853 report:

> I am convinced that a change in our Patent Laws by which the inventors of valuable machines in the United States could obtain the protection of a patent in Canada for a short period . . . would be the means of readily introducing numerous American inventions which under the present system are not introduced at all; or only by individuals who, hearing of them by chance, possess sufficient enterprise to become their own importers. It is now the interest of the American inventor to keep as far away as possible from the Canadian frontier.[17]

He recommended that foreigners should get patent protection in Canada on the condition that they establish *either* a manufactory *or* a warehouse in the province; at that time the influx of technology itself was the objective regardless of whether it came via imports or by local production. He further recommended a system of £100 bonuses for the introduction of certain types of machinery by private enterprise.

The extension of general patent protection to American "inventors" was not forthcoming, and as a result the American government retaliated by withdrawing patent privileges to Canadians. This left Canadian patent legislation in a completely unsatisfactory position. The inability of Americans to get patent protection deterred them from exporting their machinery and equipment to Canada, while the inability of Canadians to secure a patent for pirating American patterns impeded them from copying and reproducing American technique. A partial solution evolved in the form of a series of special Acts of the Provincial Legislature granting patent protection in special cases to Canadian "representatives" of U.S. patent-holders. Each of these

required a separate vote of the Legislature, and they always stipulated that the patent had to be manufactured in Canada
within two years to retain its validity. This two-year clause was
unique to the special Acts: it was not part of the general legislation.

While in theory American inventors could directly apply for a
vote of special patent, in fact they were virtually always refused.
The result was to foster a system of patent brokerage with Canadians acting as agents, or sometimes buying up American patents
cheaply. Success in obtaining the special Acts depended much
less on the merits of invention than it did on the parliamentary
influence of the foreign inventor or his Canadian agent. And of
course it failed to secure for bona fide Canadian inventions any
protection abroad. During the 1866 session, eight special patent
Acts passed the Legislature, all of them involving processes for
refining, smelting, etc. of primary products; a reflection, in part
at least, of the opening of the petroleum boom in southwestern
Ontario. One Quebec resident secured a patent for petroleum
refining as Canadian representative of three U.S. inventors
including his brother. Two other petroleum refining patents were
secured by other Canadians on behalf of foreign inventors.
Another case involved a process for turning peat into coal,
another iron smelting, another a pulping process for wood, and
two others were for mineral refining. Of the eight only one went
directly to the U.S. inventors: all others had Canadian intermediaries and in four of the seven intermediated cases, the Canadian
agents were members of the Canadian Parliament.[18]

Post-Confederation Patterns

In 1869 the first federal patent act was passed, modelled, predictably on the Province of Canada legislation, and stipulating that
only residents of the Dominion could take out patents. British
subjects had to fulfil a one-year residence requirement, and
manufacture had to occur within three years of the patent being
granted. [19] While the intent was to facilitate the imitation of U.S.
patents or the inflow of American entrepreneurs, in reality the
domicile clause was easy to evade, a simple affirmation legally
sufficing. With the 1872 Patent Act a radical new departure
occurred.

In the debates concerning amendment to the law, the leader
of the opposition, Alexander Mackenzie, asked for an amendment that would stipulate that no patent be granted if a manufacturer was already in the process of producing in Canada.[20]

This and other protective clauses were built into the new act. Patents could be granted to an inventor if his invention had not been in public use or for sale in Canada for more than a year prior to the application, thus protecting the Canadian "owners" of already pirated inventions. Patents, too, could not be given if a patent existed for the device in another country for more than twelve months prior to application in Canada. This clause not only protected past thefts but opened the door to copying all patents from the U.S. that were already established in functioning industry. Moreover, it forced the Americans in the future to seek immediately a Canadian patent. And if, during that twelve months, any person in Canada commenced to manufacture in Canada, the manufacturer retained the right to continue to produce. Thus, once the Americans sustained the risk and the expense, the Canadian manufacturers could take advantage of it free of charge *in the home market,* helping to free Canadian industry of the need to put money into industrial research, and Canadian governments of the need to invest in technical education. If a foreign patent also existed, the Canadian patent expired at the earliest date of expiry of any foreign patent. Patents too, could be taken out by designated agents of the inventor and joint applications were permitted.

But the most important section of the Act was clause 28:

> Every patent . . . shall be subject . . . to the conditions that such patent and all the rights and privileges therein granted shall cease . . . and the patent shall be null and void, at the end of two years from the date thereof unless the patentee, or his *assignee or assignees* shall, within that period have commenced; and shall after such commencement continuously carry on in Canada the construction or manufacture of the invention or discovery patented . . . at some manufactory or establishment for making or constructing it in Canada, and that such patent shall be void if after expiry of twelve months from the granting thereof, the patentee or his assignee or assignees for the whole or a part of his interest in the patent *imports,* or causes to be imported into Canada, the invention for which the patent is granted.[21] [Emphasis added.]

The use of agents, the two-year manufacturing stipulation (some politicians had pressed for one year), and the import nullification facets of the Act all assured that it would have an enormous impact on Canadian industrial development. Under its effects, as much and perhaps more than under the tariff of 1878-79, there occurred a proliferation of American branch plants, joint ventures, and licensing arrangements. American technology for British markets became Canada's industrial *raison d'être.*

And this result was consciously solicited. The Canadian Manufacturers' Association from its inception had proudly declared its adherence to a philosophy of industrial continentalism and second-hand technique:

> In certain realms of thought we may follow Oxford or Cambridge, or Edinburgh, or Dublin, but when it comes to driving shoe pegs by machinery we follow Massachusetts. . . Our cotton machinery, brought from England, though it may be, is worked so as to produce goods like those of Lawrence and Fall River, not like those of Blackburn and Preston. Our agricultural machinery is made after Ohio and Illinois patterns, with perhaps a few Canadian improvements: our stoves are copies from Albany and Troy. [22]

The impact on Canadian innovative capacity of the ease of access to American industrial technology was negative. In 1869, when only Canadians could take out patents, 588 were granted. By 1899, 30 years later, Canada's population had doubled, its GNP per capita had risen sharply, and it had felt the first four years of the great expansion of the pre-war period, but the number of patents granted to Canadians stood at 701, while that same year Americans were granted 2,312 in Canada.

TABLE X (1)

Patents Issued by Country of Residence

Year	Total	Canada	U.S.	Britain
1855	92	92	—	—
1860	150	150	—	—
1865	162	162*	—	—
1870	556	556*	—	—
1875	1,323	523	n.a.	n.a.
1880	1,408	492	843	50
1885	2,447	610	1,498	85
1890	2,428	620	1,623	116
1895	3,074	707	1,980	179
1900	4,552	707	3,216	254
1905	6,647	888	4,451	309
1910	8,233	1,198	5,021	342
1914	9,241	1,334	5,220	558

*Province of Canada until 1865, thereafter Dominion.

Some of the most restrictive clauses of the 1872 Act were modified slightly. Some exceptions were granted for short periods in the case of non-manufacture. In a few cases, imports were permitted without nullifying the patent if the importing was of

TABLE X (2)

Patents Issued to Canadians, 1868-1885

Year	No.	Year	No.	Year	No.
1868	546	1874	530	1880	492
1869	588	1875	523	1881	558
1870	556	1876	575	1882	538
1871	509	1877	533	1883	612
1872	671	1878	454	1884	607
1873	n.a.	1879	479	1885	610

TABLE X (3)

Provincial Distribution of Patents in Canada, 1874-1885

	1874	1875	1876	1877	1878	1879
Ontario	344	348	340	340	315	308
Quebec	147	136	153	132	102	134
New Brunswick	19	24	19	22	16	16
Nova Scotia	14	14	21	34	17	16
Prince Edward Island	4	—	—	2	3	2
Manitoba	1	—	1	—	—	2
British Columbia	1	1	2	3	1	1
Total	530	523	536	533	454	479

Sources for all tables: *SYB*, 1888-1904; *CYB*, 1904-1914; Dept. of Agriculture, *Annual Reports*, 1881-1914.

short duration, and designed to build up a domestic market for a product prior to undertaking full-scale manufacturing.[23] Over time, the courts tended to modify the manufacturing clause so that all that was required was that the patentee advertise himself as willing to supply on demand, with no need for manufacturing in the absence of demand for the patent to retain its validity.[24] These modified interpretations were built into the Patent Act Amendment in 1903[25] along with abandonment of the clause that held a patent to be void as soon as its earliest foreign patent expired.[26]

Nonetheless, the effects of the policy were the submergence of Canadian innovative capacity under a flood of American-imported techniques. The pirating process and the emigration of American entrepreneurs paled by comparison to the deluge of assembly operations established by American firms in Canada; the assembly bias of the operations ensured both by the fact that simple assembly sufficed to maintain the patent and by the increase over time in the staggering of tariffs with low or zero rates for inputs and semi-finished goods.

While the total number of patents granted rose quickly after the 1872 act, the proportion going to Canadians fell from 100% in 1869 to 33% by 1884 to 16% by 1908. The fastest rate of growth of Canadian patents occurred from 1855 to 1872, thereafter leveling off until 1903, followed by an acceleration. But the rate of acceleration of Canadian patents was less than that of foreign, especially American, and the gap widened. Furthermore, the most striking fact to emerge from the figures is that patents issued to Canadians fell absolutely after the 1872 patent act, and fell absolutely again after the high tariffs of 1878-79. In 1876 at the bottom of a great recession, Canadian patents stood at 576. Not until 1883, at the very top of the much vaunted National-Policy-CPR boom, was the figure again reached. Apart from one unusual year in 1886, not until 1895 was the level of patents issued to Canadians to reach and maintain itself at the level achieved in 1869.

One major problem impeding Canadian innovation was the lack of financing available to the industrial sector. Not only did it suffer from the indifference of the commercial banks, but direct aid to industry from the federal and provincial governments was absent, apart from primary iron and steel at the end of the century. Few private banks too were of any use, apart from such spectacular cases as Daniel Stewart of Aylmer who bankrupted himself by dealing in patent rights in 1878 and absconded leaving $21 in the till.[27]

Under the terms of the 1872 Act, U.S. manufacturers had to begin manufacturing in Canada within two years at a time when direct investment was possible by only an elite of firms, and when the supply of Canadian entrepreneurs with access to venture capital to join in licensed ventures was short. The Canadian inventor, too, had to find an assignee to undertake manufacture if he could not afford to do so himself. As a result a class of professional patent dealers sprang up, who perpetrated frauds on such a magnitude that, within ten years of the Act that gave them birth, new legislation to curb them had to be considered. These patent jobbers, especially in agricultural implements and similar lines of tools, would obtain patents, usually American, and sell the rights to farmers, by convincing the farmers that they could manufacture it themselves as cheaply as they could buy the product. Inevitably the cost of handicraft manufacture would far exceed the means of the farmer, who would be left with a worthless patent. The promissory note with which he paid would be taken and immediately discounted. The contemplated legislation stipulated that any promissory note issued in conjunction with the sale or rental of a patent had to be clearly marked as pertaining to a patent, and when the patent turned out to be valueless the note was null and void.[28]

Over time, more legitimate forms of patent jobbing emerged whose effect was to facilitate the exploitation of foreign, especially American, inventions in Canada. For example, in 1895, a Toronto firm, Dominion Specialty Manufacturing Company, was formed for this express purpose,[29] joined two years later by a Montreal firm, Universal Patent Developing Company.[30]

Financing of indigenous innovation, on the other hand, continued to be a major problem. In 1902, a bill was presented to the Commons proposing to extend the life of patents from 18 to 30 years to assist the Canadian inventor who needed more time to get an enterprise on its feet. The Toronto Board of Trade objected to the extension, since it would mean "the possible tying up for a very long term of valuable inventions of British and foreign patentees, thus depriving the people of the Dominion of the benefit of them."[31] This bill did not pass.

The blatant theft of patents from poor inventors who could not afford the legal expenses or other commitments necessary to secure a patent was a common phenomenon, the benefit accruing to the manufacturers who secured the invention without the need for royalties.[32] Nor did the international theft of patents entirely disappear, though it did diminish considerably. The courts, and even the Judicial Committee of the Privy Council, still had their share of contentious patents to consider.

The International Movement of Patents: I

In the area of agricultural implements, the difficulties experienced by farmers over the activities of professional swindlers dealing in implement patents, and in fact in fraudulent obtaining of notes in conjunction with all manner of implement transactions,[33] were no doubt made worse by the fact that American implement manufacturers had particular difficulty in getting adequate patent protection. Even after the National Policy they were reluctant to build branches in Canada.[34] Canadian firms using pirated or rented U.S. patents with minor modifications had already cornered the market which, in Canada, was an extremely large and therefore lucrative one. It was the patent system, not the tariff, that was responsible for "Canadian" firms established by émigré Americans using American techniques, maintaining control of the Canadian market, when so many

other industries were swamped. It also remained the most con-
tinuously prosperous industry in Canada, flourishing throughout
the 1870's depression when commerce was totally disrupted.[35] It
continued to grow and prosper, and in the first decade of the
1900's the Massey-Harris merger accounted for a full fifteen per
cent of the value of Canada's total manufactured exports.

The essential pattern of reliance on U.S. patents in the agricultural implements industry did not change after Confederation.
In 1882 John Watson of Ayr secured the use of Deering models.[36]
He was not alone; for virtually every firm in Canada advertised
its ability to produce on American patents during the 1880's,[37]
including a firm of post-Confederation American émigrés, Patterson and Bros. Ltd. of Woodstock, Ontario,[38] and the Noxon
Bros. of neighbouring Ingersoll.[39] When Edward Gurney
attempted to enter the field of agricultural implement production, his strategy was to attempt to have a harvester patent secured by A. Harris Son and Co. invalidated on the grounds of
non-manufacture in Canada. This suit was unsuccessful.[40]
Thereafter Gurney remained out of the implement field. It was
clear that securing patents was more than just the key to finding
markets, but also an effective barrier to keep new entrants out of
the industry.

The actual efforts of American firms to break into the field
with branch plants were few and far between. As early as 1860 a
branch of a Rochester firm, Hall Bros., was established in
Oshawa, the first American branch plant in Canada, but it was
short-lived.[41] Two other attempts were made by joint ventures in
the early 1880's. The North American Agricultural Implement
Co. established in London in 1883 was based on the patents of
the John Deere Plow Co. and the Moline Wagon Co., and its
board of directors included the presidents of both of these American firms. But it soon abandoned the field and moved to other
forms of toolmaking. The other effort was the Toronto Reaper
and Mower Co., a partnership based on Whitby patents —
Whitby had been careful to secure full patent protection in
Canada before joining the joint venture.[42] The firm built the
largest harvester factory in Canada before being absorbed by the
Massey company in 1881.

As in other industries, the patent law provided room for
intermediary and jobbing activities. In 1878 for example, a
Truro, Nova Scotia, businessman secured American patents and
instead of manufacturing himself he advertised his willingness to
enter into an agreement with a Canadian firm for their manufacture.[43]

In 1890, the Deering Co. purchased a site at Hamilton for a branch plant, but not until 1904 did International Harvester, which had absorbed the Deering firm, actually build a branch plant. Ironically, Deering's strength was due to one of the rare instances of a flow of Canadian innovation to the United States. The Harvester was invented by Charles and William March, whose father had joined William Lyon Mackenzie's rebellion against British rule in 1837, and had subsequently moved with his entire family to Illinois. Their patents turned out to be defective and open to infringement; and many U.S. firms made open use of them in the 1870's and later.[44]

But Deering and International Harvester remained an exceptional and very late case, the norm being Canadian use of U.S. patents. About the same time as International Harvester began to make its move, the first successful takeover of a Canadian firm occurred when the John Abell Engine and Machine Co. of Toronto could not secure enough funds in Canada to continue to operate and was forced to sell to an American merger, producing the American-Abell Engine Co.[45] But after the merger the implement business of the Canadian branch seems to have been discontinued. In the 1870's, during a very brief period when there was some significant competition from imports from the U.S., Cossitt and Bros. called for increased protection, not through tariff increases but by alterations in the laws governing trade marks to prevent foreign firms from being able to register words as trademarks in Canada if the word had been in use in Canada for a number of years. This would ensure that brand loyalty built up by U.S. firms would accrue to the Canadian patentee, an especially important factor in light of the number of American farmers settled in the Ontario agricultural frontier. Other implement firms called for strengthening of patent protection. The demand for tariff increases was conspicuously absent.[46] The use of patents continued to grow, and thereby blocked out American branch plants. The McCormick Machine Co. of Chicago tried to establish a branch plant in the early 1890's, and then simply licensed Cossitt Bros. to manufacture the McCormick Binder.[47] American patents also lay at the basis of the establishment of the Bissel Manufacturing Co. in 1901.[48] Massey-Harris in 1902 became involved in a lawsuit launched by the inventor of the Hancock plough for alleged infringement of his patents.[49]

Another industry closely linked to agriculture was the manufacture of barbed wire. The same pattern prevailed, but with even closer dependency since the firms making barbed wire in

Canada were all licensed by U.S. firms,[50] rather than involving some pirating as well. The Dominion Wire Manufacturing Company, founded by Montreal wholesale hardware merchants F. Fairman and J. Cooper,[51] and the firm of H. Ives and Co., established by the American émigré wholesale hardware dealer under the auspices of the Washburn and Moen Manufacturing Co. of Worcester, Mass.[52] were both examples of the use of American industrial techniques to make the transformation in Canada from commercial to industrial capital. The main burden and risk of the innovation had already been absorbed by the American inventors.

The industry's development was a fairly involved process, with considerable legal entanglement resulting from the operation of patent laws. In 1879 the Canada Wire Co. was incorporated by H. R. Ives and his associates as a Montreal-American joint venture.[53] The firm immediately began production by copying the barbed wire of Washburn and Moen, the leading U.S. producer. Washburn was so zealous to protect its patents that it ran a series of threatening advertisements in Canadian papers as follows:

> You are hereby notified that in putting *barbs upon wire,* or in making a *barbed wire fence,* or in using or dealing in barbs for wire or barbed fence wire, not under license from us, you are infringing upon our patents, and we shall hold you accountable for damages for all infringements . . .[54]

The threat seems to have been aimed at Ives in particular, for apart from Washburn's licensees in Montreal, the only other producer was the Dominion Barb Wire Fence Co. of Montreal. The firm was established by the wholesale hardware merchants, Cooper and Fairman, to produce yet another American patent. And in fact in 1881 Washburn launched a suit against Ives for infringement.[55] Ives promptly launched a countersuit against Washburn's Montreal licensee on the grounds of importation and non-manufacture within two years,[56] suggesting that the licensee was really a front operation only pretending to manufacture in order that the American firm would maintain its patent.

In the early 1880's there were many Canadian firms who secured access to patents from the several existing U.S. producers,[57] and to consolidate the Canadian market Washburn and Moen had to first effectively cartelize the American producers under its leadership. This was done very effectively, and the American competitors were brought under a strict price and patent arrangement.

By the late 1880's, Washburn and Moen had extended into

Canada the hold they had achieved on the American barbed wire market. Against the Lyman Manufacturing Company they had obtained an injunction to stop it from making more wire than their licence agreement stipulated.[58] H. R. Ives and Co. had become a licensee.[59] Several Canadian firms had been proceeded against to prevent them from manufacturing anything but Washburn and Moen patents, such an exclusive contract having been part of the patent arrangement.[60] In 1888 there were but three Canadian firms manufacturing wire,[61] that of Fairman and Cooper, the Ives company, and the Ontario Lead and Barb Wire Co., which was licensed by another American firm.[62] Not until 1893 did an American branch plant become established for the purpose of barbed wire manufacture, and by 1896 it was in liquidation.[63]

In Ives's case, he paid royalties well above those paid in the U.S. by licencees, the difference undoubtedly due to the tariff. This firm needed the tariff to justify its existence, for under the terms of the licence the U.S. firm agreed not to export to Canada, but nothing in the agreement prevented Canadian retailers from going to the U.S. and buying the products there. Only the tariff would permit the Montreal wholesalers-turned-manufacturers to control the retail trade. The barbed wire cartel simply passed on the higher licence fees to Canadian consumers (farmers and retailers) through higher prices possible behind the tariff wall,[64] part of the tariff protection thus accruing to the American firm which held the patent.

In other facets of wire or cable production the same pattern of licensing existed. The Canada Screw Co. of Hamilton was established as a de facto branch plant of the American Screw Co., and made use of its patents, including those for cutting and pointing wire.[65] In 1898, however, the American parent sold the firm to a Canadian group headed by its Canadian manager, C.A. Birge,[66] and only licensing remained as a formal connection between them.

In fence wire and similar products there were several American licensees active. The B. Greening Wire Co. of Hamilton got the sole Dominion rights from one U.S. firm to manufacture its steel wire chains. The American Braided Wire Co. successfully sued its licensee for patent infringement on the basis that he had cut prices on the parent, and this price cutting was contrary to the contract. The judge ordered the defendant to repay to the licensor all the profits the licensor had lost by the price cutting of its licensee.[68] Also linked to agricultural development, in part at least, was the growth of the Canadian Fairbanks-Morse Co. Ltd. which began as a branch plant in 1900 and was taken over by a local board headed by an American émigré in 1905, becoming a licensee. Its output included a wide range of machinery and mechanical equipment. Almost all of Canada's grain output was weighed on its scales, and its ploughing and other engines were among the most widely used in the country.[69]

The flow of American patents into Canada occurred in virtually every conceivable industry, occasionally without bothering to inform the American inventors. For example, the largest and most successful firm in Canada's eminently prosperous musical instruments industry, the Bell Organ Co. of Guelph, produced organs that were copied from American models by William Bell, the American immigrant who founded the firm.[70] But licensing was much more the rule after the 1872 Patent Act. Samuel May, who built the first billiard tables in Canada copying U.S. models, diversified his imitations in 1886 when he used U.S. patents in the Dodge Wood Split Pulley Co. of Canada in Toronto.[71] Both of May's industries were described as "unique," an early euphemism for monopoly. May was so successful an imitator that he was heralded by the CMA as a true "captain of industry"; the patent pulley was soon supplying not only many "Canadian" firms like the Ottawa lumber industry, but even got on an export basis through its London agents.[72]

Furniture firms too used American patents for all manner of operations. The Edgar Manufacturing Co. of Hamilton produced a patent spring support for chairs under licence from a New York firm.[73] James Hay of Woodstock was sued by an American firm for infringement of patents for a machine to prepare cane for furniture.[74] Hay's firm later became locked into long-term supply contracts with Singer's Canadian branch plant.[75]

Moncton as early as 1877 had a licensee of a U.S. firm producing plumbing equipment,[76] a field into which the Ontario Lead and Barbed Wire Co. branched, also under licence, in 1887. There were even American licensing arrangements and joint ventures in the overcrowded stove, foundry, and boiler business.[78] And in 1890 a joint venture of New York and Canadian capital was formed to buy and sell patent rights for explosives,[79] another industry which Americans operated in Canada through patent arrangements.[80] Even cheque books were made in Canada by the Carter-Crume Co., a wholly Canadian-owned licensee.[81]

Bicycles were a tremendously successful Canadian industry by the turn of the century, and many of the firms, including the misnamed Canadian Typography Co., produced American patents in Canada for export to Empire markets.[82] The CCM merger too was built on patents from the American Bicycle

Company, which granted the firm the rights to the Canadian market. And of the wave of failures that struck in 1896 following a great rush of capital into the new industry, at least one was caused by the firm having locked up its capital in the purchase of patent rights.[83]

The international patent system worked asymmetrically. Gurney, the stove maker and founder in the 1870's, complained that the U.S. patent office was hostile to Canadian industry, that he could not secure patents to his inventions in the U.S. Of course, Gurney's inventions may have been based in no small measure on earlier pirating from the period when he first migrated to Canada. The boot and shoe industry had similar complaints.[84] One of the pioneers of the industry in Canada, Louis Coté, had worked as a hired hand in the boot and shoe factories in New England before returning to St. Hyacinthe, where he set up his own factory in 1863. He was already a leading "inventor" of machinery by the time the firm was established. Subsequently he became involved in legal battles over patent rights in the U.S.[85]

Although the boot and shoe industry was exclusively Canadian-owned, the use of American machinery had been absolutely essential to its early development, and it was via the producers' goods, rather than the consumers' goods production, that American influence was exercised. One American patent pool, the Mackay Association, leased boot and shoe machinery to little factories all over the U.S., initially for a royalty payable per pair of shoes, later an annual lump sum rental.[86] These machines were also standard in Canada, and the early 1870's saw several factories established in Montreal to make the machinery. The Mackay group did not have a Canadian patent, and hence the Canadian companies — notably one that included Guy Boivin, the rather unstable Montreal manufacturer — simply copied the American machinery. But the U.S. firm so drastically undercut prices on the machines that the Canadian firms failed.[87]

A critically important change in the industry occurred in 1891 when the Goodyear Shoe Manufacturing Co. of Canada was established in Montreal to buy patents in shoe machinery. Charles Goodyear, the American rubber magnate, had for several years been in control of the Canadian rights for boot and shoe machinery, and had been manufacturing. The new reorganized firm included among its Canadian participants, James C. Holden, partner of H. B. Ames in one of the largest Anglo-Canadian shoe manufacturing firms.[88] Ames-Holden now had direct control over the use in Canada of the American machinery, and quickly came to achieve a near-monopoly in the industry so long dominated by small semi-handicraft firms, despite efforts by French firms to get control of the vital patents and stage a come-back.[89]

The Migration of Patents: II

While there was considerable inflow of American inventions into basic and mechanical industries of an earlier vintage, or even later ones like typewriters,[90] it was in the new high-technology industries of the second industrial revolution that the depen-dence grew to an absolute. In these industries, applied science was extremely important, and in this regard the Canadian educa-tional system was an abysmal failure. Canada entered the second industrial revolution suffering simultaneously from an anti-quated educational system, a shortage of industrial capital, and an entrepreneurial class of which a large part had already acquired the habit of dependence.

The shortage of skilled labour was a problem in many indus-tries by the end of 1870's, necessitating imports of skilled labour, while at the same time a surfeit of unskilled existed.[91] Many of the great public works too were designed and supervised by American engineers.[92] By 1900, with industrial expansion well under way on a major scale, many employers who had tried to provide on-the-spot training to fill the need for skills abandoned it in favour of imports of skilled men from the United States and Germany: on-the-job training of men who had no occupational training at all was too slow.[93] By 1913, the situation was chronic in virtually every major industry; in some, orders were refused because of the lack of trained personnel.[94]

The educational system of Canada was more a hindrance than a help. It was made provincial jurisdiction under the terms of Confederation at the same time the provinces were stripped of adequate sources of funds to support it, provincial revenues being diverted by the federal government into the construction of commercial infrastructure. In the prairies, the situation was exa-cerbated by the lack of revenue from natural resources, the public lands being in the hands of the federal government, the CPR, the Hudson's Bay Company, and a host of eastern land-speculating firms.

As early as 1882, the CMA began to point with anxiety to the lack of facilities for technical education,[95] and its admonitions continued, to little avail.[96] In central Canada, the tax system usu-ally exempted real estate held as an investment by the classically and professionally oriented colleges [97] while technical and vocational schools were starved of funds. In contrast to the United States, where a series of land grant colleges turned farmers' sons into engineers, the Canadian educational system blocked the vocational training of the offspring of people from lower-middle-class and working-class backgrounds in favour of refining the deportment of the children of the commercial elite, who eschewed any vocation that resembled work. As a result, there was a glut of professionals—doctors, lawyers and clergymen—such that, according to the CMA:

> Lawyers' offices are overstocked with impecunious new graduates, so too physicians' . . . It is this surplus in an honourable profession that supplies the demand for abortionists and similar questionable characters.[98]

Until World War I, no industrial research was done in Canada. [99] The ease of access to foreign technology and the facility with which skilled labour could be imported combined with commercial domination of the educational system to prevent the necessary adaptation.

The impact of the imported second industrial revolution effected a considerable transition in Canadian industrial structure, producing a series of new industries and transforming many old ones. Drugs and chemicals, for example, were very much affected by the inflow of American patents and technology. The first chemical-based fibre production occurred under license to George Drummond and John MacDougall in 1882.[100] Even in fuel oils some of the technological advance was derivative, with the Rathbun Co. producing under licence, while ironically one of the kerosene pioneers had been the Nova Scotia engineer Abraham Gesner.[101]

The rubber industry in Canada began on a small scale in the 1880's, making fire and garden hose, bicycle tires, and similar mechanical products. Some licensing arrangements existed; some of the firms were independent. Gutta Percha, for example, began as a branch plant but was so successful that in 1884 the Canadian firm was incorporated separately,[102] and by 1887 its sole association with the parent was via licensing. In 1899 a syndicate including George Cox and Edmund Gurney, Jr., was formed to establish the Dunlop Tire Co. of Canada, taking over the business formerly done in Canada by American Dunlop,[103] while the same year the stock broker Senator Robert Mackay headed the Montreal group who promoted the Boston Rubber Company's Canadian affiliate.[104] These firms, especially Dunlop, were tied into the bicycle industry as well as producing consumer goods.

But with the advent of the automobile the industry was transformed from one producing light consumer goods to one manufacturing producers' goods tributary to the automobile industry,
and a wave of takeovers and branch plant establishments
occurred.[105]

The automobile industry itself forms a case par excellence of
licensed ventures being converted into wholly-owned subsidiaries. The automobile industry was in Canada exclusively
foreign in origin, largely American with some early British presence. Patent protection seems to have been the cause of the
foreign domination, for there were fruitless efforts of Canadian
capitalists to enter the field. As early as 1896 a group of
Québécois entrepreneurs subscribed $150,000 for the Moto-cycle
Company of Canada to make "horseless vehicles,"[106] but this
firm seems to have come to naught.

The Canadian roots of the industry were twofold: first, distributing outlets of U.S. firms which later undertook manufacturing; second, the outgrowth of Canadian carriage works[107] or,
in one case, a bicycle manufacturer. The first group evolved
more or less directly into branch plants once a local market of
sufficient size to justify manufacturing was assured; the second
group formed joint licensed ventures with the American producers and later regressed to branch plants.

Ford of Canada was founded by a Canadian carriage maker,
Gordon McGregor, in 1904 who turned over 51% of the equity
to the parent firm in exchange for Ford patent rights in perpe-
tuity and control of Canada and the empire markets, excluding
Britain. Robert McLaughlin too began as a carriage maker and
entered a joint venture with Buick in 1907. Everett-Metzer was
established on a licensed basis in 1908 evolving into Studebaker-
Canada by 1911. The story of Willys is a little more complex,
though essentially the same. In 1896 the Lozier Manufacturing
Company was established in Toronto Junction as a joint venture
of Canadian and American capital to build bicycles, typewriters,
and motor vehicles, all under American patents.[108] It became part
of the CCM merger in 1899, and CCM thereafter formed a division known as the Russell Motor Company which acquired the
Willys and Overland patents. Duryea too came to Canada as a
joint venture. One early case of British involvement came with
the Still Motor Co. Ltd., of Toronto formed by a Toronto group
to make the English Still patents. By 1900 the English firm had
bought out the Canadian interest, converting the firm into a
branch plant.[109]

In the case of the joint ventures of Canadian carriage or

bicycle works with American automobile factories, a strict division of labour was usually worked out, leaving the Canadian interest to build the chassis, while the engines and more technically advanced parts were imported from the American parent.[110] For despite early growth with a number of major firms established and flourishing,—one of the most outstanding of which was the Waterous Engine Works established by an American immigrant in 1884 at Brantford[111]—the Canadian machine and engine works industry seemed to regress late in the century. At the same time a flow of American branch plants and licensed ventures began.

In 1882 the Ingersoll Rock Drill Company was formed to make machine drills and air compressors based on the models of the Massachusetts Ingersoll firm, its Canadian promoters being the Montreal wholesale hardware merchants F. Fairman and James Cooper.[112] In 1889 the Canada Rand Drill Co. followed at Sherbrooke to make machinery on the Rand patterns; it was a joint venture of A. C. Rand of New York with S. W. Jencks, a Sherbrooke engine manufacturer.[113] Many other cases appeared subsequently, [114] especially in mining machinery, and particularly after 1896 when the new mineral boom began. James Cooper reorganized in a larger scale as the James Cooper Manufacturing Co. [115] Waterous too moved into mining machinery. In Nova Scotia, the old Robb Engineering Co. in Amherst began manufacturing engines under licence from their American controllers.[116]

In flour milling machinery the same patterns emerged. Many innovations were brought to Canada in the early post-Confederation period by the American E. W. Rathbun, among the many new techniques he introduced into Canadian industrialism.[117] In 1885, a joint venture of John Bertram of Dundas with American capital established a roller flour mill machinery company.[118] Then in 1896 a Stratford company secured the patents of a Milwaukee mill machinery firm to manufacture in Canada.[119]

In several other machinery fields the same pattern occurred. In 1898, a large rotary engine works opened under licence, ranging from machines for foundries and metal works[120] to the early gasoline engines for industrial use.[121] American technology, capital, and patents were involved in a Montreal joint venture with A. F. Gault in 1898 in the first attempt to introduce textile machinery manufacture into Canada.[122]

The electrical products industry is, along with automobiles, virtually synonymous with the second industrial revolution.

Patents and patent laws were instrumental in creating a "Canadian" electrical industry in both the utility and the manufacturing facets. American Bell in 1880 established and initially wholly owned all the equity except for that needed to qualify a local board in the Bell Telephone Co. of Canada. The local board was headed by an American, along with Montreal wholesale dry goods men J. R. Thibodeau and Duncan McIntyre.[123] The company immediately acquired the telegraph properties of four Canadian companies as well as several Canadian telephone firms.[124] It followed a policy of encouraging Canadian stockholding, and by 1885 it was majority-controlled in Canada.[125] But the patents remained American-controlled. In telegraphs the same setup prevailed. Dominion Telegraph Co., established in 1881, had 4,250 of its 5,000 shares owned in Canada, but Western Union controlled the firm through the patent rights it leased.[126] In production of electrical components, Westinghouse entered Canada via a licensed venture wholly owned in Canada in 1882, while Canadian patent laws forced Edison to establish a Canadian branch plant within two years of building his American one.[127] Bell, too, was forced to build a manufacturing subsidiary in Montreal because of patent restrictions, and a licensed joint venture tied into the Bell system was established later to make cable and wire.[128]

Access to American patents was essential to success in the industry from an early date, not only in manufacturing, but also in the utility aspect. And the big companies used their control of patents to try to defend and augment their position in the industry. In 1883, a Canada-U.S. joint venture, the Sperry Electric Light and Motor Co., was established in Toronto to try to acquire patents to manufacture electrical machinery and parts, without apparent success.[129] The next year saw the establishment of a rival telephone company and a new telephone exchange in Toronto, both infringing on Bell patents.[130] Although one of Bell's patents was voided on the grounds of non-manufacture and continued importation the next year,[131] it did not seem sufficient to ensure its rival's success. The Sperry case was only the first of a long series of patent battles launched in Toronto by Bell's rivals —all were largely unsuccessful.[132]

Similarly, the Montreal-based oligopoly run by Edison Electric Light Co. successfully battled against locally owned firms to establish its hegemony and extend it. In 1889, the Royal Electric Co. fought the Edison Electric Light Co. over a patent for the manufacture of electric lights. The patent however was upheld.[133] By 1900, the Royal Electric had abandoned all efforts to manufacture parts and the Canadian company became purely an electric light and power supplier.[134]

The 1900 capitulation of Royal Electric came at the same time another Canadian-owned operation, the Toronto Street Railway Co., was forced to abandon the manufacture of electric parts and confine itself to utility operations because of patent infringements,[135] and in both cases the successful party was the firm that grew out of Edison's Canadian branches, Canadian General Electric. The merger of Edison's two plants with two other licensed ventures was effected in 1892 by a syndicate headed by Senator Frederic Nicholls at the same time as the American merger. The Canadian group at first held only a minority of the shares with an option to buy out the American equity. This option was exercised by 1899, and Van Horne and Herbert Holt joined the directorate of the firm whose sole linkage with the parent firm thereafter was through licensing.[136] Following the consolidation of its manufacturing rights in 1900, the board by 1902 consisted of Nicholls, George Cox, Rodolphe Forget, Herbert Holt, E. B. Osler, Robert Jaffray, James Ross, W. D. Matthews and Van Horne.[137]

In 1896, Westinghouse and American General Electric formed a patent pool arrangement,[138] and this arrangement was extended to Canada. Westinghouse in Canada evolved from simple licensing into a joint venture heavily dominated by its American parent at the same time Canadian General Electric moved in the opposite direction.[139]

Canadian Marconi, a relative latecomer, was set up as a licensed joint venture under Andrew Allan in 1907.[140]

In every facet of the electrical industry, American dominance manifested itself.[141] The year 1890 saw the establishment of a Montreal firm planning to go into the business of building underground telegraph and telephone cable systems. The list of promoters and their vocations spells out clearly the relations of Canadian and American capital in the industry: one American civil engineer, one American mechanical engineer, one American "capitalist," one Montreal contractor, and one Montreal merchant.[142] Even for a little local utility company like the Reliance Electric Co. of Waterford, access to American technique was essential to success, so much so that the company locked up half of its capital in patents and failed in 1894 in the wake of the collapse of the local private bank that had kept it afloat.[143] Gurney, who had tried unsuccessfully to break into agricultural implements by contesting the Harris company's American patents, spared himself the ignominy of defeat and simply secured a licence to manufacture arc lights from a U.S. inventor.[144] The only significant example of the flow of technology working in reverse was the Wanzer lamp, invented by R. W. Wanzer of Hamilton. It was the exception that proved the rule, for Wanzer, the sewing machine magnate, was an American who retired back to the U.S. at the end of his Canadian business career.[145]

Canadian Industry and Its Northern Vision

Branch plants, joint ventures, licensing arrangements — in one very important respect the difference between them is negligible. All represent a form of industrial dependence and a stifling of indigenous innovative capacity. The greater the success achieved in introducing American technology, the poorer became the record of Canadian achievement.

The Canadian strategy was a conscious one. Canada refused to join the International Union for the Protection of Industrial Property, a patent union which included the U.S., Germany and Britain, the three principal sources of supply of patents for Canadian industry, because under the terms of the union, each country afforded to the others' citizens the same patent rights as it gave their own. For Canada to have joined would have precluded the enforcement of the prohibition of imports clause in its patent law. And when at the Colonial Conference of 1907 the idea of uniformity of patent laws throughout the Empire was considered, Laurier contended it would only be an acceptable move if Britain included for the first time a compulsory working-up clause in its patent legislation.[146]

One British commentator, Sir Lloyd Wise, pointed out to the CMA in 1904 what he thought to be the danger of such clauses. He noted that similar clauses in French patent law had led earlier to a migration of German dye firms into France and that these had outcompeted and destroyed the French industry. "Surely," he said, "that cannot be the sort of effect which you, as manufacturers, would desire to see brought about in any branch of Canadian industry?"[147] It was, of course, a rhetorical question, but the rhetorical answer would have surprised Sir Lloyd, for the CMA, which he was addressing, was dominated by the representatives of branch plants, joint ventures and licensed firms who required precisely such a migration of American industry at the expense of independent development to justify their existence.

As the barbed wire case showed, the licensing system was not completely independent of the existence of high tariffs between Canada and the U.S. Reciprocity of tariffs was anathema to the licensees. One early exception was the Massey firm in agricultural implements, long free trade inclined. But by the late 1880's even this firm was beginning to have second thoughts.[148] In all probability this change of heart had something to do with the new U.S. patents the firm had begun to lease with less leniency or permanence than that which had accompanied its early borrowings. Sewing machine makers were adamantly opposed to Reciprocity,[149] with the noteworthy exception of Charles Raymond.[150] Raymond, the American émigré, had earlier acquired absolute patent rights while the newer firms were totally subservient to the American parents.

Many other industries in the 1880's counted themselves opposed if their goods were covered by U.S. patents. For the legitimately licensed firms making goods in U.S. patents, Reciprocity would pass them by, leaving them corralled in the Canadian market, while they were blocked by the licence from taking part in the American one. And in the long run there would be no reason for the American manufacturers to renew the licence arrangement. For other Canadian manufacturers, who made goods on U.S. models either because the U.S. patent did not extend to Canada or because it had lapsed through non-compliance with Canadian law, Reciprocity spelt immediate doom. U.S. firms would then enter Canada, while they themselves would be blocked from entering the U.S. by American patent laws.[151]

Conclusion

Canada's technological dependence was both deep-rooted and consciously cultivated. Technology, like capital and labour, was something to be attracted from a more developed area, and Canadian government policy from an early period assiduously solicited an influx of American techniques.

In the pre-Confederation period, the inflow of American technology was in part an incidental by-product of the migration of American master-craftsmen to Canada. In part it was the result of the pirating of American inventions. Occasionally both processes went hand in hand — most notably in the agricultural implements industry. So eagerly did the province seek to aid the inflow of American technique that it even refused to allow Canadians stealing American technology to patent it, and thus inhibit others in the province from copying the same technique.

After Confederation the patterns changed. Retaliation from the U.S., and the failure of the laissez-faire approach to patent-pirating to engender a sufficiently rapid diffusion of American technology into Canada, led to the Patent Act of 1872. Under this Act, Americans could protect their patent rights in Canada if and only if they manufactured the product in Canada either by themselves or via Canadian licensees, within two years of the patent being issued. As a result, a pattern of licensed ventures sprang up in Canada in a variety of fields.

Initially the northern migration of American technique was a general phenomenon, not centring on any particular field. But as the century drew to a close distinct patterns emerged. In particular the high-technology, capital-intensive, rapid-growth industries of the second industrial revolution made their appearance in Canada via the licensing of foreign, chiefly American techniques. Automobiles, machinery production (especially for modern mining technique), electrical apparatus, and chemicals were all almost completely derivative arrivals in Canada.

The impact on Canadian development patterns was enormous. The share of patents granted in Canada to Canadians fell sharply after the 1872 Patent Act and continued to follow a downward trend. Even in absolute terms, the number of patents granted Canadians declined for many years. The possibility of indigenous technological development was cast to the winds in favour of hothouse growth based on dependence on American technique.

Notes to Chapter X

1. L. Jenks, *The Migration of British Capital, passim.*
2. T. Ashton, *The Industrial Revolution,* Chap. I.
3. *CLRI,* p. 75.
4. See for example S. Hymer, *The International Operations of National Firms.*
5. M. Wilkins, *The Emergence of Multinational Enterprise,* pp. 30-31.
6. H. A. Innis and A.R.M. Lower (eds.), *Select Documents in Canadian Economic History,* p. 20.
7. See for example H. Marshall, F. Southard, and K. Taylor, *Canadian-American Industry,* p. 11; "Captains of Industry," Series, *CM,* June to November, 1888.
8. H. A. Innis and A. R. M. Lower, (eds.) *Select Documents,* pp. 243-4.
9. K. Lewis, "The Significance of the York Foundry and Steam-Engine Manufacturing" gives details of the early establishments.
10. *CM,* July 6, 1888, p. 42.
11. *MT,* Jan. 27, 1882, p. 910.
12. *MT,* March 30, 1900, p. 1277.
13. *CM,* Aug. 17, 1888, p. 112.
14. M. Denison, *Harvest Triumphant,* p. 30.
15. *SCCD, Evidence,* p. 119.

16. M. Denison, *Harvest Triumphant,* p. 42.
17. Canada, *Journals of the Legislative Assembly, XIII,* 1854-5, App. II. 3.
18. *Globe,* Oct. 29, 1866.
19. *HCD,* April 18, 1872, p. 64.
20. *HCD,* April 18, 1872, p. 67.
21. *Statutes of Canada,* "An Act Respecting Patents of Invention", *CAP, XXVI,* June 14, 1872.
22. *CM,* Jan. 6, 1882, p. 2.
23. Dept. of Agriculture, *Annual Report For 1885,* p. xvii.
24. *MT,* Feb. 17, 1904, p. 1098.
25. *HCD,* March 16, 1903, p. 97.
26. *HCD,* May 28, 1903, p. 3622.
27. *MT,* Dec. 6, 1878, p. 716.
28. *HCD,* March 29, 1882, p. 621.
29. *CE,* April, 1895, p. 351.
30. *CE,* June 1897, p. 87.
31. Toronto Board of Trade, *Annual Report,* 1902, p. 53.
32. *RCRLC, Quebec Evidence Part I,* p. 413.
33. Select Committee . . . Fraudulent Obtaining of Promissory Notes from Farmers, *Report,* pp. 5-12.
34. W. G. Phillips, *The Agricultural Implements Industry In Canada,* p. 10.
35. *SCCD, Report,* p. xiii.
36. *MT,* Dec. 15, 1882, p. 659.
37. Farmers' Advocate *(FA)* May 1880, p. 144; Oct. 1880, p. 246, Sept. 1889, p. 297, *et passim.*
38. *MT,* March 11, 1887, p. 1064.
39. *MT,* June 22, 1888, p. 1570.
40. Department of Agriculture, *Annual Report for 1886,* p. xvi.
41. R. Jones, *History of Agriculture in Ontario,* pp. 202-3.
42. *MT,* May 23, 1902, p. 1523.
43. *MT,* Nov. 8, 1878, p. 667.
44. M. Denison, *Harvest Triumphant,* p. 78.
45. *MT,* May 16, 1902, p. 1491.
46. *SCM,* (1874), p. 7.
47. *CE,* April 1894, p. 356; *MT,* March 9, 1894, p. 1117.
48. *MT,* Aug. 23, 1901, p. 229.
49. *CE,* Aug. 1902, p. 220.
50. *SCC, Evidence,* 1888, p. 361.
51. W. Kilbourn, *The Elements Combined,* p. 40.
52. *SCC, Evidence,* pp. 371-2.
53. *MT,* Dec. 26, 1879, p. 743.
54. *FA,* May 1880, p. 144.
55. *MT,* Aug. 5, 1881, p. 156.
56. *MT,* Nov. 11, 1881, p. 57.
57. *FA,* Oct. 1880, p. 242, *et passim.*
58. *MT,* Oct. 5, 1883, p. 373.
59. *SCC, Evidence,* pp. 371-2.
60. *MT,* July 8, 1887, p. 38.
61. *SCC, Evidence,* p. 361.
62. *MT,* March 11, 1887, p. 1071.
63. *MT,* Jan. 27, 1893, p. 874; May 8, 1896, p. 1423.
64. *Globe,* Dec. 10, 1890.
65. *MT,* Sept, 23, 1892, p. 348.
66. *MT,* Oct. 14, 1898, p. 516; Jan. 13, 1899, p. 924.
67. *MT,* Oct. 24, 1890, p. 495.

68. *MT,* Aug. 15, 1890, p. 194.
69. A. G. Brown and P. H. Morres, *Twentieth Century Impressions,* p. 432.
70. *SCM,* 1874, *Evidence,* p. 44.
71. *CM,* June 1, 1888, p. 369.
72. *CE,* April 1894, p. 355.
73. *CM,* Jan. 20, 1893, p. 48.
74. *CM,* March 17, 1882, p. 97.
75. *CE,* March 1894, p. 325.
76. *MT,* Sept. 28, 1877, p. 387.
77. *MT,* March 11, 1887, p. 1064.
78. *MT,* July 7, 1882, p. 8; Sept. 23, 1892, p. 348.
79. *MT,* April 11, 1890, p. 1253.
80. M. Wilkins, *The Emergence of Multinational Enterprise,* p. 62.
81. *MT,* Sept. 15, 1899, p. 339.
82. *CE,* Jan. 1898, p. 276.
83. *MT,* July 16, 1897, p. 75; July 23, 1897, p. 102.
84. *SCM,* 1874, *Report,* p. 8.
85. *CM,* Oct. 19, 1888, p. 273.
86. *MT,* Aug. 26, 1881, p. 242.
87. *SCCD, Evidence,* pp. 91-2.
88. *MT,* Aug. 28, 1891, p. 247; Sept. 4, 1891, p. 277.
89. *MT,* June 10, 1898, p. 1606.
90. *CE,* Sept. 1895, p. 129.
91. *CM,* May 26, 1882, p. 199.
92. Anon., *Canada Under the National Policy,* p. 102.
93. *IC,* Sept. 1900, p. 57.
94. Royal Commission on Industrial Training . . ., *Report,* p. 2156.
95. *CM,* July 14, 1882, p. 313.
96. *IC,* Sept., 1900, p. 56; Nov. 1901, pp. 120-1; Sept. 1903, p. 57.
97. *CM,* Jan. 19, 1894, p. 51.
98. *CM,* Jan. 19, 1894, p. 54.
99. *FP,* June 3, 1927, p. 14.
100. *MT,* April 14, 1882, p. 1260.
101. *CE,* Dec. 1896, p. 240.
102. *CM,* March 20, 1891, p. 198.
103. *MT,* Jan. 20, 1899, p. 954.
104. *MT,* May 12, 1899, p. 1476.
105. Commission, Combines Investigation Act, Investigation into the Alleged
     Combination . . . Rubber Products, *Report,* p. 8.
106. *CE,* Oct. 1896, p. 180.
107. C. Aikman, *The Automobile Industry of Canada,* p. 15.
108. *CE,* Sept. 1896, p. 152.
109. *CE,* April 1900, p. 333; Dec. 1897, p. 243; *MT,* Oct. 25, 1913, p. 679.
110. D. McLaughlin Henderson, *Robert McLaughlin — Carriage Builder,*
     passim.
111. G. B. D. Roberts and A. L. Tunnell (eds.), *Standard Dictionary of Cana-*
     dian Biography, II, p. 458.
112. *MT,* Dec. 8, 1882, p. 624.
113. *MT,* June 20, 1890, p. 1574.
114. E. S. Moore, *American Influences in Canadian Mining,* p. 90.
115. *MT,* Nov. 26, 1896, p. 208.
116. *CE,* March 1894, p. 313; *MT,* Aug. 4, 1899, p. 179.
117. *MT,* Nov. 27, 1903, p. 678.
118. *MT,* Oct. 30, 1885, p. 484.
119. *CE,* Sept. 1896, p. 151.

120. *CE,* March 1898, p. 333; April 1898, p. 367; Sept. 1900, p. 109.
121. *CE,* Sept. 1900, p. 109; *MT,* Aug. 17, 1900, p. 199; May 16, 1900, p. 619.
122. *MT,* June 10, 1898, p. 1604.
123. *MT,* July 30, 1880, p. 121.
124. *MT,* Dec. 17, 1880, p. 692.
125. M. Wilkins, *The Emergence of Multinational Enterprise,* pp. 50-1.
126. *MT,* Dec. 2, 1881, p. 668.
127. M. Denison, *The People's Power,* p. 20.
128. *MT,* July 7, 1899, p. 10; H. Marshall, F. Southard, and K. Taylor, *Canadian-American Industry,* pp. 69-70.
129. *MT,* Nov. 2, 1883, p. 484.
130. *MT,* July 25, 1884, p. 99.
131. *MT,* Jan. 23, 1885, p. 854.
132. Some of the patent arrangements were complex and not all one-way. In 1882, the Canadian Telephone Co. tried to prevent Bell from infringing on its patents. The case was settled out of court by an agreement between the two and the Electric Despatch Co., whereby the contested patent was transferred to Bell who agreed to sell it for ten years to the despatch company. Bell further agreed to stay out of that line of business except for message services. All telegraph lines and wires of cabmen, carters, and others were transferred to the central office of Electric Despatch, but most were transferred back to Bell in 1883. In 1887, the Great North Western Telegraph Co. opened — under American licence —and it got a telephone from Bell which it used for special messenger services. Electric Despatch objected and sued to block it, but failed to do so. Electric Despatch soon faded from the scene (*MT,* Dec. 7, 1888, pp. 649-9). In 1887 came another major effort to break Bell's hold, when on behalf of the Toronto Telephone Manufacturing Company Bell was taken to court over one patent granted Alexander Graham Bell and three granted Thomas Edison which Bell owned; and voidance of the patents on the grounds of importation and non-manufacture was sought. It won the right to use the Bell patent, but lost the three Edison ones. (Department of Agriculture, *Annual Report for 1887,* p. xvi; *Annual Report for 1888,* p. xviii).
133. Department of Agriculture, *Annual Report for 1889,* p. xv.
134. *MT,* Dec. 14, 1900, p. 751.
135. *MT,* Oct. 12, 1900, p. 457.
136. C. L. Barber, *The Canadian Electrical Manufacturing Industry,* pp. 1-2; *MT,* Dec. 15, 1899, p. 772.
137. *MT,* Feb. 28, 1902, p. 1126.
138. *MT,* March 27, 1896, p. 1254.
139. *FP,* Aug. 4, 1908.
140. *MT,* Nov. 30, 1907, p. 871.
141. Another sorely contested technique was that revolving about an electric process for calcium carbide production. One Boston entrepreneur secured a patent and decided to set up a Canadian plant in conjunction with another American, H. N. Whitney, and the Montreal financiers Louis Forget, J. N. Greenshields, and Herbert Holt. In 1896 they found that their patents conflicted with those of Thomas Willson of St. Catharines, who already had a plant in operation in conjunction with another American group (*MT,* Oct. 30, 1896, p. 581). The quarrel was settled by the Whitney syndicate's leasing Willson's patents. It was one of the very rare cases where American control of the Canadian industry relied on a Canadian patent (J. H. Dales, *Hydroelectricity and Industrial Development in Quebec,* pp. 51, 54).
142. *MT,* Jan. 3, 1890, p. 796; April 11, 1890, p. 1252.
143. *MT,* Aug. 3, 1894, p. 137.

144. *CE,* May 1894, p. 14.
145. *MT,* March 30, 1900, p. 1277.
146. Colonial Conference, 1907, *Minutes,* p. 493.
147. *IC,* Nov. 1904, pp. 267-8.
148. *SCC, Evidence,* p. 356.
149. *CM,* May 15, 1885, p. 1185.
150. *Globe,* Jan. 5, 1891.
151. *CM,* April 15, 1887, pp. 111-2.

Whenever a man comes to Canada to live and to contribute in any manner to the material success of the country, he may very properly be considered a Canadian. His birth place may be Europe, Asia, Africa, an isle of the sea, or even the land of the Yankee, and protectionists will be ready and willing to acknowledge him a Canadian. There would be no objection to him whatever because of his nationality. And the same as regards his money.

Canadian Manufacturers' Association, 1893

CHAPTER XI
Commercial Policy and Direct Investment

Manufacturing Investment, 1878-1895

One key objective of the National Policy was to shift the locus of industrial production from the U.S. and Britain to Canada. It also aimed to shift Canadian commercial patterns so that manufactured goods flowed on an east-west nexus, while industrial capital in Ontario and Quebec would be able to capture both the Northwest and the Maritime market. It mattered little if the capital invested in manufacturing was of Canadian or foreign origin. In fact, given the underdevelopment of Canadian industrialism, an inflow of foreign direct investment was an obvious prerequisite if the strategy was to succeed. As the CMA quaintly phrased the matter, "The market is reserved for Canadian manufacturers. The way for our Yankee friends to obtain a percentage of the Canadian trade is to establish their works in Canada."[1]

While the National Policy was not as successful in forcing a rapid reorientation of Canadian commercial patterns as its architects had boasted it would be,[2] some impact was felt immediately, and it grew steadily. In the East, some industries felt the effects of central Canadian competition very quickly; in the West, "Canadian" firms began to displace imports from the U.S. And the branch plant movement began with, and even in anticipation of, the high tariff.

In some cases, American firms were quick to make their move, and the migration was welcomed in Canada with enthusiasm. A Halifax journal made a formal appeal to American manufacturers to move in as soon as the tariff went up on the grounds that, with their superior access to capital, better management, and technical expertise, they would have a considerable edge over all competitors, notably local firms.[3] The *Monetary Times* fretted, lest the tariff be inadequate to tempt firms to jump over it.[4] The *Journal of Commerce* noted:

> There are fourteen pin factories in the United States, nearly all located in New England. . . .Canada should support one or two. Here is a hint for St. Hyacinthe or St. Jerome with their splendid local privileges.[5]

But most enthusiastic of all was the Canadian Manufacturers' Association, which decreed,

> It is of small moment where the capital comes from that may be employed in developing our industries. When it is invested it at once becomes Canadian capital. . . .We gladly welcome all American capitalists who desire to join our procession in our march to industrial development and national greatness.[6]

The first wave of American direct investments in Canada was largely involuntary. The U.S. was a substantial net debtor throughout the late nineteenth century, and not until the turn of the century had the process of consolidation of the American industrial giants been completed, and with it their willingness to migrate on any scale. American firms preferred to export, and at most to invest in distributing agencies. Furthermore, during the early period, given the underdevelopment of Canadian intermediaries and the lack of access to British portfolio capital to support the American direct investment, the migration of American firms meant the export of scarce capital from the parent. After the turn of the century, the burden on the parents' capital resources was lightened by the expanded availability of Canadian bank loans and British bond capital.

American branch plants began with Hall Bros., the short-lived agricultural implement firm established in Oshawa in 1860. The next instance seems to have been a file works in St. Catharines in 1870. Before the 1879 tariff, only eleven branch plants were operating, of which five were erected in 1878, in the midst of a depression, — indicating that the expected fiscal changes affected the decision for at least some of them. The inflow was sustained by the prosperity phase until 1883, and thereafter it tapered off until 1895, when a new rush began. The initial burst favored the border towns, Windsor in particular,[7] but also Chatham, Walkerville, Sarnia, and others in Ontario. The president of the CMA, Fred Nicholls boasted in 1889 that "there is hardly a town in the province of any importance but has a

branch of an American factory that has started in it." His asser-
tion seems somewhat exaggerated, but it was as much a statement of hope as of fact.

TABLE XI (1)

U.S. Branch Plants Established 1870-1887

1870-1875	1
1876	2
1877	3
1878	5
1879	13
1880	4
1881	1
1882	4
1883	5
1884	2
1885	5
1886	2
1887	1
Total	48

Source: H. Marshall *et al, Canadian-American Industry,* p. 12.

In this first period, the bulk of the foreign migrations —
whether branch plants, joint ventures, or wholesale movements
of the entire company — were caused by the desire to recapture
markets threatened by the tariff. Textiles, one of the industries
most favoured in terms of domestic growth by the National
Policy, attracted the largest share of American, and to a lesser
degree, British attention. A branch plant of a cotton batting factory in St. Catharines was established by an American group in
1879, followed by another New York syndicate exploring the
possibility of a shoddy factory there.[8] In 1881, an American knitting mill was projected for Montreal, and the following year the
American silk firm, Belding Bros., established a Montreal branch
in the form of a joint venture with a local capitalist, Belding,
Paul and Co.,[9] a private partnership, as were many of the early
joint ventures. In the Maritimes, both the Yarmouth, N.S.,
Cotton Duck Co. and the St. Croix Mill at St. Stephen, N.B.,
were joint ventures of local capital with Massachusetts cotton
mill men who wanted to recapture lost markets,[10] while the
Parks' Cotton Factory at St. John, N.B., although its equity was
locally held, was financed in part by portfolio capital from a
Boston capitalist who held a first mortgage on the property.[11]
British capital was represented not only by the involvement of

the British cotton machinery industry from afar, but also by the migration to Canada of Clayton Slater, who began a cotton and a wincey mill in Brantford,[12] and the Riverside Worsted Company in Quebec, whose equity was largely held by woollen industrialists in Bradford.[13]

In Ontario, where most of the branch plants located, there was a tendency for the Americans to try to straddle the border, which made Windsor a prime location for Detroit firms.[14] In the Maritimes, the American presence was much more often in the form of joint ventures with local capital than branch plants on the Ontario model, as with three new investments in New Brunswick in 1883, including the Harris Manufacturing Co.[15] which soon became one of the country's largest manufacturers of railway cars.

In Quebec, the joint venture again seemed more common, but with British capital represented as well as American along with local business. Sheffield manufacturers, who had been vehement antagonists of the National Policy and who had petitioned the Colonial Office for interference along with Yorkshire woollen and cotton manufacturers[16] (as they had against the Galt tariff of 1859), found a similar solution to their lost markets. In 1883 a joint venture of Sheffield and Canadian capital established a cutlery firm in St. Henri, while in 1888 Sheffield steel makers joined T.J. and W.H. Drummond, metal merchants of Montreal, in the Montreal Car Wheel Co.[17]

The branch plants established across Canada covered a wide range of products, consumer and producer goods ranging from car wheels to woollens. One American firm making organettes shifted bodily to Montreal in 1880[18] to join Canada's highly successful musical instrument business, whose leader, William Bell, had got his start by copying American models. While not a branch plant originally, Bell's firm in 1891 became incorporated and largely owned in Britain.[19] The branch plants also included a contingent of drug manufacturers who followed the leader after it arrived in 1879.[20] Vancouver managed to attract the branch plant of an artificial ice company in 1891,[21] and a wandering American soda water factory settled there a few years later.[22]

Manufacturing Investment, 1896-1914

Towards the end of the century, new influences began to affect the flow of American direct investment to Canada. The great merger waves in the U.S. spilled across the border. The American multidivisional firms began their international march; the

Canadian economy moved into a prolonged prosperity phase which attracted both American direct and British portfolio investment which also helped support the American influx; and the new industries of the second industrial revolution began to replace the older mechanical and consumer goods industries as objects of the American investors' attentions.

Some observers looked askance at the new inflow. The *Monetary Times* welcomed portfolio investment and new direct investment, but opposed takeovers. It pointed out the ample supply of Canadian savings, and castigated Canadian investors for their timidity. It was not, it felt, a shortage of capital but of entrepreneurs willing to assume risk that led to the American invasion.[23] Only after the Americans initiated ventures did Canadian investors seem to interest themselves in it. The *Monetary Times* supported the American entrepreneur Francis Clergue, who was then domiciled in Canada, in his castigation of the Canadian capitalists' recalcitrance:

> Canadian businessmen, in their cautiousness, have carried their slowness to decide upon a matter too far for their own good, and have in their desire to be absolutely safe let pass many a good opportunity.[24]

These sentiments, of course, overlooked completely the critical role of the banks and intermediaries in mobilizing savings and putting them to work in staple production and commercial infracture, rather than assisting industrial capital formation.

The new wave also represented a closer integration of parent and subsidiary than did the old, with the result that the branch plants were highly dependent on the parents for parts, semi-finished materials, and machinery,[25] a result facilitated by the lowering of raw material rates in the Canadian tariff since the National Policy had come into effect.

But pressures for more and more branch plants increased. The CMA called for even higher tariffs to draw more foreign industrial migrants:

> We do believe that by revising the tariff and bringing it up to the requirements of present conditions we could cause many more industries to be brought into the country and we would thus aid in the development and upbuilding of Canada.[26]

The laggard British investors were urged to follow the Americans' example and take advantage of the high rates of return prevailing on investments in Canada. British direct investment was urged by the Canadian Bankers' Association and the Association of Canadian Engineers to help preserve the Empire from the menace of American rivalry.[27]

The new branch plants obligingly poured into the country. By 1914, American branch plants in Canada totalled 453, while British branch plants numbered only 20. American branch plants represented an investment valued at $135 million, while British but six million. Of the influx, the Ontario border cities and the other major urban centres received the largest share. Toronto, Montreal, Hamilton and Winnipeg got the most, followed by Windsor, Walkerville and Niagara Falls with Calgary, Guelph, Brantford, St. Catharines, Sarnia and Welland well down the list.[28]

The exodus began to cause some consternation in American circles: Eugene Foss, the Governor of Massachusetts and himself a direct investor in Canada, predicted that Canadian industrial growth based on American branch plants would soon outdistance that of the U.S. itself. The *Wall Street Journal* lamented the outflow in 1913, expressing the fear that it would be followed by a migration of skilled labour as well.[29]

In fact, precisely such a movement occurred. Early propagandists for the tariff had held out hopes of deflecting the flow of emigrants from Europe away from the U.S. and into Canada. American branch plants too were expected to bring labour from the U.S.[30] On both counts the policy initially failed, and the loss of Canadian population to the U.S. continued. Detroit and similar towns in the U.S. attracted the residents of nearby Canadian towns to their factories.[31] But by the turn of the century the process was operating in reverse. Not only did the bulk of European migration now flow to Canada, but American farmers migrated to the Canadian prairies and skilled workers to Canadian branch plants. Instances were noted where the American immigrant workers and executives of branch plants and their families formed the majority of the population of Canadian villages.[32] The American farm population growing in the Canadian West helped to attract American firms as well. In 1913, the little town of Redcliffe, Alberta, boasted nine new firms, of which $600,000 worth of capital was Canadian and $1,150,000 American. Medicine Hat had 18 new firms, mostly American. Winnipeg and Calgary were the western cities most favoured by the American manufacturers.[33]

Given the new importance of the West, with the opening of the prairie agricultural frontier, it was not surprising that wire-and-fencing and agricultural implements firms in the U.S., which previously had been content simply to license, now began to move towards full-fledged branch plants. Wire-and-fencing branches were projected and established in a number of towns by the major American producers in the follow-the-leader pattern typical of direct investment by oligopolies.[34] Although the implement manufacturers made preparations to do likewise just after the turn of the century, the merger of the big American firms staved it off, and only International Harvester itself entered Canada by taking over the Deering site.[35] The rationale for the International Harvester migration was the growing importance of the Empire market. For by shifting to Canada, after its failure to take over the Massey-Harris firm, it got rebates on imported inputs for exported output and very soon began exporting to South Africa and Australia.[36] In 1911 it diversified by taking over an old Chatham wagon firm and began building lorries for the Canadian and Empire markets.[37]

Another industry linked to the expansion of grain cultivation in Canada was the American milling business, the great oligopolies of which, Quaker Oats and the American Cereal Co., descended on Peterborough in 1901. The objective of the plants was to mill Canadian crops of various sorts, partly for domestic consumption and partly to service the Empire market. Quaker Oats arrived as a joint venture of the parent with Edmund Walker, J. H. Plummer, George Cox and Joseph Flavelle, while American Cereal seems to have begun as a branch plant and been absorbed by a new syndicate partly representing Canadian capital into the Dominion Cereal Company.[38]

There were many examples in this period of new American migrants whose objective was, as of old, simply to capture markets in Canada cut off by the tariff and representing a wide range of consumer and producer goods. There were, too, examples of the old pattern of licensing the Canada-U.S. joint venture. 1898 saw the formation of Page-Hersey Iron & Tube Co. by Randolph Hersey of Montreal with E. N. and G. H. Page of Cohoes.[39] But there were distinctly new features to the post-1896 movement. The growth of the West, the rise of new industries, the American merger wave, and the new importance of the Empire market were additional push or pull factors. Moreover, the relative incidence of British industrial investments declined, with notable exceptions such as the Ross Rifle branch plant,[40] or the joint venture of the Lever Brothers with a Toronto syndicate.[41] The Ross Rifle branch was particularly remarkable since Sir Charles Ross was reputed to keep the Minister of Militia in Sir Robert Borden's cabinet, Sam Hughes, on his payroll to advance the Ross product in the Canadian defence establishment. But in terms of percentage of total, there seemed a distinct decline, at the same time the volume of British portfolio investment grew enormously.

TABLE XI (2)

American Investments In Canada, 1911 and 1913

Type (Value in $ millions)	1911	1913
Branch plants and other industrial	$135.4	$151.5
B.C. mills and timber	65.0	70.0
B.C. mines	60.0	62.0
B.C. land	8.5	60.0
Prairie land	25.0	40.0
Prairie lumber	10.0	10.5
Theatrical	n.a.	3.0
Packing plants	6.0	6.8
Farm implement distribution	8.6	9.3
Life and fire insurance firm investments	43.3	67.8
Municipal bonds sold privately	27.0	n.a.
Purchase of government or corporate bonds	n.a.	123.7
Purchase of urban property	15.5	20.7
Investments in Maritime provinces	12.9	14.1
Total	$417.2	$639.4

Source: F. Field, *Capital Investments in Canada*, p. 24; *MT Annual*, Jan. 1914, pp. 24-28.

TABLE XI (3)

Distribution of U.S. Manufacturing Investments in Canada, 1913

(Branch plants, affiliates, and major warehousing operations)

Province	No.	Leading Cities	No.
Ontario	317	Toronto	94
Quebec	78	Montreal	53
Manitoba	33	Hamilton	46
Alberta	14	Winnipeg	30
New Brunswick	6	Windsor, Ont.	26
Nova Scotia	2	Calgary	9
British Columbia	2	St. John, N.B.	4
Saskatchewan	2	Edmonton	1
Prince Edward Island	0	Vancouver	1
		Charlottetown	0
		Halifax	0

Foreign Investment and Resource Development: Forest Industries

While direct investment in manufacturing was greeted with almost unqualified delight, attitudes towards foreign investment in the resource industries were more critical and divided, and on this issue the antagonism between commercial capitalists and manufacturers surfaced frequently. The railwaymen, bankers, and land companies were eager to abet the rapid exploitation and export of raw materials, while manufacturers called for processing at home.[42]

For the most part, those interested in alienation of resources won out, though there were exceptions. As early as 1836, an attempt was made in Upper Canada to open the door to American takeover of the timber lands by permitting foreigners to hold land.[43] While that act failed to pass by the time of Confederation, the principle of absentee foreign (non-British) ownership was accepted throughout Canada, and early efforts were made by provincial governments to attract American as well as British capital into timber resource exploitation.[44]

Policy towards timber lands varied among the various levels of government. The Dominion Government did not alienate the timber lands it controlled in fee simple, but licensed them. In Nova Scotia, all timber lands were disposed of in fee simple until 1899. Thus, the Dominion Lumber Co., a U.S. firm, bought up 860,000 acres of alienated timber lands from a local syndicate in 1895 and, with it, no less than sixteen lumber mills with already established markets in England.[45] This firm was organized by B. F. Pearson of Halifax on behalf of the Boston syndicate of H. N. Whitney, which was at the same time busy trying to monopolize Nova Scotia coal lands.[46] By 1899, when restrictive measures were finally enacted, 83% of the provinces' timber lands were already in private hands. Even then the leasing policy was a thinly veiled give-away. Leases were for twenty years, renewable for another twenty at 40¢ an acre.

In Quebec, while little outright alienation had occurred, the licence fees were outrageously low, in part a tribute to the political power of the Timber Limit Holders' Association. In New Brunswick, alienation was common, and so too was outside takeover. As early as 1880 the big New Brunswick Land and Lumber Co. fell into the hands of a joint Montreal and New York Syndicate, headed by George Stephen and J. S. Kennedy.[47] In Ontario, the rate of giveaway via licensing went much further than the other provinces, for central Canadian financiers were

eager to alienate timber lands or limits into foreign hands.
George Cox promoted a firm to deal in pine lands in 1881[48] and
huge sales or leases to American or British firms occurred all
over the province, sometimes forced by the banks.[49] By 1892, a
growing shortage of pine lands in Ontario led eastern capital to
move west, building branch saw mills in B.C. In B.C., the vast
timber resources were not regarded as having any value at all
until 1888, when a royalty of 50¢ per 1,000 board feet was
charged on Crown land. And until 1896 alienation in fee simple
continued to be standard practice.[50]

In light of the profligate resources policy, it is not surprising
that the pulp and paper industry in Canada had a slow and unstable development. The first paper mill in Canada was established in 1804 in Quebec by two Americans who had already
established a number of mills in New England in conjunction
with a Montreal merchant. The Americans provided the
expertise and the Montreal capitalists much of the finance and
the marketing facilities. In Nova Scotia, the first paper mill was
erected in 1817, and in Upper Canada the Hon. James Crook
converted his grist mill into a paper mill in 1825. The Crook mill
operated on rags which it paid for in cash or in finished paper,
and like all the early mills it turned out only coarse brown wrap-
ping paper until 1828 when it began producing white paper. In
the Maritimes, not until 1867 was paper for printing and publishing locally made.[51]

In the provinces of Canada, the industry made little progress
for some time. The Montreal-U.S. joint venture died out in 1837.
Then in 1865 duties on paper were raised, as a result of this,
together with the burning or closing of many American mills in
the Civil War, the Canadian industry expanded rapidly on both
a domestic and an export basis. By the time of the crash in 1873,
there were thirty mills in Canada producing pulp and/or paper.
By 1878, ten had failed and seven were idle; only thirteen were
operational. Thereafter, the industry underwent some recovery as
newsprint prices rose. In 1879, before the tariff, came the first
American direct investment in the industry with the takeover of
a Nova Scotia mill.[52] By 1882, there were 32 operational pulp or
paper mills; four more, including George Cox's Peterborough
Pulp Company, were added that year.[53]

In the lumber industry in central Canada, the commercial orientation shifted after Confederation to serving American rather
than British needs with the opening of larger settlement areas in
the American western farming states. Capital followed, first in
the form of outright migration of entrepreneurs (E. B. Eddy, J.
R. Booth and others) into the Ottawa and Lake Superior areas.

Capital equipment and skilled labour were largely imported, but a Canadian industry making light tools for lumbering did grow up. The 1873 collapse of primary product prices disrupted the industry; by 1876 even the big E. B. Eddy firm joined the ranks of the insolvent.[54] But by 1880 prices of lumber too were rising quickly, and a wave of prosperity swept over the industry.[55] American capital moved into the Ontario timber limits. The Michigan lumber industry became totally dependent on Canadian supplies, and by 1886 Michigan firms held 1,750,000,000 feet of standing timber in Ontario, virtually all of the output of which was exported as unmanufactured sawn logs.

While export duties had existed on various wood products since 1874, their effect had been mainly to raise revenue. Not for some time were the duties high enough, or applied in the right directions to force processing in Canada. In 1882, the threat of an export duty on elm logs led to an American stave bolt manufacturer migrating to Wallaceburg, Ontario.[56] In 1886, an export duty of $2.00 per 1,000 board feet was imposed on sawn pine logs, forcing a number of Michigan firms to shift the locus of their sawing and planing operations to Ontario.[57] Then began a ludicrous see-saw battle of tariffs between the U.S. and Canada to shift the locus of milling activity back and forth across the border.

In 1888, the duty was raised from $2.00 to $3.00 over the objections of the Canadian lumbermen, whose Lumbermen's Association campaigned for repeal.[58] The U.S. retaliated with an import duty, and the Canadian government capitulated. The export duty was removed, the McKinley tariff in the U.S. reduced the import duty, and the American lumbermen began exporting the best logs to the Michigan mills, dumping the inferior grades in Canada. As the milling industry began to shift back to the U.S., a migration of Canadian lumbermen followed and many towns in Northern Ontario became depopulated.[59]

Pressure for government action mounted. In the House of Commons in 1897 an opposition member called for export duties on logs as

... the means of bringing hundreds of thousands of dollars of capital from the other side to be invested in the sawing of logs on this side ... this would give employment to our own people.[60]

The new movement towards export restrictions derived from the threat of a new tariff in the U.S., which proposed a $2.00 per 1,000 feet import duty. The Ottawa valley lumber industry opposed any retaliation, as it was closely tied to American mills, but the Georgian Bay producers pressured the federal government for an export duty on pine logs and pulp wood, applicable to any country whose import duties on Canadian lumber exceeded one dollar per 1,000 feet on white pine. They also requested an import duty on lumber entering Canada equal to the duty on Canadian logs imposed by other countries.[61] In 1898, the pulp manufacturers (including those headed by American émigrés like Francis Clergue and E. B. Eddy) met to demand export duties on pulpwood until the U.S. admitted Canadian pulp free.[62] The Canadian Furniture Manufacturers' Association the same year faced problems from the growing shortage of elm and other raw materials because American firms had moved in and cleared out accessible stands.[63] The Association urged restrictions on the export of certain types of Canadian lumber. On the American side, the newspapers pressed for free entry of newsprint to break the hold of the American paper trust.[64]

Ontario made the first restrictive moves. Under the existing American law, import duties would be raised automatically if Canada imposed a new export duty on logs.[65] An Ontario government commission headed by John Bertram and E. W. Rathbun proposed avoiding export duties by instead requiring that all logs cut in the province be manufactured there.[66] Late in 1897, Ontario first prohibited Americans not domiciled in Canada from working the lumber lands in the province, in order to cut off the use of imported seasonal labour, and then proceeded to enact the Rathbun-Bertram plan.[67] Other provinces and the Dominion followed suit. Both soft and hardwood were affected, and American capital poured into lumber mills and pulp and paper plants.[68] Pulp and paper became one of Canada's largest staple exports, especially after the U.S. lowered its import duties.

TABLE XI (4)

The Pulp and Paper Industry

Year	No. of Mills	Capital Employed	Employees
1870	21	610,400	760
1880	36	2,237,950	1,520
1890	58	6,574,121	2,757
1900	53	19,066,319	6,236
1910	72	53,886,933	9,766
1915	80	133,736,803	15,308

Source: N. Reich, *The Pulp and Paper Industry,* p. 68.

The effects of the federal export duties or their equivalent by the provinces was simply to accelerate already existing trends. Investment in the industry had been expanding rapidly even before. And while the industry was largely Canadian and organized into small mills prior to the new duties, there was already some American direct investment as well as British, and it was growing, especially in the late 1890's.

In 1895, the Sault Ste. Marie Pulp and Paper Co. established mills on both sides of the border.[69] *The Empire* protested that the mill would pollute the rivers and destroy the fish, to which the Canadian Manufacturers' Association prophetically replied that "Canada could well afford to have a hundred fishing streams thus ruined on such terms, even if American capitalists were the investors."[70]

In that year another American pulp and paper mill was projected for Arnprior, Ontario,[71] and several others, too, were put into operation. In early 1897, General Russell Alger, Governor of Michigan and Secretary of War in the McKinley cabinet, made a move into the Grand Mère area, subsequently collaborating with Van Horne in Laurentide Pulp and Paper.[72] That year too a British company, the British Columbia Wood Pulp and Paper Co., was formed to buy up an old and small local mill operating on rags and convert it into a pulp mill.[73] After 1898, control of the industry was increasingly lost to Canada as a series of American and British, or joint ventures with Canadian minority participation were formed in Ontario, the Maritimes, and B.C. In Quebec the main rush came after 1906, when restrictions on export were imposed.[74] In 1899, the Ontario government signed an agreement with an English syndicate, the Sturgeon Falls Pulp Co., for the erection of a one million dollar mill. The company got the right to cut and remove wood along the Sturgeon River and its tributaries at twenty cents per cord for spruce, and ten cents for hardwood.[75] This company initially had Canadian minority participation, but in 1907 it was taken over completely by an American syndicate.[76] In 1899 another huge grant was made in the Petawawa area to a U.S.-Canada joint venture on the same type of terms as Sturgeon Falls.[77] By that year the International Paper Co. alone held 1.6 million acres of timber lands.[78] Ontario was by no means the sole beneficiary of the influx[79] — which was aided by the fact that after 1900 the Grand Trunk Railway abandoned its policy of giving special low rates on the export of pulp wood from Canada.[80] In B.C. a great deal of American investment occurred. One U.S. firm bought Prince of Wales Island from a Vancouver group who had gotten it free from the province. In return for cutting rights, the province got one cent an acre plus 25c per cord.[81] In Cape Breton, a New York and Boston group which had sent their logs to Maine mills were forced to build a $750,000 pulp mill.[82] Quebec received the bulk of the American investors' attention, and by 1911 half of the 60 mills in Canada were in Quebec.[83] As an additional dividend, a firm producing capital goods for the industry, the Union Paper Machinery Co., began searching for a suitable branch site in Quebec in 1901.[84]

Over-entry was an immediate problem, and by 1901 many firms had watched profits dwindle to nothing as the price of pulp dropped from $2.50 to $1.70 in 15 months and several failures followed. Part of the big surge of investment had been caused by an enormous demand for newsprint due to the Cuban and South African wars.[85] And peace brought a recession. In Britain, several pulp and paper mills had overcome the usual resistance to Canadian industrial bonds, and by 1906 three of the mills that had successfully floated there had failed.[86]

Foreign Investment and Resource Development: Mining

Salt Mining

The northward migration of the lumber industry produced another spin-off in Canadian industry. The Canadian salt wells in southern Ontario had been languishing for years, with several mines shut down completely; Michigan salt wells, on the other hand, were flourishing by the use of refuse from the lumber mills as fuel. In 1892, salt was discovered on the CPR's property in Windsor, but was not immediately exploited, since estimates at that time placed existing Canadian capacity at three times domestic consumption.[87] In early 1894, when the CPR Salt Well Co. made its first shipment, it was crude salt used only for cleaning purposes.[88] The Windsor Salt Co. was incorporated in 1895 by Van Horne at the head of a group of American capitalists with some Windsor participation,[89] but expansion of the salt industry did not come until after 1897 when the Michigan wells were cut off from their fuel source by the movement of the locus of saw milling into Canada. The immediate result was a major expansion of the Canadian industry.[90]

Oil and Gas

The Canadian petroleum industry, too, remained centred in the southwestern tip of Ontario, with a few minor exceptions.[91] For most of the industry's early history, the producers of crude and the refiners remained largely independent. The wells were generally owned by the farmers on whose land the strikes were made,[92] while the refining aspect of the business attracted outside capital. Initially the refineries were controlled by Canadian capital largely from the urban centres near the wells, though Montreal was represented as early as 1881, when David Morrice got into the refining business behind the new tariff.[93] But American money began to move in in the 1880's. Buffalo and Michigan capital, in which General Alger was heavily interested, established the Sarnia Oil Company which failed in 1890.[94] That year too the Bushnell Oil Company was created by New York refiners with some minority Montreal hangers-on in the form of two oil merchants.[95]

By 1892, the refiners in the Petrolia area began to feel the shadow of Standard Oil looming over them.[96] But for the time being Standard seemed to confine itself to the natural gas fields, working through its subsidiaries in the Essex County fields, to feed its consumers in Buffalo in competition with other American firms already draining Ontario gas off to Detroit.[97]

In the mid-1890's, the Ontario industry began its last boom period, and American capital began to move in on a large scale. There was one critical difference between the new boom and those of old. Parallelling the integration of crude production and refining by then typical in American operations — Standard Oil being the major pioneer in this development — American refining companies led by Standard and followed by others like Bushnell began boring wells.[98] The new wave of strikes began in Essex County and from there spread to Kent and Lambton counties, with American firms the most active in all the new areas.[99] The depth of the new wells and the rising capital intensity of crude production was an effective barrier to the old farmer-operated crude producing units that were still the principal mode of production. But while the American firms were drilling for crude in Ontario, they were not yet active in refining within Ontario, and the vertical integration of the industry took place across the border. By 1899, however, the situation had changed. Standard, through its subsidiary Imperial Oil, had become a virtual monopolist of the refining capacity of southwestern Ontario. So complete was its control that any further crude-producing companies contemplating drilling had to be sure of a long-term contract with Standard to justify their investment. Such was the case, for example, with the Dominion Oil Company, which drew up a phony prospectus claiming to

have such contracts with Standard, sold stock widely in the U.K.
and U.S. based on that prospectus, and collapsed in a few
months after the truth was revealed.[100]

Adverse reaction to Standard's monopoly from Ontario industrialists who were its leading customers led the federal government to reduce duties on imported refined oil. Standard reacted
by shifting increasing amounts of refining capacity out of
Canada and lobbying for lower duties on imported crude and
higher ones on imported refined. The implication was that
higher refined duties would lead to an increase in refining operations in Canada and concomitantly to an expansion in employment in the area. A Tory M.P. called for a policy of higher
duties that would "transfer that refining interest from the United
States to Canada to give labour to our own citizens."[101] The
lobby of Ontario industrialists, however, seemed to win the day.
The refined duties remained low. And in their stead the Laurier
government instituted a system of bounties to crude oil production to try to maintain a flow of oil from the rapidly depleting
Ontario wells and to keep down the price to consumers,[102] especially Ontario industrial users. Standard's monopoly otherwise
went unchallenged.

Gold

Gold mining in British North America began in 1858 in Nova
Scotia, followed by Ontario and British Columbia in 1860. In
1870, another major rush in Ontario left in its train a series of
swindles but little production. In 1878 miners began to enter the
Yukon. Little gold was produced until the mid-1880's, except for
B.C.'s brief rush in the pre-Confederation period. By the mid-
1880's, however, the strikes in Nova Scotia had begun to assume
a major importance.

American capital was involved in the Nova Scotia gold rush
from its beginning in the 1850's, and the importance of New
York and New England capital increased with the second rush
of the 1880's. What little placer gold had existed was exhausted
by the 1880's, and with the change in techniques called forth by
the need to extract gold from quartz and other ores, American
capital became ever more active.[103]

There was of course some participation by local capital both
in Nova Scotia and in the few strikes that were made in neighbouring New Brunswick areas,[104] but by the time central Canadian capital was ready to migrate, attention was again shifting to
B.C. and subsequently the Yukon. In 1894, eastern and central
Canadian money along with British capital began its headlong
rush to the Pacific coast.[105]

Foreign capital dominated Pacific mining of all sorts from the start. By 1896, two-thirds of the 125 mining companies registered in B.C. were foreign.[106] And by 1911 over one-half of the total of mining capital in the province was American-owned.[107] In the intervening years there had been a relative displacement of British by American money.

For some time, the typical pattern of B.C. gold investments was similar to that of the Maritime Mining and Development Co., the first Maritime syndicate to invest in B.C. gold. It was headed by a group of eminent political figures including two provincial cabinet ministers, as well as the private banker Hon. L. E. Baker.[108] Though in fact most of the promotions were of Toronto origin, the same format was used — a group of well known politicians in collaboration with a private banking and brokerage firm — and bond capital would then be solicited in Britain or elsewhere in Europe. The Colorado Gold Mining and Developing Co. was headed by one federal minister and the Lieutenant Governor of Ontario with a large number of British and American shareholders and directors. The Gold Hills Exploration and Developing Co. included one Laurier cabinet minister, the Acting Premier of P.E.I., the Mayor of Quebec City who was also a member of the Quebec Legislature, along with the president of Imperial Oil (before the Standard takeover) and Dr. Oronhyatek of the IOF. Another promotion featured Sir William Howland, former Lieutenant Governor of Ontario, an ex-Minister of the Interior, and Senator Robert Jaffray; while the North Star Mining & Developing Co. was headed by Sir Adolphe Caron and Sir Adolphe Chapleau, both former federal Tory ministers and one the former Premier of Quebec, along with Edward Gurney and a group of New Yorkers.[109] The Big Three Gold Mining Co. was the creation of the former Tory Railway Minister J. H. Pope, another Conservative M.P., and an American syndicate.

Such star-laden bodies, at first, had ease of access to the British bond market, and in 1897 and 1898 nearly £2.5 million was raised there. But by 1899 the stream dried up almost completely, and from 1900 to 1910 there were no public issues by Canadian mining companies in Britain.[110] British funds for equity investment were difficult to raise from the start: the Canadian companies adopted the American system of issuing shares at discounts, a practice unused in Britain, as well as denominating the shares in dollars rather than sterling.[111] But the sudden curtailment of bond capital was due to other causes, notably the disasters that befell the early investments. A series of four major failures struck the British-Canadian mining ventures in the first few years, beginning with the Empire Gold Field, which had issued £200,000 in bonds in 1898 for a saw mill that never operated, a compressor that never ran, and other equipment that never got into the mine. By 1901 all the equipment was abandoned. Three other ventures issued shares at one pound each at the beginning of the boom, shares which by 1901 were worth 2/6, 1/0, and 1/6, making a total loss of £4.5 million.[112]

A great deal of American and Canadian money went into the gold fields as well, part of it to back claims illegally filed by clerks in the employ of the Ministry of the Interior who used their positions to get the best lands.[113] Most of the Canadian funds, and some of the American, came via Toronto and Toronto-based financiers — Pellatt, Cox, Mackenzie and company.

Once mined, the gold was largely exported in an unrefined state. During the Klondike rush none of it was minted into coin in Canada, for until 1908 there was no mint operating in Canada: all gold coin was struck in the Royal Mint in London, or the mint in Birmingham. And when minting facilities were brought to Canada in 1908, it was as a branch of the Royal Mint, whose officials were all appointed by the British government and whose operations were conducted directly under the regulation of its parent. Moreover, during its early existence all the coins struck were British sovereigns from gold refined abroad. Not until 1911 did gold refining auxiliary to the mint begin, and not until 1912 were Canadian gold coins struck.[114]

TABLE XI (5)

Royal Mint Canada Branch Gold Coinage

Year	Sovereigns	Canadian
1908	3,095.20	—
1909	79,195.27	—
1910	136,325.07	—
1911	1,247,789.00	—
1912	—	1,477,710.00
1913 (3 months)	18,079.67	323,020.00
	1,484,484.21	1,800,730.00

Source: Public Accounts 1914, p. xiii.

Copper and Nickel

A copper rush took place in northern Ontario in the 1840's, par- allelling the contemporary one in Michigan, but little American capital moved in at that point; the field was dominated by

British and Canadian firms. A huge bout of speculation resulted
from the strike: immense tracts of land north of Huron and
Superior were alienated into the hands of a few companies, but
very little mining was actually done, and the few fortunes made
were largely derived from swindles.[115] Refining was confined to
one British firm whose little smelter continued in operation until
1864.[116]

A later strike, this time in Quebec, led to a second wave of
speculation, which likewise collapsed, though it tended to leave
in its wake a few more permanent investments than the first.
Even during its peak the ores were all shipped out to the U.S. or
the U.K. for refining, apart from a small amount of work carried
on at Canadian sulphuric acid producing plants. The Orford
Nickel and Copper Co., an American firm, purchased a property
in Quebec in 1877 and built a refinery in New Jersey to process
the ore. In 1879 it sank its first shaft.[117] The Canadian Copper
Co., another U.S. firm, was also active by that date, and in 1878
it made arrangements to use Orford's New Jersey smelter. In
1882 yet another American syndicate bought a large property in
Megantic County.[118] Unlike the first strike American capital, not
British, dominated this second rush, though there was some
British investment as well.

The British investments were largely the work of L. S. Huntingdon, the Liberal M.P. who, with such fervour and righteous
indignation had unveiled the Pacific Scandal in Parliament.
Such time as he could spare from saving the nation from the corruption of the Macdonald Tories he spent swindling Scottish
investors in two Eastern Townships copper mines. One was sold
to a Glasgow group, with Huntingdon acting as broker and
receiving a commission from the purchasers. At the same time,
by deliberate misrepresentation, he was collecting another commission from the vendors and thus diverted nearly a quarter of a
million dollars of the sale money into his own pocket. Suits were
launched by the directors, but were stopped when Huntingdon
and some friends purchased enough of the by then badly depreciated stock to secure the election of directors friendly to him. In
the second mine job Huntingdon appeared as more than just an
intermediary, for he added to the property being transferred
some 5,000 acres of his own land for $47 an acre, land whose
value was independently appraised at 80¢ an acre. The mine too
was virtually valueless, contrary to the enthusiastic predictions of
the prospectus which Huntingdon had written. It closed shortly,
and a suit was launched against him by the second set of
outraged directors — but, it seems, to no avail.[119]

In 1886, most of the activity switched to Superior again following a new strike. The CPR immediately began building a feeder line into the new find, and Duncan McIntyre got to work soliciting investments with his glowing report.[120] From the beginning of the rush, most of the best lands were grabbed by merchants and little capitalists from Pembroke, Ottawa, Sudbury, and Sault Ste. Marie, and held for speculation. Unlike the first Superior copper strike, the Canadian presence in mining was marginal and short-lived. Within five years, the leader in the area was Canadian Copper, which had in 1886 passed into the hands of S. J. Ritchie and an Ohio group. Its refining was all done in Orford's New Jersey copper smelters.[121] There were, of course, many other efforts to break into copper by American and British capital, including the Lake Superior Queen Mining Company floated by a St. Paul group in London in 1890. In this case, £155,000 of the £175,000 subscribed went directly to the promoters and vendors of the property, leaving £20,000 only for working capital.[122]

Once the main focus of mining activity shifted to B.C., a great deal of British and American funds moved into the copper mines there.[123] The smelting of copper also tended to be concentrated in B.C., for both the Sudbury and the Quebec ores were exported to American smelters. The Boston group who controlled a large slice of the Eastern Townships deposits and exported the ores to Staten Island tried for several years to secure a Quebec government bounty for refining with the province, without success.[124]

Nickel became important as a corollary of the third round of copper explorations, and Canadian Copper was in the forefront from any early period. Other early entrants included the Welsh firm of H. H. Vivian and Co., which did all its refining in Wales,[125] and the American Drury Nickel Co., which built a smelter in the U.S. in 1892 and connected it to the CPR, along which it sent its ores from the mines to smelter. Several Standard Oil magnates were involved with this operation.[126] The Canadian nickel fields became something of a battleground of competing foreign concerns anxious to secure their raw material supplies.

Nickel was a mineral whose economic and political significance had grown dramatically by the end of the nineteenth century with technological breakthroughs in the production of the nickel-steel so much in demand in the armaments industry that boomed during the scramble for colonies and markets in the pre-World-War I period. At the same time, in Canada, pressure began mounting for government action to shift the locus of refining to Canada to generate employment during the critical years of high unemployment and population loss. By 1890, Canadian manufacturers were objecting to the tax treatment of foreign mining operations who received customs rebates on their imports of American machinery and who were granted federal government cash bounties on their iron and steel output.[127] The argument that the export of raw ore meant the export of employment opportunities was a powerful one, though not sufficiently so to offset the political power of the big mining companies.

In 1890 Ritchie, on behalf of his Canadian Copper, applied for a federal subsidy of $200,000 per annum for ten years plus another $6,000 per mile for a resource railway in order to build a functioning smelter. Ritchie, however, was foolish enough to let the information become public; the result was the immediate formation of a rival Canadian syndicate claiming preference over foreign operators, and no help could be given to Ritchie.[128] Moreover, in 1890 he was dumped from the board of Canadian Copper by the American steel producers who controlled it. Then began a long series of legal wrangles which Ritchie lost, including a suit over one-and-one-quarter million dollars that he had voted himself as a reward for services rendered the company. An effort to sell the company in England was also blocked by his partners, and Ritchie retired after a spate of accusations about bribery, corruption and theft.[130]

In the meantime, Canada Copper was still not refining, despite the fact that it was legally obligated to do so by the terms of its charter. It lacked patents for refining techniques. The English firm headed by Dr. Ludwig Mond would only sell its patents for refining to the company at such a high price as to give it control. A German inventor and holder of a patent for refining, Carl Hoepfner was hired in 1895, but it was stated his process was inadequate. Refining techniques had to be learned by stealing an engineer from Vivian,[131] whose diggings in Canada were closed by 1894. Drury also ceased operations in 1894,[132] and apart from a few small firms, Canadian Copper-Orford had a virtual monopoly for several years. That year a further request was made for a federal subsidy for a smelter, again to no avail.[133]

The Sudbury nickel ranges continued to attract considerable outside attention. British capital was represented by both British American Nickel, an English and Canadian operation in fact controlled by the British government, and after 1899 Mond Nickel, incorporated under imperial statute, itself joined the field.[134] In 1899, Ritchie, Carl Hoepfner, and some Hamilton iron and steel men backed by British steel manufacturers created a group of companies in a new effort to establish a nickel-steel complex in Canada,[135] and these companies purchased large ranges in Sudbury in 1901,[136] the same year that Thomas Edison, a former associate of Ritchie's, paid a visit to the area looking for a source of nickel for his new storage battery.[137]

The campaign for export duties on nickel matte had continued until the federal government passed the requisite legislation in 1897. It was not, however, proclaimed and if it was intended a threat to impose the law if Canadian Copper failed to refine in Canada, it was not taken seriously by the company. In 1898 another American firm offered to build a smelter if the duties were imposed. As early as 1896 Francis Clergue had advocated such duties,[138] and Ritchie and his syndicate now joined him, along with such bodies as the Toronto Board of Trade.[139] Clergue argued that if the smelting of nickel in Canada was inhibited by the lack of access to patents — as had the New Jersey smelter a few years before — the clauses in the Patent Act that stipulated forfeiture for non-use and non-manufacture could be used to force local development.[140]

When the federal government refused to act, Ritchie and his group used their political clout with the Ontario government to have the licence fees and royalties raised for ores exported from Ontario in unrefined form. By 1901 both Canadian Copper and Orford — who merged into International Nickel (Inco) the next year — and Mond Nickel did the first stages of concentration in the Sudbury area, but all the higher stages of refining were still done in the U.S. and the U.K. respectively.[141] There were immediate protests from the companies affected, and efforts to have the federal government disallow the Ontario legislation. Inco for a time switched much more of its activity to its New Caledonia deposits, reducing the amount of mining done in Ontario.[142] True to form, the big banks sided with the nickel firms against the Ontario government and the CMA. Sir Edward Clouston of the Bank of Montreal contended that

> the inevitable result, if it is permitted to remain on the Statute Books, will be the closing of the doors to the flow of English capital into this country. Dr. Mond is a very prominent man, not only in the scientific, but also in the manufacturing world, and if it is known in the London market that, after investing very largely in this country, his property was practically confiscated by the Ontario Legislature, it will have a very serious effect on future English enterprise here.[143]

Other bankers such as Edmund Walker, expressed similar sentiments.[144] The Ontario government was forced to back down, and the familiar threat of closing the London capital market must have helped in forcing that decision.

Lead and Silver

A silver boom occurred in Ontario in 1868 and again in 1906. Americans were first in, and reaped the greatest profits,[145] while the small Canadian firms followed. During the Cobalt silver rush the Canadian banks were flooded with requests for aid which, with the rather bizarre exception of the Farmers' Bank, they refused.[146] The industry quickly passed into American control, with a series of sellouts of established mines with excellent ore bodies.[147] British capital was also active in Cobalt[148] though less so than American.

Silver also figured heavily in the B.C. mining boom, but there it was linked closely to the lead industry. Prior tò 1897, all of the lead ores of B.C. were drawn off via the CPR to American smelters for refining, and the large mills, including the North Star Mining Co. controlled by Van Horne, Donald Mann, and others, had contracts with the American smelters for delivery of lead and silver ores.[149] In 1897, with growing pressure for local refining, the CPR agreed to alter its rates to cease subsidizing the export of ore, and the next year it took over a smelter which had opened at Trail a few years before.[150] In 1899 began the first of a series of consecutive federal bounties to encourage lead refining. The Hall Mines smelter at Rossland, established in 1895 to smelt copper-silver ore, added lead in 1899.[151] There were only two other smelters in the province at the time: the Pilot Bros. operation, which was seized in 1898 by the Bank of Montreal and thereafter ceased production and a by then defunct smelter established in 1889 at Revelstoke. Despite pressure from Vancouver and from the Kootenay Board of Trade among others, very little actual refining was done, and the outward flow of ore continued.[152] Under the Dingley tariff, the American smelters could import Canadian ore in bond as long as at least 90% of the product was exported.

Two events intervened. Late in 1901, the bottom fell out of lead, copper, and silver in B.C. followed by a series of liquidations of overcapitalized firms. In January 1901, the London price of pig lead was $77.78 per short ton; by February of 1902 it was $44.03. A surfeit of lead ore now afflicted the American smelters who began to boycott the B.C. product, and new higher duties on ore and pig lead were imposed in the U.S.[153] In 1903, the Canadian government put a bounty of 75¢ per 100 pounds on lead from lead-bearing ores refined in Canada: output rose 500% and the number of mines doubled in two years. By 1905, $20 million was invested in the Kootenay mines and concentrating mills and another $15 million in infrastructure to service the mines.[154] Typically, the smelting interests — namely Consolidated Mining and Smelting, the reorganized CPR-owned firm that owned the Trail smelters — immediately asked for a tariff to supplement the bounty.[155] From 1903 to 1913, when a total of $1,967,708 was paid out in lead bounties, there were only two beneficiaries: Consolidated, and a small Kingston smelter — the successor to Canada's first lead smelter which had operated in Kingston from 1879 to 1882. By 1913, not only was the flow of lead ore to the U.S. stopped, but American ores were coming to the Trail smelters for refining. [156] The recovery of the industry under the bounty plan helped attract British funds in the B.C. mines.[157]

Iron and Coal

The ebb and flow of iron mining in Canada tended to follow that of the primary iron and steel industry more than the demand from the U.S. for ores, for American ores were abundant and more easily accessible than Canadian. There were a few exceptions, however, and by the 1880's some American iron and steel interests in border interests were beginning to register an interest in Ontario ores.

American, and indeed British capital had first ventured into Ontario iron lands during the Marmora and Madoc boom of the 1840's, a boom whose collapse frightened foreign capital away from Ontario iron mines for some time thereafter. By the late 1860's and 1870's, small mines in northern Ontario were exporting to the U.S. on a minor scale.[158] And after the National Policy tariff, American funds began to flow into mining at the same time they were moving into primary iron and steel production, though different groups tended to be involved in the two cases.

The most ambitious of the new American operations was that mounted in 1882 by S. J. Ritchie and his Ohio associates, which involved nothing less than an attempt to monopolize all the available iron lands in Ontario — with the active co-operation of the provincial government. They began with a magnetite site in Hastings county. A resources railroad was taken over and extended to the mine to facilitate the export of ore.[159] Permission was then secured from the Ontario government for the promoters to expropriate all properties along the right-of-way of an enormously expanded railway which was to link up to the CPR. The right-of-way was planned to pass through all the properties that the syndicate desired to secure. But the second thoughts of the

Ohio partners and their growing interest in the copper-nickel belt ended the project.[160]

The primary iron and steel industry in Canada remained rather primitive and small-scale until after 1897. Imports continued to satisfy a large part of the demand for steel products — the CPR, for example, proudly advertised that the wheels on its rolling stock were the finest of Krupp products. As a result, local demand for iron ore was restricted. Exports to the U.S. continued until 1890, but they were not of great significance — from 1868 to 1888 the total value of Ontario iron ore exports to the U.S. came to only $1,300,000, an average of $65,000 per annum. Even that small flow was terminated by an American duty of 75¢ a ton. By 1895 exports to the U.S. ceased altogether.[161] But the revival of iron and steel smelting in Canada after 1897 led to an expansion of mining as well, and American capital figured heavily in the subsequent expansion of both.

Nova Scotia was the only other part of Canada where iron mining was of consequence. Unlike those in Ontario, Nova Scotia iron mines saw little new foreign investment in the period after the National Policy tariff, though not for lack of effort. In 1885, for example, a Pictou company was formed to try to raise foreign funds to exploit a rich mine which had great potential for developing into a primary iron and steel producer. Within fifteen miles of the mine there existed ample coal, limestone, and water power, but American and British capital refused to invest.[162] At the same time the Londonderry steel plant was languishing, robbing that area of a potential market for iron ore. But after the new iron and steel policy, American money, notably that of the H. N. Whitney syndicate, began moving in.[163]

Nova Scotian coal had more consistent success in attracting foreign capital. Apart from the General Mining Association, there were instances of other British investment.[164] And in 1893 the Whitney syndicate, in close co-operation with the Fielding government, began its systematic effort to monopolize the Nova Scotian fields.[165]

Heavy reliance on foreign capital was in fact typical of coal mining operations all across Canada. In 1895, American capital was involved in at least eight of the eleven largest coal mining operations.[166] And British capital figured in A. T. Galt's Albertan empire. One of the larger coal mine operations, the Anthracite Coal Mine Co. in B.C., fell into the hands of foreign investors in 1889 when its Canadian owners were unable to secure further operating funds. It was a profitable operation, which the new owners immediately began to enlarge.[167]

Coal was one of the objects of J. J. Hill's attentions on the

Pacific coast once he began his major campaign against the CPR. In addition to his aquisition of the Dunsmuir collieries on Vancouver island, Hill was heavily involved in the Crow's Nest Pass Coal Company. This was a largely Toronto-based operation headed by George Cox, and including the elite of the Toronto Liberal Party-big business establishment: Joseph Flavelle of National Trust; Plummer of the Bank of Commerce; Henry Pellatt, the broker; E. S. Cox, Canada's leading bucket shop operator; Elias Rogers, Toronto's leading coal merchant; E. R. Wood; and Robert Jaffray.[168]

The CPR-Great Northern fight for the Pacific coal fields began even before J. J. Hill's line entered B.C. Rumours of his planned entry were sufficient to bring the CPR into full battle dress. The Crow's Nest Pass Coal Company initially provided coke and coal to the CPR smelters at Trail. But a wrangle over long-term contracts led to a rupture, and the company began cultivating closer ties to Hill's railway. This relationship was doubly alarming for the CPR. Not only would the coal supplies ease Hill's entry into B.C., but the threatened loss of control of cheap coal and coke supplies meant a blow to CPR-linked smelting and refining operations at a time when rumours were afoot of a conspiracy to capture B.C. mines by J. J. Hill, J. P. Morgan and the Standard-Oil-controlled American Smelting and Refining Co. This alliance was credited with instigating earlier American efforts to destroy the B.C. lead smelting operation conducted by the CPR with federal government subsidies.

The CPR's efforts to stop the Crow's Nest Pass Coal Co. alliance with Hill failed. George Cox and Robert Jaffray fought back: the company was incorporated with Hill securing 30% of the stock.

Miscellaneous Minerals

The lack of Canadian refining or smelting facilities, coupled with foreign control of the mines — either directly through ownership of the equity or indirectly through long-term contracts for the export of raw output — were traits found in many mineral industries. They were typical, too, of virtually every province where mining was an important part of economic activity.

In the era between the decline of copper and the post-war rise of iron mining, Quebec was the chief Canadian source for two minerals, phosphates and asbestos. Phosphate mining on a large scale began by 1880 with French, German, British, and American capital all involved.[169] After 1885, world phosphate prices began rising sharply and the industry grew.[170] Despite the abundance of the material, all processing into fertilizers was done abroad. The Quebec government in the 1880's was in the habit of distributing prizes at agricultural exhibitions in phosphates rather than in cash, and found itself in the embarrassing position of having to import the processed fertilizers from abroad.[171] In 1881, an agreement with a French fertilizer firm was worked out for the erection of a plant in Quebec, but nothing concrete materialized. After 1890, world prices began to slip, and the industry declined.[172]

The same pattern, albeit on a much greater scale, typified asbestos mining. The first strike in the province came in 1878 at Thetford — by an American company which exported the raw asbestos to the U.S.[173] A series of other American investments occurred, in one case with the help of the Bank of Montreal, which sold a mine property it had seized to a New York syndicate.[174] However, both British and Canadian capital were quick to follow the Americans. The United Asbestos Corp., the Anglo-Italian conglomerate which had monopolized the world's supply before the discovery of the Canadian deposits took over a going mine in Canada in 1889.[175] In 1891 a group of Quebec cabinet ministers and other notables headed by Adolphe Chapleau promoted the Coleraine Mining Co. By that year the largest of the Eastern Townships asbestos mines were British or British-Canadian joint ventures.[176]

But despite their ownership the bulk of the output went to the U.S. for processing. At its peak the secondary industry in Canada employed 150 people long after Canada had replaced Italy as the world's leading producer.[177] And during the 1890's the American secondary industry led by the H. W. John's Manufacturing Co. of New York began to cartelize to end competitive bidding for output, forcing the burden of carrying stocks onto the mines. This drove out the small Canadian operators, who had to rely on selling output in advance to secure working capital, and many mines passed into the hands of the American secondary industry.[178]

Some phosphate mining occurred in Ontario, too — by 1894 an American syndicate was digging near Kingston.[179] But most of the early activity remained in Quebec. Where Ontario did have a monopoly was in the surge of interest in arsenic in 1902 when British and foreign capital invested heavily in Hastings County. Its request for an Ontario government bounty for arsenic reduction was not granted.[180] By 1914 the only arsenic produced in Ontario was the by-product of Cobalt's silver-cobalt ores which were smelted in several Ontario locations.

Mining in the Maritimes tended to be controlled to a great degree from New England. Boston capital figured heavily in

New Brunswick's gold, antimony, copper, and manganese.[181] Manganese ores were being exported in a raw state to Boston from as early as 1879.[182] Not until 1903 did the provincial government make a serious move to secure smelting activities by offering a monopoly of the right to search for bog or wad ore on Crown land to any firm undertaking to build a smelter.[183] None did.

In all manner of mining industries the pattern repeated itself. As late as 1914, all feldspar was shipped to the U.S. for processing and use in its potteries. Zinc ore went exclusively to the U.S. from B.C. Of the gypsum produced, largely in the Maritimes, only a tiny percentage was worked into fertilizer or plaster of paris in Canada. Smelting of antimony took place exclusively as a by-product in B.C. lead refining — efforts to smelt in the Maritime mines failed. And of the tungsten output of Nova Scotia not until 1913 was there even a concentrating mill operating.

Conclusion

The policies adopted by Canadian governments to attract American and other foreign direct investment into the country's manufacturing and resources sectors were vigorous and varied. Apart from the patent laws, direct investment in Canadian secondary manufacturing industry from abroad was most energetically cultivated by tariff policy beginning in 1878.

The initial influx of foreign direct investment was not of major import economically; but it was politically, for it whetted appetites for more. Initially the bulk of the influx of foreign capital came in to recapture markets lost because of the tariff. Subsequently more complex forces were at work. After 1896, the export-staple-led prosperity wave induced American direct investment, while the growth of American big business led to a "natural" spill-over across the border. At the same time, the void that was filled by foreign investment can only be accounted for by the pattern of Canadian development, particularly its concentration on staple exports which diverted Canadian capital away from the industrial sector, thus opening it up to the American penetration.

In resource-extracting industries, both federal and provincial policies were more complex, and their precise motivation was often uncertain and subject to change. While the accolades that greeted the migration of direct investment were virtually unanimous, the movement of foreign capital into natural resources was often regarded critically. In the forest industries, a virtual give-away program by the provinces and the Dominion began to change by the turn of the century. The new policy promoted stricter husbanding of resources, with a view to relocating the primary processing of the natural resource inside Canada. This of course induced the desired influx of foreign capital into saw milling and pulp and paper mills, and in turn sparked a boom in the lagging Ontario salt mining industry.

In petroleum and gas, foreign capital was active from the 1890's. A policy of keeping the Canadian refiners in operation to maintain employment in the processing of Ontario's petroleum resources took the form of subsidizing the production of crude oil once the Ontario wells began to exhibit serious signs of exhaustion. In lead mining, the federal government instituted subsidies for smelting to maintain and expand the industry. Iron and steel was the most spectacular case of a resource-based industry expanding subject to government encouragement.

But in other instances federal policy was conspicuously lacking. Gold was not refined in Canada until 1912, as a result of the power of the chartered banks who frowned on any potential competition to their note issue power. Nickel, as well, continued to be exported in its crude state: this reflected a power-play of big international financial interests directed at the Ontario government through the instrumentality of the federal government. And a wide range of other minerals were exported in a raw state.

On balance, Canadian government resource policy was no policy at all. In certain instances, efforts were made to stimulate resource-based processing industries: in others, the exigencies of government finance or private corporate power led to the replication of the traditional policy of rapid alienation and quick resource depletion.

Notes to Chapter XI

1.   *CM,* Jan. 16, 1891, p. 44.
2.   *HCD,* April 5, 1888, p.556.
3.   *MT,* Oct. 11, 1878, p.977.
4.   *MT,* March 7, 1879, p. 1113.
5.   *JC,* June 3, 1881, p.491.
6.   *CM,* March 2, 1894, p. 188.
7.   *RCRLC, Ontario Evidence,* p. 370.
8.   *MT,* April 4, 1879, p. 1238.
9.   *MT,* July 22, 1881, p.95; July 21, 1882.
10.   *JC,* Oct. 26, 1883, p. 306; *MT,* Dec. 23, 1881, p.763; July 20, 1883, p. 64.
11.   *MT,* July 31, 1885, p. 121.

12. *MT,* Dec. 15, 1882, p. 652.
13. *MT,* June 26, 1885, p. 1456.
14. W. W. Johnson, *Sketches,* p. 173; *MT,* April 25, 1884, p. 1198.
15. *MT,* Feb. 23, 1883, p. 930.
16. *JC,* May 2, 1879, pp. 338-9.
17. *MT,* July 6, 1883, p. 9; July 13, 1888, p. 36.
18. *MT,* Dec. 31, 1880, p. 748.
19. *MT,* April 10, 1891, p. 1239.
20. M. Wilkins, *The Emergence of Multinational Enterprise,* P. 58.
21. *MT.* Feb. 27, 1891, p. 1062.
22. *CE,* Sept. 1895, p. 129.
23. *MT,* April 11, 1902, pp. 1326-7; Jan. 3, 1902, p. 851; Aug. 22, 1902, pp. 241-2.
24. *MT,* March 8, 1901, p. 116.
25. *MT,* Oct. 27, 1916, p. 6; J. Viner, *Canada's Balance,* p. 12.
26. *IC,* Oct. 1906, p. 239.
27. H. M. P. Eckhardt, "Americanizing Influence," p. 293; *CE,* March 1901, p. 226.
28. *MT,* Annual, Jan. 1914, pp. 28-30.
29. *MT,* Annual, Jan. 1914, p. 25.
30. *CM,* May 6, 1887, p. 263.
31. *RCRLC, Ontario Evidence,* pp. 369-70.
32. H. M. P. Eckhardt, "Americanizing Influence," p. 293.
33. *IC,* March 1913, pp. 1035-6.
34. *CE,* June 1901, p. 315; March 1901, p. 245; Nov. 1901, p. 448; Oct. 1902, p. 278; *MT,* July 23, 1897, p. 99; Oct. 21, 1898, p. 527; May 24, 1901, p. 1573; Oct. 4, 1901, p. 437.
35. *CE,* May 1902, p. 219; Aug. 1902, p. 219; *MT,* April 25, 1902, p. 1383.
36. *MT,* Annual Jan. 1914, pp. 25-6.
37. W. G. Phillips, *The Agricultural Implements Industry,* p. 62.
38. B. E. Walker to R. Stuart, June 26, 1901, *Walker Papers; MT,* June 7, 1901, p. 1638; Jan. 11, 1901, p. 895; Dec. 27, 1901, p. 809; Feb. 28, 1902, p. 1112.
39. *MT,* Dec. 16, 1898, p. 791.
40. *CE,* Jan. 1902, p. 14; W. T. R. Preston, *My Generation,* p. 325.
41. *MT,* Aug. 4, 1899, p. 137.
42. *CM,* Feb. 3, 1882, p. 36; July 4, 1890, pp. 8-9; Nov. 7, 1890, p. 295; Dec. 5, 1890, pp. 364, 371.
43. H. A. Innis and A. R. M. Lower, *Select Documents,* p. 253.
44. *MT,* March 21, 1881, p. 1092.
45. *CE,* Feb. 1895, p. 302.
46. *MT,* Sept. 14, 1894, p. 350.
47. *MT,* Dec. 3, 1880, p. 636.
48. *MT,* July 29, 1881, p. 127.
49. *MT,* Sept. 24, 1880, p. 357; Oct. 25, 1889, p. 489; July 8, 1892, p. 7.
50. *MT,* Nov. 18, 1892, p. 572; L. Knowles, *The Economic Development of the British Overseas Empire,* pp. 558-60.
51. N. Reich, *The Pulp and Paper Industry,* pp. 13-14; W. W. Johnson, *Sketches,* p. 156; *MT,* Dec. 31, 1897, p. 861.
52. *MT,* Feb. 21, 1879, p. 1043.
53. *MT,* May 25, 1883, Supplement; July 27, 1883, p. 91; *CM,* June 15, 1888, p. 406; July 6, 1888, p. 7.
54. *MT,* Dec. 8, 1876, p. 642.
55. *Ec,* March 6, 1880, p. 265.
56. *CM,* April 14, 1882, p. 138; *MT,* Aug. 27, 1897, p. 262.

57.   *MT,* July 23, 1886, p. 95.
58.   *MT,* Nov. 23, 1888, p. 587; Feb. 15, 1889, p. 937; March 1, 1889, p. 999.
59.   *CM,* Oct. 16, 1891, p. 244; *MT,* Oct. 10, 1890, p. 435.
60.   *HCD,* April 28, 1897, p. 1418.
61.   *MT,* April 9, 1897, pp. 1341, 1343.
62.   *MT,* Sept. 16, 1898, p. 373.
63.   *MT,* April 15, 1898, p. 1362.
64.   *MT,* Dec. 30, 1898, p. 863.
65.   *MT,* April 1, 1892, p. 1190.
66.   *MT,* Aug. 6, 1897, p. 170.
67.   *MT,* Sept. 24, 1897, p. 406; Dec. 24, 1897, p. 821.
68.   A. R. M. Lower *et al, The North American Assault On The Canadian Forest,* pp.154-7.
69.   *CE,* Dec. 1895, p. 220.
70.   *CM,* Jan. 18, 1895, p. 72.
71.   *CE,* Jan. 26, 1896, p. 252.
72.   *MT,* Feb. 5, 1897, p. 1036; W. Vaughn, *Van Horne,* p. 287.
73:   *MT,* Oct. 15, 1897, p. 505.
74.   *Globe,* Jan. 1, 1911.
75.   *MT,* March 31, 1899, p. 1282.
76.   *CE,* Jan. 1900, p. 258; *MT,* July 20, 1907, p. 92.
77.   *MT,* April 7, 1899, p. 1317.
78.   F. W. Field, *Capital Investments In Canada,* p. 138.
79.   *MT,* May 18, 1900.
80.   *CE,* Feb. 1900, p. 282.
81.   *MT,* April 18, 1902, p. 1363.
82.   *CE,* Nov. 1902, p. 310.
83.   *Globe,* Jan. 12, 1911; *CE,* July 1901, p. 351; April 1901, p. 268; *MT,* Sept. 13, 1901, p. 332.
84.   *CE,* Feb. 1901, p. 215; *MT,* Oct. 4, 1901, p. 433.
85.   *MT,* March 9, 1900, p. 1186.
86.   *Ec,* July 8, 1911, p. 62.
87.   *MT,* Dec. 2, 1892, p. 636.
88.   *CE,* Jan. 1894, p. 266.
89.   *MT,* May 17, 1895, p. 1487.
90.   Salt existed all over Canada. It had been mined in Manitoba, for example, as early as 1820. But there was little activity apart from the springs at Cardwell, N.B., which began a new phase of growth after 1902 when an English syndicate took it over — the province assisting by exempting it from all royalties for ten years (*MT,* Aug. 25, 1902, p. 1383). In Nova Scotia, a series of efforts to commercially exploit its salt wells proved unsuccessful. By 1914 only southwestern Ontario was producing.
91.   The exceptions included a short-lived operation in Cape Breton born out of the desire to break the hold of the Ontario combine in 1876. The company remained in operation for a few years and had some successful strikes but never became of any great importance. (See *MT,* Sept. 1, 1876, p. 240; Aug. 20, 1880, p. 203.) An English operation explored the Gaspé, looking for a source of oil for export to Britain, but failed in 1909. In 1899, another New Brunswick organization was put together by a syndicate headed by the Premier. Despite hopeful reports from experts, Canadian money could not be found and drilling was delayed for two years. By 1905, oil and gas finds were verified and the syndicate went to England unsuccessfully seeking funds. In 1909, an English syndicate took over the operation and, while petroleum remained dormant, its gas operations were a huge success. The English syndicate quickly achieved a high degree of monopoly

through an alliance with an American-owned utility firm, Moncton Tramways, Electricity and Gas Co., which undertook distribution throughout the province.

92. *Ec,* Jan. 26, 1901, p. 119.
93. *MT,* May 6, 1881, p. 1285.
94. *MT,* Jan. 25, 1889, p. 842; Sept. 12, 1890, p. 308.
95. *MT,* Feb. 14, 1890, p. 988; *Canada Gazette,* Feb. 8, 1890, p. 1625.
96. *MT,* Dec. 9, 1892, p. 667.
97. *CE,* Sept. 1894, p. 160; Jan. 1895, p. 272.
98. *MT,* May 10, 1895, p. 1444.
99. *MT,* Aug. 7, 1896, p. 168; Jan. 22, 1897, p. 976.
100. *MT,* April 3, 1903, p. 1346; Oct. 9, 1903, p. 446.
101. *HCD,* Aug. 4, 1904, p. 8443.
102. *HCD,* June 7, 1904, p. 4359; July 28, 1904, p. 7785; *Ec,* July 17, 1909, p. 129.
103. A. G. Brown and P. H. Morres, *Twentieth Century Impressions* pp. 254-6; *MT,* Oct. 14, 1870, p. 166; Oct. 9, 1885, p. 400; Nov. 30, 1888, p. 613; Jan. 4, 1889, p. 747; Oct. 9, 1891, p. 430; May 10, 1895, p. 1445; *CE,* Jan. 1894, pp. 265-6; Feb. 1894, p. 296.
104. *MT,* July 27, 1894, p. 104.
105. *CE,* April 1894, p. 358.
106. *MT,* Aug. 30, 1896, p. 1394.
107. *MT, Annual,* Jan. 1914, p. 32.
108. *MT,* March 12, 1897, p. 1220.
109. *MT,* Aug. 14, 1896, pp. 212-14; Jan. 22, 1897, p. 978; Feb. 5, 1897, p. 1056; Feb. 26, 1897, p. 1139.
110. *Ec,* July 8, 1911, p. 62.
111. *MT,* Jan. 13, 1899, p. 930.
112. *MT,* July 12, 1901, p. 48.
113. *MT,* April 7, 1899, p. 1320.
114. Public Accounts, Sessional Papers 1914, p. xiii.
115. *MT,* Oct. 8, 1886, p. 412.
116. O. W. Main, *The Canadian Nickel Industry,* p. 7.
117. *MT,* Feb. 7, 1879, p. 976; Feb. 24, 1871, p. 550.
118. *MT,* May 9, 1878, p. 1383; *MT,* Feb. 10, 1882, p. 972.
119. *HCD,* May 10, 1878, pp. 140-2.
120. *MT,* July 15, 1887, p. 68.
121. O. W. Main, *Nickel,* p. 12.
122. *MT,* June 20, 1896, p. 1572.
123. *MT,* May 13, 1898, p. 1477; Dec. 13, 1901, p. 746; March 10, 1899, p. 1195; Dec. 23, 1904, p. 806, Dec. 30, 1904, p. 845.
124. *MT,* Aug. 29, 1902, p. 280; May 20, 1904, p. 1539.
125. Ontario, *Report of the Bureau of Mines,* 1903, p.287.
126. *MT,* April 1, 1892, p. 1189.
127. *CM,* May 16, 1890, pp. 328-9.
128. Macdonald to Tupper, Nov. 22, 1890, *MacDonald Papers.*
129. *CE,* Nov. 1894, p. 248.
130. *MT,* Jan. 11, 1895, p. 901.
131. O. W. Main, *Nickel,* pp. 27-8.
132. *CE,* July 1894, p. 94.
133. *CE,* April 1894, p. 358.
134. E. S. Moore *American Influences on Canadian Mining,* p. 32.
135. O. W. Main, *Nickel,* pp. 33 *et passim.*
136. *MT,* April 19, 1901, p. 1374.
137. *CE,* Oct. 1901, p. 422.

138.   *CM,* June 5, 1896.
139.   *MT,* April 29, 1898, p. 1415.
140.   *MT,* May 11, 1900, p. 1482.
141.   *MT,* March 8, 1901, p. 1151; July 12, 1901, p. 42.
142.   Ontario, *Report of the Bureau of Mines,* 1903, p. 17.
143.   V. Nelles, *The Politics of Development,* p. 171.
144.   B. E. Walker to Dr. B. Mohr, Jan. 3, 1913, *Walker Papers.*
145.   E. S. Moore, *American Influences,* p. 41.
146.   *MT,* Dec. 14, 1910, p. 2615; Jan. 14, 1911, p. 210.
147.   *MT,* Sept. 21, 1906, p. 387; Dec. 1, 1906, p. 784.
148.   *MT,* March 16, 1907, p. 1454.
149.   *MT,* May 14, 1897, p. 1511.
150.   *MT,* July 30, 1897, p. 146; Dec. 23, 1904, p. 806.
151.   *MT,* March 10, 1899, p. 1195; Sept. 14, 1900, p. 330; May 31, 1901, p. 1601.
152.   *HCD,* Aug. 6, 1903, p. 8196; *MT,* Dec. 28, 1900, p. 819; May 29, 1901, p. 1277.
153.   *Ec,* Feb. 22, 1902, pp. 280-1.
154.   *Tariff Enquiry Commission Papers,* vol. X, pp. 28-9; *HCD,* July 3, 1903, p. 6170.
155.   *Ec,* Feb. 28, 1903, p. 382.
156.   Department of Trade and Commerce, *Annual Report for 1913,* Part IV, pp. 9, 35.
157.   *Ec,* Jan. 25, 1908, p. 173.
158.   *MT,* June 17, 1869, p. 699; May 16, 1879, p. 1413.
159.   *MT,* Feb. 10, 1882, p. 972.
160.   O. W. Main, *Nickel,* p. 12.
161.   Ontario, *Report of the Bureau of Mines,* 1903, p. 19.
162.   *CE,* Aug. 1894, pp. 104-5.
163.   *MT,* March 10, 1899, p. 1187.
164.   *MT,* Sept. 5, 1890, p. 279.
165.   *MT,* Jan. 27, 1893, p. 878.
166.   *CE,* April 1895, p. 355.
167.   *MT,* Aug. 2, 1889, p. 141.
168.   *MT,* March 14, 1899, p. 1204; March 24, 1899, p. 1273; Dec. 14, 1900, p. 752; Jan. 11, 1901, p. 891; Feb. 15, 1901, p. 1046; May 3, 1901, p. 1478.
169.   *MT,* July 23, 1880, p. 91; Aug. 5, 1881, pp. 149-50; Sept. 28, 1883, p. 344; March 27, 1885, p. 1082.
170.   *MT,* Jan. 22, 1886, p. 820.
171.   *MT,* Aug. 26, 1881, p. 239.
172.   Quebec, Commissioner of Crown Lands, *Report for 1889,* p. 90; Quebec, Commissioner of Colonization and Mines, *Report,* 1897, p. 278.
173.   *MT,* May 31, 1878, p. 1401; Nov. 29, 1878, p. 686.
174.   *MT,* Jan. 20, 1882, p. 879; Oct. 4, 1889, p. 398.
175.   M. Mendels, *The Asbestos Industry of Canada,* p. 18.
176.   *MT,* Sept. 1891, p. 366; Aug. 14, 1891, p. 194.
177.   M. Mendels, *Asbestos,* p. 36.
178.   M. Mendels, *Asbestos,* pp. 19-21.
179.   *MT,* July 13, 1894, p. 40.
180.   *MT,* Feb. 21, 1902, p. 1079; A. G. Brown and P. H. Morres, *Twentieth Century Impressions,* p. 265.
181.   *CMJ,* Nov. 1909, p. 547; *MT,* July 19, 1889, p. 64.
182.   *CM,* May 26, 1882, p. 199; *MT,* April 25, 1879, p. 1326; April 30, 1880, p. 1286; Aug. 6, 1880, p. 148.
183.   *Statutes of New Brunswick,* 3 Ed. VII 1903, Chap. 17.

Now Mr. Mackenzie said he looked with loathing upon money raised by this "legalized robbery." Gentlemen, we are not so particular.

John A. Macdonald, 1881

Chapter XII
Federalism and the Rise of the Corporate Welfare State

Bounties and Bonuses

In addition to tariff and patent laws, the federal government granted bounties of various orders of magnitude to some primary processing industries, such as the lead and iron and steel refiners and smelters. Occasionally the provinces followed suit. But most prolific of all the levels of government in the granting of largesse to corporations were the municipalities, and of all the multitude of techniques used by various levels of government in Canada to increase the rate of industrial capital formation none was as bizarre as the system of municipal bonusing. In large measure, bonusing was a stop-gap policy to plug the hole in the capital market left by the banks, the financial system in general and the federal government, which channelled funds off into commerce and the construction of commercial infrastructure. Bonusing of industry in effect converted the municipality into an investment banker, facilitating industrial capital accumulation by redistributing income and by providing a further attraction to foreign capital.

It began in a modest way, but soon degenerated into a vicious system of intercommunal warfare. Municipalities competed to drive each other into bankruptcy in order to benefit a few industrial capitalists who often had no need of the gifts. Lured by bribes of every description, capital was tempted to move from other municipalities, from other provinces, from the United States, from Britain, and even from France. The bonusing system encouraged chronic overexpansion of many industries, notably cotton, canning, iron and steel, sugar, furniture factories, and others, helping to precipitate cartelization. Beginning innocently enough with small cash grants or tax exemptions, it grew inexorably. As one municipality succeeded in building or attracting a new industry, others would follow, and the handouts grew. Cash gifts, interest-free loans, free sites, long-term tax exemptions, low or free water, gas and electricity rates, railroad spurs, bond guarantees, even cases of towns paying for dredging occurred regularly. The system passed the bounds of what little reason it might have possessed with subsidies to wages, poor law fashion, and even a case of guaranteeing dividends.

Federal tariff, patent law, and bounties were central to encouraging the inflow of foreign investment, but they seldom determined the actual location of the new industry. This was left to the bonusing system in a great many cases. Railroads, too, clearly affected the distribution of industry, but since federal railway policy aimed at creating trunk lines, it was often left to the municipality to bribe the railway companies into building feeder lines. Within the context set by the federal tariff, patent, and railroad policy, firms would actively solicit bonuses and go shopping for the best terms. Their requests for bonuses were almost invariably granted,[1] at least in the early years, and this would provide them with ammunition with which to exact an even larger offer from another village or town.

But bonusing played a role over and above the distribution of industry: it was accessory to tariffs and patent laws in actually encouraging the migration of foreign firms.[2] While it is unclear whether bonusing — apart from the federal government's iron and steel bonuses — would by itself have actually brought in foreign capital, nonetheless on top of the other policies it helped to induce the entry of firms who were reluctant to move because of tariff protection alone. Canadian industrialization tended to show distinct waves which centred on a particular industry, and these waves of follow-the-leader investment were usually related to some facet of government policy. Bonusing, too, came in complementary waves. Thus, in 1879, tariffs led to a rapid cotton expansion fed by bonusing. Iron and steel, meat packing, pulp and paper, and beet sugar came in waves at the end of the century; and in the case of iron and steel, pulp and paper, beet sugar, and others, a conscious federal or provincial policy change preceded them.

After Confederation, bonusing seems to have been initiated by the Quebec towns, which by the late 1860's were offering tax exemptions on a wide scale[3] — apparently illegally, for in 1870 a bill authorizing the tax exemptions was passed in the Quebec Legislature. The Act, "for the purpose of encouraging the introduction and establishment of new manufactures of all kinds," permitted the municipalities to grant tax exemptions of up to ten years. If any already established firm was injured by the giveaway to the newcomer, the town was granted the authority to extend the bonus to the old firm as well.[4] In southern and western Ontario, the cash bonus system came into vogue quite early.[5] These practices spread to eastern Ontario and to the Maritimes. The West came later, of course, but it too got actively into the game of bonusing eastern manufacturers to move,[6] and there were frequent cases of grants to agribusiness.

That the Eastern Townships of Quebec and southwestern Ontario should be the initiators is readily explicable. Employment was the burning political issue of the day, and these areas suffered the most serious drains of population to the United States. Agitation to stop it began early, well before the National Policy. The Quebec 1870 legislation had just this problem in mind.[7] At its first annual meeting, the Dominion Board of Trade, while still antiprotectionist, had called for an industrial development policy to stop the outflow.[8] Sir John A. Macdonald, in 1876, used the fact that bonusing had become prevalent to "prove" that the farming population wanted protection. Since they had put a tax on themselves by bonusing, they would be willing to accept a tax via a protective tariff.[9] Even before the National Policy, towns had begun to openly advertise their willingness to bargain with industry over the terms of the bonus. Early in 1879 the following advertisement appeared in the *Monetary Times:*

TO MANUFACTURERS

The Council of the town of Chatham, Ont. is prepared to treat with manufacturers looking to the establishment of manufacturing industries in that town in offering a reasonable bonus therefor.

Parties prepared to establish such on the guarantee of a bonus are invited to communicate with the undersigned . . .

Town Clerk,
Chatham, Ont., March 18, 1879[10]

The abuses of the system mounted, and opposition grew. Efforts by legislatures, especially Ontario's, to curb it were futile. The individual municipalities dared not desist: the very competitive character of the bonusing craze locked them into a system of Hobbesian behaviour. They could deplore it, but only after working hours, for some other town might take advantage of their hesitation to attract away one of their prize catches. St. Jean, Quebec, a town that was exceptionally active in the bonusing craze, declared in 1888 that "St. John's is not strong enough yet to stem the tide in such matters. We must, to some extent, do as others do or lag behind in the race."[11] In 1910, an Ontario town council concurred that even at that late date "Woodstock must do likewise or remain at a standstill."[12]

The principal beneficiaries were the large American and Canadian firms to whom the bonuses meant simply expanded profit margins. The losers were those who paid for it. The burden fell on the poorer citizens, who paid the highly regressive taxes, and on established local firms, whose rates and taxes went up to support the gifts to newcomers.[13] The costs fell on future generations as well, for despite the exactions from the taxpayers and existing firms, current resources were inadequate to sustain the mammoth barbeque, and debenture issues by the municipalities were a standard and escalating means of fund-raising.

Many of these debentures were taken up in Britain, and formed an important part of the inflow of British portfolio investment of the period. British finance capital was thus made available to the Canadian municipalities, who converted it into industrial capital with the town, not the British investor or the firm, bearing the risk. In this way, much of the British funds went indirectly to support American direct investment in Canada, thus effectively doubling the net international indebtedness that resulted from a particular level of capital inflow.

Most of the municipal debentures, however, were taken up in Canada, by insurance companies and more especially by the chartered banks. The municipality, not the bank or the firm, still bore the risk. A myth promulgated by the bankers in this period to defend the branch system was that no one local bank could sustain the demands for capital typical of the era, but that branch banking could by moving funds from "surplus" savings areas to "deficit" areas. The interregional movement that resulted drained the Maritimes and the small towns of Ontario of the funds to sustain industrial capital formation, and hence increased the burden that had to be carried by such gimmicks as bonusing via debenture issues, which locked the locality into a debtor relationship with Britain or the main urban financial centres of Canada. To the extent that funds flowed back to these areas via debenture purchases by the chartered banks, the banks were often lending back funds already derived from that area, and simply adding another level of intermediation and therefore higher credit costs.

Bonusing Before Confederation

Pre-Confederation patterns are precisely the reverse of those afterward. Before Confederation, the municipalities were heavily involved in financing commercial infrastructure, while the few instances of industrial bonusing that occurred were the prerogative of the provincial governments.

The dubious distinction of being the first industrial panhandler in Canada seems to go to the Acadia Paper Mill, established in Nova Scotia in 1817, which in 1823 received a £100 gift from the Nova Scotia Legislature. In 1825, James Crook, the founder of Upper Canada's first paper mill, was similarly rewarded by his province.[14] In 1834, in Upper Canada Charles Perry, the pioneer of steam engines received £50.[15] In Lower Canada in 1844, a case of private bonusing by a subordinate arm of government occurred when A. T. Galt's British American Land Company gave free water privileges to the A. T. Galt-Massachusetts joint venture in cotton.[16]

Hence, in a very limited way, the elements of the future industrial bonusing system had already taken shape in the form of cash grants and utility privileges. But these were very scattered cases, for large-scale industrialism was still some decades away, and competition among municipalities for industry was nonexistent.

For infrastructure, it was a different story. In fact it was the result of municipal bonusing in the form of the huge pork barrel called the Municipal Loan Fund that gave so much impetus to the Confederation movement. Each municipality was authorized to issue debentures to pay for canals, harbours, roads, and railroads. The debentures of each were pooled in the Municipal Loan Fund, and the Receiver General of Canada was authorized to issue provincial debentures in proportion to the size of the fund. The pooling was expected to increase their saleability in London, and the proceeds of the sale were to be transferred back to the municipalities for investment in railroads and other public works. Each municipality contributed to a sinking fund to redeem the debentures at maturity.[17] The plan was short-lived and not very successful, for it was linked to the free banking system's requirements for a bond-backed currency, and the free banking system tended to frighten away British capital.

Nonetheless, large sums were raised. By 1859, the municipalities of Upper Canada had raised $5,600,000 for railroads alone, on which arrears of interest totalled nearly $2,400,000. Lower Canadian municipalities raised a total of less than one million,

with arrears of interest reaching nearly $350,000. Efforts to cover
the arrears led to the tariff increases of 1858-1859, a regressive
tax to transfer large sums to a few railroad magnates. Small
municipalities subscribed sums out of all proportion to their
resources, a few examples of which are given in Table XII (1).[18]

TABLE XII (1)

Railway Bonuses, 1859

Town	Population	Loan
Port Hope	3,000	$740,000
Cobourg	4,000	500,000
Brockville	4,000	400,000
London	10,000	375,400
Ottawa	10,000	200,000
Brantford	6,000	500,000
Niagara Falls	2,500	280,000

One village ran up debts of $300 per capita. The waste
involved was enormous. One of the most flagrant examples was
the competition between Port Hope and Cobourg, situated only
seven miles apart and servicing the same lumbering area. Both
invested heavily in feeder lines to the towns to bring traffic into
their respective lake ports. Instead, traffic flowed out, and the
ports lost all their lumber traffic. The towns became depopulated, and the per capita debt rose as their capacity to bear it
fell.[19] It was a portent that was ignored.

Bonuses to Infrastructure
After Confederation

Railway construction at municipal expense and to the companies' enhanced profits continued after Confederation,
oblivious to earlier expenses. Even before the CPR construction
began, the townships and villages of Lanark, Frontenac, Hastings, Addington, and Peterborough — most of which had run up
debts to the Municipal Loan Fund — gave a total of one million
dollars to the Toronto and Ottawa Railroad Co.[20] With the emergence of transcontinentals, municipalities once again began to
build competitive feeder and branch lines to try to tilt the industrial balance in their favour. These lines were largely a gift to the
CPR for, unable to cover their fixed costs, most were absorbed at

bargain prices.[21] Sometimes of course the CPR got the municipal
bonus directly, as in 1882 when it squeezed $100,000 out of
Morris, Manitoba,[22] which went into bankruptcy a few years
later. However, the direct grants were minor compared to the
bonuses given it via acquired lines. By 1916 the CP main line
had received $488,458 in municipal cash gifts, while its acquired
and controlled lines had got $3,279,605. Nor was the CPR alone.
By 1916, the CNR had gotten from various Canadian municipalities some $751,704, while the GTR's total, including its pre-
Confederation grants, came to $5.5 million.[23] Some of these
grants were not strictly voluntary. The Erie and Huron, which
the GTR absorbed, won an 1885 court decision against
Chatham, Ontario, forcing it to honour an earlier bonus commitment.[24]

   The rationale behind the municipal railway bonus was to provide commercial access to the main lines of traffic. The trunk
lines built with federal government assistance were planned with
a view to long-distance trade and staple movements. The burden
of financing the feeder lines fell upon individual municipalities
seeking markets for their industrial or agricultural produce or
working to lower freight costs to attract industry. American lines
were not left out of the effort to render the municipalities attractive to industry or to break the monopoly of the big trunk lines.
The tiny municipality of Amherstburg, Ontario, gave $25,000 to
the Windsor, Sandbrook and Amherstburg Railway and a further $5,000 to the Michigan Central to extend into the town.[25]
Sherbrooke had paid a total of $150,000 to the CPR main line,
to the Boston and Maine, and to the Quebec Central by 1900.[26]

   The demands made upon the municipalities by the railway
companies for bonuses went far beyond just financing feeder
lines: money to build depots and car shops was a frequent
request. In some cases the negotiations were complex. The
Grand Trunk owed Montreal $700,000 deriving from its take-
over of the assets and liabilities of the Atlantic and St. Lawrence
in 1853. In 1881, the GTR offered the city $400,000 in equity in
payment for the debt; the equity at that time was trading at 23
and the city refused. Montreal made a counter offer of $100,000
cash plus the expenditure of $400,000 by the GTR on a new
depot; in effect the city would have paid $600,000 for a $400,000
depot.[27] But the offer was refused and the debt remained outstanding for many years. In 1882 the city of Montreal turned to
the CPR and voted it $350,000 cash plus a site that had cost the
city $200,000 to build a new depot.[28] The CPR also secured
$200,000 from Winnipeg for a depot along with a site and a per-

petual tax exemption. In addition, the CPR promised to build its car shops in the city.

Car repair shops, and rolling stock and locomotive manufacturing works with which they were often integrated, were eagerly sought by municipalities to generate employment, so much so that, when Winnipeg was considering bonusing the rival Manitoba and Southwestern railroad, the CPR used the threat of shifting the proposed car shops to Selkirk to stop the bonus. The Winnipeg ratepayers voted 130-to-one in favour of accepting the CPR's terms.[29]

The tug-of-war over the GTR's Point St. Charles car shops began in 1881 when Kingston ratepayers offered it a loan of $250,000 for ten years, and another $125,000 for another two with interest fixed at five per cent, along with the gift of a ten-acre site.[30] The same year, Carleton Place and Perth began competing for the CPR shops, and Carleton Place won.[31] In 1882, Belleville and Montreal began battling to move the Ontario Car Works out of London. Montreal's victory was considerably assisted by the fact that R. B. Angus had secured majority control of the firm, which was then integrated into the CPR's rolling stock program.[32] London did not secure a replacement until 1895, when it gave the Grand Trunk $100,000 to move its car shops from Brantford where they had ended up after Kingston's early offer was rejected.[33] A year later, Van Horne and Shaughnessy caused a lot of commotion by touring Ontario looking for a site for a CPR rolling stock manufacturing plant. Carleton Place won again for $20,000, and the CPR car works in North Bay and Chapleau were closed down. At the ratepayers' meeting the Carleton Place bonus carried 493 to six.[34]

Car works were an early recipient of bonuses in the form of the municipal stock subscription. Thus in 1882, during the early rage for railway manufacturing and repair plants, Peterborough subscribed $20,000 in equity in its firm, though it was a difficult fight at the ratepayers' meeting.[35] Not so for Kingston, which the same year subscribed $35,000 and granted an eighteen-year tax holiday to the Canada Locomotive Company, [36] a reorganized version of the old engine firm under George Stephen's control.[37] It was a bad decision.

As soon as the needy firm opened, it received an offer from a railway company to take all of its output for the next two years.[38] All proceeded well until the late 1890's, when it began to mutter threats about leaving Kingston if a bonus of $50,000 was not paid. This sum escalated in a month to $75,000, the car company claiming that it had an equivalent offer elsewhere. The nature of the offer was revealed in another month's time, when the Bank of Montreal announced that the firm was insolvent.[39] The threats to leave had been a bluff to force the municipality to cover its debts. When this failed, the firm went into assignment. With the growth of the new railways, recovery seemed possible, the car works attracting a number of offers included one from the Mackenzie and Mann syndicate.[40] Another offer from an American syndicate requested a tax exemption, free water, and the town's guarantee of interest on a $100,000 bond issue.[41] The firm was reorganized by a Canadian group headed by an Ontario cabinet minister, [42] and by early 1901 it was again threatening to leave Kingston if its bonus demands were not met.[43] By this time the firm was in such financial need that it would attract and decline a New York offer of $500,000. It had back orders for 103 locomotives, enough to keep it operating for several years. [44] Kingston apparently paid up again, for the car works stayed.

Shipbuilding firms became an attractive proposition for some cities, as witnessed by the extravagant terms they offered to attract them. In 1885 Owen Sound, Ontario, led the way by getting the Polson Iron Works, a firm established in Toronto in 1882, [45] to move its shipbuilding activities in exchange for a ten-year tax exemption, a nine-acre site, and dredging for a launching site done at municipal expense, the launching site being for ships built under CPR contract.[46] This was followed by a gift of $4,000 in 1888 and another of $15,000 in 1889. [47] In 1889 the firm announced it was in financial difficulty and secured a $50,000 loan from the city repayable over 25 years. Its profits for the year before it got the loan were $100,000; its surplus before the loan $188,000; hundreds of thousands of dollars worth of work had been turned down for lack of capacity; and it was paying dividends at fifteen per cent on stock that had been doubled without subscription the year before.[48] Even given the possibility that the firm had faced a genuine short-term liquidity squeeze and that the municipalities frequently had to play the role of investment banker in light of the structure of the chartered banking system, the firm reorganized within a year after which the remaining 24 years of five per cent money from the town was a completely unnecessary gift which would be expected to yield at least fifteen per cent return to the firm's stockholders.

Once its exemption ran out, the firm demanded an extension, which was refused.[49] It then sued the town for recovery of taxes it had paid after establishing itself in Owen Sound but before its exemption became operational — that is, during the period before the production of ships actually occurred. However, the judge ruled that the exemption was only binding on the town for the period that Polson actually produced.[50] The company moved back to Toronto and into liquidation.

TABLE XII (2)

Federal Iron and Steel Bounties, 1896-1912

Type	Period Paid	Total
pig iron	1896-1911	$7,047,041
puddled iron bars	1896-1907	113,674
steel	1896-1911	6,706,990
steel manufactures	1905-1912	2,868,122
		$16,735,827

Source: Department of Trade and Commerce, *Annual Report, 1913*, Part IV.

In 1889, Collingwood followed Owen Sound's inspiring example by granting $50,000 to a steel shipbuilding firm,[51] followed by a tax exemption.[52] But it was in the Maritimes that the bulk of the steel shipbuilding bonuses were offered. These came on a competitive basis after the turn of the century, when Maritime port cities struggled to restore some of the wealth they formerly had in the era of wooden ships in international commerce.

Halifax started the scramble in 1901 with an offer of $2.00 per ton for ten years and another dollar per ton for the next ten on each ship built. This brought an immediate response from an American company, and bargaining began. Halifax changed the terms to an immediate $100,000 subsidy with another $100,000 payable after the installation of plant and equipment. But the deal was not closed. Nova Scotia offered another $100,000 on top of the Halifax offer, and efforts were made to extract an equivalent sum from the Dominion. Not until 1902 was a taker found, and then only for the less-desired Dartmouth shore, for which Halifax would grant only $100,000.[53] Halifax was not alone. Sydney, Dartmouth, and St. John all offered a substantial bonus.[54] St. John agreed with a British firm for a bonus of $200,-000, half in land, half in cash to be used for equipment and machinery.[55]

Along with shipbuilding came demands for bonuses from private docking companies. A British firm began negotiations with Halifax in 1880, and an agreement was reached for a subsidy of $20,000 per year for ten years along with a complete tax exemption for five years and a one-third valuation thereafter. But the Nova Scotia Legislature rejected the arrangement.[56] Not until 1889 was the docking firm established, under much the same

terms as those originally worked out. The firm also secured a
heavy subsidy from the Royal Navy, and once its original grant
from Halifax ran out it asked for another $5,000 per annum for
twenty years as well as additional aid from the federal government.[57] The Halifax grant was acceded to, and the use the firm
made of it may be inferred from the fact that the year after the
new grant the docking company began paying dividends for the
first time.[58]

Another sphere of activity linked to the movement of goods
was in cold storage warehousing, which began to spread across
Canada in the mid-1890's. One of the earliest and largest of these
companies was the New Brunswick Cold Storage Co., which in
1897 secured a bond guarantee from the provincial legislature of
up to $150,000. Its headquarters was in St. John, but the firm
had branches in Sussex, Chatham, Moncton and Halifax. It secured as well a Dominion Government guarantee. The Dominion
was immediately faced with demands for bond guarantees from
cold storage warehouses in Toronto, Quebec, Charlottetown, and
Halifax.[59]

All manner of public utilities, which were almost invariably
privately owned before 1900, were voted cash aids to construction and operation, despite the fact that they were run on a
profit-making basis. Gifts ranged from a cash grant of $5,000 to
the private owners of a dam by Richmond, P.Q.,[60] to a bonus by
Rosseau, Manitoba, to start a local newspaper,[61] a somewhat
more defensible grant.

Waterworks got all manner of assistance, from cash gifts by
Sarnia[62] to tax breaks by Campbellton, N.B.,[63] to a stock subscription by Lindsay, Ontario. Why Lindsay did not proceed to
full municipal ownership was unclear, especially to the people of
Lindsay after stock juggling by the private firm cost the town
$24,000.[64]

After the turn of the century, electric railways and tramways
became the rage, and municipalities usually carried the expense
of constructing and then let a private firm run it for private
profit.

Primary Iron and Steel Subsidies

Next to the railways, those receiving the greatest amount of government largesse were the American bonus hunters who were
responsible for the creation of a Canadian primary iron and steel
industry. After its slow start, the industry blossomed by the turn

of the century. The principal handouts were federal, but the provinces and the municipalities too were active in pouring forth an unending stream of gifts into the industry to such a degree that the Grain Growers' Association dubbed it "the Steal Industry."[65]

The expanded primary iron and steel scheme introduced by the Laurier government, with its bounties to pig iron products, was supplemented in 1900 by a railway subsidies act that required the railroads to use only Canadian-made iron and steel. This act was passed largely at the insistence of Francis Clergue. Despite the bounty system, the iron and steel industry was hampered by high overhead costs due to the smallness of the home market,[66] and Clergue felt the problem could be solved by linking primary iron and steel to railway development and therefore to the opening of the new staple-producing areas of the West. For the first few years there were difficulties in steel rail production which seriously affected Clergue's operations. Other producers were also in trouble.[67] But after the new round of transcontinental railway building got well underway, the industry prospered thanks to its huge grants and links to the railway companies. The railroads and the new primary iron and steel firms were closely interlocked, and once again the Montreal commercial capitalists made the transition to industry via joint ventures with American industrialists in a sea of government largesse. Americans created the Hamilton Iron and Steel industry by taking over and rejuvenating a rolling mill abandoned by the Great Western Railway; the American promoters, Francis Clergue and H. N. Whitney, were responsible for Algoma Steel and Dominion Iron and Steel respectively. In addition to these three major works, Americans took the lead in virtually all the smaller smelter operations that sprang up under the Laurier government's "fostering care." The new schedule of subsidies offered $2.70 per ton for pig made from Canadian ores, $1.80 for that from foreign, $2.70 for the manufacture of steel ingots and for puddled iron bars. The puddled iron bar subsidies were discontinued in 1907, while those for pig and steel continued to 1911. Of the bounties given out, the great majority went to the companies created by American promoters. Between 1883 and 1906, a total of sixteen companies had qualified for about nine million dollars, of which six million went to the three large American-derived firms, DISCO, Hamilton Iron and Steel, and Clergue's Algoma.[68] The 1909-1910 distribution of subsidies, together with the nationality of the principal initial promoters of the firms, is given in Table XII (3).

TABLE XII (3)

Iron and Steel Bounties, 1909-1910

Company	Nationality of Promoters	Amount
Algoma	U.S.	$ 318,815
DISCO	U.S.	1,029,504
Hamilton	U.S.	238,408
Canada Iron	U.S.-Can.	40,149
Nova Scotia	Can.	97,346
Lake Superior	U.S.	54,629
Ontario	U.S.	4,404
Atikokan	Can.	15,100
Deseronto	U.S.	10,120

Source: *MT,* Dec. 31, 1910, p. 271.

The provincial governments also gave ample assistance. Between 1897 and 1901, Ontario added its own bounty on pig iron, if it was made from Ontario ores. In 1897, too, a bill had been placed before the Ontario Legislature proposing that provincial railway bonuses be paid in iron and steel made in Ontario from ores of which at least two-thirds were mined in Ontario, and that money voted be given directly to the iron manufacturers instead of the railway companies.[69] But this bill did not pass. B.C., though it had no iron smelters of its own, stipulated in 1902 that all railways of the province subsidized with cash or land had to use rails, spikes, etc. made in Canada as long as prices in Canada were no greater than the "open market price" in Great Britain or the U.S. plus the cost of freight.[70] New Brunswick added iron to its offer of a monopoly of rights to manganese bog ores in an effort to attract investment into a local blast furnace, but to no avail.

Nova Scotia was especially compassionate to the new industry. Rather than give a subsidy to pig iron, however, it chose to cut the royalty payable by DISCO on provincial coal in half[71] while all other industries in the province continued to pay the full rate, including Nova Scotia Steel and Coal, which unlike DISCO was locally owned. In addition, DISCO got low dock duties and special low toll charges.[72]

The purpose of both federal and provincial subsidies, as was typical of the whole period, was as much to earn a return on political capital as to build up an industry. The principal beneficiary in the short run was Nova Scotia, which had received the greatest amount of federal aid and therefore hosted the largest iron and steel capacity. The federal aid was in part a delayed reaction to a secessionist movement in the province triggered off by the destruction of several major industries by central Canadian competition, and the rising tide of resentment against the uneven terms of the federation. Such investments drew fire from Toronto capitalists, who opposed the implied infringement of their hegemony and objected to having to pay a disproportionate amount of the subsidy and heavy freight costs for the benefit of a "far eastern" industry.[73]

The municipalities were actively involved in a scramble for a share of the industry. The bonusing craze began shortly after the 1874 tariff revision brought enquiries from foreign firms. In 1876, Toronto began to consider a bonus for an iron furnace at a time when Canada had enough capacity to satisfy its demand already.[74] In 1879, the American group who had revived the abandoned rolling mill in Hamilton asked for and got a tax exemption and free water.[75] Though primary producing facilities were not added for several years, this was effectively the beginning of Hamilton's integrated primary and secondary iron and steel industry.

The prosperous year of 1882 saw the beginnings of the iron rush. Belleville, Ontario, gave fifteen acres, an access right of way, water frontage, and a ten-year tax exemption to an American firm promising a blast furnace.[76] The terms were light, but the furnace was never built. The same year, Kingston and London quarrelled over who would secure another itinerant foreign blast furnace and rolling mill,[77] but again neither was successful.

With the revival of Londonderry and the Quebec forges and the advent of a newcomer in New Glasgow after the National Policy there was little room for new capacity for the time being. In 1885 Selkirk, Manitoba, offered cash and local capitalists offered land for a smelter, but found no takers.[78] In 1889 Lindsay, Ontario, began agitating for a smelter to provide an outlet for the output of its languishing iron mines. An American syndicate offered to construct it and a resource road in exchange for large railway subsidies from the surrounding counties and the province and the right to buy 30,000 acres of iron mine lands.[79] The Ontario government aid requested by Lindsay was not forthcoming.

The Ontario industry began in 1893, when an Ontario group began to pressure the province for a bounty of $2.00 per ton on iron manufactured from Ontario ores and asked Toronto for 100 acres plus $75,000. The same year, with considerably more success, an American group reached an agreement with Hamilton after being pursued by a number of municipalities. Hamilton granted a $35,000 site plus $40,000 in city debentures for a blast furnace, and another $60,000 cash for a steel oven. And Ontario assured it a bonus of $1.00 per ton on the production of iron from Ontario ores.[80] Most of the American money planned for the venture was cut off during the 1893-4 crisis in the U.S., but American promoters remained in charge of the Hamilton Iron and Steel Co.[81] which finally began producing in 1897. It was regarded as a great acquisition for the city, for other industries consuming pig iron would cluster about it, and it was the means by which a number of branch plants were attracted to the city.

The bounty offer by the Ontario government set off a spate of other ventures. In 1895, Kingston was pronounced "jubilant" over the fact that an American blast furnace operation, the Ontario Iron and Steel Co., decided to locate there. It secured a bonus of $250,000 in exchange for first mortgage bonds. It also demanded $50,000, or free water for ten years while Kingston offered $3,000 a year for ten years.[82] Within a few months the terms had escalated, and now included a free site and a bounty of ten cents a ton on iron manufactured over the first five years of operation.[83] Kingston failed to secure the firm, which, after the new federal subsidy program came into effect, located instead at the mouth of the Welland Canal.[84]

Kingston, however, did not give up the battle for a blast furnace. A Montreal firm, Abbot and Co., was offered $50,000 cash plus a site worth $10,000 in 1898.[85] It accepted, then changed its mind and moved on to Belleville. In 1900, Kingston offered $4,000 per year for fifteen years plus a $9,000 site to get another blast furnace operation.[86] Again the bribes failed, and Kingston had to be content with the part-time lead smelter that grew up under the federal lead bounty program in 1908.

Belleville, which had tried to attract American capital into iron smelting in 1882, tried again in 1895. An American promoter was at that time flooding Ontario towns with propositions for a smelter for a site, a tax exemption, and $5,000 per year. The *Belleville Intelligencer* remarked,

> From the letter it would appear that he wants the industrial committee to give him the city, without even a receipt in return. Belleville don't [sic] want industries on such terms.[87]

Others in the town disagreed and, though that particular deal was not closed, in 1898 a fresh proposition from some American promoters was debated. In return for $50,000, a free site, a ten-year tax exemption, and the duty that had to be paid, they would undertake to move the plant of a Connecticut firm bodily into Canada.[88] The Mayor of the city, who led the pro-bonus forces, called for a policy of "nursing industries" and cited the example of Sherbrooke, Quebec, as a town built up by bonuses. Another factor in favour of the project was the fact that Deseronto had just secured an iron furnace which threatened to divert all the iron ore trade off to that town. The opposition stressed the folly of giving $50,000 for a plant that the federal government evaluated at $12,000 for customs purposes.[89] Nevertheless the deal went through; not only did the Connecticut firm migrate, but a rolling mill from New Hampshire was acquired along with the Abbot company of Montreal, which had stopped off in Kingston briefly to pick up a bonus en route.[90] By 1901 the new Abbot-Mitchell Iron Co. had collapsed, and the plant was taken over by another American firm.[91]

A number of towns had followed Belleville and Hamilton. Bancroft tried in 1896 to attract American money into smelting at the instance of local railwaymen, but none materialized.[92] Others were more successful. In Deseronto, the American émigré E. W. Rathbun began the establishment of a smelter which was finished by a new American entrepreneur, F. B. Gaylord, head of Detroit's Gaylord Iron Co. At first the town offered a paltry $20,000. But by raising the bid to $25,000 plus assuring a local market for at least 25% of the output in the form of a contract with the Rathbun Manufacturing Company, the smelter was built and put into operation. [93] In 1899, Fort William granted $50,000 to an American group who created the Mattawa Iron Co. Another $25,000 to the same firm for a silver smelter was added shortly after. [94] Midland got into protracted negotiations with the Canada Iron Furnace Company, a joint venture of American capital with A. F. Gault and the Drummonds of Montreal. The company demanded $80,000 and eventually settled for $50,000, a ten-year tax holiday, and freedom to get its ore from anywhere and thus not be restricted to the output of nearby mines.[95] Collingwood was blessed with the Cramp Steel Co. in 1900 for a cost of a mere $115,000 and 80 acres on the waterfront. It was the creature of an American steel magnate from Philadelphia, though local colour was provided by Sir Charles Tupper and Sir Sandford Fleming on its board.[96]

Some efforts by promoters to secure bonuses came to naught. In 1901, a Toronto and London syndicate began soliciting in Ottawa without success.[97] A pretentiously entitled operation, the Canadian International Banking and Investment Syndicate, claimed to represent Canadian and Mexican capital and offered to erect iron furnaces, precious metal smelters, and a rolling mill for $125,000 plus 110 acres. [98] No one seems to have taken it very seriously.

Bonusing activity occurred in Nova Scotia as well. DISCO, in addition to its provincial coal royalty reduction, secured the right of eminent domain, freedom from all provincial and county taxes, the amazing concession of power to pay dividends on preference shares while its Sydney plant was still under construction, and a relaxation of the provincial laws to allow Americans to sit on its board of directors. The city of Sydney in turn gave the company a free site, which had cost the city $370,000 and which had been purchased with the proceeds of a special debenture issue. It also gave a 30-year municipal tax exemption.[99] North Sydney then gave $30,000 cash to the Nova Scotia Steel and Coal Co., with the pledge of another $20,000 once the firm began production, and a twenty-year tax exemption.[100] Even little Pictou got into the act, giving the Pictou Charcoal Iron Co. $20,000 and a twenty-year tax holiday.[101] At the same time, the old Londonderry iron works were again in complete collapse. They were sold in 1899 by the liquidator to Herbert Holt for $153,000. For this pittance Holt secured a blast furnace, a foundry, a coke oven, a railway and rolling stock, 30,000 acres of iron land, town lots in Londonderry, houses, buildings, plant and machinery, the mines plus an enormous colliery of four square miles of coal leases, 2,200 acres freehold and all the other claims, materials and cash of the company[102] into which so much public money had been placed, over half a million dollars in iron bounties alone, and countless millions indirectly via the tariff.

Such were the origins of the Canadian primary iron and steel industry. Apart from the Nova Scotia Steel and Coal Co., and the British-controlled Londonderry firm, all the largest works and most of the smaller ones were the creation of American bonus hunters who migrated north and sometimes brought the plant with them. There were no actual corporate linkages via branch plants, and hence, like agricultural implements, the industry over time was "Canadianized." The level of subsidies involved in the creation of the "Canadian" industry was largely unnecessary. For despite the long period over which bounties were offered, it was after the new round of railway contruction began in the late nineteenth century that the industry got firmly underway with an assured market. But the firms pressured for the continuation of the system of bounties. In 1902, DISCO deliberately held off building a new plant, which it was planning to set up in any event to coerce the federal government into a renewal of the subsidy scheme. All levels of government contributed to a bonusing scheme on such an order of magnitude that, as one newspaper commented, "Banana growing in Manitoba could be made profitable on the same terms."[103]

The Beet Root Sugar Industry

The system of federal, provincial and municipal subsidies granted in an effort to establish a beet root sugar industry in Canada was second only to primary iron and steel in complexity, and an unmitigated failure in terms of results.

In 1871, the Dominion Parliament exempted from excise all sugar made from domestic beet and granted the potential industry free entry of the necessary machinery for ten years.[104] In 1877, the Quebec government promised a bonus of $70,000 to a beet root sugar refiner[105] but not until 1879 did the predictable scramble begin behind the new sugar duties. It was reinforced in 1881 when the Dominion extended its tariff concession for another five years.

Most of the early activity was in Quebec, where refineries sprang up in Farnham and Coaticook in 1879. Immediate disagreement arose as to who should get the Quebec government bonus; after a great deal of contention it was given to A. F. Gault's Farnham Beet Root Sugar Co.[106] In addition, this firm had secured a $25,000 stock subscription from the town and another of $10,000 from the parish.[107] And in the interim, until the Quebec bonus was paid, both Coaticook and Farnham gave loans to their respective refineries of $7,000 per year for ten years.[108] The early prosperity of the two firms, plus the tariff and hopes of a bonus, attracted foreign capital. In France, L'Union Sucrière du Canada was formed by a group of French sugar industrialists who proposed the establishment of a series of refineries under special tax concessions commencing in Berthierville, in addition to investing in others. In 1881, Belgian capital began exploring the possibility of a refinery at Beauharnois.[109] But by early 1882 the collapse began.

The Farnham refinery got into financial difficulties and was bailed out temporarily by the Quebec government's agreement to pay $40,000 worth of bonuses all at once — out of the $70,000 fund which was to have been stretched over ten years.[110] A few months later, a writ of attachment was issued against the Coaticook refinery, followed within a few weeks by the failure of Union Sucrière with losses of over $150,000.[111] Both the Coaticook and Berthier refineries were sold at liquidators' auctions, with large debts due to the German and Belgian machinery firms who had supplied their equipment; they were then seized by the Dominion government for customs claims.[112] To avoid their fate, Farnham's refinery had switched to cane sugar refining for half the year to avoid having its machinery idle after the beet season was over. But by 1884 it too was closed.[113]

For the next several years the factories and machinery passed from hand to hand. The federal government established its prior claim over the Belgian creditors to the Berthier plant and sold it to a group of Québécois small businessmen who proposed reopening it in 1887.[114] Negotiations stretched on for several more years through Alphonse Desjardins and La Banque Jacques Cartier[115] until the plant was secured and reopened in 1893 by the Montreal food processing firm of M. Lefebvre and Co.[116] Even before that date, as early as 1890 the Farnham refinery began to plan for a reincarnation, placing orders with farmers for beets at $4.50 a ton and negotiating with town councils for an additional one dollar a ton for the farmers. Prospects appeared so bright that the promoter contemplated buying and resuscitating Coaticook as well.[117]

The immediate cause of the new burst of activity in sugar beet refining was that the Dominion Government had capitulated to a then-current trend in European countries of subsidizing beet sugar production over the years 1892 to 1896. For the fiscal year 1892-3, the Farnham refinery got $20,560, while over 1893-1896 Lefebvre received nearly $49,000.[118] Farnham however collapsed once more in 1892. Built at a cost of $250,000, the refinery fetched $26,000 at a sherriff's auction.[119] The Berthier refinery carried on for three years after the expiry of the federal bounty program, then failed along with M. Lefebvre and Co. in the wake of the Banque Jacques Cartier collapse in 1899. In 1900, the town of Farnham bought its local refinery from the Gault Bros. for $25,000 and began looking for a company to revive it for a bonus. Pressure was put on the Quebec government for yet a third effort at beet refining,[120] but by 1901 the action had switched to Ontario, following the federal government's decision to put beet sugar machinery back on the free list.

Efforts to establish the industry in Ontario date as far back as those of Quebec, but not until after the turn of the century was any significant success achieved. In 1878, following the announcement of the Quebec provincial bonus, promoters in Ontario sought a similar grant.[121] Although none was given, Tillsonburg established a beet refinery in 1879, a year before it built a cane refinery, and plans were made to convert an old cheese factory near Galt into a refinery.[122] But these early efforts came to nothing. Some success was achieved in growing cane and sorghum in the province, and for a time a grape sugar refinery operated.[123] In 1890, Ontario government experiments to grow beets were successful, though despite the federal government subsidy no refineries sprang up until Owen Sound secured a short-lived one in 1896.[124] In 1900, a group of promoters asked St. Catharines for $40,000, 20 acres, three million gallons of water a day and a guarantee of 4,000 acres of beets to supply the refinery.[125] This was refused. But that year a beet root sugar association was formed to pressure the province into establishing a bounty system.[126]

In 1901, the province set up a fund of $225,000 to give three-year bounties to beet sugar refineries to be divided among those established, to which another $150,000 for a further two years was added in 1904.[127] The result was sheer pandemonium as municipality after municipality pursued itinerant sugar factories. Refineries sprang up with fat bonuses of cash or stock subscriptions all over the province. Foreign promoters had a field day. A Detroit firm wooed Chatham; a British firm asked for $25,000, water, a free site, and a tax exemption from London; a Pennsylvania syndicate created a scramble among Ontario towns with the ultimate winner being Baden; another Pennsylvania promoter asked Berlin for a $150,000 stock subscription. This was refused, and Berlin then got into a tug of war with neighbouring Waterloo for another refinery. After Berlin won, the syndicate spent $350,000 to import a sugar refinery bodily from Michigan. When another Pennsylvania syndicate announced it would build not one but two refineries, the shock wave spread from one end of the province to the other, Wallaceburg securing one, Brockville the second, for $30,000 each. The surfeit of American capital was due to the fact that the American sugar trust at that time was in the process of squeezing out the little refiners who thus needed but little incentive to migrate north en masse. And they were joined by numerous Ontario promotions in the hunt for the biggest municipal bonus and shares of the provincial bounty fund. Within two years of the establishment of the bounty, the beet association was asking the Dominion Government to bail them out. Even the extension of the Ontario bounty could not protect the industry from a drastic liquidation following the chronic expansion that saw at least seventeen municipalities scramble for the refineries, most successfully.[128]

Other provinces had been active in the struggle to establish a refinery system, albeit not quite so spectacularly. Before the National Policy, New Brunswick farmers exported beets to Maine and early in 1879 an attempt was made to erect a refinery at Digby; later that year the province imported seed from Germany for experiments. Cane sugar was also subject to early attempts to cultivate it within the province, [129] and municipal tax exemptions were offered to cane or beet refineries.[130] But no beet refinery took hold in the province, although the Ontario scramble provoked a bit of jealousy in 1901.[131] Winnipeg tried to secure a refinery in 1898, and P.E.I. bargained with an American beet refining firm in 1900,[132] but apart from Ontario and Quebec only Alberta succeeded in establishing the industry.

The Alberta refinery was established at the same time as the Ontario industry, and was also a case of American surplus capacity migrating north. Alberta's single refinery was established at Raymond in 1901 by a Utah beet refiner.[133] To keep the industry afloat the province initiated a system of bounties to the firm in 1906; they totalled $63,000 before being discontinued in 1910.[134]

The parallels between the primary iron and steel industry and beet sugar refining are striking. Both were subject to a battery of subsidies, bonuses, tariff, and tax concessions from all levels of government. Both represented spillovers of American surplus capacity in response to an active subsidy system at a time of cartelization in the U.S. Both were the creation in large measure of itinerant American promoters and/or migrating plant and equipment, but without formal ties to an American parent corporation. Both, too, greatly overexpanded. The liquidation came early in sugar beets, for by 1913 there were only three producers left in the Dominion, at Raymond, Alberta, and in Ontario at Wallaceburg and Berlin.[135]

Notes to Chapter XII

1.   *CM,* Aug. 5, 1887, p. 76.
2.   *RCRLC, Ontario Evidence,* p. 179.
3.   Dominion Board of Trade, *First Annual Meeting,* 1871, p. 28
4.   *Statutes of Quebec,* 1870, 34 Vic. Chap. 18.
5.   *MT,* April 18, 1879, p. 1296.
6.   *GGG,* Aug. 21, 1912, p. 6.
7.   *MT,* Dec. 2, 1870, p. 304.
8.   Dominion Board of Trade, *First Annual Meeting,* pp. 27-38.
9.   *HCD,* March 10, 1876, p. 572.
10. *MT,* March 28, 1879, p. 1220.
11. *MT,* Sept. 21, 1888, p. 331.
12. *MT,* Oct. 1, 1910, p. 1417.
13. *MT,* March 10, 1899, p. 1185.
14. N. Reich, *The Pulp and Paper Industry in Canada,* p. 14.
15. K. G. Lewis, "The Significance of the York Foundry," p. 6.
16. H. A. Innis, and A. R. M. Lower, Select Documents, p. 301.
17. W. T. Easterbrook and H. Aitken, *Canadian Economic History,* p. 315.
18. H. Y. Hind *et al, Eighty Years of Progress,* pp. 216-7.
19. E. B. Biggar, *The Canadian Railway Problem,* p. 84.
20. *JC,* Nov. 21, 1879, p. 444.
21. H. A. Innis, *History of the CPR,* p. 273.

22. *MT,* Sept. 1, 1882, p. 231.
23. *RCRTC,* pp. xiii, xvii.
24. *MT,* Nov. 27, 1885, p. 599.
25. *JC,* Jan. 13, 1893, p. 50.
26. *MT,* March 23, 1900, p. 1268.
27. *MT,* July 1, 1881, p. 8; Sept. 1, 1882, p. 240.
28. *MT,* Nov. 17, 1882, p. 540.
29. R. C. Bellan, *The Development of Winnipeg,* p. 38.
30. *MT,* July 8, 1881, p. 37.
31. *MT,* Nov. 4, 1881, p. 542; March 3, 1882, p. 1076.
32. *CM,* May 12, 1882, p. 181.
33. *CE,* Dec. 1895, p. 220; *MT,* July 2, 1897, p. 7.
34. *CE,* Oct. 1896, p. 180; Dec. 1896, p. 272; Jan. 1897, p. 293.
35. *CM,* April 14, 1882, p. 137.
36. *CM,* Feb. 3, 1882, p. 41; Feb. 17, 1882, p. 56.
37. *MT,* April 22, 1881, p. 1233.
38. *CM,* March 31, 1882, p. 119.
39. *CE,* Dec. 1899, p. 233; Jan. 1900, p. 258; Feb. 1900, p. 283.
40. *CE,* Oct. 1900, p. 125.
41. *MT,* Oct. 19, 1900, p. 491.
42. *MT,* Nov. 9, 1900, p. 585.
43. *CE,* June 1901, p. 315.
44. *CE,* Jan. 1902, p. 14.
45. *SCM* (1885), p. 9.
46. *MT,* June 22, 1888, p. 1568.
47. *MT,* Dec. 28, 1888, p. 729.
48. *MT,* Dec. 6, 1889, p. 683; Dec. 27, 1889, p. 774.
49. *CE,* Dec. 1895, p. 219.
50. *MT,* July 14, 1889, p. 43.
51. *MT,* Feb. 1, 1901, p. 979.
52. *Statutes of Ontario, 1902,* 2 Ed. VII Chap. 45.
53. *MT,* Feb. 22, 1901, p. 1079; March 8, 1901, p. 1159; Sept. 13, 1901, p. 342;
    May 9, 1902, pp. 1448, 1450.
54. *MT,* April 26, 1901, p. 1428; May 31, 1901, p. 1603.
55. *MT,* May 15, 1901, p. 1212.
56. *MT,* May 7, 1880, p. 1316; March 13, 1885, p. 1025.
57. *MT,* Sept. 24, 1910, p. 1315.
58. *Ec,* Sept. 24, 1921, p. 473.
59. *Statutes of Canada,* 1897, Chapter 7; 1898, Chap. 7; *MT,* June 18, 1897, p.
    1661.
60. *CE,* May, 1894, p.25.
61. *MT,* April 18, 1879, p. 1295.
62. *CM,* May 12, 1882, p. 179.
63. *CE,* April 1894, p. 355.
64. *CE,* Jan. 1894, p. 264.
65. *GGG,* April 5, 1911; March 23, 1910.
66. *MT,* April 21, 1899, p. 1384.
67. *Ec,* Oct. 17, 1903, p. 1754.
68. *HCD,* Feb. 14, 1907, p. 2979.
69. *CE,* April 1897, p. 374.
70. *Statutes of British Columbia,* 1902, Chap. 61.
71. *CE,* April 1899, p. 354.
72. *MT,* March 10, 1899, p. 1187.
73. Toronto Board of Trade, *Annual Report* 1906, pp. 9-10.
74. *MT,* Feb. 25, 1876, p. 982.

75. *MT*, March 21, 1879, pp. 1173-4.
76. *CM*, April 28, 1882, p. 145.
77. *MT*, Oct. 13, 1882, p. 400.
78. *MT*, Feb. 13, 1885, p. 910.
79. *MT*, Oct. 18, 1889, p. 465.
80. *Statutes of Ontario*, 1896, 59 Vic. Chap. 80; *MT*, April 14, 1893, p. 1221; May 12, 1893, p. 1343; May 18, 1894, p. 144.
81. *MT*, Aug. 23, 1895, p. 232.
82. *CE*, May 1895, p. 22.
83. *CE*, Sept. 1895, p. 130.
84. *CFC*, June 23, 1900, p. 1251; *MT*, Feb. 9, 1900, p. 1034.
85. *CE*, Jan. 1898, p. 52; *MT*, Jan. 14, 1898, p. 917.
86. *CE*, July 1900, p. 33; *MT*, June 10, 1900, p. 1639.
87. *MT*, Aug. 2, 1895, p. 135; Aug. 9, 1895, p. 165.
88. *CE*, Jan. 1898, p.52.
89. *MT*, Sept. 23, 1898, p. 407.
90. *MT*, Nov. 4, 1898, p. 607.
91. *CE*, Nov. 1902, p. 309.
92. *MT*, Sept. 4, 1896, p. 321.
93. *CE*, March 1898, p. 333; April 1898, p. 367; Oct. 1898, p. 143; *MT*, Oct. 6, 1899, p. 433.
94. *CE*, Oct. 1899, p. 174; March 1900, p. 33; *MT*, July 22, 1898, p. 115.
95. *CE*, March 1899, p. 326; *MT*, Feb. 17, 1899, p. 1091; March 3, 1899, p. 1160.
96. Ontario, *Report of the Bureau of Mines*, 1903, p. 23; *MT*, July 6, 1900, p. 21.
97. *CE*, May 1901, p. 293.
98. *MT*, May 3, 1901, p. 1474.
99. E. C. Porritt, *The Revolt In Canada*, pp. 114-5.
100. *CE*, Jan. 1901, p. 13; *MT*, Dec. 13, 1901, p. 761.
101. W.J. Donald, *The Iron and Steel Industry*, p.90.
102. *MT*, Nov. 10, 1899, p. 618.
103. *Toronto Sun*, Jan. 23, 1907.
104. *MT*, Jan. 8, 1881, p. 867.
105. *MT*, Dec. 14, 1877, p. 696.
106. *MT*, July 23, 1880, p. 91; Jan. 27, 1882, p. 909.
107. *JC*, Jan. 9, 1880, p. 671; *Statutes of Quebec*, 1880, Chap. 89.
108. *MT*, Jan. 16, 1880, p. 832.
109. *MT*, Sept. 10, 1880, p. 306; Nov. 5, 1880, p. 528; March 25, 1881, p. 114; *MT*, Dec. 9, 1881, p. 699.
110. *MT*, April 14, 1882, p. 1268.
111. *MT*, July 21, 1882, p. 71; Aug, 18, 1882, p. 176.
112. *MT*, July 28, 1882, p. 98; Sept. 22, 1882, p. 319; Oct. 20, 1882, p. 428; Jan. 26, 1883, p. 819; July 20, 1883, p. 64.
113. *MT*, Aug, 4, 1882, p. 120; July 25, 1884, p. 91.
114. *MT*, Oct. 2, 1885, p. 375; April 9, 1886, p. 1148; Oct. 8, 1886, p. 406; Sept. 9, 1887, p. 330.
115. *MT*, April 27, 1888, p. 1331; Oct. 25, 1889, p. 488.
116. *MT*, Oct. 12, 1894, p. 474.
117. *MT*, April 18, 1890, p. 1287; Sept. 19, 1890, p. 338.
118. Canada, Auditor General, *Report*, 1893, 1896; *HCD*, March 31, 1897, p. 265.
119. *MT*, Feb. 26, 1892, p. 1020.
120. *MT*, Oct. 26, 1900, p. 537; March 1, 1901, p. 1123.
121. *MT*, Feb. 8, 1878, p. 929.

122. *MT,* Oct. 29, 1880; Dec. 3, 1880, p. 643.
123. *MT,* May 21, 1880, p. 1376; *FA* May 1880, p. 112; June 1880, p. 124; *MT,* Aug. 26, 1881, p. 242; Sept. 23, 1881, p. 371; Aug. 17, 1883, p. 176; Jan. 11, 1884, p. 763.
124. *MT,* Nov. 14, 1890, p. 590; Aug. 14, 1896, p. 199.
125. *MT,* April 20, 1900, p. 1374; May 4, 1900, p. 1441.
126. *MT,* Sept. 7, 1900, p. 294.
127. *Statutes of Ontario,* 1901, Chap. II; 1904, Chap. 9.
128. *CE* April 1901, p. 269; May 1901, p. 292; Oct. 1901, p. 423; Dec. 1901, p. 476; Jan. 1902, p. 16; April 1902, p. 107; Nov. 1902, pp. 44-6; *MT,* Feb. 8, 1901, p. 1011; March 1, 1901, p. 118; March 22, 1901, p. 1238; May 3, 1901, p. 1473; July 12, 1901, p. 53; April 23, 1901, p. 244; Aug. 23, 1901; Aug. 30, 1901, p. 274; Sept. 13, 1901, p. 342; Nov. 22, 1901, p. 647; Dec. 13, 1901, p. 743; Jan. 10, 1902, p. 886; Feb. 21, 1902, p. 1087; Feb. 6, 1903, p. 1058.
129 *MT,* Jan. 3, 1879, p. 834; Jan. 31, 1879, p. 945; April 18, 1879, p. 1296; May 16, 1879, p. 1414.
130. *Statutes of New Brunswick,* 1879, Chap. 59.
131. *MT,* Feb. 8, 1901, p. 1011.
132. *MT,* Oct. 28, 1898, p. 572; Oct. 26, 1900, p. 505.
133. *CE* Oct. 1901, p. 424; Feb. 1902, p. 45; *MT,* Nov. 1, 1901, p. 555.
134. *Statutes of Alberta,* 1910, Chap. 20.
135. *MT, Annual,* Jan. 1913, p. 250.

We have discovered that most of these great fortunes have been made by plundering the public; that as fast as we produce wealth, others take it from us; that the conditions that create millionaires and multimillionaires also create city slums and the depopulation of our rural districts.

Farm and Dairy, January 5, 1912

CHAPTER XIII
The Bonusing Craze and Secondary Industry

Even without the existence of federal or provincial subsidies, the competitive system of bonusing industry thrived in all facets of secondary production. Bonusing served to build up local industry, to attract it away from neighbours, and to draw in foreign direct investment. It was partly done on a free-for-all basis, but often distinct patterns would emerge. A particular industry would be regarded as crucial for a municipality's development plans, and one town's success in attracting it would spark a wave of competitive bidding from others.

Bonusing Agribusiness

There were two distinct patterns to municipal efforts to induce the location of food processing industries. In the western provinces, a great number of efforts were made to secure mills of various sorts for the primary processing of grains. Some mills, too, were given central and eastern municipal subsidies, but not on the scale of the West. Instead, the secondary food processing industry, especially meat packing, canning, and beet sugar refining, occupied the attention of central Canada, along with elevators and other means of tapping the western grain trade. .

The demand for local milling facilities in the West is at first glance surprising. For with the wheat staple large elevator firms and grain dealers of all types were active there. But these were all geared to exporting wheat. Very little flour was processed for export, and, if left to the devices of the elevator and transportation firms, none of the western wheat and other grains would have been milled for local consumption. The anomaly of being one of the world's largest wheat exporters and at the same time requiring to import flour from central Canada must have struck the western towns, for from a very early date they offered bonuses for the establishment of small, local mills.

One of the first to do so was Rosseau, Manitoba, which in 1878 offered a bonus of 1,000 bushels of wheat and $1,000 worth of real estate for the building of a mill.[1] In 1894, for a similar mill, Brandon offered $6,000.[2] With the growing settlement of the West and the rise of wheat prices, the demand for local mills became more insistent. Offers of bonuses for flour or oatmeal mills came from Rapid City, Wawanesa, Cardiff, Assinaboia and North Cypress by 1898[3] followed shortly by Miami, Alameda, Calgary, and others.[4] But the wheat boom led to the destruction of many local mills by the competition of those of the eastern-based milling companies like Ogilvie's or by the expansion of the western Lake of the Woods Milling Co., which controlled the purchase and distribution of grain for milling within Canada.[5] Increasingly, the prospects of a local mill — especially for flour — became contingent upon securing a branch of one of the milling chains. In 1909, a Saskatoon group headed by its major "waited on the Ogilvie company at Winnipeg to secure a flour mill for the city."[6]

Grain mills of various sorts were built in the central and eastern provinces as well. In the early period these were oriented towards providing for local consumption. One of them, the oatmeal mill in Norwich, Ontario, was ruined in 1879 by the National Policy oat duties and forced to refund its bonus.[7] While efforts to create local mills continued,[8] the rise in grain prices in 1896 led to a new emphasis on bonusing facilities to service the export trade, such as Fort William's gift of $50,000 that year to build a flour mill.[9] More common, however, were bonuses for elevators. The CPR extracted $40,000 from Owen Sound for an elevator and flour shed in 1897, and another $25,000 from Windsor the same year.[10] Also in 1897, Kingston gave a gift of $35,000 to a Montreal elevator company, while Goderich in 1898 took $50,000 in stock in a local elevator promotion.[11]

Secondary food processing industries were also in great demand. Shortly after one of its periodic failures in Montreal, M. Lefebvre and Co. was voted unanimously $22,500 to shift to St. Jean in 1897. Within two years it had failed again.[12] Somewhat more durable, though not by much, was the meat packing industry that went through a period of rapid growth around the turn of the century.

The canning of meat for export was attempted in eastern Canada and Quebec in the 1870's. The last of Quebec's efforts, a

Sherbrooke company bonused by the town, failed in 1878, and thereafter canning for export occurred only in two small factories in New Brunswick and P.E.I.[13] Canadian livestock moved into the U.S., especially Chicago, for packing or canning, and in 1878 David Morrice and Co. developed a trade in exporting ice to that city.[14] Small packing firms, of course, were active in serving local needs, and by the early 1890's some of them began to attain a fair size. There were also a few new spectacular promotion jobs such as the Canada (Direct) Meat Co. of Trois Rivières set up to export to Britain in 1890. Its directors included one British cabinet minister, one Canadian federal minister — Sir Hector Langevin, whose corruption was outstanding even among MacDonald's ministers — and the mayor of the city, who helped secure "concessions" from Trois Rivières which were capitalized by the firm. Of £90,000 paid in Britain, the chief promoter (who bore the appropriate name M. Eugene Prosper Bender) pocketed one-half, and the company came to an inglorious end in an English bankruptcy court.[15]

Three events intervened to give the industry a new lease on life. The B.C. mining boom, the railway construction in the West,[16] and the spurt of investment in the forest industries following the new restrictions on export around the turn of the century — all operated to generate a great expansion of demand. In addition, the American tariff of 1897 raised rates on Canadian livestock to such a degree that, whereas formerly immature cattle were sent to the U.S. for maturing and sale to European markets, Canadian farmers and dealers began maturing them themselves.[17] This helped considerably to wipe out the advantage given American stockyards and packing firms by the Canadian railways' discrimination in favour of American routes. Also, the Ontario government planned a $100,000 bounty system to the meat packing industry, of the same type as that given to sugar beets. Although this was not granted,[18] it probably helped create the climate for overinvestment in the industry. In addition, the reawakening of the Canadian salt wells that followed the movement of pulp and lumber mills north may have assisted the industry. And by 1899 in Ontario a pork packing rage had broken out. Farmers in Ontario rural communities were the leading shareholders in the new firms, and fed by municipal bonuses, the industry soon spread to Quebec and the Maritimes, but within a year of the burst of activity it showed signs of over-capacity.[19] By 1903, paralleling the beet root sugar liquidation, a number of these pork packing firms were in bad shape, some had failed, and others followed.[20]

In fruit and vegetable canning a similar pattern occurred, though it began earlier. By 1896 some fourteen companies in eleven Ontario municipalities had received aid, mainly in the form of tax exemptions but occasionally in cash as well — and by that date the industry was already overcrowded.[21] Yet the encouragement of new firms continued,[22] including roving Americans like the Heinz Company.

Another popular acquisition, but in Quebec more than Ontario, was the tobacco factory, and a number of Quebec towns secured small firms with the help of bonuses. At least two towns secured their tobacco firms at the expense of Montreal. Granby paid $25,000 to the Empire Tobacco Co. in 1895.[23] St. Jean gave a bonus of $10,000 to secure H. S. Swain and Sons in 1898 — the town bonus paid for the fixed capital, circulating capital was acquired by accommodation paper, and within a year the firm had failed. The bank's claim was preferred, while the rest of the estate paid about ten cents on the dollar.[24] Some Ontario towns were also "lucky." Guelph joined in, and its bribes secured it the only pipe tobacco firm west of Montreal in 1902.[25] Leamington added an American cigar tobacco firm to its industrial base in 1901.[26]

The Textile Industry

The oracle of the Canadian Manufacturers' Association in 1882 declared that "we cannot by any trick of Protection or National Policy produce crops of cotton on the banks of the St. Lawrence. But we can set up cotton machinery in Cornwall or Montreal."[27] And the municipalities did their best to make that boast come true. For no industry received the amount of attention and handouts with such an assortment of gimmickry as cotton. Other textiles were well treated, too. The industry was centred in Quebec, but by no means confined thereto, and the keen competition for mills was felt everywhere in the central and eastern provinces.

The fun began even before the National Policy. In 1877 St. Jean, Quebec, voted $20,000 in a stock subscription to its local woollen factory.[28] Norval, Ontario, also had one in operation until the next year, when Cobourg, Ontario, bribed it to leave with $2,500.[29] This was one of the earliest cases of subsidized internal migration in the industry. It was a bad choice. After two subsequent bonuses, the firm was taken over and closed up by a Montreal competitor. The influx of foreign firms into textiles also preceded the high tariff. In 1878, a New Yorker was given

$10,000 by Ottawa plus a free 99-year lease of a site and a ten-year exemption from taxes to move his mill there.[30] The stakes were mounting.

After the tariff went up, all restraint was abandoned and the systematic beggaring of neighbours began. In 1879, an English manufacturer, Clayton Slater, offered to migrate to Brantford with his woollen mill "provided he can secure favourable terms."[31] It seems that he could. On the other hand, Yarmouth, Nova Scotia, issued a blanket offer of a ten-year tax exemption to any woollen mill in 1881.[32] Such paltry terms were easy to refuse, however, and local capitalists rather than outside firms had to be relied on to build up Yarmouth's textile industry. That year, Sarnia granted a demand for $20,000 for a woollen mill, meeting it in part out of $13,500 that had been voted previously for a malleable iron works and a match factory, neither of which materialized.[33] Before the recession set in in 1884, at least a dozen Ontario municipalities had voted cash to woollen mills, several others had given them tax exemptions, and some bonusing had spilled over into Quebec and the Maritimes as well. Some of the bonuses turned out disastrous for the towns, not simply because of financial failure. In 1879, Napanee's woollen mill had secured $4,000 and a ten-year exemption. In 1881 its promoters bolted town, leaving a lot of unsettled accounts behind.[34] And in 1887 Markham, Ontario, gave $5,000 to a woollen mill, secured by a mortgage on the plant and equipment to be foreclosed if the mill ceased production. Markham was wise by the standards of the day to have gotten a mortgage, but other parties were wiser. A prior manufacturer's lien existed on the equipment. There was clearly collusion between the mill owner and the equipment manufacturer for the mill packed up and moved to another town offering a bigger bonus.[35] Markham got nothing for its $5,000; the process, one supposes, simply began again in another location.

The woollen mills were generally a small, local industry in the 1880's and 1890's, though there were examples of branch mills of Montreal textile houses or of migrating American and British promoters. As local industries, they provided an excellent example of the municipal government's role as an investment banker. In 1882, a Simcoe small businessman proposed to start a worsted mill but had only $10,000 of his own and his partner's money, while the estimate of fixed capital requirements came to $30,000. The town lent the extra $20,000 interest-free for two years, at three per cent for the next three, and six per cent thereafter.[36]

Other textile firms, too, benefited from the orgy of bonusing.

Strathroy's knitting mill in 1878 got $10,000 and closed down shortly after.[37] A. S. Beauchemin got $2,000 and a ten-year exemption from St. Hyacinthe to build a shirt factory in 1892; it failed in 1883.[38] Victor Hudon secured $8,000 in cash, $20,000 in a stock subscription, and a twenty-year tax holiday from Beauharnois to build a cashmere factory in 1883.[39] After the migrating Englishman Clayton Slater built a wincey mill in Brantford, numerous other towns made him offers.[40] Corset and button factories and all manner of knitting mills were eagerly sought.[41] One Frenchman secured $25,000 from Roxton Falls, Quebec, for a hosiery mill.[42] In 1891 Sherbrooke gave $25,000 to a worsted company, and in 1894, perhaps to commemorate the hundredth anniversary of the Speenhamland decision, it gave a corset company a five per cent subsidy to its wage bill.

But it was to the cotton industry that the municipal cornucopia poured forth its greatest fruits. Most of the Ontario mills got bonuses in cash and tax exemptions to start proceedings.[43] In the case of the Galt, Ontario, mill, failure ensued as soon as the bonus was used up. Sarnia was a pioneer in the process, giving $20,000 to a firm which had demanded $25,000.[44] Sarnia's success in 1879 in the "bargain" was probably due to the fact that the great cotton binge had not yet begun in full steam. Later that same year, Farnham, P.Q., had to pay the full $25,000 for its cotton mill.[45]

Kingston at first was reluctant, and despite its cotton mill's active politicking it twice rejected demands for a cash bonus.[46] The issue was forced when the mill burnt down. The town council and individual citizens subscribed stock to rebuild it "sooner than see it go elsewhere." An eighteen-year tax exemption was added.[47]

The cotton craze spread to the Maritimes as well. In 1879 Truro, Nova Scotia, offered a ten-year tax holiday to a proposed cotton mill.[48] However, the Nova Scotia Legislature intervened and decreed that year that any cotton mill built in Nova Scotia within three years would get a twenty-year provincial, municipal and local tax exemption.[49] In 1885, the city of Halifax was granted permission to go into debt to give $7,000 to the Nova Scotia Cotton Manufacturing Co. under the terms of an 1882 agreement, the funds to be used for such things as railroad spurs.[50] In 1899, too, the tax exemption given to all firms was extended another twenty years for the Windsor Cotton Mill.[51] Nor were New Brunswick firms omitted from the bonusing system.[52]

It was in Quebec, however, that the most active cotton campaigns were mounted. Cornwall, while politically part of

Ontario, was economically tributary to Montreal, and even
before the National Policy it gave cash grants to the Canada
Cotton Co. and the Stormont Cotton Co. Coaticook contemplated a bonus in 1878, but it had just been robbed by a boot
and shoe promoter and hence was hesitant.[53] Farnham, however,
was "agitating" for a mill in the face of 100 unemployed
labourers in the town[54] — at a time when New England cotton
mills, with their great lure to Québécois workers, were booming.
The Gault brothers secured yet another cash gift from Cornwall
for Stormont Cotton early in 1879.[55] After the National Policy
all hell broke loose.

The Montreal wholesalers, turned manufacturers with the aid
of English investment and machinery, were now besieged with
offers from various municipalities. In 1879 Farnham offered
$20,000, but was forced to raise it to $25,000 when St. Jean
entered the bidding at that higher level.[56] Canada Cotton the
next year squeezed another cash bonus from Cornwall.[57] Also in
1880 Trois Rivières and St. Hyacinthe began competing for the
affections of a mill demanding fifteen per cent of capital costs
plus a twenty-year exemption.[58] It was a ludicrous proposition,
for the firm, the Merchant's Cotton Co. of Montreal, could have
inflated nominal capital cost by any amount of scamping or
stock watering. In any event, they lost to St. Henri, which offered
$10,000 and a ten-year exemption[59] — and lived to regret it, for
the company exacted further exemptions as the old ones
expired.[60]

St. Hyacinthe was apparently soured on bonusing by its experience, for along with Sorel and Halifax in 1881 it refused to
offer any cash, only an exemption, to another potential visitor.[61]
Trois Rivières, by contrast, had learned its lesson well, and voted
$25,000 for its first mill, easily outbidding Sherbrooke, which
was offering only $5,000 and a ten-year tax break.[62] Sherbrooke,
however, had other tricks up its sleeve for future use.

Coaticook got over its initial reluctance after the boot and
shoe swindle and joined the parade in 1882. Its cotton bonus of
$7,500 paid off handsomely — for the firm, which in its first six
months of operation earned 43½% profit.[63] Whether this figure is
gross or net is unclear, and not particularly important since the
company paid no taxes.

Hochelaga refused to be left out of the bidding for the presence of the transmogrifying Montreal merchants. After Victor
Hudon was dumped from the presidency of his mill by a stockholders' coup organized by the Gault brothers, he joined with
Louis Forget and another Montreal wholesaler to organize a new
mill with the town's kind assistance.[64] In 1883 Longueuil kicked

in $35,000, plus a site on a railway spur, and taxes and water free for eleven years.[65] But these terms were rather high for the time.

Montreal was a less-than-enthusiastic witness to the exodus of manufacturing capacity, and had to take steps to preserve and build its own cotton industry. A group of wealthy merchants of the city offered in 1882 to build their cotton mill there if the city paid what seemed to have become the standard terms — $25,000 cash and a ten-year tax holiday.[66] Another group offered what seemed to be more modest terms, a twenty-year tax exemption and a free site. However, as matters turned out, the desired site belonged to the British American Land Company and its asking price was, not surprisingly, $25,000.

The enormous overexpansion of mills in the period, which later led to drastic liquidation and cartelization, is generally attributed to the tariff, but it is clear that competitive bonusing must bear part of the responsibility. And just as expansion had provided a golden opportunity for the cotton firms to squeeze high and rising terms from the municipalities, so did the contraction that followed. The municipalities had had to pay to attract the mills, and then pay again to hold them.

The chief extortionist in the 1890's was the Dominion Cotton Mills combine, which owned, among others, the Kingston and Brantford factories. Both cities were faced with demands for bonuses in 1898, the alternative being to see the mills closed down and production shifted to Trois Rivières, which was offering cheap power from Shawinigan Falls.[67] In Kingston, where the mill had largely been built by municipal stock subscription, it demanded $50,000 to replace the machinery. From Brantford it demanded that the old site and factory be purchased by the town, the proceeds to be used for a new one, else the old one would be sold for whatever it would fetch and the machinery moved out to Trois Rivières.[68] Both cities capitulated.

The late 1890's were an active time for bonusing. Huntingdon, Quebec, seeing that the cotton mills were on the move again, secured the Montreal Cotton Co. for the gift of a mill property plus 25 years tax exemption in 1898.[69] Longueuil had to pay another $15,000 to hold its earlier acquisition in 1899,[70] while in 1906 the Manufacturing Cotton Co. demanded of Lachine $25,000 and 25 years free of taxes to finance extensions to its plant.[71]

Cash grants to establish firms, cash grants to cover depreciation and/or to expand, cash grants to move, cash grants not to move, free sites, tax exemptions, subsidies to wages — the cotton nightmare repeated itself in all manner of industries, and the municipalities, in general, caught in a trap of their own devising, meekly submitted.

Bonusing In Ontario

While in Quebec the textile industry led the recipients of municipal largesse, that role was taken in Ontario by secondary iron and steel, though it was certainly not the only industrial beneficiary. As in Quebec, the rationale of bonusing was seldom questioned in its early stages, and the practice was widespread and competitive.

One of the earliest to plan a general campaign was Mitchell. In 1876, following the loss of one of its firms to Stratford, it offered $10,000 in municipal debentures to any firm employing more than 60 persons; within a year it had raised the offer to $15,000.[72] The linkage of the bonus directly to the firm's capacity to generate employment grew more common over time, as did the practice of stipulating its use for fixed capital formation. After the tariff went up, of course, the practice of competitive bonusing spread. In 1882, Sarnia ratepayers voted on a group of bonus requests, and the results of the balloting reveal much about the attitudes of the time. For a stove works 460, against 19; for a malleable iron works 459, against 17; for a water works bonus 436, against 42.[73] Almost simultaneously, Stratford held a meeting of leading citizens to plan a bonusing campaign based on free sites and tax exemptions.[74] Private bonuses too made their appearance. One Toronto real estate speculator offered a rolling mill a site for one dollar an acre a year in 1882 in the hope that it would attract other industries [75] — a precedent followed to good effect by Hamilton some years later. Naturally, the terms of Ontario bonuses were inflated over time.

Rolling mills, foundries, and the like were all the rage in Ontario, bringing hefty bonuses with their fair share of bad investments. In 1896, Guelph received a visit from an American promoter who persuaded the town to subscribe $20,000 in equity in his rolling mill while he and his partner took a like amount. Guelph subscribed cash, while the Americans "paid up" by transferring a lot of old iron from Michigan which they then sold to the company as machinery. Two more local stock subscriptions of $20,000 each were raised before the firm foundered. Of the $60,000 paid in, $8,000 was recovered.[76]

Even with such horrors coming to light, the municipalities were caught in a vicious circle, and would not desist, for to stop the give-aways was to lose a firm or firms to another town. Hence a huge wealthy firm like the Massey Manufacturing Co. could squeeze special tax rates and cheap power from Toronto, better rates than smaller and poorer firms, simply by threatening to leave.[77] It did not even need another concrete offer. And if one firm got a bonus, other newcomers would often follow. In 1907, St. Thomas gave $50,000 to a firm formed to build railroad passenger cars. Another group of citizens quickly organized to form a company to build passenger cars, and demanded equal treatment for their infant.[78]

Agricultural implement firms received a lot of attention in Ontario. Haggart Bros. secured a $75,000 loan from Brampton in 1883.[79] Brockville gave a cash gift to Cossett Bros. in 1892, Woodstock to the Patterson Bros. in 1885; Sarnia, Forest, and Grimsby all bonused local firms with cash. And in 1901 when Frost and Wood, a long-established and wealthy firm, proposed to expand, the town of Smith's Falls gave it $20,000 plus the right-of-way of a railway siding.[80]

Many other industries in Ontario received bonuses — salt refiners, tanneries, rubber factories, even little handicraft industries like masons' shops. Distinct waves of bonusing manifested themselves around particular innovations in industry. Pulp and paper began to flourish in Ontario after the 1898 duty changes, and the bonuses flew fast and furious.[81] Cement manufacture became a craze in 1900, and bonuses were on hand to assist its early overexpansion.[82] Carriage works were popular in many towns, to the regret of some like Brockville who spent $50,000 to move a carriage works from Gananoque only to have part of its bonus diverted into the firm's operations elsewhere, and to see Gananoque secure a replacement for only $10,000.[83]

But next to iron and steel, furniture factories seemed most beloved by Ontario towns, and the infatuation was of long duration. The process of bonusing was well underway before the National Policy. Almonte, for example, saw a bonus voted to its local furniture factory in 1877 by a town council composed largely of the shareholders of the firm. One ratepayer took exception and got a court order quashing the bonus, and the firm promptly failed.[84] In the early 1880's, a furniture maker migrated from England to set up shop in Owen Sound, then moved to Toronto and failed. His next stop was Oshawa in return for a $15,000 bonus, which kindness he repaid by failing again.[85] Not intimidated by such experiences, the towns continued to vote aid on a grandiose scale. In 1888, Wingham bonused three furniture manufacturers with cash gifts.[86] And once the new prosperity got underway no small amount of its fruits was obligingly passed on by the towns to local or itinerant furniture companies.[87]

Legislation to curb bonuses in Ontario was introduced in 1888, but to little avail. In 1892, Toronto launched a wholesale campaign to attract new industry, followed by other towns.

Toronto's campaign was based on a blanket tax exemption in manufacturing machinery and plant.[88] Plots were hatched to go even further. The Toronto Ratepayers' Association envisaged a scheme whereby the city was to give free land sites taken from vacant lots plus fifteen years' initial tax exemption followed by 21 years of low frozen assessment to any firm employing more than 20 people. It also proposed a fund of one million dollars be set up to provide interest-free loans to cover up to fifty per cent of fixed costs.[89] The group put in charge of the fund included Sir Casimir Gzowski, Senator George Cox, Hon. Sir Frank Smith, G. R. Cockburn, Sir William Howland, and George Gooderham. Four of them had been implicated in frauds surrounding bank failures, one was later the main object of a Royal Commission enquiry, and the other was a principal Tory backroom dealer in CPR contracts. It was like putting a gang of convicted rapists in charge of a girls' school. But the proposal was not put into effect, and Toronto bonuses were restricted to tax exemptions and services.

Such a planned campaign coming from a metropolis like Toronto is a little surprising. But Toronto, despite its size, did not develop into a major industrial centre for some time. While Toronto dominated much of southern Ontario financially and commercially, it was Hamilton where the greatest amount of industrial activity tended to be centred.[90] Part of Toronto's problem lay in its tax system, which permitted land speculators to acquire great tracts of potential industrial land and drove up the price of sites. In addition, costs of gas and electricity were raised to excessive levels by the control of Toronto utilities by the Mackenzie-Mann group, including George Cox.

Bonusing in Quebec

In Quebec, bonusing spread from textiles to include all types of industry. Among the towns that bonused cotton mills and then went on to bigger, but seldom better things were Farnham, Coaticook, Hochelaga, St. Jean, Longueuil, and Lachine.

Farnham, in addition to cotton and beet sugar, gave $20,000 to a Montreal furniture company to build a branch and got into a tug of war with Roxton Falls over another one.[91] Coaticook, after its cotton "success," announced it was eager for more factories, especially boots and shoes and a tannery, but that all manufacturers would find the town "most liberal."[92] Hochelaga followed its cotton bonus with a cash gift to a rolling stock company in 1882.[93] Longueuil in 1882 gave H. R. Ives of the Dominion Barbed Wire Co. $10,000 to "establish" a foundry in the town.[94] He took the bonus funds and used them to buy up an existing defunct foundry.[95] A few years later Lachine gave Ives $5,000 to build them a branch too.[96]

Lachine's efforts did not end herein. Over the next fifteen years its handouts included $35,000 to James Cooper (another hardware merchant who, like Ives, moved into manufacture under American licence) $25,000 to a tannery, and $15,000 to a furniture factory.[97]

St. Jean competed successfully with Trois Rivières for a carriage factory in 1888 at a cost of $25,000.[98] But most of the town's activities seemed to gravitate towards the enamel works in that area. As early as 1877, it debated rescuing the St. Jean Stone Chinaware Co. with a municipal stock subscription. It decided against the move and the firm went into assignment,[99] though in 1882 another pottery was rebuilt after a fire with a municipal loan.[100] The Stone Chinaware Co. passed into the hands of Charles Arpin, the private banker who restored its fortunes, but it collapsed once more. In 1893, it tried to rebuild itself again with a municipal bonus, again failing. In 1896, it passed into the hands of a French firm who received a bonus to take it over. Three years later it was again wound up, the works being taken over by a New Brunswick senator who asked for a bonus to revive it.[101] His request appears to have been refused. The pottery, rebuilt at municipal expense in 1882, passed into the hands of an American firm two decades later.[102]

All manner of other Quebec towns went on bonusing binges, including Megantic, which in 1882 offered $5,000 and a twenty-year tax holiday to any new industry with a "capital" of $100,000 or more.[103] Rimouski offered a twenty-year blanket tax exemption to all comers in 1881, followed by a string of cash gifts; it was a lumber area and announced that it wanted to industrialize.[104] Huntingdon guaranteed interest on the bond issue of a match factory.[105]

Pulp and paper mills, after the turn-of-the-century change in federal regulations, became popular in Quebec towns. Hapless Danville, in 1900, gave $10,000 to a pulp mill. A few months later Danville and the township of Shipton were called upon to guarantee the company's bonds to an amount of up to $30,000.[106]

But if any industry in Quebec, apart from cotton and other textiles, could be regarded as a favourite of the towns, it was boots and shoes. Both bonusing and the concomitant frauds began early: in 1877 Coaticook was swindled out of $20,000 by a boot elastic firm.[107] The migration of firms began at least as early as 1880, when Charles Arpin and Louis Coté, then partners, took over a defunct factory in Waterloo, Quebec, and moved it to St.

Jean.[108] Four years later their successors, Séguin, Lalime et Cie., moved from St. Jean to St. Hyacinthe, and St. Jean contemplated a bonus of $10,000 to get them back.[109] St. Hyacinthe, however, had paid them $12,000 to make the move, and they stayed there — for a while.

In 1881 Longueuil, always an easy mark, gave G. Boivin a $20,000 bonus to move from Montreal. Within a few months Boivin was in the midst of one of his periodic failures.[110] The year 1888 saw both Trois Rivières and Lévis bribe Montreal factories to shift[111] while in 1890 St. Hyacinthe added Louis Coté and Bros. to its inventory, another acquisition at the expense of St. Jean.

The year 1895 saw a great burst of activity in the boot and shoe industry, with towns falling all over themselves to acquire members of the overcrowded field. In the first ten months of the year, upward of a dozen firms had failed[112] including Séguin, Lalime and Co. of St. Hyacinthe. The town paid up another $15,000 in the form of a "loan" while the people of the town subscribed $15,000 in stock to save it. But by 1902 it was in liquidation.[113]

The next few years saw the continuation and escalation of the boot and shoe mania. St. Henri acquired a Montreal firm in 1897; St. Jean finally secured a replacement for the firms stolen from it earlier by bribing away Terrebonne's factory; Lachine got a Sorel firm which failed almost immediately.[114] The town of Lévis also regretted its choice in a new bonus, for a new acquisition took the town to court for failing to pay up its bonus on time, and seized town property including the fire engine.[115] St. Henri promptly announced it would grant no more bonuses. The situation was rendered all the more ludicrous by the fact that in 1898 when Lévis made the bonus offer, neighbouring Quebec City alone had 32 boot and shoe firms.[116]

Still, others failed to follow St. Henri's example. St. Louis, Quebec, voted a bonus in 1900, the same year Maisonneuve voted two, and the same year that St. Hyacinthe lost its second acquisition from St. Jean when the Coté firm failed.[117] Delormier voted a bonus to the big James McCready boot and shoe establishment to secure a branch in 1901, and in 1903 St. Hyacinthe replaced its two failures by bribing Ames, Holden and Co. to move their main plant from Montreal.[118] The important distinction between the early and the later thefts was that now it was the growing anglophone boot and shoe firms that were securing aid, while the smaller Québécois ones were falling by the wayside.

The most blatant example of bonusing run amock in Quebec

is provided by Sherbrooke. It began innocently enough, with three bonuses in 20 years. But the year 1892 saw it lose a corset company to St. Hyacinthe, and an electrical supply company to Peterborough, while the next year Waterville stole a wooden ware firm.[119] Thereafter, Sherbrooke began a widespread campaign of "nursing" its industrial base, and its record to 1900 is summarized in Table XIII (1).

TABLE XIII (1)

Sherbrooke Bonuses

Firm	Year	Bonus
Paton Manufacturing	1871	site and $5,000
Meat Factory Co.	1875	$20,000
Worsted Co.	1891	$25,000
Royal Corset Co.	1894	5% on wages
Hovey Bros. Packing Co.	1895	5% on investment
Jencks Machine Co.	1896	$30,000
Gardener Tool Co.	1897	$30,000
Walter Blue Co.	1899	10 year tax break
Brussel Carpet Co.	1899	$17,500
Quebec Central R.R. Shops	1899	$15,000
Rand Drill Co.	1900	$15,000

Source: *MT,* March 23, 1900, p. 1268.

Some of these firms were not newcomers; the Paton firm, a woollen mill, was established in Sherbrooke five years before it received its bonus, and Jencks was founded in 1846, fifty years before.[120] Jencks, one of the largest machinery firms in Canada, was deluged with orders from the mining districts. In December 1894 it asked the town for a bonus to pay for extensions and was granted it.[121] Since it clearly had no need for the extra funds, the bonus was simply a subsidy to profits.

Some of Sherbrooke's bonusing endeavours had a less than happy ending. Gardener Tools had originally established itself in Brockville with the aid of a healthy bonus. It then asked Sherbrooke to raise the ante, and delayed accepting its terms until it was clear that Brockville could not match them. But the plant it finally moved to Sherbrooke was that of the Beaver Saw Works of Hamilton, which it bought out using the bonus funds. Within a year of the money being paid, the firm was in liquidation,[122] a fate it shared with two other of Sherbrooke's efforts.

Bonusing in the Maritimes

Bonusing in the Maritimes was conducted on a far less profligate
scale than in the central provinces. In Prince Edward Island it
seems to have been totally absent, apart from a couple of early
tax exemptions from Charlottetown to local handicraft-style
firms.[123] In Nova Scotia, cotton and primary iron and steel
absorbed a disproportionate share of what bonuses were voted.
There were, though, instances of grist and flour mill subsidies,
and spillovers from Ontario into pork packing and canning late
in the nineteenth and early in the twentieth centuries were
recorded in both Nova Scotia and New Brunswick.

In 1879 the creation of the Halifax Sugar Refinery was
greeted by the Nova Scotia Legislature with a twenty-one year
exemption from all county rates and local taxes. All future sugar
refineries were accorded equal treatment.[124] For the Halifax
refinery, the city added free water from each main adjacent to it
for ten years.[125] Two decades later, Halifax voted a blanket tax
exemption to all firms investing $10,000 or more in plant and
equipment.[126] It also attempted to bribe away from Amherst the
car works of Rhodes, Curry and Co. The city offered twelve
acres of land, DOMCO was to give cheap coal, and the People's
Heat and Gas Co. offered gas at nominal rates. In addition the
firm, of course, qualified for the tax rebate. The total value of
the bonus was about $100,000, but the firm declined.[127] As late as
1909, Halifax endorsed plans for a new bonusing blitz.[128]

Sydney, which topped the Maritime list with its iron and steel
give-aways, secured permission from the Legislature in 1904 to
give a tax exemption and $10,000 cash to a firm to make cement
out of the slag and waste of DISCO. It was a time of rapid
expansion of the cement industry throughout Canada, and
Sydney was determined to get its share. In the same bill,
authority was granted to give a cash gift to the Sydney Manufacturing Company to build railway cars, another booming Canadian industry, and to give a twenty-year tax exemption to the
Dominion Glass Company.[129] A few years later the city offered
half a million dollars in cash, "and other concessions" to any
firm building it a shipbuilding plant,[130] five times the standard
level of shipbuilding bonus that had typified the early round of
competition in 1901.

The usual type of bonus was handed out to small, local industries in small towns, though with remarkable restraint in comparison to Ontario and Quebec. Amherst in 1896 gave cash gifts to a

grist and to a woollen mill. Pictou in 1899 bonused a boot and shoe firm.[131]

In New Brunswick, apart from cotton and little gifts to local industry by small towns, there were a few outstanding cases, for instance, in fish packing or paper. In Fredericton in 1895, one firm received a tax exemption and up to 250,000 gallons of water a year for twenty-five years to build a canning factory.[132] Another cannery got a tax exemption, a free site, free water and a $10,000 loan on which the city guaranteed the interest to build a factory valued at $15,000.[133]

Woodstock, New Brunswick, decided to join its Ontario and Quebec counterparts and get a share of pulp and paper following the export duty alterations, offering one firm $50,000 in 1899. When the deal fell through, it promptly offered the money to a furniture factory.[134] In 1907 Moncton, joined by St. John and Chatham, announced new bonus campaigns based on free sites.[135]

Bonusing in the West

In the West, bonusing was even more restricted than in the Maritimes, and, of course, such bonusing as did occur had to follow the course of settlement. This automatically restricted the time period in which a giveaway program could be mounted.

The first general campaign to be planned seemed to be that of Portage la Prairie in 1886, when ratepayers authorized a debenture issue to buy land to give to manufacturers.[136] This scheme was stopped short by the town's financial straits at that time. St. Boniface in 1895 gave $10,000 to a boot and shoe factory; two years later its efforts to bonus a tin can factory were blocked by the Manitoba Legislature, which frowned upon bonuses.[137] Winnipeg was frequently asked for bonuses, especially by American firms, but it followed the Manitoba pattern and granted few, if any.[138]

In Alberta much the same was true. Calgary gave cash to a local tannery and a creamery in 1894.[139] Medicine Hat gave tax exemptions, utility concessions, and free sites to a number of firms.[140] Again the over-all importance was minimal.

In B.C., bonusing was a little more energetic. Victoria, for example, came close to financial collapse after an orgy of bonusing from 1888 to 1892.[141] In West Kootenay, a municipal stock subscription and a site to build a branch of a Vancouver foundry were granted in 1896.[142] Most noteworthy among B.C.'s

bonuses were the efforts to induce municipalities to grant bounties to smelters. In 1895, Vancouver received an offer from an
English syndicate to build a smelter for a bonus of five dollars a
ton on the first 5000 tons of ore refined. It did not accept this
proposition. Two years later, the company had raised its terms to
a bonus of $1.00 per ton for the first 65,000 tons, in return for
which the city would get $65,000 worth of equity. But instead,
Vancouver accepted the bargain offered by an American copper
and gold company of a smelter in return for a bonus of 50¢ a ton
for 100,000 tons.[143]

Municipal "Fire Insurance"

One of the stranger uses of the municipal bonus was to rebuild
factories and mills destroyed by fire. That such was necessary at
all reflected the state of fire insurance in Canada, the onerous
rates charged by the cartel, the inadequacy of the coverage
offered by American underground companies, and the very
extent of the great conflagrations that intermittently engulfed
Canadian towns because of the nature of the construction of factories and mills. Not surprisingly, too, fires in one town tended
to set aflame the competitive industrial ambitions of others, and
each conflagration touched off a round of bidding for the pleasure of rebuilding.

For some firms it seemed almost a pleasure to be burned out.
Welland Vale Manufacturing, for example, was destroyed in
Kingston in 1877 and asked for a $15,000 gift to rebuild.[144] When
this failed to materialize, it moved to St. Catharines. A fire destroyed the new plant in 1900, and complicated bargaining
resulted. St. Catharines refused it a $100,000 loan, but gave it an
eight per cent subsidy on its wage bill for up to $4,000 per year
for fifteen years, plus a fifteen-year tax exemption. In the same
vote, the St. Catharines ratepayers gave $10,000 to a paper mill
and defeated a $2,200 grant for a new collegiate,[145] — illustrating
well the industrial priorities of the time, for the entire range of
Welland Vale's output was produced under American licence.[146]

Instances of municipalities taking the role of, or supple-
menting fire insurance companies, occurred all over the country.
In Moncton, the town made offers for the rebuilding of a sugar
refinery.[147] In 1894, Brandon had to make a loan to rebuild a mill
it had bonused to build in the first place only a few months
before.[148] Quebec saw a rash of competitive offers following fires.
In 1887, the destruction of a Montreal tannery led to renewed
economic warfare between St. Jean and St. Hyacinthe.[149] St. Jean

had to offer loans to rebuild its pottery and enamel works several times.[150]

In Ontario the same phenomena occurred. A Clinton fire, for example, destroyed an organ factory worth $70,000. Its insurance with ten British and three Canadian companies came to but $30,-000, and the town had to make up most of the difference.[151] The penalty for failing to do so was, of course, to lose the factory. This was especially evident when the McLaughlin carriage factory burned down in Oshawa in 1899 and many towns offered assistance. Belleville made an especially tempting offer of cash and a special bond issue, but McLaughlin "felt a deep loyalty to Oshawa," especially in the face of a $50,000 interest-free loan to be repaid "as convenient." The loan carried at the ratepayers' meeting 572 to ten.[152]

Subsidizing Internal Migration

The most insidious facet of the bonusing craze was the competition between municipalities to bid industry away from each other, a practice that began in textiles and spread rapidly. The *Monetary Times* insisted that only "lame ducks" went bonus-hunting.[153] These "lame ducks" included Massey, Dominion Cotton, the CPR, the Grand Trunk, DISCO, Stelco, Heinz, Yale, the Lever Brothers, McLaughlin, and many more. The rumours of any prospective acquisitions sent town councillors tumbling over each other to attract it. And as the industrial hopes of one town went up in smoke, dozens of others descended on the ruins before the ashes had cooled to offer all manner of inducements for rebuilding.

In Quebec, the typical pattern was towns stealing industry from Montreal, and to a much lesser degree from each other, as with St. Jean and St. Hyacinthe. Montreal was the source not only of a seemingly never-ending supply of textile firms, but also of tobacco factories and many others. Both St. Jean and Granby, for instance, secured their tobacco factories from Montreal in addition to several other firms. St. Jean over 1897 and 1898 secured three other firms from that city, while Granby got a rubber plant, perhaps intended to make up for the fact that it had just lost its enamel works to St. Jean for $20,000 plus the cost of moving.[154] St. Henri secured a biscuit factory from Montreal.[155] Côte St. Paul gave an agricultural implements firm $10,000 to set up in the village: the plant never arrived, and the municipality had to sue for recovery of its bonus.[156] A foundry moved from Maisonneuve to St. Jérôme for a bonus in 1896, moved back to

Maisonneuve for a larger bonus in 1898, and failed in 1899.[157]

Ontario patterns were very different. There was no systematic movement of industry out of Toronto, for Toronto did not exhibit nearly the same degree of industrial development as Montreal, and hence the scope for pilfering its industry was much less. Ontario manufacturing developed in a more decentralized way in a number of major urban centres who raided each other, over and above their energetic efforts to attract American branch plants.

Hamilton had a long history of successful bonus campaigns. As early as 1887 it had moved the Dundas Screw Works away from its home with a tax concession.[158] Dundas was clearly frightened by its burgeoning neighbour, and when John Bertram and Sons, one of Canada's largest and wealthiest machine shops, asked for a bonus, it quickly gave it $12,000.[159] One month later, Bertram announced that it had been the most prosperous year in their history.[160] The bonus was evidently a reward for doing so well. It might too have had something to do with the fact that John Bertram in 1889 had been unanimously elected mayor of the town, whose council now voted the bonus, while his eldest son became president of the Board of Trade.[161]

The habit of attempting to beggar your next-door neighbour afflicted others besides Hamilton and Dundas. Waterloo and Berlin engaged in a contest over a brick company which moved to Waterloo when Berlin failed to meet its terms.[162] The Woodstock, Ontario, wagon works announced it was unhappy over the treatment accorded it by the town, and threatened to move to Ingersoll if it did not improve. Ingersoll, in turn, had to give bonuses to a fruit basket firm and a metal foundry to keep them quiet.[163] In 1889, Collingwood placed an advertisement in the *Monetary Times* extolling its own virtues as an industrial site and offering to bargain with manufacturers over bonus terms. Immediately, Trenton and Belleville placed their own ads claiming similar attractions, including the prospect of bonuses.[164]

Even Hamilton had to be careful. Woodstock voted by a huge majority to try to steal a foundry from it for $25,000 in 1891, while in 1900 Welland and Port Colborne cast covetous eyes on its iron and steel plant.[165] But on balance Hamilton was the biggest gainer, for in addition to attracting a series of Ontario firms it secured a number of branch plants. Some of its transactions were curious. In 1896, the local glass works was compelled to close for lack of orders.[166] Hamilton secured a replacement in the form of the Diamond Glass Works, which bought out the Toronto Glass Works in 1896 and moved it to Hamilton. The firm then purchased the Burlington Glass Works and moved it to Toronto, which by then seemed more willing to be reasonable in the matter of bonuses.[167]

But if the outcome of bonusing was pleasing to the Hamilton authorities, it was quite otherwise with Brantford. In 1895, the Waterous Engine Works, a very large, well established firm, threatened to leave; the city offered it $40,000, another ten-year extension to its existing tax holiday, plus free light and water. Waterous accepted,[168] then promptly raised the terms, demanding that the city buy its old site and grant it another year's tax exemption.[169] Brantford ratepayers voted 1,230 to 179 to comply.[170] It was a mistake, for within a year the Verity Plough Works demanded $15,000 for its old site, a tax exemption, free water, and new main installed at the city's expense. The terms were accepted, and Verity kindly consented to stay in Brantford.[171] Within another year, Dominion Cotton had begun to make its demands, and Brantford acceded. Again in 1898 it gave a ten-year exemption to a screw factory and the Nott Bicycle Co.[172] Less than two years later, Nott demanded a $5,000 cash gift and a $10,000 "loan" to stay.[173] As to the old Waterous building, it was given by the city to a new machine and tool firm among whose promoters was C. H. Waterous, and later became a site for a carriage factory.[174]

Subsidizing Foreign Immigrants

While the habit of subsidizing intercommunal movements was publicly deplored as often as it was privately practiced, the use of bonusing to attract foreign firms, especially American, but also British and French, was almost always lauded. It was the field where bonusing was expected to yield the highest dividends which, for the firms, it often did; while for the municipalities it generated some of the worst abuses.

Again it began innocently enough. Thorold, Ontario, gave a free site and minor tax concessions to a wealthy American glucose manufacturer in 1882.[175] In 1887, Toronto gave an American furniture firm a ten-year tax exemption: when the exemption ran out, the firm moved to Walkerton.[176] In 1888, Brantford raised the terms considerably, giving $20,000 to a New York carriage company.[177] All the border towns of Ontario actively competed to secure their share of itinerant firms.[178] In 1887, a Detroit firm asked London for $50,000 towards its planned investment of $100,000.[179] This, however, was not granted, for London, like Toronto and Hamilton, as a major centre, could usually safely restrict its bonuses to large, valuable tax concessions and avoid the abuses of the cash grant.

It was in the 1890's that the main scramble began, and it increased in intensity with each American firm that announced its intent to make the move.[180] The American firms followed the leader. In 1893 the Odell Typewriter Co. of Chicago went shopping for a site in Canada,[181] followed the next year by the Oliver Typewriter Co. of Iowa, which asked Toronto to make it an offer it could not refuse.[182] Terms were often announced in advance and offers then awaited. [183] One case that illustrates well the financing techniques of the American immigrants came up in the negotiations between Carleton Place and Iver-Johnson of Massachusetts. The firm proposed a joint venture, capitalized at $100,-000, to be made up from a $5,000 cash bonus from the town, $5,000 stock subscription by the town, $30,000 subscribed by the citizens of the town, $25,000 by a local firm whose works would be absorbed by the new venture, and $25,000 by Iver-Johnson in the form of "plant" and any stock that could not be marketed at a good price.[184]

The give-aways by Ontario municipalities embraced all manner of gimmicks. Leamington gave $10,000 to the impoverished Heinz Company,[185] later adding an American tobacco firm to its bonus list. Heinz had initially wooed Hamilton, but the bonus vote failed to secure the required majority, in part due to the active opposition of two established canneries who complained of the discrimination in favour of Heinz.[186] Sarnia guaranteed $30,000 worth of bonds for a Detroit firm.[187] Peterborough secured a lock company, and then paid even more to keep it.[188] St. Catharines gave the needy Yale and Towne Company nine acres, free water, a ten year tax exemption and a fixed low assessment. The firm had been founded in 1868, had since absorbed most of its competitors, and by 1911, when it got the handout, had a capital subscribed of five million dollars. [189]

Hamilton again proved eminently successful. The Westinghouse Co. began roving Ontario in 1895 looking for a site and "creating quite a stir in several Canadian towns."[190] It ultimately settled in Hamilton. Hamilton also got a branch of the Mansfield Glass Co. of New York. [191] Why Hamilton needed another glass firm is beyond comprehension. It tempted a large carriage firm from Plattsville to settle, and picked up the Canadian Meter Co., which had stopped over briefly in Windsor in the process.[192] Its most spectacular acquisition since the Hamilton Iron and Steel Co. was undoubtedly the Deering Plow Co. branch, which became part of International Harvester. In fact, the plant was almost lost to Brockville, for Hamilton ratepayers voted only 2,819 to 632 in favour of a $30,000 bonus, while under Ontario statute 3,858 positive votes were needed from Hamilton's ratepayer population. But Deering came in any event.[193]

The credulity of Canadian town councillors spread throughout the northeastern United States, whose firms had only to indicate they were interested in establishing a Canadian branch to be inundated by offers. One Michigan firm was especially adroit at playing the various towns off against each other, and got a free site worth several thousands, free power, a twenty-year tax exemption, and an interest-free "loan" of $13,300 for a factory whose total cost was only $16,000.[194] One Mr. Thomas of Cleveland, a total stranger to the town of Lindsay, offered to build a tannery and a boot and shoe factory. Lindsay "knew" that many other towns and cities would grab at his offer, and gave him a free site. He then borrowed $900 from one chartered bank, $550 from another, and when one of the managers became suspicious, he left town in a hurry.[195]

Canada's fame spread abroad. The Imperial Starch Company got an $8,000 site, a twenty-year tax exemption, electricity for 100 bulbs, and 100,000 gallons of water free per year for twenty years from Prescott.[196] Quebec City gave $12,500 to the Globe India Rubber Manufacturing Co. of Manchester.[197]

French capital, too, became interested in the bonusing system, and it was an important factor in attacting several firms in the late nineteenth and early twentieth centuries.[198] St. Jean, Quebec, was foolish enough to give $20,000 to a French firm to *take over* one of the pottery and chinaware firms with which it had been cursed long before.[199]

The ultimate absurdity came as a result of Toronto's big bonus campaign of the 1890's, which, by 1900, had netted it Lever Brothers. The firm bought a 23-acre site. In turn, Toronto agreed to keep the assessment fixed for ten years regardless of improvements, exempted the firm from local rates for roads, sewers, and sidewalks, agreeing to maintain them free for ten years, and undertook to crib and pile a frontage of several hundred feet along the Don River, and to dredge and maintain a channel fourteen feet deep for ten years.[200] This plan was approved by the Ontario Legislature, subject only to the condition that not more than $60,000 be spent on improvements to the Don, and not more than $1,500 a year in maintaining the improvements.[201]

No other soap maker in Canada had ever received a bonus or concession, apart from one case of a ten-year tax exemption.[202] And the Toronto give-away was illegal under the terms of the 1888 Ontario legislation which forbade bonusing newcomers in an industry where firms had already been established without assistance. Some firms had been established in Toronto making soap and glucose, the Lever Brothers' planned output, for over forty years, and had paid full taxes for that entire period. The Lever plant was built to a capacity capable of supplying five million people with laundry soap. Yet within a hundred-mile radius of Toronto there were fifteen domestically-owned soap firms and no export market existed. Moreover, it was a relatively capital-intensive industry. One firm in Hamilton, operated a plant with one-fifth the capacity of the Lever plant on only twenty-five hands. [203]

Costs of the Bonusing System

Antagonism to the bonusing system began almost as soon as bonusing itself. In 1871, the president of the Dominion Board of Trade condemned it as "protectionism in its worst form, because the poorer classes are thereby compelled to pay the taxes properly due from the factory." [204] In 1906, the president of the Toronto Board of Trade echoed these sentiments, calling bonusing "one of the worst forms of class legislation." [205] In the intervening thirty-five years a great deal of redistribution of income from the poor to the rich, and from established firms to newcomers, had occurred in the name of industrial development.

The municipal tax systems of the period were extremely regressive even without the costs of bonusing. In Montreal between 1876 and 1886 landed proprietors, including businesses, saw their property taxes fall by $82,723 annually, while merchants' annual business taxes were $10,673 less in 1886 than in 1876. The value of property over the ten-year period for assessment purposes had been reduced by $6,898, 578, while 3,600 new buildings had been constructed and rent receipts increased by $477,733. However, only small rents had risen; larger rents had been stationary or falling. Over the same decade, Montreal tenants were paying $49,000 more per annum in water rates. Montreal water rates were so oppressive that working-class families often could not meet them; the water would then be shut off, and the family's furniture seized for the debt and auctioned off at a sheriff's sale. "If a charitable neighbour gave them a bucket of water, the neighbour was liable to a fine of $20 and a month in prison." [206] At about the same time, private firms were getting upwards of a quarter of a million gallons free of charge.

Railways, too, in addition to their hugh cash bonuses, benefited from the tax structure. The CPR began with a blanket tax and tariff exemption. As late as 1900, it refused to pay the Winnipeg school tax and the Supreme Court of Canada upheld its refusal. [207] In 1909, in the states bordering Ontario, the CPR and Grand Trunk had 5,120 miles of line on which they paid taxes of $2,440,000 or $471 per mile. They had 5,320 miles in Ontario, on which they paid $452,000, or $85 per mile. In 1906, the assessment on Ontario farm property was $5.33 per $1,000, while on railway property it was $1.55. [208]

Another important redistributive effect was from the old established firms to the newcomers of which Lever, while a particularly startling example, was hardly unique. One city in 1887 gave $20,000 and a ten-year tax break to bring a newcomer into an industry which already had twelve firms in the city. [209] One of London's victories secured it a cigar box firm which had asked for free water and a twenty-year tax exemption. For a year the request was in abeyance because of the vehement objection of a firm already established. But fortunately for Adam Beck, his rival failed, the bonus was carried, and Beck moved from Galt to London, having gained an indispensable lesson in industrial development policy. His system of cigar box factories stretched to Toronto and Montreal well before he seized upon the idea of a province-wide utility rate bonus to manufacturers. [210]

Complaints from established manufacturers were heard all across Canada. Meaford in 1890 gave a bonus to a stove foundry to move into the village which already had had one such for 23 years; the old firm had through its taxes to pay an annual subsidy of $200 to his rival. [211] Moncton manufacturers in 1899 organized a protest against discriminatory bonuses. [212] In Francis Clergue's fiefdom of Sault Ste. Marie these problems did not arise, for so strong was his hold over the town that the municipal authorities had to consult with him and obtain his clearance before they brought any new firms into the area. [213]

But the competitive nature of the system forced the municipalities to continue the practice despite the patent absurdities. As early as 1881, the village of Elora, Ontario, brought itself to the brink of bankruptcy by issuing debentures at seven per cent, "loaning" the proceeds to a firm which failed, following which the town was then unable to recover the loan. It repudiated the debt and was hauled into court by the debenture holders. Its plea was that (1) the town really had no authority to make the loan; (2) even if it did, it had no authority to issue debentures to pay for it; and (3) the rate of interest of seven per cent was illegal. All were refused by the court and the town had to honour its debts. [214] Another absurdity was revealed by the results of Whitby's bonuses. The town had paid $110,000 to secure railway

shops and an organ factory each to employ 50 men — a total
cost of $1,100 per job to be created, by itself ludicrous. But a
contemporary report noted that "today there is said to be but
one man employed in the railway works, while the sole occupant
of the organ factory is a cow." [215]

In addition to rich American firms like Yale, Heinz, Westinghouse etc., a number of American carpetbaggers enriched themselves on a grab-and-run basis. As late as 1910, the *Monetary
Times* reported, "Our towns are being exploited . . . by men
without cash, credit, or reputation."[216] And the competitive
system led to all manner of abuses. Intercommunal visits were
profitable to the firms, the costs of duplication falling on the
municipality. Moreover, many cases occurred in which large
sums were paid to shift factories from one town to another, only
to have the municipality discover it was the victim of a put-up
job, the machinery being virtually valueless.[217] The sole factor
mitigating the waste seems to have been the fact that, due to the
inadequacy of fire insurance facilities, many factories were built
as flimsily as possible — which also made them easier to move.
It thus seemed very appropriate that in 1897, after the ratepayers
of Port Dalhousie had just voted the necessary bonus to shift a
boot and shoe factory out of Toronto, "the people celebrated the
event by having a large bonfire."[218]

In 1879, the *Monetary Times* began an anti-bonusing campaign, berating the municipalities for their overzealousness. As
the inequities grew, so did the campaign against them.[219] In 1888,
the Ontario Legislature received petitions from 45 municipalities
and a number of labour organizations asking for severe curbs or
abolition of the power to grant bonuses.[220] For the towns had
realized that only legal restraints applying all across Ontario
could remove the abuses by relieving the municipalities of the
fear that, if any of them desisted, some competitor would get
ahead. And for the unions the problem of the "runaway shop"
was already a serious one. An amendment to the Municipal Act
was passed stipulating that:

(1) Two-thirds of the ratepayers had to vote in favour of a
bonus;
(2) No bonus could be granted to a firm to establish itself in an
industry in which firms had set up in the municipality
without bonuses;
(3) No bonus could be given to move a firm from one part of
the province to another;
(4) The maximum value of any bonus, principal and interest,

could not exceed ten per cent of the total municipal tax receipts.[221]

In 1899 Quebec passed a similar act.

The legislation was largely ineffectual, for there were many ways to avoid it. Guelph, Ontario, for example, purchased a piece of land for $15,000 and "sold" it to a firm for $250 to move from Galt to Guelph.[222] Changing the name of a firm often sufficed to escape the law. Then too, it was an era when many firms were changing from private to public, and incorporation sufficed to avoid the provisions of the statute. Again, a firm might start a new branch in a bonusing community and gradually withdraw from the original.[223] In 1899, a bill was proposed in the Ontario Legislature stipulating that bonuses could be paid only in the event of loss by fire.[224] But it never passed. In 1902, an amendment was passed to include under the provisions of the 1888 Act all firms who simply switched to an incorporated basis or changed partners, or underwent some other minor alteration of form.[225] In addition, Ontario moved to restrict the amount of the bonus even further by extending the ten per cent maximum to include the value of exemptions, utility rate reductions, services provided, and any other concessions, and it tried to eliminate an obvious and old abuse by prohibiting stockholders in the firms concerned from voting on their own bonuses.[226]

By the turn of the century, Quebec also began to move towards restricting the system. A series of statutes were enacted, aiming, like those of Ontario, to prohibit subsidized intra-provincial migration and the voting of bonuses for firms in industries already established in the town, and to stop the obvious conflicts of interest.[227] These restrictions were vehemently opposed by Sherbrooke, whose real estate speculators saw in bonusing the key to keeping up real estate values by raising industrial demand for sites and increasing the population.[228]

In the West, where bonusing was not rampant in any event, it was further inhibited by legislative discouragement. A number of cities in Alberta had clauses placed in their charters expressly forbidding the granting of any sort of bonus.[229] Some bonusing still went on in the western provinces, serving to transfer income, in the words of the *Grain Growers' Guide,* into "pockets already bulging with the gains of an unjust economic system."[230]

Bonusing was an exceedingly wasteful process, fraught with abuses. Yet it is clear that bonusing fulfilled a need. The great majority of bonuses were voted for *fixed* capital formation. The municipalities were performing an important role in filling a gap in the capital market left by the private intermediaries, who channelled off funds to commerce, and at best advanced to industry only circulating capital — and reluctantly at that. Furthermore, the bonusing system was central to determining the distribution of the existing industrial capacity. Ontario's bonuses favoured such things as secondary iron and steel and agricultural implements; Quebec's tended to develop textiles, boots and shoes, and other consumer goods industries. Within Quebec, bonusing helped diffuse industry from Montreal to other towns. In Ontario it moved industrial capacity from the U.S. and it redistributed it among various major centres, but not out of Toronto. Some Ontario cities, like Hamilton, gained; others, like Brantford, lost heavily and went into secular decline.

Notes to Chapter X111

1.   *MT,* April 18, 1878, p. 1295.
2.   *CE,* June 1894, p. 89.
3.   *CE,* Aug. 1894, p. 126; May 1895, p. 22; June, 1896, p. 55; March 1898, p. 332; *MT,* Aug. 12, 1898, p. 203.
4.   *MT,* April 5, 1901, p. 1319; Dec. 13, 1901, p. 757; March 28, 1902, p. 1269.
5.   W. L. Morton, *Manitoba, A History,* p. 260.
6.   *CMJ,* Nov. 1909, p. 546.
7.   *MT,* July 26, 1878, p. 119; April 18, 1879, p. 1296.
8.   *CE,* June 1896, p. 55; Aug. 1896, p. 118.
9.   *CE,* March 1896, p. 312.
10. *CE,* Jan. 1897, p. 272; *MT,* March 19, 1897, p. 1251.
11. *MT,* Sept. 24, 1897, p. 403; March 4, 1898, p. 1155.
12. *MT,* Dec. 3, 1897, p. 720; Nov. 17, 1899, p. 648.
13. *MT,* Aug. 18, 1878, p. 1296; Dec. 26, 1879, p. 744; Jan. 2, 1880, p. 771; Aug. 13, 1880, p. 176.
14. *MT,* Oct. 25, 1878, p. 529.
15. *MT,* Feb. 14, 1890, p. 995; June 13, 1890, p. 1548.
16. *MT,* July 14, 1899, p. 49.
17. R. Radosh, "American Manufacturers, Canadian Reciprocity and the Origins of the Branch Factory System," p. 34.
18. *Farming World,* June 15, 1906, p. 413.
19. *MT,* Feb. 23, 1900, p. 1112; Sept. 14, 1900, p. 337; *CE,* Jan. 1899, p. 264; Feb. 1899, p. 294; Dec. 1899, p. 233; Feb. 1900, p. 281; July 1900, pp. 62 - 3; Aug. 1900, p. 81; March 1901, p. 245; June 1901, p. 315.
20. *MT,* Feb. 27, 1903, p. 1164; April 24, 1903, p. 1446.
21. *CE,* Jan. 1896, p. 252; Sept. 1896, p. 152.
22. *CE,* Feb. 1900, p. 281.
23. *CE,* Aug. 1895, p. 100.
24. *MT,* March 10, 1899, p. 1185; Nov. 17, 1899, p. 648.
25. *LG,* Sept. 1902, p. 138.
26. *MT,* April 12, 1901, p. 1342.
27. *CM,* July 21, 1882, p. 345.
28: *MT,* Oct. 27, 1876, p. 474.

29.   *MT,* March 16, 1877, p. 78.
30.   *MT,* Nov. 22, 1878, p. 99.
31.   *CM,* Feb. 3, 1882, p. 41.
32.   *JC,* Jan. 3, 1881, p. 90.
33.   *MT,* Jan. 12, 1882, p. 771.
34.   *MT,* July 8, 1881, p. 36.
35.   *CM,* Nov. 18, 1887, p. 328.
36.   *MT,* Jan. 27, 1881, p. 917.
37.   *MT,* April 5, 1878, p. 1172; May 10, 1878, p. 1314.
38.   *CM,* Jan. 20, 1882, p. 25; *MT,* Nov. 9, 1883, p. 512.
39.   *MT,* July 6, 1883, p. 9.
40.   *MT,* March 3, 1882, p. 1077; Sept. 21, 1888, p. 322.
41.   *MT,* Jan. 6, 1882, p. 817; Aug. 5, 1881, p. 158; Feb. 9, 1883, p. 875; Oct. 29,
      1886, p. 490; *et passim.*
42.   *MT,* Sept. 25, 1891, p. 366.
43.   *RCRLC, Ontario Evidence,* p. 975.
44.   *JC,* Dec. 26, 1878, p. 606.
45.   *JC,* June 3, 1881, p. 489.
46.   *MT,* April 19, 1881, p. 1263; July 22, 1881, p. 95.
47.   *CM,* Feb. 17; 1882, P. 56; *CM,* Feb. 3, 1882, p. 41.
48.   *MT,* May 9, 1879, p. 1383.
49.   *Statutes of Nova Scotia,* 1879, 42 Vic. Chap. 27.
50.   *Statutes of Nova Scotia,* 1885, 48 Vic. Chap. 50.
51.   *Statutes of Nova Scotia,* 1899, 62 Vic. Chap. 24.
52.   *MT,* May 20, 1881, p. 1346; *CM,* May 26, 1882, p. 199.
53.   *MT,* Dec. 6, 1878, p. 717.
54.   *MT,* April 12, 1878, p. 1201.
55.   *MT,* Jan. 24, 1879, p. 918.
56.   *MT,* Oct. 3, 1879, p. 407; Oct. 31, 1879, p. 520.
57.   *MT,* April 23, 1880, p. 1254.
58.   *MT,* Dec. 24, 1880, p. 726.
59.   *MT,* April 21, 1881, p. 1232.
60.   *CE,* Oct. 1899, p. 174.
61.   *MT,* May 13, 1881, p. 1321.
62.   *CM,* March 17, 1882, p. 99; *MT,* April 14, 1882, p. 1260.
63.   *CM,* Aug. 4, 1882, p. 410; Aug. 18, 1882, p. 430.
64.   *CM,* March 31, 1882, p. 120.
65.   *MT,* May 25, 1883, p. 1319; July 6, 1883, p. 9.
66.   *CM,* March 31, 1882, p. 119.
67.   *CE,* June 1898, p. 52.
68.   *MT,* May 27, 1898, p. 1546.
69.   *MT,* April 8, 1898, p. 1317.
70.   *CE,* July 1900, p. 62.
71.   *MT,* Dec. 1, 1906, p. 784.
72.   *MT,* April 21, 1876, p. 1213; Oct. 13, 1876, p. 419; April 20, 1877, p. 1200.
73.   *CM,* May 12, 1882, p. 179.
74.   *CM,* Feb. 17, 1882, p. 58.
75.   *CM,* Feb. 3, 1882, p. 41.
76.   *MT,* Sept. 30, 1898, p. 438.
77.   *CM,* Jan. 20, 1893, p. 37.
78.   *MT,* July 20, 1907, p. 103.
79.   *MT,* April 13, 1883, p. 1144.
80.   *CE,* Oct. 1901, p. 424.
81.   *MT,* April 10, 1896, p. 1295; July 29, 1898, p. 136; Dec. 13, 1901, p. 761.

82.   *MT*, July 6, 1900, p. 11; July 19, 1901, p. 74; Aug. 23, 1901, p. 229.
83.   *CE*, April 1896, p. 339; May 1895, p. 21; Nov. 1902, p. 307; *MT*, Jan. 8, 1892, p. 807.
84.   *MT*, March 16, 1877, p. 1051; May 25, 1877, p. 1352; Nov. 16, 1877, p. 584.
85.   *MT*, Sept. 14, 1888, p. 294.
86.   *MT*, Oct. 5, 1888, p. 380.
87.   *CE*, April 1896, p. 340; April 1899, p. 354; Oct. 1900, p. 126; Jan. 1901, p. 192; Nov. 1901, p. 449.
88.   *CE*, Dec. 1894, p. 245; *MT*, May 27, 1892, p. 1425; *CE*, Feb. 1898, p. 299.
89.   *CM*, Jan. 20, 1893, p. 37.
90.   See esp. T. W. Acheson, *The Social Origins of Canadian Industrialism*, p. 204.
91.   *CE*, Dec. 1898. pp. 230, 232.
92.   *CM*, Aug. 18, 1882, p. 43.
93.   *CM*, Jan. 6, 1882, p. 6.
94.   *MT*, April 21, 1882, p. 1289.
95.   *CM*, March 31, 1882, p. 120; *MT*, July 4, 1879, p. 35.
96.   *MT*, April 17, 1885, p. 1193.
97.   *CE*, Aug. 1898, p. 114; Nov. 1899, p. 214; July 1900, p. 63.
98.   *MT*, Sept. 21, 1888, p. 331.
99.   *MT*, Oct. 27, 1876, p. 474; July 27, 1877, p. 123; Oct. 12, 1877, p. 471.
100. *MT*, May 26, 1882, p. 1443.
101. *CE*, Aug. 1902, p. 222; *MT*, Sept. 1, 1893, p. 253; June 5, 1896, p. 1564; April 14, 1899, p. 1345.
102. *MT*, May 23, 1902, p. 1523.
103. *CM*, Feb. 3, 1882, p. 41.
104. *MT*, Aug. 26, 1881, p. 255; Sept. 9, 1881, p. 309.
105. *MT*, May 16, 1902, p. 1481.
106. *CE*, Aug. 1900, p. 81; Feb. 1901, p. 215.
107. *MT*, Dec. 6, 1878, p. 717.
108. *MT*, May 5, 1880, p. 1047.
109. *MT*, July 4, 1884, p. 8.
110. *MT*, May 20, 1881, p. 1345; Nov. 11, 1881, p. 570.
111. *MT*, March 9, 1888, p. 1124; Nov. 23, 1888, p. 583.
112. *MT*, Nov. 22, 1895, p. 660.
113. *MT*, Oct. 11, 1895, p. 463; June 6, 1902, p. 1573.
114. *CE*, Oct. 1897, p. 175; *MT*, Sept. 24, 1897, p. 402; *MT*, Jan. 14, 1898, p. 915; July 6, 1900, p. 7.
115. *CE*, Jan. 1900, p. 257.
116. *MT*, June 3, 1898, p. 1579.
117. *MT*, Aug. 10, 1900, p. 171; Oct. 12, 1900, p. 463; Oct. 26, 1900, p. 505; Nov. 23, 1900, p. 651.
118. *MT*, Dec. 20, 1901, p. 776; Jan. 16, 1903, p. 942.
119. *MT*, Nov. 4, 1892, p. 515; Dec. 8, 1893, p. 698.
120. *SCM* (1885), p. 16.
121. *CE*, Dec. 1894, p. 245; March 1895, p. 329; Jan. 1896, p. 251; March 1896, p. 312; Oct. 1896, p. 179.
122. *CE*, Nov. 1895, p. 193; Dec. 1895, p. 219; Nov. 1896, p. 210; March 1896, p. 313; Dec. 1898, p. 231.
123. *MT*, Dec. 9, 1881, p. 698.
124. *Statutes of Nova Scotia*, 42 Vic. Chap. 27.
125. *MT*, March 21, 1881, p. 1093.
126. *CE*, March 1899, p. 325.
127. *CE*, Jan. 1896, p. 253.
128. *CMJ*, April 1909, p. 172.

129. *MT*, Feb. 12, 1904, p. 1059.
130. *CMJ*. Oct. 1909, p. 506.
131. *CE*, Aug. 1896, p. 118; *MT*, March 24, 1899, p. 1251.
132. *CE*, Feb. 1895, p. 302.
133. *MT*, Sept. 24, 1910, p. 1315; Oct. 1, 1910, p. 1417.
134. *CE*, Oct. 1899, p. 156; *CE*, March 1902, p. 74.
135. *MT*, Nov. 9, 1907, p. 741.
136. *MT*, Dec. 10, 1886, p. 661.
137. *MT*, April 26, 1895, p. 1382; April 2, 1897, p. 1317.
138. *CE*, Aug. 1898, p. 113; Nov. 1898, p. 202; *MT*, April 27, 1894, p. 1350.
139. *CE*, Dec. 1894, pp. 245 — 6.
140. *MT*, Sept. 28, 1900, p. 392; *CMJ*, Nov. 1909, p. 547.
141. British Columbia, Royal Commission of Inquiry into the Conduct of the
     Affairs of the Municipal Council of Victoria, *Report*, 1892, p. 484.
142. *CE*, March 1896, p. 313.
143. *MT*, Oct. 5, 1895, p. 439; Oct. 29, 1897, p. 560; May 13, 1898, p. 1477.
144. *MT*, Feb. 16, 1877, p. 925.
145. *MT*, July 6, 1900, p. 12; July 20, 1900, p. 75.
146. *CM*, April 15, 1887, p. 111.
147. *CE*, Dec. 1896, p. 240; Jan. 1897, p. 272.
148. *CE*, Oct. 1894, P. 188.
149. *MT*, Nov. 11, 1887, p. 605.
150. *MT*, May 26, 1882, p. 6; Sept. 1, 1893, p. 253.
151. *MT*, Feb. 4, 1898, p. 1017.
152. D. M. Henderson, *Robert McLaughlin*, p. 17; *CE*, Jan. 1900, p. 257; *MT*,
     Jan. 19, 1900, p. 933.
153. *MT*, Jan. 3, 1890, p. 802.
154. *CE*, June 1901, p. 305; April 1901, p. 269; *MT*, Feb. 12, 1897, p. 1072.
155. *CE*, Oct. 1897, p. 175.
156. *CE*, June 1895, p. 48.
157. *CE*, Dec. 1899, p. 234.
158. *MT*, May 6, 1887, p. 1308.
159. *CE*, Nov. 1898, p. 202.
160. *CE*, Dec. 1898, p. 230.
161. *MT*, May 24, 1889, p. 1350; Sept. 13, 1887, p. 320.
162. *CE*, Dec. 1898, p. 230.
163. *CE*, Dec. 1901, p. 478; March 1902, p. 74.
164. *MT*, May 10, 1889, p. 1294; July 6, 1889, p. 19.
165. *CE*, Jan. 1900, p. 258; *MT*, Oct. 16, 1891, p. 455.
166. *CE*, Jan. 1896, p. 251.
167. *CE*, Nov. 1898, p. 213.
168. *CE*, Jan. 1895, p. 269.
169. *CE*, May 1896, p. 23.
170. *CM*, Jan. 18, 1895, p. 74.
171. *CE*, Dec. 1897, p. 243; Jan. 1898, p. 274; *MT*, Dec. 3, 1897, p. 753.
172. *CE*, Nov. 1898, p. 202.
173. *CE*, Sept. 1900, p. 109.
174. *MT*, Jan. 25, 1897, p. 1695; Aug. 4, 1899, p. 139.
175. *CM*, April 14, 1882, p. 138.
176. *CE*, Oct. 1897, p. 175.
177. *RCRLC, Ontario Evidence*, p. 179.
178. *RCRLC, Ontario Evidence*, pp. 180, 364-374, 389; *MT, Annual*, Jan. 1914,
     pp. 28-30.
179. *MT*, May 20, 1887, p. 1368.
180. *CE*, Nov. 1896, p. 210.

181. *CM*, Jan. 6, 1893, p. 18.
182. *CE*, Jan. 1894, p. 263.
183. *CE*, Aug. 1896, p. 118.
184. *CE*, Sept. 1896, p. 151.
185. *CMJ*, Feb. 1909, p. 73.
186. *MT*, Dec. 3, 1897, p. 722.
187. *MT*, Oct. 1, 1901, p. 1417.
188. *CE*, Nov. 1895, P. 192.
189. *MT*, April 29, 1911, p. 1711.
190. *CE*, Jan. 1896, p. 253.
191. *LG*, May 1904, p. 1104.
192. *MT*, May 19, 1905, p. 1557.
193. *CE*, June 1902, p. 168; July 1902, p. 193; *MT*, April 25, 1902, p. 1383.
194. *MT*, May 10, 1895, p. 1453.
195. *MT*, Dec. 3, 1910, p. 2314; see also Nov. 26, 1910, p. 2215.
196. *CE*, June 1900, p. 37.
197. *CE*, Dec. 1894, p. 245.
198. *MT*, June 3, 1911, p. 2211.
199. *CE*, July 1896, p. 88.
200. *MT*, March 30, 1900, pp. 1288-9.
201. *MT*, April 13, 1900, p. 1356.
202. *CE*, Nov. 1897, p. 21.
203. *MT*, April 6, 1900, p. 1314.
204. Dominion Board of Trade, *First Annual Report*, p. 28.
205. Toronto Board of Trade, *Annual Report*, 1906, pp. 9-10.
206. *RCRLC, Report*, pp. 33-34.
207. *MT*, Oct. 19, 1900, p. 492.
208. *FA*, March 3, 1908, p. 1842.
209. *MT*, March 16, 1887, p. 185.
210. *MT*, July 18, 1884, p. 63; W. Plewman, *Adam Beck and Ontario Hydro* pp. 19-21; *MT*, June 24, 1898, p. 1676.
211. *MT*, Dec. 5, 1890.
212. *MT*, June 16, 1899, p. 1641.
213. *CE*, Aug. 1902, p. 202; Dec. 1901, p. 477.
214. *MT*, Dec. 9, 1881, p. 696.
215. *MT*, July 29, 1887, p. 128.
216. *MT*, Dec. 3, 1910, p. 2314.
217. *MT*, June 3, 1890, p. 802.
218. *MT*, Aug. 27, 1897, p. 262.
219. *CM*, Aug. 5, 1887, p. 76; *MT*, April 18, 1879, p. 1296; Nov. 18, 1887, p. 328.
220. Ontario Legislature, *Journals*, vol. 21, 1888, *passim*. vol. 22, 1889, *passim*.
221. *Statutes of Ontario*, 1888, 51 Vic. Chap. 28.
222. *CE*, Aug. 1900, p. 81.
223. *MT*, Jan. 3, 1890, p. 802.
224. *CE*, March 1899, p. 324.
225. *Statutes of Ontario*, 1902, 2nd Ed. VII Chap. 29.
226. *Statutes of Ontario*, 1900, 63 Vic. Chap. 33.
227. Statutes of Quebec, 1899, 62 Vic. Chap. 41; 1901, 1st Ed. VII Chap. 28.
228. *MT*, March 27, 1900, p. 1268.
229. *MT*, Dec. 13, 1913, p. 893.
230. *GGG*, Aug. 21, 1912, p. 6.

We are rapidly passing to the same condition as that which obtains in the United States; corporations control the legislature, they control the government, they get everything they ask; the people get nothing. More and more of the heritage of the people is being handed over to the companies.

W. F. Maclean
House of Commons, 1904

Chapter XIV
The Rise of Big Business

Industrial and Commercial Organization

Whenever competition existed in Canada, so too, it seemed, did an effort by businessmen to avoid it. In this they were powerfully assisted by government policy, both by its presence in the form of high and rising tariffs and by its absence in the lack of enforceable combines legislation. Many combines from the beginning were continental in scope, involving associations of manufacturers, wholesalers, and retailers in Canada with manufacturers in the U.S. and even, on occasion, in Britain. The devices for the regulation of competition were many and varied, ranging from the gentlemen's agreement, to formal trade associations (often under the auspices of the Canadian Manufacturers' Association), to exchanges of directors. It included the vertical and/or the horizontal merger. And, less easy to document, but powerful in its economic impact in those few clear cases that did exist, was the interlocking of directorships and of stockholding between corporations performing ostensibly different economic functions but in fact mutually complementary.

Employers' associations were the most important basis for cartelization. An organization created nominally for such mundane purposes as tariff lobbying or quality standardization quickly became an association for normalizing the credit offered to customers, and from there formal price fixing was a logical next step. Quantity regulation and profit pooling often followed. The extent of employers' associations is impossible to document. In 1905, the Department of Labour published a list of 200 such associations, of which 80 claimed to have been formed since 1901. It was an incomplete list.[1] Just how much it underestimated the extent of association may be judged from the CMA's reaction to the formation of the Department of Labour and the questionnaires the new department circulated. At the 1901 general meeting of the CMA, the following exchange occurred with regard to one of the questionnaires.

> J.R. Shaw: I have never gone to the bother of filling it out myself, but have put it in the waste-paper basket, and I would like to know if that is the course that manufacturers are usually pursuing?
>
> The President: Mr. Shaw wished to know if the form is generally filled up, or consigned to the waste-paper basket.
>
> Chorus of Voices: The waste-paper basket.[2]

One rather characteristic sequence among combines was the transformation from cartel to merger. Initially, loose associations would exist, especially in industries or trades characterized by many small firms. Drop-outs would lead to problems of enforcing the rules, and a formal merger was frequently the only solution.

Mercantile Cartels

The largest and most powerful of the mercantile cartels was the Dominion Grocers' Guild, which had two roots in the early 1880's. In 1883, Toronto and Hamilton wholesale grocers formed a guild to stabilize prices and stop price cutting,[3] while in 1884 Montreal grocers organized their wholesale association to control the dating-ahead of invoices and other aspects of the long credit system. By 1887 their union had 95% of the wholesale grocers in Ontario and Quebec under control, as well as agreements with the sugar refiners and other producers to discriminate in favour of guild members in their pricing policy.[4] There was a striking similarity between developments in the grocery business and those in textiles two decades earlier: in both cases the wholesale merchants were able to assure their control over both producer and retailer by driving a wedge firmly between them. Individual industrialists agreed to deal exclusively with the Guild, and direct connections between retailer and industry were effectively blocked.[5] The Guild was sufficiently powerful to be able to force some English export houses to conform to its rules.[6]

Refined sugar was the most important single item in the grocery trade, and around it the combine arrangements tended to coalesce. Loss-leader sales and price cutting of sugar were curbed at the 1886 meeting of the Guild, with the co-operation of the refiners.[7] The curbs were renewed and the combine steadily expanded. In 1890, seemingly to celebrate the passage of Canada's first so-called anti-combines legislation, the Guild began openly advertising in newspapers the terms on which its members were bound to do business.[8]

The point of the agreement with the refiners was to stop the ruinous competition among the army of retail merchants, and to maintain retail prices. After the combine was effected, retail prices were closely controlled, and price increases exacted from the retailers by the wholesalers were uniformly passed on to the consumer.[9]

In 1892 the agreement on sugar was broken, and cut-throat competition emerged among the myriad of petty retailers backed by the big wholesale houses. Order was restored; then, in late 1894 and early 1895, the combine again broke down, partly because of the dumping of German beet sugars. In early 1897, many wholesale grocers stocked up on sugar, awaiting the tariff *increase* that the Conservatives had led them to expect. The Liberal victory led to tariff decreases, and a lot of dumping resulted. But the cartel got back into business within a few months.[10]

The organization spread from coast to coast, and its stranglehold over trade increased. The principle of strict division of function between wholesaler, retailer, and producer remained its fundamental tenet. In 1904, the Wholesale Grocery Company was refused supplies from the sugar refineries, canneries, starch manufacturers, and other suppliers because the firm was not a member of the Guild, and the Guild refused it membership on the grounds that part of its business was retail.[11] This firm, a co-operative, filed an information against the Guild with the Attorney-General of Ontario, and the Guild was charged with combination in restraint of trade. The case was dismissed by the Court, who contended that

> the proper method of distribution of goods is from the manu-facturer, through the wholesale dealer, to the retailer, then to the consumer, because *this is the most economical* method.[12]

The logic was bizarre, for if the division of function were the most economical, it would hardly have required a combine to maintain it. And in any event, it was a rear guard decision, for the tendency was already underway for the elimination of the middleman in industrial and commercial organization. The decision simply helped delay this rational reorganization of the Canadian distributive mechanism whose absurdities played a major role in raising retail prices. It also opened the door for further exactions of the Guild.

The wholesalers' organization provoked a defensive move on the part of those retailers who were in a position to combine. In 1886 a Retail Grocers' Association met in Montreal to complain of manufacturers and jobbers in certain lines selling direct to customers, and of the effects of the wholesale combine on prices. The sugar cartel with the refiners brought renewed protests in 1887, and in 1891 a new, more complete association was formed to offset the power of the combine.[13] In 1910 the Retail Merchants' Association of Canada received a federal charter, and this far-reaching and powerful reorganization celebrated its birth by trying, albeit without success, to block the passage of a co-operatives bill sponsored by the Grain Growers' Grain Association in the federal Parliament.[14]

While not cartels in the strict sense of the term, a series of commercial travellers' associations sprang up to bargain collectively with the railways and to regulate trade conditions. These tended to follow regional patterns, headquartered in various cities which aspired to commercial leadership of their environs. The first was the Commercial Travellers' Association of Canada, formed in 1871 after Hamilton, Toronto, and Montreal commercial houses began to become active in the Maritime market.[15] It was a Toronto-dominated association, and in 1875 A. F. Gault, James Cooper, Robert Simpson, and other Montreal notables in drygoods, groceries, and hardware broke off to form the rival Dominion Commercial Travellers' Association. It was followed by the London-based Western Commercial Travellers' Association.[16]

In addition to bargaining with railroads for special rates for the commercial travellers and their merchandise, the associations were important political lobbies for breaking down regional barriers to commerce. Cases were fought in the courts to stop Maritime and Quebec municipalities from imposing discriminatory taxes against commercial travellers in favour of their own merchants.[17] To defend local prerogatives, new associations sprang up: the leading wholesale merchants of Nova Scotia, including T.E. Kenny, formed the Eastern Commercial Travellers' Association in 1881, and by 1887 the North West Commercial Travellers' Association was in operation, though the Western had since been absorbed by the Toronto-based organization.[18] To increase their bargaining power with the railways, the associations began to negotiate as a unit with them in 1887,[19] the first step towards full integration. Another of their functions requiring collective regulation was long credit. During boom and bust alike, great armies of commercial travellers were sent out by the wholesale dealers, and their dispensation of credit to their customers led to serious losses.[20]

A powerful mercantile combine existed among the coal dealers of Toronto, Ottawa, Montreal, London, and other major central Canadian cities. In Toronto, the Board of Trade was a veritable incubator of cartels, and the Coal Trade Branch was one of its more insidious offspring. All of Toronto's coal was American anthracite. In 1881, a coal ring was formed among the Toronto dealers led by Elias Rogers to push up prices following the tariff, but it was broken by one firm. Another attempt followed in 1883, broken once again by the same firm.[21] Later that year, the U.S. anthracite producers sent representatives to Toronto to impose order among the dealers, who had been engaged in price cutting, by threatening to curtail supplies.[22] Subsequent arrangements embraced the American suppliers in a wholesale price fixing arrangement, and this proved more successful. If any retailer broke the rules, he was fined and the proceeds were divided among the import cartel.[23] Again the objective was to drive a wedge between producers and retailers. The American producers' combine, the Western Anthracite Association, co-operated because of earlier enormous losses from failures of retailers running amok in Canada under the aegis of the long credit system.[24]

In Ottawa, London, and Montreal, the same pattern existed of a coal combine affiliated with the Board of Trade and with connections to the American exporters.[25] No coal combine operated in the Maritimes, and in central Canadian cities where it was inoperative, prices were much lower. Where the cartels did function it was common practice for manufacturers and other large organizations to import their own coal, the burden of the combine thus falling on the working-class consumer.[26]

Mercantile combines with international connections operated in a number of fields in central Canada from the late 1880's, including egg dealers, watch jobbers, and undertakers who were notorious for their frauds.[27] In some cases more than one combine existed, but with market division agreements between them.

Formal reorganization of merchandising in the central and eastern provinces into the department store and chain store was slow. To the extent that restructuring did occur, it involved both the growth of industry into assuming its own sales function and the squeezing of the myriad of petty traders by corporate chain stores.

One example of the first of these trends had occurred in the meat packing industry. In 1890, Ontario émigré Patrick Burns established himself as a livestock dealer in Calgary, and in 1894 he acquired his first packing house. Thereafter he began a series of retail operations in the mining districts of B.C. and later on the prairies. Two further packing plants were added in Vancouver and in Edmonton, such that by 1914 the Burns system embraced three packing plants and over 100 retail shops. Similarly, Gunn's Ltd., the Ontario firm that had produced the Maple Leaf brands of meats since 1873, formed a partnership in 1901 with Charles Langlois and Co., a large Montreal retail food firm, to supply Quebec. The new enterprise, Gunn, Langlois and Co. Ltd., established a series of cold storage plants and branch packing houses across Ontario and even into the Maritimes, as well as warehouses in major centres. By 1911 they had branched into poultry and egg plants throughout Ontario and Quebec, making the firm probably the Canadian leader in the evolution of the new integrated agribusiness mode of production.[28]

In some small towns in Ontario the department store idea grew up as a defensive move by small shopkeepers who merged their various lines of business into one store to cut overhead and fight the drain of business to the big cities.[29] In 1897, too, legislative authority was sought in Ontario to enable any municipality with over 30,000 people to impose special taxes on stores doing more than three distinct kinds of business.[30] Nonetheless, until the war, the small trader remained the dominant mode of distributing commodities.[31]

In the West there were two outstanding contributions to Canada's roster of commercial cartels. 1892 saw first meeting of an organization that long after blighted the prairie farm community, the Western Retail Lumbermen's Association.[32] At first the association embraced the three prairie provinces, but the Alberta dealers broke off to form their own cartel, with no effect on the structure of prices since the dealers respected each others' territory. Both cartels had combine arrangements with the B.C. timber and shingle mills to deal only with their members,[33] and the CPR collaborated by posting combine price lists in its stations — until a commission of enquiry was established, at which point the railway ordered the price lists torn down and destroyed lest they fall into the investigators' hands.[34] Besides price maintenance, the lumber dealers regulated credit conditions. Farmers in the West bought lumber on credit and paid ten per cent on their notes to the lumber firms before the due date, twelve per cent after, and gave the dealers lien notes on almost all their property not tied up already by the banks, mortgage companies, or implement dealers.[35]

The CPR was also active in the creation and maintenance of

the western cattle dealers' combine arrangements. In 1906, the Gordon, Ironside and Fares Co. controlled 75% of the cattle exported from Canada. They also had market sharing arrangements with the other dealers and packing firms. The CPR gave the firm secret rebates on the export of horses and cattle under an agreement negotiated by Van Horne. In addition, the CPR's own stockyards were managed by the company.[36] The result was solid price maintenance. Farmers who brought livestock for sale received only one bid. The agreements covered all facets of packing as well as dealing and distribution. The big abattoirs were controlled by the large cattle dealing firms, though the extent of the integration was sometimes hidden. Gordon, Ironsides, for example, adopted the rather modern trick of paying higher prices on the cattle "bought" from their own ranches than from independents to hide their profits.[37] The result of the integration and price maintenance was that butchers who did their own buying, slaughtering, and retailing could make 46% profit and still retail cheaper than the big abattoirs sold wholesale. The problem was to find such an independent firm. In 1908 the big abattoirs were recording profits of up to 60%.[38] What the real rate of profit was, after allowance for manipulation of transfer prices, is impossible even to begin to estimate.

The Cotton Industry

Among the most strenuous cartelization attempts by an important industry were those made by the chronically over-extended cotton producers. Efforts had begun after the crisis in 1883. Several banks, including the Federal, the Nova Scotia, and the Montreal, had made heavy advances to some of the mills and insisted on cartelization and cutbacks as a precondition of further advances.[39] Under David Morrice's auspices, a meeting of the major producers proposed several solutions, including closing the mills one week per month (which held the danger of having the unemployed operatives drifting off to the New England mills) and an eight-hour day (which met with considerable opposition).[40] Agreement was finally reached, and quickly broken, for the mills to shut down each Monday and each Thursday night, to cut output by one-third, and to try to diversify as much as possible. The Canadian mills were all built to produce the same run of grey goods thanks to the energetic sales pitch of the English machinery manufacturers. A bond was posted by all the members, with penalties for breaking the rules, and an association known as the Cotton Manufacturers' Association was established to police the arrangement. Its president was D. McInnis; A. F. Gault held the vice-presidency; and Clayton Slater and David Morrice were among its executive committee members.[41]

With Morrice's assignment came the end of the first cotton cartel, and despite the tariff being increased to 35%, *ad valorem* conditions in the industry were chaotic for sometime. The Park and Sons mill in St. John cut back capacity in 1884 and began to lose its skilled operatives, who drifted back to England from where they had been imported.[42] Then in 1885 it failed completely, with heavy stockholder losses.[43] Its American mortgage holdee foreclosed, then reorganized and reopened the mill a few years later.[44] In the interim the Galt mill had also failed, while that of Windsor, Nova Scotia, ran up heavy losses following Morrice's assignment.[45] Despite the difficulties of the industry, Alex Gibson, the New Brunswick lumber king, built a new mill at Marysville in 1885 , and imputed all contrary advice to a conspiracy by the central Canadian mills to keep out new entrants.[46]

In 1886, another conference with all the mills represented was held in Montreal to try to achieve a consensus on prices and credit terms, to cut back output, and to prohibit practices like dating-ahead of invoices or altering the terms of sales by gifts, etc. Proposals were made for Saturday closure, with the association's officers being empowered to order one-week shutdowns at their discretion.[47] Agreement proved impossible. But the next year a new conference of all the mills but the Gibson did manage to fix prices and renew a bond of agreement.[48] Sixteen mills, including four in the Maritimes, were included. The Gibson mill stayed out, but promised to adhere to the rules.[49] The Chambly mill made the same promise but did not honour it. By 1888 the agreement was in disarray again, though some diversity of output had been achieved.[50]

The Dundas mill announced in May it would pull out of the combine.[51] While the Gibson mill agreed to join, the St. Croix mill immediately pulled out because of an intense rivalry between the two New Brunswick mills.[52] The final breakup led to price declines,[53] but even then the deflation continued. The Windsor, Nova Scotia, mill collapsed. Ontario mills cut back to only partial capacity without any combine agreement. Over the period 1882-1889 the Moncton mill paid only one dividend of two and one half per cent, while those in Stormont, Brampton, Dundas, and Merriton paid none at all.[54] A new cartel agreement was formed in 1890 under A. F. Gault's tutelage to regulate prices and output,[55] but by then the lessons had been learned. Cotton illustrated well the difficulty of maintaining a cartel in an overextended industry during a period of secular deflation. As long as costs and prices in general are falling, the incentive to break ranks and cut prices is considerable: during a period of steady inflation the probability of such break-aways is considerably reduced. In this case it was clear that merger was the only solution to the stabilization problem, and for cotton, with its interlocking directorships at least in the Montreal area, its links to the banks, and its corporate organization, merger was a relatively easy step.

Efforts to merge the cotton mills actually began as early as 1884, when Clayton Slater began to pronounce in its favour following the Morrice failure. Slater's Brantford mill was one of those hit by serious problems of over-production.[56] In 1885, two of the mills, Hudon Cotton Co. and the St. Anne Spinning Co. merged under A. F. Gault, David Morrice, Jacques Grenier, and others. But virtually all directors of the two had been shared anyway,[57] so it was really more a minor reorganization than a serious merger effort. The first of these came in 1889 with a group of New York and English financiers.[58] It failed to materialize, but in 1890 A. F. Gault and David Morrice merged seven grey mills into Dominion Cotton Mills Ltd., and another seven mills into Canada Coloured Cotton Ltd. in 1892.[59] The Bank of Montreal provided interim financing until the bonds were sold.[60]

William Park's mill and that of Alex Gibson stayed out of the mergers. The Bank of Montreal and the combine tried without success to crush Park's mill, but it survived. In 1896 it took on Canada Coloured Cottons in a round of price cutting that became known as the Flannelette War.[61] Gibson's mill was really under combine control indirectly through the Bank of Montreal.[62] Many of the smaller Ontario and Quebec mills were closed down, including those at Merriton, Dundas, Chambly, Coaticook, and even Brantford despite the combine's promise at the time of purchase to keep it operational,[63] and despite the fact that the city fathers had obligingly offered to perform financial cartwheels on command to save it. Windsor, Nova Scotia, and Moncton were closed soon after, and the Gibson mill in 1910.[64]

In 1904 came the final solution to the cotton problem. Despite the 1890 and 1892 mergers, textile prices, including cottons, continued to fall. There was some rallying after 1896, but the price increases did not keep pace with those of other industrial products. In 1904 the major operations, Dominion Cotton Mills, the Merchants' Cotton Co. Ltd., Montmorency Cotton, and Colonial Bleaching and Printing Co., were merged into Dominion Textiles

Co. Ltd. by a syndicate of professional promoters headed by
Louis Forget. The earlier cotton merger had been typical of the
conservative, industrial merger of the era: the new one was an
omen of what the future held in store. For a total investment of
one million dollars, the syndicate of outside promoters under the
auspices of Royal Trust secured control. The common stock was
purchased for $500,000 and immediately paid dividends of 89%.
Then an enormous watering operation was mounted, with the
common stock revalued at $4.5 million and issued to the direc-
tors.[65] To pay dividends on such an overissue, prices had to rise
— and rise they did. In 1906 the industry appeared before the
Tariff Enquiry Commission pleading for higher protection on
the pretext that the mills could not run steadily and that the laid-
off workers tended to drift off to the U.S. With higher tariffs and
higher prices it was claimed they could pay higher wages.[66] And
to prove the point, in the 1907 crisis, in order to generate revenue
to pay dividends and interest on the enormous capitalization, a
wage cut of ten per cent was introduced.[67]

The Agricultural Implements Industry

The first successful efforts to cartelize the agricultural implements industry came in 1879 with the formation of the Ontario
Agricultural Implement Manufacturers' Association under the
presidency of James Noxon of Ingersoll.[68] Agreements to fix
prices, curtail output, and contract long credit followed in 1883.[69]

Mergers began early. The industry was superficially like
cotton, insofar as it made use from an early period of the corporate form in some of the leading firms — though John Watson,
and Frost and Wood, did not incorporate until the late 1890's
during a rush of industrial reorganizations among many firms.[70]
But in fact stockholding was largely confined to the family of the
entrepreneurs who had built up their firms from the handicraft
stage. The first major consolidation was the North American
Agricultural Implements Company at London in 1883. Although
the firm quickly moved out of implement manufacturing completely, the merger had several important characteristics. It was a
conglomerate merger of several firms in diverse lines of production, including, besides implement makers, a foundry and a
wagon manufacturer. And it was organized around American
patents, its directors including Charles Deere of the John Deere
Plough Co. who became president, and the president of the
Moline Wagon Co. of Illinois. Also included were Charles

Murray, president of the notorious Ontario Investment Association, one private banker, Winnipeg distributors, and the brewer John Labatt.[71]

The late 1880's were critical years for the industry as the decline in farm produce prices and consequent rise in the real burden of fixed interest debt brought distress to farm communities. Cut-throat competition prevailed for the existing trade, with a resultant squeeze on profits. Selling costs mounted, due to the expense of maintaining a vast array of dealers throughout Ontario and the Northwest.[72] Small towns could have up to a dozen different dealerships, each tied to a particular manufacturer. And the harvester price war that had broken out in the U.S. spread to Canada. E. Maxwell and Sons, which had shifted from Paris to St. Mary's in 1888 for a $30,000 bonus, failed in 1890. The next year John Watson was pronounced in financial difficulties. The Haggart Bros. of Brampton were rescued from failure by a loan of $75,000 from the town in 1888, exhausted the loan, and collapsed in 1891.[73]

That year saw the merger of Massey and Harris. In contrast to the cotton amalgamations of the period, this one was completely industrial in origin and involved no outside capital, and no water.[74] No plant closure followed. In fact, the year before Massey had absorbed a Sarnia implement firm. The only rationalization involved cutting back on the proliferation of agents in the Northwest.[75] A defensive merger of Woodstock's Patterson and Bros. and Brantford's J. O. Wisner and Son followed, both formerly private firms, now merged as an incorporated enterprise. But the new firm was absorbed by Massey-Harris the next year.[76]

Conditions for the smaller firms did not improve for some time. Farmers were still unable to meet their debts to the implement firms which, like the private bankers of the period and with identical results, had extended them credit. Just as the falling grain and produce prices brought down major Ontario private bankers, the firm of John Watson failed in 1895, followed by a smaller firm in Alliston, Ontario, and by one at St. Thomas in 1896.[77] In 1899, Canadian and American implement firms met in Chicago to fix prices,[78] but by then the deflation had given way to a secular rise in grain prices and the conditions of the industry had improved. A price advance of a mere 20% was decided upon for the year.

The big J. P. Morgan-inspired International Harvester merger in the U.S. spilled over to Canada only via the Hamilton branch plant, and by the takeover of Toronto's John Abell Engine and

Machine Co. and its integration into another American implement complex in 1902.[79] No further major merger effort among
the Canadian producers themselves was successfully mounted.
Instead, integration took two forms: diversification of product
lines and integration of complementary plant by takeover, or
cartel arrangements for marketing finished product. In 1901,
Frost and Wood moved into the production of seeding and cultivating machines by absorbing an Oshawa firm.[80] Massey-Harris
bought part control of the Bain Wagon Works of Woodstock,
and an interest in Brantford's Verity Plough Co. Cockshutt completed its range of output in 1912 by buying an interest in a
wagon factory and a carriage factory, both of which had been
previously tied to Cockshutt by an agreement whereby the
implement firm marketed their output in the West.[81] A year earlier, Frost and Wood and Cockshutt had merged their sales
departments and divided up the market, Cockshutt getting all of
Canada west of Peterboro and functioning there as Frost's exclusive agent, while Frost and Wood occupied a similar position for
the East.[82] On the international front, export price fixing arrangements were maintained. At one point, Ingersoll's Noxon Bros.
refused to participate, and pressure had to be mounted through
their banker to get them back into line.[83]

One industry inextricably related to agricultural implements
but which remained independent of them in organization was
the binder twine and cordage makers. In 1885 there were but two
such manufacturers in Canada, in Montreal and in New
Brunswick, joined by a Brantford firm in 1886 [84] and two others
by 1888. The costs of the output tended to be lower in Canada
than in the U.S., since hemp entered Canada free, but prices
were kept up by a cartel arrangement that embraced both the
Canadian producers and the American companies who controlled the world supply of raw material from the Philippines.[85]
The final product was subject to a tariff in Canada until 1897.

In 1890, American manufacturers and merchants joined
Montreal cordage merchants to create two new joint stock firms,
Dominion Cordage and Consumers' Cordage, the last of which
included J. F. Stairs as a participant. Within a year all of the
independent companies had been absorbed by Consumers'.[86]
Two thousand farmers reacted by establishing a co-operative in
1893 in Brantford, the city which had hosted the last of the string
of firms absorbed by the mergers in 1891.[87] And to meet short-
ages that tended to emerge at harvest time, some production was
undertaken with convict labour in Kingston.[88] The growth of
prairie demand, too, led the New Brunswick plant to shift its

focus from the declining market in the shipbuilding industry to the grain growing areas of Canada — until it was absorbed by Consumers' Cordage.[89]

The removal of the duty on binder twine in 1897 led to sharp protests and threats of closure from the combine and its affiliates. None in fact closed, and in 1900 the Brantford co-operative declared a 90% dividend.[90] With the expanding demand from the improvement in primary product prices and increased grain cultivation, a series of new firms were established in Ontario.[91]

By 1903 most, if not all, of the producers were involved with the American producers in a price fixing and market division arrangement.[92] Then the American firms became greedy, and had the American government impose an export duty on manila fibre sent from the Philippines to non-American manufacturers.[93] At that time the Canadian market was already glutted: the Chatham plant which had opened only two years before had shut down completely, and even the Montreal combine was operating on a part-time basis only. Beginning in 1904, to avoid alienating farmers by the imposition of countervailing duties, the Laurier government instituted a system of subsidies equal to the American export duty to offset its effects. From 1904 until the U.S. tariff was withdrawn in 1913, $344,224 in subsidies were paid to the industry.[94] The withdrawal of the duty was followed by the restoration of the former system of direct control by American firms of the raw material, and therefore of the firms in the Canadian market dependent upon it. The Grain Growers' Association tried to induce British capital to establish a factory, but to no avail as the raw material monopoly of the American firms blocked them. Late in 1913, the Grain Growers' Grain Company, the western co-operative, tried another route by buying the Canadian rights to a U.S. patent of a knotter attachment that used binder twine made from threshed flax straw.[95] Whether the new technique succeeded in breaking the cartel is doubtful.

The Resource Industries

Early organization in the petroleum industry reflected the dichotomy that long existed between producers of crude and refiners. In 1869, the refiners organized on prices and output, and this immediately called forth a cartel among the well owners to do likewise. The crude association, however, wrecked itself very quickly by contracting to sell at $1.25 per barrel, only to have prices in the open market advance beyond $1.50.[96] Subsequent efforts to regulate the industry were made, especially after the tariff hike of 1873. Both crude and refined associations emerged, and succeeded in keeping Canadian prices more than 100% above American.

Canada was at that time the cheapest crude producer in the world, the costs of production averaging about two cents a gallon. But in Toronto a gallon of refined sold at 35-40¢, the same size gallon of Canadian refined yielding 15¢ in New York. In London, England, Canadian refined sold for 21¢; in London, Ontario, near the centre of the oil industry, it cost 35¢. These price differentials were the work of the refiners' association presided over by Major John Walker of London, (who was also vice-president of Hugh Allan's abortive CPR syndicate). The cartels collapsed after duties were cut by the Liberal administration in 1874.[97] Cartels in both crude and refined emerged and collapsed intermittently until the National Policy gave them a new lease on life.[98]

The immediate effect of the tariff was to produce a merger of four of the leading Canadian refiners into Imperial Oil in 1880.[99] The merger still did not control the majority of the refining capacity in Canada. An effort to coalesce 50% of the total refining plant in 1888 was unsuccessful.[100]

American capital moved into Canadian oil in the 1890's, including the Bushnell Oil Co., which soon became the centre of a coal oil cartel.[101] Standard Oil itself did not appear to be represented in oil refining, though by 1897 it had control of a gas company supplying Detroit, and it had a distribution system for its products throughout Ontario, including market sharing arrangements with local firms.[102] But the facts were somewhat different, for Bushnell had since become part of Standard and was secretly operating as its agent in the Canadian refining centres. Bushnell began a mini-merger movement among the small Canadian refiners, and a series of them were soon absorbed. Standard then set out to acquire Imperial. It secured from the Laurier government a change in the import regulations regarding containerization, which permitted it to undercut the Canadian tariff and swamp the market with cheap oil.[103] After Imperial was forced to sell, Standard arranged with the CPR and the Grand Trunk for special discriminatory rates against other American refiners which were equivalent to an increase in the tariff. Secured in its Canadian monopoly and insulated from American competition, Standard began putting the squeeze on Canadian consumers and manufacturers by raising fuel oil prices or cutting off supplies altogether.[104] The refining industry in Petrolia was eliminated as refining operations were centred in one Sarnia plant, and Petrolia began to depopulate. Objections from Canadian manufacturers led to a reduction in import duties from five to two and one half cents a gallon, just equal to the increase imposed by Standard after achieving its monopoly, and this was followed by crude oil bounties to stimulate production.[105]

The Nova Scotia coal mines had a long history of successful collective bargaining with Canadian governments on coal tariff levels. In 1885, an effort was made by a combine of mine owners to band together to raise money for a railroad to give them better access to the Intercolonial Railway.[106] But co-operation and integration do not seem to have gone beyond this stage until 1893, when the H.N. Whitney syndicate of Boston capitalists got busy following a visit to Boston by W.S. Fielding, then premier of the province. Under the terms of agreement with the Dominion Coal Company, the Nova Scotia government, direly in need of revenue, accepted an increase in coal royalties from ten to twelve-and-one-half cents in return for the granting of a 99-year lease on coal lands acquired, with provisions for another 20-year extension. All of the funds required to purchase existing leases, which had 54 years to run, and which would then be nominally surrendered to the province in return for new and longer leases, were acquired at inflated prices from their English and American owners by a bond issue. Thus a near-monopoly was achieved without any real investment by the promoters.[107] In addition, the province pledged itself to build a railway to move the coal to a Cape Breton port.

For a province which had just won a long and expensive struggle to extricate itself from the cupidity of the General Mining Association, it was a ludicrous arrangement. There was nothing in the lease which precluded the promoters from pocketing a large amount of the capital, and this was promptly done. The lease itself was bonded for $6.5 million.[108] And fifteen million in common shares were issued, plus three in preferred of which $12.5 million represented promoters' stock.[109] U.S. coal duties were obligingly lowered in 1894. Only the prospect of the increased exports following the tariff reduction would seem to justify the enormous amount of water in the stock. Nor did the correlation of American ownership and the reduction of duties pass without notice. The *Globe* took a dim view of the proceedings:

It will be noticed how cleverly the Yankees transact their affairs. They want our coal and pass a law to admit it to the United States free of duty. But it will be observed that before passing this law, they had already annexed our most valuable

coal mines. . . . The removal of their duty on coal is a rounda-
bout way of annexing a portion of our territory.[110]

Despite the fact that the duty was slashed from 75¢ to 40¢ per
ton of bituminous, the export trade growth was very slow. And
in 1897 the Dingley tariff restored the 75¢ duty. The Nova Scotia
syndicate then faced certain catastrophe with its absurdly
watered capital. It requested higher Canadian duties to give it
the Ontario market to offset the American loss.[111] This was
granted by the Laurier government: the Minister of Finance who
cheerfully introduced the legislation to tax Ontario consumers
and industry for the sake of a handful of Boston promoters was
none other than Whitney's old friend, W.S. Fielding.

Salt mining was another resource industry which, like coal,
had been plagued by overexpansion. A combine was active in
1871,[112] and the tariff and the assurance of higher prices led to a
round of undercutting of cartel rates,[113] but by 1882 the combine
was reconsolidated. This new cartel began openly to advertise its
existence and its terms of organization in newspapers, the following notice appearing in the Monetary Times.

SALT! SALT! SALT!

The Salt Manufacturers of Ontario having formed an Association and established a central office from which all sales will
be made except Table and Dairy Salt sold by proprietors, beg
respectfully to announce to the trade that all enquiries as to
prices and orders addressed to the Secretary will receive
prompt attention.[114]

The combine collapsed, re-established itself in 1885, and collapsed again. A new combine emerged in 1886[115] and was active
in the campaign for Reciprocity in 1890. In 1892 in the face of
sagging demand, new restrictions on output and the fixing of
prices were imposed. One firm broke the cartel, but was barred
by an interim injunction issued by a Goderich judge from doing
business contrary to the combine agreement.[116] So effective was
Canada's anti-trust legislation that cartels were enforceable in
court!

With the creation of Van Horne's Windsor Salt following the
strikes on CPR property, a new element was introduced into the
combine picture. The 1895 price hike[117] was broken by the
newcomer — without, it seems, any legal interference. By 1901,
Van Horne and other CPR magnates, Strathcona, Angus and
Shaughnessy together with George Cockburn, president of the
ill-fated Ontario Bank, organized a highly watered merger of salt
wells around the Windsor company, known as the Canadian Salt
Company.[118] It immediately entered an international salt cartel

with the British, American, and some other European producers, which held almost a complete monopoly of the world's salt refining capacity.[119]

In lumbering, the most effective efforts to organize the industry came in B.C., and dated from the virtual opening-up of the province to large-scale timber exploitation for export in 1892. That year, Victoria-based lumber firms formed an exchange to stabilize prices. Shingle mills began to organize in 1893 to prevent price cutting and overproduction. The American mills then began to export and undercut the B.C. mills, who were forced to follow suit or lose their prairie clientele.[120] From this flowed the cartel arrangements between the B.C. shingle and lumber mills and the prairie lumber dealers' associations. The results were sufficiently impressive to spark imitators, and in 1900 shingle manufacturers in New Brunswick, Quebec, and Maine formed a cartel and jumped their prices.[121] In B.C., however, shingle makers were still troubled by overproduction. In 1901 a centralized distribution plan through a Chicago agent was put into effect to try to stabilize prices.[122] In 1903 overproduction again threatened the cartel, and output was restricted by eliminating night shifts and one day shift in four in all mills.[123] More success seems to have crowned the lumber mills' restrictive efforts, for by 1901 they had formed an Association with their American Pacific Coast confreres, and in any event J.J. Hill was making moves towards buying up a lot of the milling capacity,[124] along with his myriad other Pacific Coast ambitions.

By that date two American monopolies had established themselves in mining. From 1900 on, Aluminum Ltd., the Canadian refining subsidiary of the Aluminum Company of America, sat on the international cartel as its parents' representative.[125] And in 1902, J. P. Morgan effected the merger of the American nickel mines and smelters in Canada along with a string of other companies into International Nickel,[126] giving U.S. Steel a virtual monopoly of the mining, refining, and sale of nickel. The only other large firm was the English Mond, and the two colluded effectively.[127] With their connections with the federal and Ontario governments in Canada, and the New York and London capital markets, they blocked any new entrants.[128]

The Food Processing Industry

Developments in cane sugar refining parallel those in cotton — rapid expansion after the National Policy, then drastic liquidation. Over 1884, sugar prices fell 40% and the Kenny-Stairs Nova

Scotia Sugar Refinery alone lost over $200,000. Difficulties were compounded by the fact that due to the method of customs valuation Montreal refiners paid lower duty on their raw requirements, and by the discrimination on the Intercolonial Railway, which gave better rates on raw than on refined sugar moving west.[129] The Moncton Refinery also lost heavily with the fall of prices.[130]

By 1886 some improvements were apparent. The Halifax refinery had absorbed the Woodside Sugar Refining Co. and closed it down, later selling the property in which $750,000 had been invested for $180,000.[131] The Halifax firm then reorganized and refinanced itself with the backing of the Merchants' Bank of Halifax.[132] The Maritime refiners secured the prohibition of yellow sugars, which competed with the low-grade Canadian, an increase of the tariff to 35% *ad valorem* plus one cent a pound, a reduction in freight rates from Halifax to Montreal, and the exclusion of imported beet sugar. As the refiners stressed, "the exclusion of beets means a West India trade for Nova Scotia."[133] Over 1887 the Halifax refinery paid thirteen per cent dividends, while Montreal's Canada Sugar Refinery declared only its usual ten. By late 1888 all debts incurred in reorganizing the Halifax refinery were discharged while the dividend over the year rose to 20%.[134] No cartel was actually required to squeeze out these dividend levels: in addition to the higher tariff, output for the industry as a whole was cut 20% by the burning down of the St. Lawrence refinery, to which the other refiners responded by advancing prices.[135] The Maritime refineries were able to exploit the space created and export to the Northwest.[136]

By 1890, conditions had improved sufficiently for reactivation of the Woodside refinery, which passed into the hands of an English syndicate formed to try to merge all the Canadian refineries, beginning with those in the Maritimes.[137] Permission for the merger of the three Maritime refineries was refused by Ottawa; to circumvent the ban of the merger the syndicate simply had the Acadia Sugar Refinery chartered under imperial statute and proceeded with the consolidation.[138] While the remaining refineries were not incorporated into the merger, a combine arrangement to fix prices was operational.[139] Further merger activity was probably impeded by changes in the tariff. In 1895, to raise badly needed revenue, the Conservative government taxed raw sugar,[140] while Laurier in 1897 kept the raw sugar tariff intact and reduced the refined duty. This drew immediate protests from the West Indies merchants of Halifax, who feared for the loss of their carrying trade in the face of a growing world supply of bounty-fed beet sugar, especially from Germany.[141]

Response to the tariff of 1879 in the milling industry was mixed. Some firms took exception, and in 1886 the oatmeal mills of Ontario formed a combine[142] to lobby for Reciprocity. Before the Association was formed, Ontario alone had 60 mills. The four largest mills alone could have fulfilled the Dominion's total needs. In 1888 an arrangement was entered into whereby the mills ran only one day every two weeks, prices were fixed, and subsidies were paid to some mills not to run at all.[143] The arrangement proved unenforceable and quickly collapsed.[144] Difficulties were compounded by the subsequent establishment of branch plants of the big American cereal companies.[145]

Flour mills began to organize in Ontario in 1881, to regulate the use of credit in their sales. The competition of many small mills made the agreement to restrict credit unenforceable.[146] Excess capacity was again a problem. By 1890, the mills were running full time only two months a year.[147] Led by Ogilvie's, a flour milling merger was attempted in 1890 with the help of an English promoter, but without outside capital. This failed, but a cartel arrangement was evolved including the Hudson's Bay Milling Co., Lake of the Woods, and other leading producers.[148] At the same time the miller's association, now Canada wide, was agitating for tariff reform, for a new duty on American flour, and a change in the spread between the flour and wheat duties, which discriminated in favour of the maintenance and extension of the entrepot trade in American flour.[149] This was a long-standing complaint among Canadian millers, and it continued to be voiced, in addition to the fact that preference was given to the export of Canadian wheat over Canadian flour.[150]

The canning and packing industries fitted the familiar pattern of small firms, ease of entry encouraged by municipal bonusing, and resultant excess capacity and efforts at cartelization. In the vegetable canning industry there were 25 failures from 1885 to 1897, costing shareholders $300,000, yet new firms kept emerging.[151] The first to organize in the packing industry were the Ontario Pork Packers. In response to the tariff issue, they formed an association including both packers and wholesale distributors in 1879, calling for tariff stability.[152] In 1880, it made its first restrictive moves by agreeing on shorter credit conditions.[153] By the late 1880's, it had congealed into an effective unit lobbying for tariff increases, bitterly opposed by the lumbermen whose shanties were the source of much of the demand for the pork packers' products.[154]

Canada's fruit and vegetable packers and canners met first in 1883 to form a price fixing arrangement.[155] In 1894 came the creation of the more permanent Canadian Packers' Association including all but one of Canada's fruit and vegetable packers. The association agreed to make sales only through the wholesale grocers and appointed brokers, with a cash penalty for anyone breaking the arrangement. Output was to be cut 25%, and prices stabilized.[156] Over-entry was still a problem, and bumper crops led to releasing of the members from the combine agreement.[157] By 1905, in the first of a series of mergers, 24 Ontario factories were rolled into Canadian Canneries Company, a two million dollar venture.[158]

The multiplicity of salmon canneries on the Pacific Coast posed similar problems. By 1884 there were already twelve, and the province was still not opened up by the CPR. Dozens more small canneries were added over the next decade-and-a-half. In 1891 a merger of seven canners took place, the others refusing to join. In 1895 an English syndicate acquired a group of nine. But not until the 1897 cartel arrangement, fixing prices and output, was organization effectively imposed on the industry.[159] In 1902 a merger of 44 canneries into the B.C. Packers' Association was effected, with the support of the Bank of Montreal. Capital *issued* came to $2,740,000.[160] To pay dividends and interest, the corporation exploited its monopoly power to the full, reducing prices paid to Canadian fishermen until, by 1910, they fell to half the level received by American fishermen.[161]

In the tobacco industry, no cartels of any degree of success seem to have been organized before the 1900 mergers. The industry had been dominated by small firms and was one of the few in which Québécois competed on equal terms with Anglophone businessmen.[162] But by 1900 the market was consolidated and dominated by two foreign affiliates, the American Tobacco Company and the Empire Tobacco Company, American and British respectively, along with Macdonald's, the largest Canadian firm. The two foreign firms, as part of their international peace agreement, merged their Canadian subsidiaries into one firm operating under licence.[163] After the merger a number of small Canadian plants were bought up and closed to curtail output, in Joliette, Montcalm, and L'Assomption counties, including the Granby plant, and considerable unemployment as well as a substantial curtailment of farm incomes followed.[164] Competition from the remaining outside firms was reduced by the device of forcing dealers to sign exclusive contracts and to maintain retail prices. Macdonald's and the Anglo-American firms arrived at a market sharing arrangement. A Royal Commission declared the arrangements were legitimate and not in restraint of trade![165]

Iron and Steel Industries

The iron founders of Ontario and Quebec, many small firms just emerging from the handicraft stage, celebrated Confederation by the formation of the Canadian Iron Founders' Association to regulate the production of stoves. With the National Policy came the predicted flood of capital into the industry; within a decade its capacity was four times the level the Canadian market could support. By 1888 there were only 18 members from Ontario and Quebec in the Association, with at least 40 outside; hence its impact on the structure of competition appears to have been minor. Moreover, the activities of the Association were restricted to stoves, despite the fact that most founders produced a range of output including agricultural implements of a simple mechanical sort.[166]

Beginning in 1882, a parallel organization functioned in the Maritimes, with more success in fixing stove prices.[167] This association met annually to determine price adjustments and credit conditions.[168] The only early merger of consequence was the 1893 absorption by Rhodes, Curry and Co. of the St. John foundry, James Harris and Co.[169]

In Ontario by 1890 the Association was making renewed efforts to regulate the industry. As one member put it, "The tariff protected them from American competition — it was not enough. They needed protection from themselves."[170] In 1900, American promoters mounted an effort to merge all of the leading stove founders, but failed in the face of resistance from Gurney and other major firms.[171] An effort to effect a smaller merger two years later also came to naught.[172]

Several other cartels operated in various areas of the iron and steel industry. The Barbed Wire Association was a creature of the 1872 Patent Law, embracing all of the Canadian producers, all of whom were licensees of American firms.[173] The tariff of 1879 opened the way to price fixing as well,[174] and the combine succeeded in keeping Canadian prices charged to farmers well above the American level.[175]

One characteristic of the industry was the phenomenon of super-associations embracing a wide variety of interests who in turn also had sub-associations to look to their peculiar needs.[176] Thus, the barbed wire manufacturers were also members of the Iron and Steel Association of Canada. This organization held annual conventions at elegant hotels to fix prices and the terms of sale, that is, the credit terms that each firm offered — the openness of the proceedings being sufficient comment on

Canada's 1889 anti-combines legislation. Among the members of the club were the Montreal Rolling Mills, the Ontario Tack Co., Pillow-Hersey Manufacturing Co., H. R. Ives's Dominion Wire, the Canada Screw Company, the Safety Barbed Wire Co., and the Ontario Lead and Barbed Wire Co. Prices usually followed American trends. Price advances also followed the beginnings of the great expansion of the primary iron and steel industry in Canada, which, despite the switch from tariff to subsidy aid, led to a substantial increase in iron prices.[177]

One of the more volatile sub-associations was that of nail manufacturers, which regulated prices and credit conditions in co-operation with the American cartel. The American organization's exactions reached the point where American merchants were able to go to Europe, purchase nails exported there by the American combine, reimport them paying duty and transport costs, and still profitably undercut the combines' local prices. In Canada the nail makers averted dumping by the American cartel only by paying protection money in the form of a royalty on the output of Canadian factories to the American combine.

During gluts, selected factories in Canada were closed to curtail output and maintain prices.[178] It was standard practice to fix retail prices with the dealer. If stocks became excessive instead of lowering prices, the combine would announce increases. Merchants would then rush to purchase before the price hike went into effect, and the burden of carrying stock was then pushed onto the merchants. The Waterous company refused to participate in the nail combine, and the organization then sought to close it by withholding raw material, and subsidizing the nail making machinery producers not to deal with it.[179] Another problem of regulating production was posed by the Montreal Rolling Mills, which dropped out of the cartel in the face of excess capacity in 1896 and began cutting prices. Order was restored, however, and price fixing recommenced.[180]

In the pre-1907 period, two major mergers in the primary iron and steel industry occurred. In 1890, the Nova Scotia Steel and Forge Co. absorbed a New Glasgow mining company and was reorganized into the Nova Scotia Steel and Iron Co.[181] The General Mining Association properties were added in 1900, followed by a series of other local firms, and the merger was reorganized as Nova Scotia Steel and Coal Co.[182] Of its authorized capital of $9.5 million, some $4.12 million was issued. Several features of the merger stand out: its bonds were all sold in Canada, largely in the Maritimes with the help of the Bank of Nova Scotia,[183] control remained in the hands of the Maritime owners of the original firms, and a substantial sum was spent on enlarging and developing its works after the merger[184] — quite a contrast to the contractions that seemed to follow in the wake of some central Canadian efforts.

Equally successful for all but its original promoter was the reorganization of Francis Clergue's holdings into the Consolidated Lake Superior Corporation. Clergue's enterprises by 1901 represented an investment of nine million dollars, all of it from equity.[185] The 1903 reorganization valued the assets at nearly $28 million. Late in the year, scarcity of working capital was crippling the company. Wages were in arrears; workers, faced with starvation, were rioting. In 1904, the Ontario government guaranteed a two million dollar loan for the company, which fell into the hands of an American syndicate through the New York bank which made the loan. Clergue was relegated to a back seat.[186]

Consumers' Goods Industries

Cartels and mergers to achieve market power were found in virtually every facet of Canadian industry before the great merger waves after 1907. The first efforts by the paper manufacturers to organize came after the 1879 tariff, followed by similar abortive efforts in 1886 and 1892. Not until 1900 was success achieved, following a period of declining newsprint prices. The price decline was arrested and reversed by the manufacturers' cartel. The situation was also improved by the enormous demand for newspapers as a result of the Cuban and South African wars.[187] But demand factors alone did not account for the price rise, for over the same period that Canadian paper prices shot up, American prices of paper made from Canadian pulp fell.[188]

In 1889, Ontario's furniture manufacturers organized to find ways of regulating credit conditions in the industry,[189] and the association soon spread across much of Canada with price fixing power,[190] though it remained mainly based in Ontario, amply assisted by municipal bonuses. In 1899, Senator Robert Jaffray tried to promote a merger of 24 Ontario firms with the aid of British capitalists who were to take one-third of the equity. No bond issue was planned, nor were any issues outstanding, and the total mortgage debt of the component firms was only $80,-000, much of it non-interest-bearing in the form of bonus loans from municipalities.[191] But the Boer War led to an income tax hike in Britain, and the head office would have had to be located in Britain as a condition for the investment of British capital.

The Canadian manufacturers then went ahead themselves with the merger, and kept out all outside promoters. The primary objective of this company was to rationalize competition among a myriad of small firms and to develop an export trade, especially in Britain, as a vent for the surplus productive capacity.[192] The successful merger, the Canadian Furniture Manufacturers' Co., which controlled 75% of the total Canadian output, led to a scramble among Ontario towns to attract its headquarters.[193] Export trade was developed by the addition of a major exporting house to the merger, and the inclusion of a large number of independent firms into an exporting association with British agencies.[194]

One of the most spectacular and least successful of the mergers of the period was that which grew out of the bicycle manufacturers' cartel[195] when the industry began its rapid expansion near the turn of the century. Five firms were initially purchased by a syndicate headed by Senator George Cox and Sir Joseph Flavelle in a two million dollar swindle called the Canadian Cycle and Motor Co. (CCM). One of the firms was a branch plant of an American firm, most of the rest were licensed by American companies.

The five original firms were purchased for $1,397,500 and the properties were then sold by the syndicate to the new firm for $1,740,000. Of the difference of $342,500, brokers' fees were $20,400, fees to the provincial treasurer $400, and "underwriting costs" accruing to the syndicate members $250,000. Profits of the original firms in 1899, the year of the merger were $300,000; in 1900 they were $195,000; in 1901, $2,000; and by 1902 there was a loss of $130,000, part of it due to the purchase of a sixth firm at an inflated price.[196] As soon as the stock of the original merger was subscribed, it began to fall. The directors then took $450,000 worth off the market at 92 to keep up the quotation, and it was rumoured at the time that the purpose was to maintain the value so the directors could unload their holdings later at an inflated price. In fact the directors chose instead to plunder the treasury by voting $175,000 in dividends in 1901 — when total profits that year were $2,000. The directors, of course, were major stockholders. A series of suits by small stockholders were launched to try to force repayment of the $175,000 and to invalidate the purchase of the sixth firm. Severe cutbacks had to be made to save the waterlogged firm; unprofitable distribution agencies were eliminated, its foreign business reduced, and production centralized by moving the Brantford and the Hamilton plants to Toronto Junction. The only profitable part of the merger turned out to be the section that assembled automobiles on American patents from imported parts.[197] For Hamilton, it was one of its few losses in the bonusing game, for the plant which was closed down had been secured from Windsor in 1900 for a privately subscribed bonus of $25,000.

There were numerous other examples of organizations to enhance market power — efforts by boot and shoe makers and tanners to regulate credit and fix prices, by woodenware makers, by the St. Jean enamel works, the woollen mills, the various metal working industries, etc. Mergers occurred in many lines. Canadian General Electric, formed by a syndicate headed by Fred Nicholls and operating under licence granted from the American parent in 1893, was in trouble from the start; large amounts of water in its stock forced immediate and substantial dividend reductions.[198] Canada-U.S. conferences of rubber manufacturers began meeting to fix continental prices from 1879.[199] Out of this in 1906 came the Canadian Consolidated Rubber Company, a Montreal holding company under the leadership of Hugh Montague Allan and D. Lorne McGibbon. The merger parallelled that in the U.S., and in 1907 a controlling interest was acquired by the American trust. This share increased to a clear majority by 1911, when several new firms were added. The American firm then had a virtual monopoly of the continental market for an industry which the advent of the automobile had revolutionized.[200]

Industrial Mergers, 1907-1914

The early mergers, apart from the 1904 cotton effort or CCM, were largely industrial in origin, and generally conservative in their objectives, though some flagrant cases of stockwatering did occur. Most of them involved either overcrowded industries with many small firms, or the consolidation of relations between American oligopolies and their Canadian relatives. But after 1907 mergers showed distinctly new characteristics.

The new wave followed the upward revisions of the tariff in 1907, and would have been virtually unthinkable without it. The high tariff and assured tariff stability were essential in deciding upon the level of capitalization, for tariffs, bounties, municipal bonuses, and every other species of hand-out were capitalized as assured earnings in determining the water levels of the new concerns.

The new mergers involved outside promoters, generally Montreal, but to a lesser degree Toronto and Halifax financiers as well. These men had no interest in or ability at industrial management, but were interested solely in quick promoters' profits on a grab-and-run basis. The flotations often came to grief, but not before the promoters had garnered their rewards.

The new wave of amalgamation occurred, too, in the context of a confluence of ideal capital market conditions. The year 1909 saw the real beginnings of the merger movement. Industrial common stock prices, always weak, were exceptionally low in the 1907-1909 period.[201] In 1909, call money rates in Montreal reached an all-time low, falling from a monthly average of 5.47% in 1908 down to 4.21, then rising to 5.25 in 1910. And for the first time a flood of British portfolio investment was available for Canadian industrial bonds on a great scale.

It must be stressed that the mergers did not involve any sort of industrial risk capital. The risks, if any, had already been borne by the initial investors who set up the firm, which was absorbed into the merger as a going concern. The finance for the watering job came from borrowings in the form of industrial bond flotations, and included no risk to the promoters, who simply intermediated. The degree of monopoly resulting, together with the tariff, would in fact serve to reduce the risk, if the mergers were sensibly effected, by making earnings more secure.

The tariff was essential to success. The corporations had to raise prices and exact all they could from consumers in the form of oligopoly profits to ensure a sufficient level of earnings to pay dividends on the bloated stock issue and interest on the bonds. Without the tariff these firms would have collapsed. Some of the old cartels had leaned to free trade, for an assured American market would have eliminated the excess capacity that forced the combine arrangement; now they were formally merged, one and indivisible, and converted by a stroke of the pen into powerful lobbies for renewed and heightened tariff walls. Unlike the old cartels, the new mergers had chronic inefficiency built into their fabric by the actions of the outside promoters and their British backers. By 1911, the final decision was forced in the political arena by the defeat of low tariff forces in the Reciprocity campaign. Tariff stability was assured. Canadian industry was consolidated in its position of acute inefficiency, excess capacity, and high prices, with a huge burden of bonded debt for which the Canadian consumer had to pay to settle the interest claims of British financiers. In addition, the technology of the industry was confirmed as derivative of American patents and models.

The leading promoters of the era were Louis Forget and his associates, E. R. Wood of the Cox empire and several other Montreal and Toronto magnates — but above all, Max Aitken

(Lord Beaverbrook). Aitken began his career in Halifax with J. F. Stairs, president of Nova Scotia Steel and Coal and the Union Bank of Halifax. Aitken planned several mergers in Nova Scotia and the Caribbean before he shifted his Royal Securities to Montreal in 1906.[202] Thereafter came a series of mergers, many of the biggest and most controversial of the era bearing his trademark. Before he finished his promotional career he had been involved with Canada Power, Calgary Power, Western Canada Power, Cape Breton Trust, Union Bank of Halifax, Demerara Electric Co., Camaguey Electric and Traction, Puerto Rico Co., Robb Engineering, Standard Ideal Co., Canadian Car & Foundry Co., Canada Cement, and the Steel Company of Canada (Stelco).

The Fielding tariff increases of 1907 triggered off an immediate reaction. The woollen industry had gone into decline during the great expansion, with output falling absolutely from $14 million worth in 1899 to $7.6 million in 1909. The number of mills fell drastically, and employees declined from 6,956 to 4,263.[203] In 1900 the Canadian Woollen Mills Co. was organized by Manville of Johns-Manville, New York, at St. Hyacinthe. It merged five woollen mills, but failed by 1902.[204] In 1904 the British preference was largely eliminated rescuing the woollen mills from oblivion, and after the 1907 tariff changes another effort at merging was mounted. A series of independent mills at Thorold, Paris, Port Dover, Almonte, Brantford, Coaticook, and St. Hyacinthe were merged into Penman's Manufacturing Co., with six million authorized capital.[205] It was a ridiculous capitalization, given that the total output of all 87 mills in Canada in 1909 was only $7.6 million.

The next year, the still overcrowded Ontario canning industry witnessed the formation of Consolidated Canners, which, in a rare event, was forced to reduce its prices when the independent canners fought back. Other mergers occurred in 1908 in the food industry. The Atlantic Fish Co. merger, backed by the Bank of Montreal which provided interim finance until the bonds were sold in London, produced a powerful Maritime fish concentration to parallel the already existing Pacific salmon trust.[206] Over the period 1901-1911 the number of fishermen working from small boats fell by nearly 20%, while workers in canneries rose a like amount,[207] reflecting a shift in the mode of production from independent commodity producer and fish merchant to wage labour and industrial capital.

In 1908, as well, an iron and steel merger took place. The Canada Iron Corporation combined a number of primary and secondary firms, including the Drummond-New York joint venture, the Canada Iron Furnace Co. together with some Ontario mines. This and the big iron and steel mergers to follow included in their overcapitalization a generous estimate of the value of the iron and steel bounties which the federal government lavished upon them, as well as tariffs and local bonuses. The largest of these later iron and steel mergers were the union of DISCO and DOMCO into Dominion Steel, following a victory of the Canadian Northern group over the CPR forces in those concerns,[208] and Stelco, the CPR's subsequent effort to consolidate an integrated iron and steel complex of its own, combining the Montreal Rolling Mills, Canada Screw Co., the Hamilton Iron and Steel Co., Pillow-Hersey, the Hodgson Iron and Tube Works, and Dominion Wire among others. Several of the Stelco components were licensed by U.S. firms, some were the creation of American capital without ties to an American parent, and at least one was a joint venture of U.S. and Canadian capital.

It was the 1909-1912 period when the merger movement proper blossomed forth. In that four years, 58 industrial amalgamations occurred, including some 275 individual firms, with a total authorized capital of $490 million of which 337 million was issued. The new merger wave embraced every facet of industry from canneries to shoes, with iron and steel well represented. Of the nineteen largest from 1908 to 1910, the aggregate capital came to $200 million, of which $165 million was issued while the total capital of the component companies was only $65 million. And of them the total expenditure on new plant and equipment was but $1,100,000.[209] The promoters' profits poured into interest and dividend payments instead of being reinvested in plant and equipment.

One particularly notorious case was that of Max Aitken's Canada Cement operation. In 1901 there were nine plants in Canada with five more under construction, and already overproduction was noticeable.[210] Four of the earlier plants had already been merged by E. W. Rathburn and a syndicate of Philadelphia and Toronto capitalists including E. B. Osler and W. D. Matthews.[210] By early 1903, the cement firms had formed a special branch of the CMA to agitate for higher tariffs, at the same time claiming to have a great export potential.[212] Yet the flow of new capital into the industry continued.[213] Cement dealers in 1906 agitated for tariff reductions to break the cartel.[214] A period of falling prices set in, despite tariff stability;[215] the Bank of Montreal, which backed several firms, began pressuring for restrictions on production. Aitken merged eleven of the 23 existing producers into Canada Cement in 1909. The value of the assets of all 23 was only $15 million, but the new merger was capitalized at $38 million, of which $32.5 million was eventually issued. The owners of the merged factories were paid $1,348,000 in bonds, $4,316,800 in preferred, $2,155,850 in common stock, and $1,001,600 cash — a total of $14,822,250, by itself representing a large amount of water.[216]

TABLE XIV (1)

Business Consolidations 1900-1914

			($ million)	
Year	Number	Firms Merged	Capital Authorized	Capital Issued
1900-1908	8	57	$ 43	$ 33
1909	11	51	139	84
1910	22	112	157	113
1911	14	44	96	65
1912	13	37	97	75
1913	5	16	n.a	n.a.
1914	2	4	n.a.	n.a.

Sources: H.G. Stapells, *The Consolidation Movement*, p. 12; Royal Commission on Price Spreads, *Report*, p. 28; *MT,* Sept. 24, 1910, pp. 1328-30.

The merger coincided with a great building boom in Canada,[217] and as a result the average price of cement in Winnipeg rose immediately from $1.80 to $2.40 per barrel.[218] In addition, the quality of the cement deteriorated, and there were accidents to construction workers, some fatal, and attributed by building inspectors directly to the low quality of the cement.[219] Aitken was awarded a knighthood, and left Canada in 1911 to immerse himself in British politics. The *Grain Growers' Guide* greeted his departure with the prediction, "Probably he will now set out to 'save the Empire' by the cement process."[220]

Merger followed merger as the big waterlogged concerns found their financial salvation in control of markets. To the already enormous Canadian Consolidated Felt Co. in 1911 were added the Ames-Holden and McCready shoe manufacturing firms, giving D. Lorne McGibbon virtual control of the footware market.[221] Canada Leather had control of a minimum of 75% of its market by 1910. Rolling stock companies and foundries, including Nova Scotia's Rhodes, Currey and Co., merged into Canadian Car and Foundry, controlling 85% of total Canadian production. The Canadian Canneries reorganized as Dominion Canneries, adding another 24 small firms and giving it control of 90% of Ontario's output, which constituted 95% of the Canadian total. The Wholesale Grocers' Guild announced that the only way for grocers to still make a profit in trade in the face of such a monopoly was for them to "work in harmony" with the canning merger. [222] The canning merger went one better than its brethren in other industries, for it introduced water not only into its equity but into its products as well. In 1913 a series of samples of canned tomatoes were taken by Dominion government analysts, which showed that one-third of each can was water, while 60% of the samples were below American state government standards.[223] There were no Canadian government standards.

In flour milling came a series of mergers. Maple Leaf Milling issued more than treble the former capital of its constituents. It controlled, as well, a long string of western elevators, while another milling merger, Canadian Cereal and Milling Co., was largely Ontario-based. It was subsequently absorbed into an American-based consolidation, while seven more Ontario milling companies formed another merger in 1911.[224] Meat packing was added to the list of food processing consolidations, and in 1911 the B.C. lumber mills' cartel spawned two mergers.[225]

Not all of the big mergers after 1907 involved Montreal promoters. There were several cases of American-based movements in this period as well as the earlier. Sherwin-Williams Paints was a merger of three firms, one Canadian, one British, and one American, which remained under the American parent's control via licensing.[226] Two large licensed joint ventures in mining equipment and machinery, the Canada Rand Drill Co. (1899) and the Ingersoll Rock Drill Co. (1882), were combined in 1912 as the Canada-Ingersoll-Rand Co. parallelling the parent's merger.[227] In 1906 Bell Canada, one-quarter owned by ATT, bought control of Northern Electric and Manufacturing, in which Western Electric held part interest. Imperial Wire & Cable was also jointly owned and in 1914 the two were merged into Northern Electric of which 44% of the stock was held in the U.S.[228] The gunpowder manufacturers, which had long been a part of a Canada-U.S. trust, were merged under American control in 1911; the only firm not taking part was a branch plant of an American operation.[229]

Another American move that sparked a great deal of controversy was the move into Canada of the United Shoe Machinery Co. This firm, a branch plant, had quickly secured a virtual monopoly by virtue of its patents and through a system of twenty-year exclusive contracts with the lessors of its machinery.

Prices of the machines rose abruptly after the branch plant absorbed smaller Canadian firms.[230]

American moves into the resource industries also occurred as an adjunct to American manufacturing mergers. In asbestos mining, the little Canadian mines relied on advance sales for operating capital, and when a big merger of manufacturers took place in the U.S., the Canadian mines were deprived of advance sales revenue by the combine's new policy of pushing the burden of carrying stocks of ore onto the mine owners. Insufficient funds could be found in Canada to hold the ores, and most of the little Canadian operations were forced to sell high-class properties cheaply to American mine promoters.

In 1909, the Amalgamated Asbestos Co. grew out of the earlier cartel that had followed American purchases of Canadian asbestos mines with Louis Forget's assistance. The Bank of Montreal, the Bank of Commerce, and Royal Trust all supported the merger, which by 1912 had to be reorganized as the Asbestos Corporation of Canada with capital cut 50%.[231]

The merger wave led by Montreal promoters ended as abruptly as it began in 1912. Drastic liquidations portended by CCM and pioneered by Asbestos led to reorganization and capital reductions. The process of retrenchment began before the war and did not peak until 1921. Even before the war cut Canada off from British portfolio investment, British capital was frightened away from Canadian industrial bonds by the early liquidations.[232] For the fact of heavily watered equity meant that bondholders ended up putting up the money for capital expenditure and promoters' profits and expenses, with the result that bondholders had no more security than if they were actually the stockholders. If the company failed they stood to lose heavily; if it succeeded then the water became valuable. A string of firms saw their securities begin to depreciate or even go into default on interest[233] before the war intervened to save them temporarily.

In Canada widespread outcry followed the merger wave as prices of consumer goods and building materials shot up while wages lagged. But public policy was little more than incantation. Oligopoly and monopoly had been built into the fabric of Canadian economic life from the time of the Hudson's Bay Company charter in 1670 to the CPR monopoly clause in 1880 to the great mergers of the pre-war period. The anti-combines act of 1889 was never enforced, and was in any event virtually unenforceable. What little strength the original bill had was eliminated by the Senate, in which the representatives of big business held lifelong tenure. Inserted into the clauses was the word "unduly" whenever the bill decried restraints of competition, and it was

otherwise rendered innocuous by being transformed into a
hotch-potch of sunny banalities.[234] The only action ever taken
against a cartel came in 1902, when Fielding reduced the tariff
on paper from 25 to 15% in response to the complaints of the
newspapers against the paper combine. An effort to push a bill
through the Ontario Legislature forbidding stockwatering after
the Dominion Canners merger failed after a stormy session.[235]

Nor were the courts of much use. One of the rare convictions,
by the Superior Court of Quebec, held that the United Shoe
Machinery Co. was a combination in restraint of trade: it was
overturned by the Judicial Committee of the Privy Council,
which insisted that legislation rather than litigation was the
proper solution.[236] And legislation followed in the best of Canadian traditions. In 1910 the Minister of Labour, Mackenzie King,
was forced to act by the vacuum created by the court decision,
and by the mounting public pressure, which laid the blame for
the inflation of the period squarely at the feet of the great trusts
which contributed so much to Liberal Party campaign coffers.
Tabling his Combines Investigation Act, he prefaced it with the
words:

> I would like the House to understand that in introducing this
> legislation, no attempt is being made to legislate against com-
> bines, mergers and trusts . . . [237]

When the laughter subsided, the promoters got to work once
more.

The Act was aimed at abuses of oligopoly power, not oligopoly per se, and such undue abuses of corporate powers were
apparently rare indeed: the Act was never enforced, while
merger after merger was effected. As to the price rise, this was
neatly imputed to the rising volume of world gold production
and the inflow of foreign capital,[238] carefully ignoring the fact
that Canada's money supply bore little or no relation to gold
reserves,[239] and the fact that much of the inflow of capital went
to sustain the great industrial mergers. It was a piece of political
sophistry that accorded with the best principles of neo-classical
economics.[240]

Conclusions

The industrial structure in Canada until the 1890's was fairly traditional. Small firms, often with a local orientation, typified most
industries. Many of the consumers' goods industries in particular
were badly overcrowded. During the deflation phase of the long
cycle, the result was a squeeze on profit margins and vigorous,

often unsuccessful efforts at cartelization. Cartels and profit
pools were difficult to maintain during a period of secular deflation, for falling costs encouraged firms to break ranks and begin
price cutting. Mergers were occasionally attempted during this
period as methods of curbing competition, but they were relatively few and far between, partly because of the effects of the
deflation and partly because the Canadian capital market provided no scope for dealing in industrial equities. After the inflation phase began, monopolization accelerated. From 1896 to
1907 many new mergers were created, mainly by the participating firms. For secular inflation meant that the former potential for getting one step ahead of competitors by price cutting
was restricted due to the prospect of increasing costs over time.
After 1907, when tariff stability was assured and capital market
conditions improved greatly, the potential existed for a great
merger wave. The expectation of continued inflation encouraged
enormous stock watering operations, and the inflated prices at
which the components of the mergers were purchased would be
recovered in part automatically through inflation, in part
through the exploitation of the monopoly created — which
monopoly price increases in turn fed the inflation. Supported by
British industrial bond purchases, the merger wave created an
industrial structure totally dependent on the tariff to permit the
mergers earnings levels sufficient to pay interest and dividends
on their waterlogged capital.

Notes to Chapter XIV

1.   *LG,* Sept. 1905.
2.   *IC,* Nov. 1901, p. 137.
3.   *SCC, Evidence,* p. 69; *MT,* Sept. 7, 1883, p. 261; *SCC, Report,* pp. 3-5.
4.   *SCC, Evidence,* p. 76.
5.   *MT,* May 7, 1886, p. 1265; July 16, 1886, p. 70; July 30, 1886, p. 127.
6.   *MT,* Oct. 24, 1890, p. 498; Oct. 31, 1890, p. 540.
7.   *SCC, Evidence,* pp. 62, 109.
8.   *RCRLC, Nova Scotia Evidence,* p. 11.
9.   *SCC, Evidence,* p. 54.
10. *MT,* Feb. 19, 1892, p. 995; Nov. 16, 1894, p. 641; Jan. 11, 1895, p. 905; July
     16, 1897, p. 79; Oct. 15, 1897, p. 506.
11. *TEC,* p. 356.
12. Cited in O. D. Skelton, *General Economic History,* p. 267.
13. *MT,* Oct. 15, 1886, p. 436; Sept. 9, 1887, p. 330; April 17, 1891, p. 2171.
14. *GGG,* Dec. 28, 1910.
15. A. Hedley, "Canada and Her Commerce," p. 37.
16. H. W. Wadsworth, "The Dominion Commercial Travellers Association,"
     p. 56; *MT,* Jan. 4, 1878, p. 786.

17.   *MT,* Dec. 17, 1875, p. 691; Aug. 15, 1881, p. 1197; H. M. Wadsworth, "Dominion Commercial Travellers Association," p. 61.
18.   *MT,* Oct. 28, 1881, p. 519; Jan. 7, 1887, p. 790.
19.   *MT,* Dec. 23, 1887, p. 782.
20.   *MT,* March 30, 1877, pp. 1113, 1115; Jan. 18, 1878, p. 841; Sept. 27, 1878, p. 407.
21.   *MT,* Jan. 5, 1883, p. 742.
22.   *MT,* Oct. 5, 1883, p. 378.
23.   *SCC, Evidence,* pp. 159, 162.
24.   *SCC, Evidence,* p. 172.
25.   *SCC, Evidence,* pp. 174, 184, 192, 241-4.
26.   *SCC, Evidence,* pp. 197, 244.
27.   *MT,* May 18, 1888, p. 1424; *SCC, Evidence, passim; MT,* June 7, 1889, p. 1410.
28.   A. G. Brown and P. H. Morres, *Twentieth Century Impressions,* pp. 441-2, 728.
29.   *MT,* March 19, 1897, p. 1240.
30.   *MT,* April 2, 1897, p. 1312.
31.   Royal Commission on Price Spreads, *Report,* pp. 200-1.
32.   *MT,* April 8, 1892, p. 1214.
33.   Select Committee on Prices Charged for Lumber in the Provinces of Manitoba, Alberta, and Saskatchewan, *Report,* p. xxvii.
34.   Select Committee . . . Lumber Prices, *Evidence,* p. 117.
35.   *CBC,* p. 369.
36.   Manitoba, Beef Commission, *Report,* pp. 371, 374, 382.
37.   Manitoba, Beef Commission, *Report,* pp. 373, 386, 389.
38.   Manitoba Beef Commission, *Report,* p. 380.
39.   *JC,* Oct. 26, 1883, pp. 306, 312; Nov. 2, 1883, p. 342.
40.   *JC,* Sept. 7, 1883, p. 79.
41.   *MT,* Aug. 31, 1883, p. 235; Sept. 7, 1883, p. 265; Oct. 12, 1883, p. 399; Sept. 14, 1883, p. 292.
42.   *MT,* Aug. 22, 1884, p. 233.
43.   *RCRLC, Ontario Evidence,* p. 974.
44.   *MT,* July 31, 1885, p. 121.
45.   *MT,* Aug. 7, 1885, p. 155.
46.   *MT,* Sept, 25, 1885, p. 350.
47.   *MT,* Aug. 13, 1886, p. 180.
48.   *MT,* Aug. 19, 1887, p. 235.
49.   *RCRLC, New Brunswick Evidence,* p. 484.
50.   *MT,* Feb. 17, 1888, p. 1031.
51.   *MT,* May 25, 1888, p. 1451.
52.   *MT,* Aug. 17, 1888, p. 177; Sept. 7, 1888, p. 267.
53.   *MT,* Sept. 28, 1888, p. 359.
54.   *RCRLC, Ontario Evidence,* p. 975.
55.   *MT,* Aug. 16, 1889, p. 188.
56.   *MT,* July 25, 1884, p. 93.
57.   *MT,* Feb. 20, 1885, p. 950.
58.   *RCT,* p. 36.
59 . *MT,* Oct. 10, 1890, p. 428; Oct. 17, 1890, p. 462; Dec. 12, 1890, p. 710; Jan. 16, 1891, p. 864; Sept. 4, 1891, p. 976; Jan. 29, 1892, p. 898; Feb. 26, 1892; p. 1027.
60 . M. Denison, *Canada's First Bank,* p. 240.
61 . *MT,* March 1, 1892, p. 1131; May 13, 1892, p. 1364; Dec. 30, 1892, p. 759; Nov. 13, 1896, p. 682.
62 . *MT,* Oct. 13, 1899, p. 465.

63 .   *MT,* Oct. 17, 1890, p. 462.
64 .   *RCT,* p. 37.
65.   *RCT,* pp. 118-9.
66 .   *TEC,* p. 144.
67.   Royal Commission on Industrial Disputes in the Cotton Factories, *Evidence,* p. 12.
68 .   *MT,* Nov. 7, 1879, p. 549.
69 .   *MT,* Oct. 19, 1883, p. 429.
70 .   *CE,* Sept. 1898, p. 143; Nov. 1898, p. 202.
71 .   *MT,* Oct. 5, 1883, p. 373; Aug. 10, 1883, p. 149.
72.   *MT,* Nov. 27, 1891, p. 642.
73 .   *MT,* March 2, 1888, p. 1094; Nov. 14, 1890, p. 586; Feb. 6, 1891, p. 959.
74.   W. G. Phillips, *The Agricultural Implements Industry,* p. 52.
75.   *MT,* May 8, 1891, p. 1363; Oct. 16, 1891, p. 455.
76.   *MT,* Nov. 20, 1891, p. 603.
77.   *MT,* May 3, 1895, p. 1412; May 17, 1895, p. 1479; July 3, 1896, p. 10.
78.   *MT,* Oct. 6, 1899, p. 427.
79.   *MT,* May 23, 1902, p. 1523; June 6, 1902, p. 1576.
80.   *MT,* May 31, 1901, p. 1602.
81.   *MT,* Jan. 20, 1912, p. 345; Nov. 1, 1901, p. 565.
82.   *MT,* July 29, 1911, p. 519.
83.   B. E. Walker to F. H. Mattewson, July 7, 1902, *Walker Papers.*
84.   *MT,* Oct. 8, 1886, p. 409; Sept. 16, 1887, p. 365.
85.   *SCC, Evidence,* pp. 343-9.
86.   *MT,* June 27, 1890, p. 1610; July 4, 1890, p. 17; Nov. 5, 1891, p. 543; Jan. 14, 1898, p. 921.
87.   *HCD,* July 24, 1903, p. 7362; *MT,* Jan. 27, 1893, p. 873.
88.   *MT,* April 17, 1894, p. 202; Sept. 7, 1894, p. 312.
89.   *MT,* Sept. 16, 1887, p. 265.
90.   *MT,* Nov. 30, 1900, p. 683.
91.   *MT,* July 13, 1900, p. 38; March 29, 1901, p. 1270; April 16, 1901, p. 198.
92.   *HCD,* July 24, 1903, p. 7305; *MT,* July 31, 1903, p. 144.
93 .   *HCD,* July 13, 1903, p. 6438; *HCD,* July 24, 1903, p. 7362.
94.   Department of Trade and Commerce, *Report 1913 Part IV,* p. 16.
95.   *GGG,* July 13, 1913; Sept. 17, 1913.
96.   *MT,* Jan. 7, 1869, p. 330; Aug. 27, 1869, p. 24; Oct. 17, 1873, p. 373.
97.   *HCD,* Feb. 26, 1878, p. 559; *MT,* Nov. 21, 1873, pp. 490-1; Dec. 19, 1873, p. 588.
98.   *RCRLC, Ontario Evidence,* pp. 693, 725; *MT,* Jan. 4, 1878, p. 787; April 26, 1878, p. 1259; Jan. 9, 1880, p. 812.
99.   *MT,* Jan. 7, 1881, p. 784; May 14, 1880, p. 1346; May 28, 1880, p. 1045.
100.   *MT,* Oct. 5, 1888, p. 389.
101.   *MT,* Nov. 25, 1898, p. 697.
102.   *CE,* Dec. 1897, p. 115; *MT,* June 4, 1897, p. 1591; Sept. 8, 1899, p. 298.
103.   *CE,* Dec. 1897, p. 115; Aug. 1898, p. 114; Jan. 1899, p. 263; Oct. 1899, p. 156; Nov. 1899, p. 185.
104.   *MT,* Dec. 16, 1898, p. 795; Feb. 24, 1899, pp. 1113, 1119; *CE,* March 1899, p. 326.
105.   *Ec,* Jan. 26, 1901, p. 119; *MT,* March 3, 1899, p. 1155; March 17, 1899, p. 1227; July 7, 1899, p. 30.
106.   *MT,* Nov. 20, 1885, p. 568.
107.   *MT,* Jan. 20, 1893, p. 847; Jan. 27, 1893, p. 878; Oct. 6, 1893, pp. 420, 424.
108.   *MT,* Feb. 3, 1893, p. 911.
109.   E. Forsey, *Nova Scotia Coal Industry,* p. 5.
110.   Cited in *CM,* March 2, 1894, p. 188.

111. *MT,* May 29, 1896, p. 1530; April 16, 1897, p. 1374.
112. *Globe,* Nov. 20, 1890.
113. *MT,* Aug. 22, 1879, p. 232.
114. *MT,* Nov. 10, 1882, p. 527.
115. *MT,* Sept. 25, 1885, p. 344; June 4, 1886, p. 1374.
116. *MT,* July 15, 1892, p. 36.
117. *CE,* June 1895, p. 47; *MT,* Jan. 11, 1895, p. 906.
118. *CE,* June 1901, p. 315; *MT,* March 1, 1901, p. 1120; June 7, 1901, p. 1640.
119. *MT,* July 19, 1901, p. 79.
120. *MT,* June 24, 1892, p. 1550; Feb. 10, 1893, p. 938; April 13, 1894, p. 1284; April 20, 1894, p. 1316.
121. *MT,* March 30, 1900, p. 1290.
122. *MT,* Jan. 18, 1901, p. 914.
123. *MT,* June 26, 1903, p. 1745.
124. *MT,* July 12, 1901, p. 49; Sept. 27, 1901, p. 391.
125. L. Marlio, *The Aluminum Cartel,* pp. 12ff.
126. *MT,* April 4, 1902, p. 1286.
127. O. D. Main, *Nickel Industry,* pp. 56-7, 149.
128. V. Nelles, *The Politics of Development,* p. 544.
129. *MT,* Feb. 13, 1885, p. 910.
130. *MT,* Sept. 11, 1885, p. 288; Sept. 17, 1886, p. 323.
131. *MT,* Sept. 11, 1885, p. 288; Sept. 17, 1886, p. 323.
132. *MT,* March 19, 1886, p. 1062; April 2, 1886, p. 1118.
133. *MT,* Feb. 12, 1886, p. 913.
134. *MT,* Dec. 30, 1887, p. 816; Jan. 6, 1888, p. 844; Feb. 3, 1888, p. 962; Oct. 5, 1888, p. 391; Jan. 18, 1889, p. 823.
135. *MT,* Aug. 5, 1887, p. 171.
136. *MT,* Aug. 24, 1888, p. 206.
137. *MT,* Oct. 24, 1890, p. 429.
138. *MT,* March 24, 1893, p. 1134; Aug. 4, 1893, p. 131.
139. *MT,* Nov. 18, 1899, p. 669; Jan. 20, 1899, p. 966.
140. *MT,* May 10, 1895, p. 1453.
141. *MT,* April 30, 1897, p. 1430.
142. *MT,* Aug. 13, 1886, p. 176.
143. *SCC, Evidence,* pp. 375-80, 390.
144. *MT,* Aug. 10, 1888, p. 157.
145. *MT,* Jan. 11, 1901, p. 895.
146. *MT,* March 11, 1881, p. 1061; Aug. 4, 1882, p. 125; Dec. 11, 1891, p. 692.
147. *Globe,* Dec. 17, 1890.
148. *Globe,* Oct. 20, 1890; *MT,* Oct. 24, 1890, p. 497.
149. *MT,* Feb. 22, 1889, p. 969; Aug. 7, 1891, p. 166.
150. *MT,* Aug. 31, 1900, p. 279.
151. *CE,* Feb. 1897, p. 307.
152. *MT,* Jan. 4, 1879, p. 925.
153. *MT,* March 12, 1880, p. 1077.
154. *MT,* Dec. 21, 1888, p. 703; March 1, 1889, p. 999.
155. *MT,* Aug. 17, 1883, p. 176.
156. *MT,* March 9, 1894, p. 1124; Sept. 28, 1894, p. 410.
157. *MT,* May 24, 1901, p. 1583.
158. E. C. Porritt, *The Revolt in Canada,* p. 47.
159. *MT,* April 3, 1891, p. 1212; Nov. 22, 1895, p. 660; Dec. 3, 1897, p. 730.
160. *MT,* June 6, 1902, pp. 1585-6.
161. *HCD,* April 25, 1910, p. 7883.
162. *RCRLC, Quebec Evidence,* p. 33.
163. *LG,* Dec. 1902, p. 470; *MT,* June 6, 1902, p. 1586.

164. *LG,* Nov. 1902, p. 377; *HCD,* April 26, 1910, p. 7993.
165. *LG,* Oct. 1902, p. 248; May 1903, pp. 865-6; *IC,* Oct. 1903, p. 132; Royal Commission. . . Tobacco Industry, *Report,* p. 10.
166. *SCC, Evidence,* pp. 392-3.
167. *MT,* April 28, 1882, p. 1323.
168. *MT,* March 27, 1885, p. 1082; April 18, 1890, p. 1286; April 21, 1899, p. 1381.
169. *MT,* April 21, 1893, p. 1258.
170. *Globe,* Dec. 19, 1890.
171. *CE,* June 1900, p. 36; March 1901, p. 245; *MT,* April 27, 1900, p. 1407; Feb. 15, 1901, p. 1046.
172. *CE,* March 1902, p. 74.
173. *SCC, Evidence,* pp. 271-3, 360.
174. *MT,* Nov. 3, 1882, p. 491.
175. *Globe,* Dec. 10, 1890.
176. *MT,* Jan. 6, 1893, p. 788; Dec. 14, 1894, p. 763.
177. *CE,* July 1895, p. 76; May 1896, p. 24; March 1899, p. 324; Nov. 1902, pp. 308-9.
178. *MT,* Nov. 15, 1895, p. 629.
179. *MT,* Dec. 11, 1896, p. 778.
180. *CE,* June 1895, p. 47; June 1901, p. 315.
181. *MT,* April 25, 1890, p. 1319.
182. *MT,* July 27, 1900, p. 108.
183. L. M. Jones to B. E. Walker, Aug. 1, 1904, *Walker Papers;* Bank of Nova Scotia, *Annual Reports* 1908, 1909.
184. *MT,* Aug. 15, 1902, p. 215; *IC,* July 1901, p. 313.
185. F. Clergue "Address...Sault Ste. Marie," pp. 16, 29.
186. *MT,* Aug. 7, 1903, p. 170; Sept. 25, 1903, p. 380; Oct. 2, 1903, p. 413; March 4, 1904, p. 1181; May 20, 1904, p. 1539; June 3, 1904, p. 1621.
187. *MT,* March 9, 1900, p. 1186; May 25, 1900, p. 1553.
188. Royal Commission... Combination of Paper Manufacturers and Dealers, *Report,* pp. 7-8, 13, 15.
189. *MT,* Feb. 22, 1889, p. 972.
190. *MT,* April 15, 1898, p. 1362.
191. *MT,* Dec. 8, 1899, p. 735; April 6, 1900, p. 1322.
192. *CE,* Feb. 1900, p. 283; *MT,* Jan. 5, 1900, pp. 882-3; Jan. 4, 1901, p. 859.
193. *MT,* Jan. 11, 1901, p. 899; Feb. 22, 1901, p. 1078.
194. *MT,* July 27, 1900, p. 116.
195. *MT,* Dec. 6, 1895, p. 727.
196. *CE,* Sept. 1899, p. 140; July, 1902, p. 195; May 1902, p. 136; Dec. 1900, p. 165; Jan. 1900, p. 258; *MT,* Aug. 25, 1899, p. 239; Nov. 13, 1903, p. 1899.
197. *MT,* Dec. 13, 1901, p. 744; Jan. 31, 1902, p. 980; April 4, 1902, p. 1286; July 11, 1902, p. 50; Nov. 7, 1902, p. 596.
198. *MT,* April 18, 1908, p. 1756.
199. *MT,* May 23, 1879, p. 1444.
200. Royal Commission...Rubber, *Report,* p. 5; *MT,* May 26, 1905, p. 1599; *Globe,* June 25, 1908; July 27, 1908.
201. *CLRII,* p. 609.
202. A. Wood, *The True History of Lord Beaverbrook,* p. 25.
203. O. J. McDiarmid, *Canadian Commercial Policy,* p. 253.
204. *MT,* Aug. 15, 1902.
205. *Globe,* June 1, 1907.
206. *HCD,* April 12, 1910, p. 6826.
207. *CLRII,* p. 952.
208. *Globe,* Jan. 9, 1907; *FP,* May 30, 1908; June 27, 1908.

209. *MT,* Sept. 24, 1910, p. 1337.
210. *MT,* Dec. 12, 1902, p. 758.
211. *CFC,* June 2, 1900, p. 1097.
212. *MT,* Jan. 30, 1903, p. 951.
213. *MT,* Feb. 13, 1903, p. 1097; Nov. 27, 1903, p. 677.
214. *TEC,* p. 168.
215. *MT,* Sept. 24, 1910, p. 1326.
216. H. Stapells, *The Recent Consolidation Movement,* pp. 144-5; T. Driberg, *Beaverbrook,* p. 44.
217. A. Wood, *The True History,* p. 38.
218. *HCD,* April 25, 1910, p. 7979.
219. *GGG,* Sept. 27, 1911.
220. *GGG,* Aug. 28, 1912.
221. R. Cooper, *Montreal,* p. 114; O. D. Skelton, *General Economic History,* p. 261.
222. *CAR,* 1909, p. 256; *MT,* Sept. 24, 1910, p. 1327.
223. *GGG,* March 26, 1913.
224. *MT,* July 1, 1911, p. 121; July 15, 1911, p. 321.
225. *MT,* Oct. 21, 1911, p. 1712; June 17, 1911, p. 2416.
226. *MT,* June 10, 1911, p. 2321.
227. E. S. Moore, *American Influences in Canadian Mining,* p. 94.
228. H. Marshall *et al, Canadian-American Industry,* p. 128.
229. *MT,* Jan. 7, 1911, p. 150.
230. *HCD,* April 26, 1910, p. 8000; *MT,* March 4, 1911, p. 916.
231. *MT,* Jan. 8, 1910, p. 223; M. Mendels, *The Asbestos Industry,* p. 18.
232. *CF,* Jan. 7, 1914, p. 21.
233. *Ec,* Jan. 25, 1913, p. 158.
234. *Senate Debates,* April 29, 1889, p. 631 *et passim, Statutes of Canada,* 1889, 52 Vic. Chap. 41; *MT,* May 3, 1889, p. 1270.
235. *MT,* Feb. 25, 1911, p. 823.
236. H. Ferns and B. Ostry, *The Age of Mackenzie King,* p. 103.
237. *HCD,* April 12, 1910, p. 6803.
238. *HCD,* April 12, 1910, pp. 6814, 6817; *CLRI,* p. 28.
239. *CLRII,* pp. 1041-43.
240. See especially J. Viner, *Canada's Balance,* p. 2,17 *et passim.*

The big bankers are all fighting Reciprocity. It must be a splendid thing for the people.

Grain Growers' Guide, 1911

CHAPTER XV
Reciprocity

Early Debate

Because Canada remained largely an agrarian society, Reciprocity with the United States, at least in natural products, remained on the level of theory, if not in fact, the ultimate objective of federal commercial policy until 1911, when the issue was finally settled.

From an early period, leading manufacturers began to point out the difficulties inherent in Reciprocity. Aside from the issue of patents, where Reciprocity would lead to a wholesale destruction of Canadian business operating in Canada under licence from the U.S., the loss of branch plants was an early and powerful counter-argument. The possibility was also raised that branch plant closures would be followed by a movement of skilled labour and even of Canadian capital to the U.S. The chance of being out-competed by American producers whose longer production runs kept costs down was anathema to many Canadian producers. Leading industrialists like Edward Gurney and Samuel May were active in the fight against tariff reductions, as were various branch plant managers.[1] The sweated labour argument was a popular one. And faced with a drain of population to the U.S. that showed no sign of abating in spite of the National Policy, the CMA outdid its normal standards of sophistry and argued that the loss of population would be worse in the absence of protection.[2]

While farm opinion, and that of a number of export staple industries, was favourable to Reciprocity, it is important to note that in the early period a substantial body of manufacturers, too, favoured free trade with the United States. In agricultural implements, the leading firms were active in the free trade campaign until the late 1880's, when Massey began to hedge. By 1895 too, W. H. Frost, formerly a Reciprocity advocate, announced he would seek election to the Commons as a "National Policy Candidate,"[3] a rather poor euphemism for Tory. Many industries, however, did not show such a change of heart, and these cases are revealing.

In 1888, some secondary paper manufacturers declared themselves in favour of free trade provided it applied to both raw material and finished goods. From their point of view, the raw material tariff more than negated the protection to final product.[4] Nor were they alone, for free trade sentiment could be found in a large number of industries through the 1880's and early 1890's and for a variety of reasons.

A Guelph carriage manufacturer reversed the usual logic and advanced the opinion that Reciprocity would be more useful in blocking the outflow of population than the National Policy had been, and would, moreover, lead to an expanded inflow of American capital. He wanted freer access to the American market for his already substantial exports. Representatives of the organ and piano manufacturing industries also called for free trade, for without the raw material tariffs, they could compete on a continental scale.[5] A furniture manufacturer joined the chorus of complaints against the tariff on raw materials and protested the lack of access to the American market, denying that any real long-term growth of the industry had followed the National Policy.[6]

Several staple industries were strongly in favour of free trade. The malt industry, which had been virtually wiped out by American tariffs, wanted the market reopened. One planing mill operator claimed that prices would fall with Reciprocity but that expanded volume would more than offset any reduction of profit margins.[7] The flour millers called for access to the New England market to ease the excess capacity that had built up in their industry. Canadian mills by 1890 were running two months a year, while New England mills were running 24 hours a day all year and still could not meet demands.[8] The Oatmeal Millers' Association testified before the Combines Committee in 1888 that if Reciprocity existed, the oatmeal millers' cartel would not.[9] Hog producers, flax mills, and other farm-based industries wanted access to the American market, complaining of raw material duties which raised their costs and penned them up on the Canadian market.[10] The ailing salt industry, whose fate at the hands of American trusts had been lamented during the

National Policy debates in the Commons in 1878,[11] turned out to be adamant in favour of Reciprocity. The salt combine kept Canadian prices well above American; with Reciprocity, the refiners predicted the combine would vanish.[12]

While the presence of staple industries in the ranks of the Reciprocity proponents may come as little surprise, the secondary wood products industry's representatives are not so easy to explain in terms of the usual stereotypes of Canadian industry during this period. But even more noteworthy is the fact that woollen firms could be free-trade-inclined. Some small woollen mills, as distinct from those dominated directly by Montreal commerce, were not afraid of American competition but were quite eager for access to the American market. They resented the effects of the National Policy on their commercial patterns. While it assured Canadian woollen mills a market "from Charlottetown to Calgary," it raised their distribution costs considerably.[13] The beneficiaries of the high distribution costs were, it goes without saying, the railroads and the big Montreal-based wholesale distributors.

But the greatest amount of pro-Reciprocity sentiment came from the largest Canadian manufacturing industry—secondary iron and steel. Many small agricultural implement makers, despite the desertion by the leaders, continued to favour Reciprocity. The Erie Iron Works and the Macdonald Manufacturing Company of Stratford complained of high duties on iron and other parts which kept them locked up in Canada. Farran, Macpherson and Hovey had the same complaint, but managed to export in spite of their raw material costs. These firms bought bolts and other parts from the U.S., paid the Canadian duty of 50%, and still paid less than they would for Canadian products, and received superior quality. Again the burden on the consumer was cited, and its underlying cause, the high distribution costs of maintaining an east-west nexus when a large market existed just across the border.[14] Leading entrepreneurs in the industry advanced the opinion that emigration from Canada, which had reached an all-time high, would be reduced if costs of production of industry were lowered.[15]

In addition to the implement firms, many others in secondary iron and steel—stove makers and founders, tool makers and machine and engine works—denounced the raw material duties and claimed that access to the American market would bring economies of scale, cut distribution as well as production costs, and generate the potential for considerable expansion of the industry. In stove making, for example, the National Policy had led directly to overexpansion, and access to the American market was needed to relieve it. Even such specialized firms as the Waterous Engine Works and Raymond's sewing machine factory held out for Reciprocity. Raymond ridiculed the idea of Canada becoming a slaughter market, for he pointed out that under Reciprocity dumping was by definition impossible—the goods would be dumped right back into the laps of the producer again.[16]

A number of critically important points come out of these opinions. Many of the firms expressing them were headed by former National Policy advocates, especially in the secondary iron and steel industry. And their conversion to free trade indicates perhaps more than the conventional view that infants can grow up. With many firms, a more important contradiction of the National Policy came to light. Several expressed the opinion that the level of protection they enjoyed had been more than adequate under the old Mackenzie-Cartwright tariff of 17½%, and that many firms that had flourished under it were wiped out by the National Policy. This would indicate that the level of effective protection resulting from the 17½% so-called revenue tariff was greater than that of the supposedly protectionist National Policy, which had a considerable revenue-raising effect.

The Laurier victory in 1896 on an ostensibly low tariff policy came as a rude shock to some of the business world. The CMA had often noted that its membership was not so much Tory as National Policy in its allegiance,[17] and that the National Policy was the "keystone of political success." [18] It had, as usual, planned a pro-Tory strategy during the 1896 election, fearful of Liberal tariff intentions.[19] The pressure of agrarian opinion and Maritime discontent propelled Laurier into office to the considerable consternation of the CMA and other bodies like the Toronto Board of Trade, whose president, CPR magnate and financier Edmund Osler, immediately asked Laurier to be careful with the tariff.[20]

Just prior to the election, the Quebec cotton mills threatened to close if the results of the election were unfavourable.[21] And after the Laurier victory the Montreal Rolling Mills closed one of its branches, threw 400 men out of work, and announced it would stay closed until the new government's tariff intentions were made known.[22] The Pictou Charcoal Iron Company refused to fire its furnace until the tariff situation was clarified.[23]

Laurier himself was certainly amenable to cultivating the industrial community's support. Prior to the 1887 election he wrote to Edward Blake concerning a Montreal Liberal rally,

It was unanimously represented that the feeling in [the] city

would be very good, except for the fear among businessmen
that a change of administration would bring a radical change
in the tariff.[24]

And he asked his leader, Blake, for "some declaration that would
satisfy the manufacturers." During the 1896 campaign, Laurier
called for a revenue tariff, dismissing free trade out of hand, and
promised the business community a sort of permanent incidental
protection.[26] Further into the campaign he explicitly promised
that no major tariff changes would follow the election.[27]

In fact, no changes of any great economic significance were
initiated, apart from a new iron and steel policy. But a series of
minor alterations reflected an exceedingly clever political strategy. The reduction in iron and steel duties was complemented
by an expansion in the bounties to the primary industry. Refined
sugar duties were cut, as a sop to consumers, and at the same
time coal duties were raised to pay off the debt due to the
Fielding Liberal machine in Nova Scotia. To attempt to convince the farming community that the Liberal Party remained
loyal to its Clear Grit agrarian roots, the duty was eliminated on
binder twine and cut on barbed wire and agricultural implements. To try to bring a key sector of the industrial capitalist
class into the Liberal fold, increases in a range of textiles were
recorded, some of them poorly hidden behind a switch from
specific to *ad valorem* rates. An empty clause was attached to the
tariff permitting reduction by order in council where combines in
restraint of trade existed. And a new rising British imperial xenophobia was capitalized upon by the enactment of a 33⅓% imperial preference.

There were a few dissenting voices. The Dartmouth Rope
Works and the Dartmouth Sugar Refinery both announced they
were closing because of the tariff — and did not.[28] The woollen
cartel met, and graciously consented to accept their new 35% *ad
valorem* — formerly they had received 25% plus 5c per lb. —if
the government struck out the preference clause.[29] But in general
the strategy worked magnificently in shattering the old Macdonald grand alliance.

The CMA as a political force simply disappeared; it split
down the middle into its members traditional party loyalties
once its *raison d'être,* the tariff, was no longer threatened.[30] By
1899 Clifford Sifton, Laurier's new Minister of the Interior,
could claim that the tariff was a dead issue.[31] Together with the
new strategy of building transcontinental railway lines competitive with the CPR, Canadian commerce, finance, and organized
industry was effectively divided on regional lines, and as long as
that split was maintained, Laurier held office. By 1901, politics

had become so mundane that A. E. Ames, President of the Toronto Board of Trade, could comment on the upcoming election that "that tariff was one of the great questions before the country upon which the parties were able to divide with considerable fervour. . . . No such question is now before the country." The Liberal Party capitulation seemed complete. In response to a request from a reorganized and non-partisan CMA for tariff increases, the Liberal Finance Minister, W. S. Fielding, replied "Educate the people," and the CMA undertook to do just that.[32]

The new CMA owed allegiance to neither party, for it was a merger of the rump of the old Ontario-based organization (which itself was a logical outgrowth of the Ontario Manufacturers' Association) and the Montreal Manufacturers' Association.[33] The Montreal group had had its genesis in the mid-1870's under the auspices of the Montreal wholesale dry goods merchants and other members of the city's commercial elite — E. K. Greene, George Stephen, A.W. Ogilvie, A.F. Gault, D. Morrice, and others.[34] The two bodies, though assiduously cultivated by Macdonald and both tariff enthusiasts, had been sufficiently divided on other issues (particularly railways, which Montreal commercial capital tended to largely control) that the alliance between the two had been one of expediency and the National Policy. In his tariff policy Laurier accomplished what Macdonald could not — the depoliticization of *organized* industrialists.

Apart from the iron and steel policy, and a few changes in the agricultural implements tariff, the only noteworthy Fielding-Laurier departure was the Imperial Preference of 1897. While the Tory Party and the CMA were not enthusiastic, in fact the only industries really affected were cordage and twine, and woollens.[35] Canada's import pattern had increasingly shifted towards iron and steel products, coal and petroleum, raw cotton, and similar goods in which the U.S. had a substantial advantage over Britain. Holes in the tariff for raw material imports thus benefited American exports. This pattern was reinforced by a number of factors. The American branch plants which grew rapidly in Canada after 1896 had a built-in propensity to import from their parents, or their parents' relatives in the U.S.[36] In addition, the conservatism of British industrial patterns, their inability or unwillingness to adapt to Canadian requirements, and the spillover of advertising from American periodicals all helped American goods continue their steady displacement of British.[37] Hence Britain was forced to rely on its old textile export staple to try to keep up a share of Canadian trade, and the imperial preference led to such sharp protests from the big Canadian woollen mills that the tariff was revised upward in 1904. Even

the brief respite of 1897 to 1904 was regressive, for it had benefited only an upper-income class of consumers who were financially better equipped to bear the burden of the tariff than the
worker or farm consumer who bought only the less luxurious
local products.

In exports, the opposite pattern manifested itself. The traditional deficit with Britain gave way in 1891 to a trade balance
surplus, which grew steadily. The importance of the British
market for staple and manufactured output grew relative to the
U.S. during the early years of the boom, though the U.S. market
tended to regain some of the lost ground after 1900.

TABLE XV (1)

Trade of Canada

Year	% Exports to U.S.	U.K.	Other		% Imports from U.S.	U.K.	Other
1880	38	52	10		40	48	12
1885	41	48	11		46	40	14
1890	40	49	11		46	39	15
1895	32	57	11		50	31	19
1900	32	59	9		59	25	16
1905	37	51	12		60	24	16
1910	36	50	14		56	27	17
1913	39	49	12		65	27	8

Source: *CYB,* 1915, pp. 256-7.

Imperial preference was regarded with skepticism by the organized manufacturers. Imperial free trade was rejected out of
hand. The tariff was regarded as necessary to offset the advan-
tages accruing to the British producers from their cheap labour,
lower capital costs, and lower unit production costs from economies of scale.[39] The only sort of imperial preference acceptable
was one that would "raise the general tariff so high that when a
preference is granted to British manufacturers, the minimum
duties will be sufficient to safeguard Canadian industry."[40]

As to the implement industry reductions, in 1898 the tariff
was cut to 17½%, but the raw material rates were reduced by the
same proportion. In 1907, a further cut to 15% was matched by a
complete drawback on all imported inputs regardless of whether
the output was for domestic or foreign markets. The *Toronto Sun*
noted the hypocrisy involved in the supposed move towards
lower protection:

When the privilege of free raw material is taken into account it will be seen that the agricultural implements industry, instead of having what might be called a moderate rate of protection, has really a high rate of protection. This is where the "joker" in the agricultural implement tariff comes in.[41]

The Tariff Enquiry Commission of 1906 took evidence all across Canada, and the results were very predictable. Many firms demanded reductions in their raw materials, several of them insisting that the raw material taxes meant negative net effective protection.[42] A number of firms demanded higher duties on their final product, including the Raymond Sewing Machine Co., which 16 years earlier had been actively pushing for Reciprocity. At the same time, the Singer branch plant was expanding rapidly, implying that the level of duties should have been quite adequate.[43] The cotton mills were once again seeking higher duties, joined by the lumber mills, who cited the higher prairie farm incomes as justification for the price increases that would follow the tariff hike.[44] On the other hand, demands for reductions were heard from farm groups across Canada.[45] In 1907 a general upward revision of the tariff was made.

Reciprocity, 1911

During the Reciprocity campaign of 1911, the tensions and conflicts between different groups in the Canadian economy came to the surface, and the defeat of Reciprocity was a watershed point in the history of Canadian commercial policy. Reciprocity was certainly not the only economic issue to surface during the 1911 election campaign. The failure of the Farmers' Bank and Fielding's complicity probably helped to defeat the Liberal Party in several rural Ontario constituencies which would normally have been sympathetic to Reciprocity. The Ontario Hydro agitation of the Ontario municipalities and the Whitney government in Ontario combined against the Liberal Party, many of whose leading lights were directly identified with the power cartel. The Grand Trunk strike of 1910 led to mass dismissals, and the pro-company stance of the Liberal Minister of Labour, William Lyon Mackenzie King, alienated organized labour from the party. But Reciprocity, if not the sole or even the main issue, was an extremely important one, and its defeat the chief long-term result of the election.

Just why Laurier and the Liberal establishment adopted Reciprocity in 1911 is a question that has never been satisfactorily answered. There were undoubtedly a number of factors involved. Farm unrest certainly played a role — 1910 was the year of the "Siege of Ottawa" by organized farmers from across Canada, especially but certainly far from exclusively from the new staple-producing areas. And in early twentieth-century Canada organized farmers were, potentially at least, the single most powerful opposition group to big business interests. Then, too, the Cape Breton coal mines once more played an important role. H. N. Whitney had consolidated his hold on the mines and, ipso facto, on W. S. Fielding, his representative in Ottawa. Fielding seemed the leader of the pro-Reciprocity forces in the Laurier cabinet. In 1867 the coal mines of Cape Breton, led by Charles Tupper, one of the principal proprietors, pushed for Confederation to secure a Canadian market to replace the American one lost in 1866 with the abrogation of Reciprocity. This was a failure. Even after the National Policy, Ontario remained closed to Nova Scotia bituminous, for Ontario capital gradually secured free access to American anthracite. A brief period of lower American tariffs came to an end in 1897. And to salvage the fortunes of the investors in the Cape Breton mines, Reciprocity was a last resort.

American branch plants in Canada played a central role in crystallizing the issues. The American support for the treaty was in fact often based on the hope that free trade would lead to a movement of American branch plants back to the U.S.,[46] despite the fact that the treaty under consideration applied only to primary products. The Governor of Massachusetts, Eugene Foss, who himself had a branch plant in Canada, declared that

> the present tariff system has resulted in securing approximately $300 million of American capital to Canada to build up branch industry which can compete with American factories in foreign markets. It has resulted in stifling the growth of Massachusetts and kept us out of the business and commerce which belongs to us in every right.[47]

The Wall Street Journal issued a call for American firms to move back across the border.[48] Other American journals and business groups such as the New York Chamber of Commerce emphasized the access to Canadian natural resources inherent under the terms of the treaty. The president of the American Association of Manufacturers asked, "why should this country be so anxious to exhaust its mineral wealth and denude its forests that it should bar these products from other countries?"[49] The great American trusts sought expansion of their markets into Canada not only as an alternative to direct investment but also as a way of avoiding renewed outbreaks of violent price wars to extend markets at the expense of rivals at home.

In Canada, organized farmers, with a few exceptions, were the main force behind the treaty, while most business organizations — financial, commercial, transportation and manufacturing, were adamantly opposed. Only a very few resource industries indicated support. The Canadian Bankers' Association advanced the view that British investments in Canada would be injured. To prove that the great bulk of Canadian opinion was opposed, it conducted its own public opinion poll and concluded that

> the consensus of present Canadian opinion as expressed in unmistakeable terms by the Montreal Board of Trade, by the Chambre de Commerce, by the Manufacturers' Association . . .

was antagonistic to the treaty.

The strongest anti-Reciprocity arguments in Canada were precisely the strongest pro-Reciprocity arguments in the U.S. — that Canadian natural resources would be looted and branch plants would leave the country. But inside the Commons the debate was remarkable in that for the first time opinions were voiced that the loss of American branch plants might not be an unmitigated disaster. Liberal members, perhaps out of sheer opportunism, suggested that profits drained out of Canada by American branch plants exceeded the benefits they brought.[52] There was little option for the Liberal Party but to take this line of defence, for the brunt of the Tory assault focussed on the effects of the tariff on American branch plants and the resulting employment generated.[53]

Liberals who crossed the floor did likewise. Sir Clifford Sifton asked,

> Will this proposition assist in transferring American capital to the construction of factories in Canada which has been going on in Canada for several years past at a very rapid rate? Surely we cannot conclude that it will.[54]

The member for Welland, where a number of branch plants had located, broke with his party and credited the tariff with "bringing millions of dollars of capital to our shores to build up manufacturing industry in our land."[55] Quaker Oats threatened to leave Canada if the treaty went through, and this was noted in the debate. Lloyd Harris, of Massey-Harris, and the member from Brantford generalized from the Quaker case and claimed many others were on the verge of leaving. He said,

> I want American manufacturers to be forced to establish plants on this side of the line, and provide work for our Canadian workmen if they want to have the advantage of supply of our home market.[56]

To drive the point home, Massey-Harris threatened to leave Canada if the treaty passed.[57] Sir George Foster, who led the Tory attack, predicted that a drain of population would accompany the withdrawal of branch plants: "Just as the flag follows trade, just so labour follows capital."[58] Foster's denial of the trade-creating possibilities of the treaty, based on his observation that the two countries had surpluses of the same goods, wins him no points for perspicacity, since the same firms were active on both sides of the border.

Outside the House, big business waged a titanic struggle. The Laurier strategy had been to drive a wedge down the middle of industry and commerce, separating the business community into two antagonistic camps; it collapsed as their common interests transcended their sectional conflicts. The Toronto Liberal establishment staged an open collective revolt, led by Edmund Walker, E. R. Wood, and others.[59] The railroads were frightened by the knowledge that J. J. Hill (with his Great Northern system, which had already begun to build an elevator system in Canada),[60] was waiting to divert traffic into the U.S. The CPR then put Van Horne to work against the treaty.[61] Sir William Mackenzie fought it for the Canadian Northern, and while the Grand Trunk in Canada was forced to support Laurier in return for the government's assistance in smashing the strike of its machine shop employees, A. W. Smithers, chairman of the English board of directors, denounced the treaty.[62] Even Rudyard Kipling pitched in on behalf of the opposition.

There were exceptions to the hostility of Canadian secondary industry to the Treaty. One rather strange case of pro-Reciprocity sentiment came from the Patrick Burns Co., the Calgary meat packing firm which went on record as favouring the treaty[63] —at the same time, Sifton had declared in Parliament that Reciprocity would destroy the Canadian meat packing industry,[64] and the CMA did likewise, claiming as well that Reciprocity would expose the Canadian farmer to the rapacity of the American meat packing trust.[65]

Among some smaller manufacturing industries the treaty was welcomed. In Guelph, Ontario, many if not most of the firms declared in favour. Two notable exceptions were the Bell Piano and Organ Company and the Raymond Manufacturing Company, both of which had been pro-Reciprocity in 1890. While they did not actually publicly declare their intentions, both firms let their workmen off with pay during working hours to listen to Tory candidates.[66] In Goderich, a long list of firms including machinery, engine, and tool work, furniture, lumber, and planing mills, vehicle manufacturers, musical instrument makers, and others supported the treaty.[67]

That small manufacturers in highly specialized lines open to severe competition were in favour of Reciprocity, while the big manufacturing interests were almost universally opposed, calls for an explanation. Between the campaigns of 1891 and 1911, a radical change had come over the pattern of Canadian industrial organization—the creation of the waterlogged merger. With these huge mergers the tariff had been capitalized as assured earnings in calculating their water levels, and the loss of the tariff would have threatened their ability to pay dividends and interests on their bloated capitalization. Prices in Canada had to be kept up to squeeze out an earnings level commensurate with their capitalization. Firms which might well have been able to withstand price competition with the American giants with any sensible capitalization had been wrecked by the actions of the Montreal promoters who created the trusts. Strikingly absent from the list of pro-Reciprocity advocates in 1911 was the milling cartel, which had favoured the treaty in 1890. In the interim, the cartel had been replaced by several mergers, and the sole flour mill to favour Reciprocity in 1911 was a small firm left out of the merger craze. The salt cartel too had been displaced by a merger. And in primary iron and steel the only advocates of the treaty were two directors of the Nova Scotia Steel and Coal Co.,[68] the least overcapitalized of the giants in the industry.

The campaign itself led to a sharp rise in American interest in Canada, and Canadian dealers descended on Chicago and did a brisk business in selling securities tied to western Canadian development.[69] And while the CPR directors were avidly fighting the treaty, CPR advertisements in Britain for land or equity sales stated that Reciprocity would double the value of CPR land.[70]

Nor can the Laurier defeat be completely imputed to the Reciprocity Treaty. Apart from the several other economic issues, the revulsion of Quebec from his naval policy did a great deal of damage, while at the same time seven Nationalist candidates in Montreal, nominally Tory, declared for Reciprocity.[71] Moreover, Laurier appealed to the polls with the existing electoral map. A redistribution by population based on the 1911 census would have given ten more seats to the free-trade West, and ten less to the East, for a net transfer of twenty to the Liberal camp.[72]

The Tory tactics too must have helped a great deal, if two

1912 by-elections are any indication. In the appropriately named Macdonald riding in Manitoba, the Tory Minister of Public Works took personal charge of the campaign in collaboration with the provincial Premier, Sir Rodmond Roblin. The two schemers spent a great deal of time terrorizing the electorate by tales of hundreds of "thugs and thieves" from Saskatchewan and Alberta who were supposed to have descended on the riding to work for the Liberals. Roblin, putting into practice the principles he had learned in his campaign to stamp out independent grain futures dealers, ordered the police to arrest a number of Liberal campaign workers who were held without counsel or bail until the election returned a Tory. All of the arrested men were freed; only one was charged, and the case quickly dismissed. However, a court appeal subsequently overturned the election and a new contest was ordered. In the Richelieu by-election the Tory Minister of Public Works was equally active, though without success. It became clear just what the "Public Works" portfolio meant when, on the Minister's instructions, Sir Rodolphe Forget was sent to the riding to bluntly inform the voters that the promise of a subsidy of hundreds of thousands of dollars for a branch railway depended on their return of the Tory candidate.[73]

After the 1911 election produced a Tory landslide, the equity of every large trust in Canada shot up on the exchanges, while the price of wheat fell two cents a bushel in Winnipeg and rose six cents in Minneapolis,[74] and American northwestern railway shares fell while CPR shares rose.[75] No more eloquent and revealing commentary on the nature of the main forces involved, and on the victors and the losers, could have been made. Immediately after the campaign ended, a renewed inflow of branch plants occurred. The enquiries from American firms were reported as never having been so numerous.[76] And in 1913 Governor Foss began moving his machinery to Galt from Massachusetts.[77]

Notes to Chapter XV

1.   *CM,* May 6, 1887, p. 263; March 20, 1891, p. 198.
2.   *CM,* Feb. 17, 1893, p. 105.
3.   *CM,* July 19, 1895, p. 57.
4.   *RCRLC, Ontario Evidence,* p. 365.
5.   *Globe,* Jan. 9, 1891.
6.   *Globe,* Dec. 5, 1890.
7.   *Globe,* Dec. 26, 1890.
8.   *Globe,* Nov. 27, 1890.
9.   *SCC, Evidence,* p. 390.
10. *Globe,* Nov. 24, 1890.

11. *HCD,* March 7, 1878, pp. 859-60.
12. *Globe,* Nov. 20, 1890.
13. *Globe,* Nov. 27, 1890; Nov. 29, 1890.
14. *Globe,* Nov. 24, 1890; Nov. 29, 1890; Dec. 17, 1890.
15. *Globe,* Dec. 19, 1890; Dec. 26, 1890.
16. *Globe,* Dec. 5, 1890; Dec. 15, 1890; Dec. 19, 1890; Nov. 17, 1890; Jan. 5, 1891.
17. *CM,* Jan. 15, 1892, pp. 35-6.
18. *CM,* Sept. 2, 1892, p. 132.
19. *CM,* June 5, 1896, p. 468.
20. Toronto Board of Trade, *Annual Report,* 1896, p. 13.
21. *MT,* July 3, 1896, p. 14.
22. *MT,* March 19, 1897, p. 1243.
23. *MT,* March 12, 1897, p. 1220.
24. Laurier to Blake, Jan. 14, 1887, *Blake Papers.*
25. Laurier to Blake, Jan. 21, 1887, *Blake Papers.*
26. *MT,* June 5, 1896, p. 1557.
27. *MT,* July 17, 1896, p. 77.
28. *MT,* May 21, 1897, p. 1527.
29. *MT,* May 7, 1897, p. 1467.
30. See especially T. W. Acheson, *The Social Origins of Canadian Industrialism,* pp. 400, 451, *et passim,* which is excellent on this, as well as many other points.
31. *MT,* March 17, 1899, p. 1223.
32. *IC,* Nov. 1903, p. 201.
33. *MT,* Oct. 26, 1900, p. 536.
34. *MT,* Jan. 23, 1880, p. 860.
35. E. C. Porritt, *Sixty Years of Protection,* p. 389.
36. D. R. Annett, *British Preference in Canadian Commercial Policy,* pp. 43-4.
37. J. A. Hobson, *Canada Today,* pp. 72-4.
38. E. C. Porritt, *The Revolt in Canada,* pp. 20-1.
39. *IC,* Sept. 1903, p. 57.
40. *IC,* July, 1903, p. 519.
41. *Toronto Sun,* Nov. 2, 1910, cited in E. C. Porritt, *The Revolt in Canada,* p. 84n.
42. *TEC,* pp. 11, 71.
43. *TEC,* pp. 153-4.
44. *TEC,* pp. 49-51, 28-31, 48, 73, 144.
45. *TEC,* pp. 5, 125-7, 134-5, 140, 512-8, 565, 574-80, 619-21, *et passim.*
46. *IC,* May 1911, p. 1072.
47. Cited in *HCD,* March 8, 1911, p. 4905.
48. *MT,* March 4, 1911, p. 918.
49. New York Chamber of Commerce, *Reciprocity Report,* pp. 4-6.
50. *JCBA,* Oct. 1910, pp. 44-5.
51. *IC,* May 1911, p. 1072.
52. *HCD,* March 9, 1911, p. 4954.
53. *HCD,* Feb. 23, 1911, p. 4171; July 19, 1911, p. 9776.
54. *HCD,* Feb. 28, 1911, p. 4394.
55. *HCD,* March 2, 1911, p. 4484-7.
56. *HCD,* Feb. 28, 1911, p. 4395.
57. *HCD,* March 8, 1911, p. 4905.
58. M. Denison, *Harvest Triumphant,* p. 200.
59. *HCD,* Feb. 14, 1911, p. 3542.
60. *CAR,* 1911, pp. 47-8.
61. *CE,* Jan. 1900, p. 256.

62.   W. Vaughn, *Sir William Van Horne*, pp. 205-7.
63.   *Globe,* Sept. 13, 1911.
64.   *HCD,* Feb. 28, 1911, pp. 4394, 4399.
65.   *IC,* July, 1911, p. 1290.
66.   *Globe,* Sept. 12, 1911.
67.   *Globe,* Sept. 18, 1911.
68.   *Globe,* Sept. 9, 1911.
69.   *CF,* Sept. 16, 1911, p. 793.
70.   *Ec,* Sept. 23, 1911, p. 599.
71.   *Globe,* Sept. 13, 1911.
72.   *Ec,* Oct. 11, 1911, p. 825.
73.   *HCD,* Nov. 25, 1912, pp. 37-55 *et passim; GGG,* Nov. 19, 1913.
74.   *GGG,* Sept. 27, 1911.
75.   *CFC,* Sept. 23, 1911, p. 756.
76.   *IC,* Dec. 1911, p. 585.
77.   *MT,* Aug. 9, 1913, p. 287.

Canadian capital and clearer northern brains are fast turning the island of Cuba into a modern hive of industry.

Journal of Commerce, 1900

CHAPTER XVI
Canadian Commercial and Financial Expansion Abroad

Investment and Empire

During the period before World War I when Canada was a net borrower, it was also engaged in the export of capital. Nor were these international loans always minor in scale, for during the period 1895-1901 the balance of trade was in surplus over-all and an export of capital net of continued borrowings from the U.S. and Britain occurred.

Because of the unevenness of development of various sectors of the economy, capital tended to flow more facilely internationally and intrasectorally than it did intranationally and intersectorally. These tendencies were particularly acute in Canada before the war because of the sharp division between industrial capital and commercial capital. As with virtually every colonial economy, the dominant stratum of Canada's capitalist and entrepreneurial class was commercial, linked to metropolitan capital, especially British. And it was this commercial group that accounted for the overwhelmingly large share of Canadian investments abroad. Their strength in the Canadian economy in banking and finance, transportation, and utilities was reflected in their extensions abroad and their diversion of funds abroad, to the detriment of industrial capital formation within Canada.

Capital exports went almost exclusively to two areas — to the United States and to the Caribbean and South America. Since the one was a major metropolis and the others economic hinterlands, the role performed by the Canadian ventures in the two areas was very different. The American investments represented substantial outflows of capital from Canada: the others did not, for the South American and Caribbean investments were devices for draining funds from these areas. Thus, the investments in the U.S. helped to develop and strengthen American economic power, while those in the Latin American areas helped perpetuate underdevelopment. Those in the U.S. were either rentier type of investments or oriented toward servicing the movement of commodities; those in the Caribbean and South America were aggressive, domineering enterprises representing substantial economic control.

Investment tended to follow the patterns of trade. Canadian investments abroad fell into the following categories:

(1) Bank establishments in the United States to facilitate capital movements and commodity exchange between the U.S. and Canada. With these banks, and even without the actual establishment of branches, went large amounts of call money and short-term loans and deposits in New York to be used for currency speculation or call loans to stock brokers. Without the Canadian funds, Wall Street would have had difficulty conducting its operations.

(2) Insurance companies established branches in the U.S. which, unlike the banks, actively solicited business there. However, the insurance companies were substantial net exporters of capital from Canada, despite their American business, for they were holders of large portfolios of American securities, especially utility bonds and stocks.

(3) Railway extensions and operations in the U.S. were considerable. Their purpose, like that of the banks, was to facilitate the movement of commodities over long distances rather than to generate local traffic.

(4) A sizeable amount of individual, as well as institutional, portfolio investments existed in the U.S.

(5) The smallest group of Canadian investments in the U.S. were direct investments of industry, horizontal or vertical extensions of Canadian oligopolies, or investments forced by American commercial policy.

(6) A network of banks was established across the Caribbean and beyond which, unlike their American ventures, were active in developing and dominating local banking business. Insurance companies, too, established a dominant position in local business. Both extracted funds for export back to Canada, and their holdings of local securities were virtually non-existent.

(7) Railways and utility operations in Latin America also differed radically from those in the U.S. The railways were

designed to develop local traffic and resources. The utilities were generally wholly owned direct investments, rather than the portfolio investments typical of Canadian holdings in the U.S.

In terms of the chronology of investment patterns, before 1867 most Canadian investments abroad were in the form of currency speculation in the U.S., and in short-term financing of commodity movements, with a few railway extensions after mid-century. After Confederation, while short-term loans continued to bulk large, exports of long-term debt capital began to assume importance, and railway extensions multiplied. By the end of the century, the proliferation of financial institutions' branches and agencies, begun in the 1850's, reached a peak. Towards the end of the century, too, began the large-scale movements of Canadian capital into Latin America, first in the form of direct investments in branches by financial institutions, and after the turn of the century, the utility and railroad promoters. It was a period of consolidation and expansion of the British Empire in which Canada sought its own resource hinterlands.

The movements of capital at the end of the century reflected major structural changes in the Canadian payments position, in its capital market, and its financial institutions. The Bank of Montreal, for example, was the largest bank on the American continent. It had much earlier begun in some functions to replace the Barings, which came close to collapsing in 1890, after a revolution in the Argentine threatened the value of Argentine debentures in which the merchant banking firm was heavily interested. In 1892, the Bank of Montreal assumed the role of Canada's financial agent in London, a role until then exercised by the Barings and the Glyns. And in the Baring reorganization that followed the crisis, substantial shares were held by their lordships Strathcona and Mount-Stephen. The Canadian financiers' presence in such an imperial institution as the Barings reflected well the new division of power in the Empire.

As a prelude to the export of capital, too, changes occurred in the asset-liability structures of various Canadian financial institutions. During the period when the balance of trade was moving into surplus, mortgage loan companies reduced their foreign liabilities, their debentures abroad falling by $17 million from 1893 to 1899. Bank deposits grew 60% from 1896 to 1900, while bank current discounts grew only 40%.[1] Chartered banks began to usurp the great bulk of the savings deposit business, and interest rates were falling. A great increase in call loans for speculations in New York occurred. By 1900 the banks had $60 million invested abroad in call loans, short loans, or railroad securities, and the sum grew steadily.

Life insurance companies also became active in lending abroad, and curtailed their home investments, especially municipal debentures. For the earnings from assisting municipalities in building roads and sewers were a pittance compared to the attractions of foreign utility promotions. In 1891, less than one per cent of their investments were foreign, while by 1911 nearly fourteen per cent were.

TABLE XVI (1)

Life Insurance Company Foreign Investments, 1891-1911

Life Companies	% Total Investments		
	1891	1901	1911
British & Colonial Gov't Bonds	0.22	0.25	0.26
Foreign Gov't Bonds	0.55	0.18	0.21
Corporate & Railroad Bonds			
— U.S.	—	3.13	10.22
— Foreign	—	0.29	0.65
Stocks			
— U.S.	—	0.88	2.45
— Foreign	—	—	0.40
Total	0.77	4.73	14.19

Source: Superintendent of Insurance, *Report,* Vol. 11, 1929, p. xxxii.

The rise of Canada to the role of a mini-metropolis was not a sudden development. Canada's foreign adventures had long historical roots in the logic of Canadian development patterns within the international context of British imperialism, an imperialism that warmed the hearts as it filled the pocketbooks of Canadian commercial capitalism. As early as 1860, Sir Charles Tupper used the phrase "an Empire on which the sun never sets,"[2] fifty years before it became the rallying cry of another staunch Maritime imperialist, Lord Beaverbrook. By 1911 the *Globe* could seriously raise the question, "Will Imperial Government eventually be in the Dominion?" citing the opinion of Sir Frederick Young, vice-president of the Royal Colonial Institute, that Canada would soon become "the centre of the Empire."[3] A leading member of the banking establishment fought Reciprocity in 1911 on the grounds that it threatened the unity of "we, the allied and confederate races of Britain, numbering in all some 61,700,000 *whites.*"[4] Sir Edmund Walker in 1912 assured the Canadian Club of Montreal that "we are determined to do our share and eventually to pay our share towards the perpetuation of the British Empire forever."[5]

Nor were words alone offered. Colonel Garnet Wolsely, who in 1870 had brought "law and order" and an army of land speculators to Manitoba, was soon promoted to the position of chief of staff for the house of Baring. Shortly after his forays into the Canadian Northwest, Sir Garnet Wolsely led the British forces in the war of conquest against the Ashanti to seize control of the West African coastal trade and access to the gold resources of the interior. (It was during this war that Lord Baden-Powell invented his cheerful homily regarding the proper education of the English upper-class youth, pointing out that "football is a good game, but better than it, better than any other game, is that of 'manhunting'.")[6]

In 1882, General Wolsely crushed the rebellion in Egypt against the rule of British capital and assured that Sir Evlyn Baring (Lord Cromer) would be de facto the next Pasha. A regime of corrupt tax collectors were then imposed upon the captive Sudan until the people there rose up in rebellion against their exactions. It then fell to Wolsely the task of crushing the insurrection. Canada at first refused military assistance for the "Gordon Relief Mission" and its bloody aftermath. Canadian artillery battalions were not enlisted for foreign service, and high unemployment in the U.S. had stirred unrest among Fenians, who threatened to invade Canada if she sent troops against the Mahdi.[7] However, a volunteer contingent was mounted, including a large number of Indian and Québécois boatmen. After a Hamilton firm was awarded the contract to supply the Canadian Nile expedition with tobacco, the *Hamilton Times* enthusiastically declared:

> What with Canadian men, Canadian officers, Canadian clothing, Canadian canoes, and the best Canadian tobacco, Gordon is safe.[8]

On yet another imperial front Lord Wolsely was active along with Canadian troops. In addition to the regular Canadian contingent, whose lives Fielding agreed to sacrifice in exchange for the admission of Canadian-inscribed stock to the trustee list, Lord Strathcona equipped from his personal fortune a body of cavalry, known as "Lord Strathcona's Horse," to safeguard British investments in the gold mines of the Boer republics. And of course huge numbers of conscripted lives were patriotically sacrificed in the great struggle over the division of the spoils in 1914-1918.

Canada's stake in all this was far from sentimental. The president of the Canadian Bankers' Association declared at its annual meeting in 1898:

Are we not part and parcel of an empire that is world wide? . . . Can we do nothing to stimulate and encourage trade within the empire? . . . Of what use is the shedding of our best blood on the sands of Africa or on the snows of the Himalayas if nothing is to come of their sacrifice but military glory?[9]

It was of course a rhetorical question, the answer to which had long been evident.

Pre-Confederation Investments Abroad

Canadian interest in the West Indies predated the American Revolution. Nova Scotia merchants, and to a lesser degree those of Montreal, assiduously cultivated trade ties, and mercantile credit in conjunction with long-distance trade flows was the first export of Canadian capital to the area. From the Revolution until as late as 1900, Nova Scotia merchants struggled in vain against those in New England to establish their hegemony in the Caribbean. Trade in raw materials moved both ways: fish and timber to the Indies; sugar, salt, rum, and molasses back to the Maritimes. To facilitate the commodity movements, the Halifax Banking Company established a partnership in 1837 with the London-based Colonial Bank to service the area. But Nova Scotia merchants remained secondary to those of New England.

In the Far East, the trail was blazed by the Hudson's Bay Company which, while a British company, had a substantial Canadian participation that grew over time. The Hudson's Bay Company posts spread to Honolulu, and from there their trade connections reached the Orient. Canadian trade and investment followed this path.

Capital of the Province of Canada moved to the United States in several forms. One early case of direct investment occurred in 1825, when Montreal capitalists became shareholders in the Erie Canal.[10] This canal was the instrument of destruction of Montreal's commercial hegemony over the American midwestern states,[11] and the presence of Montreal capital in its construction and operation tends to confirm the view expressed some decades later by Lenin that "the bourgeoisie will compete to sell the rope to hang themselves."

Before 1840, Montreal capital played a key role in financing American international trade. The U.S. ran a steady balance of trade deficit with Europe which was covered in part by loans and investments, in part by immigrants' imports of cash, and in part by imports of specie from Spanish America. The specie moved from New Orleans to New York, where it was sold for Province of Canada sterling drafts on London. Canada ran a balance of trade surplus with the U.S., permitting an export of capital to New York for currency speculation, while it ran a deficit with Britain. The triangulation pattern permitted large and profitable foreign exchange transactions for Canadian financiers.[12] Montreal financiers invested virtually nothing in the development of their province, and infrastructure had to be built with imports of British capital. At the same time, Montreal capital moved to New York in such quantities that Canada, from an early date, assumed an importance in American money markets far out of proportion to her size and wealth, helping in the process to perpetuate Canada's relative underdevelopment.

Throughout the 1850's, Canadian commercial capitalists began extending their interests into the American northwest states and became actively involved in crop movements, the objective being to divert American agricultural produce away from New York and the Erie Canal along the St. Lawrence route. During the 1857 crisis, in both Canada and the U.S., bank credit contracted sharply and severe deflation ensued. In the U.S., bank failures were numerous. Chicago being the centre of midwestern commerce, Illinois bank notes in particular were being rejected by merchants all over the U.S., especially in St. Louis, the chief commercial outlet of the area.

But one stabilizing factor emerged. To divert the through trade to Montreal, Canadian banks drained funds from Canada to purchase large amounts of wheat in Chicago, paying for it in drafts on New York. These Canadian purchases provided most of the eastern exchange that was offered on the Chicago market at that critical time, and their operations prevented a catastrophic fall in the price of American grain. They also helped precipitate one of the worst Canadian produce price deflations in its history. Commercial and agricultural distress was widespread; failures escalated due to the credit squeeze, and the sharp reduction in dutiable commodity imports threw government finances into chaos, leading to the new demands for higher taxation through tariff increases to pay off the British investors in Grand Trunk securities.

So helpful were the Canadian banks to Chicago during the crisis that their notes were used for both currency and remittances. The leading newspaper, *The Democrat*, urged the Canadian banks to replace their agencies in the city with full-fledged branches. The Canadian banks, with their "immense control of capital" compared to the local banks, would "provide the nucleus for the establishment of mercantile houses here rivalling in extent those of Montreal, Toronto and Hamilton."[13] Despite

America's industrial strength, Canada's commercial and financial capacities were already enviable.

Thus, even before the Civil War the patterns of Canadian investment in the U.S. were established. It was investment in commerce, in facilitating the movement of commodities, or in exchange speculation associated with commodity movements. The export of capital was at the expense of Canadian development. And it created a north-south flow of funds that seriously impeded east-west integration of the Canadian economy.

The Civil War produced a bonanza for Canadian financiers. By 1863, Canadian investments in U.S. bonds were estimated to total $50 million.[14] The Bank of Upper Canada, the Commercial Bank, and the Bank of Montreal largely replaced the eastern American banks in moving western crops. During the war, too, gold reached 300% in New York, and the Bank of Montreal traded heavily. Borrowers paid in U.S. currency as security, and the bank used the currency to discount high-class trade bills, thus earning a double profit.[15]

The gold with which the Montreal speculated was derived from the Ontario banks by the bank's refusing to settle claims in notes and insisting on specie payments.[16] The result was a chronic drain on the smaller banks' reserves and a credit contraction, the burden of which fell most heavily on Ontario farmers. While the other banks were precluded from taking part in the speculation to any great extent by virtue of the fact that it was their specie that financed the Bank of Montreal's escapades, whenever spare gold could be found they would join the fun on whatever scale their resources permitted. The fledgling Bank of Toronto at one point had to replace a Montreal branch manager who proved over-anxious to commit the little bank's reserves to the speculative mania.[17]

Some of the funds drained off from Ontario also went to provide extra credits to the Montreal wholesale merchants, who were in their glory during the war.[18] For the war meant the breaking up of the marketing patterns of the American northwest farmers, and hence meant the temporary hegemony of the St. Lawrence route over its American competitors for moving American grain.[19] The ultimate result of the siphoning-off of specie from Ontario was to add another tier to the Bank of Montreal's already double profit balance by precipitating the collapse of its two leading competitors. The Bank of Upper Canada passed its dividend in 1864 and 1865. With Macdonald's ministry in office, the government accounts were obligingly shifted from the Upper Canada to the Montreal, followed by the principal railroad accounts. In 1866 the Bank of Upper Canada suspended.[20] The Commercial followed shortly. The failure of the Commercial was due to more than just the Montreal's credit squeeze and the failure of its sister institution, though these were important factors. Its collapse was also bound up with the tangled story of Canada's first railway investments in the U.S.

Railway competition in Canada at the time took the form of the two big trunk lines, the Great Western and the Grand Trunk, seeking to outdo each other in neglecting the needs of Canadian commerce to service the American entrepot trade. Between 1852 and 1853, the Great Western secured £770,000 in Government of Canada "loans" of the usually permanent variety. Of this some $1,225,000 was illegally used to construct the Detroit and Milwaukee Railroad. In addition, the Commercial Bank lent the Detroit and Milwaukee £250,000. The Great Western subsequently foreclosed on its mortgage on the Detroit and Milwaukee and repudiated the £250,000, transferring its account to the Bank of Montreal in the process.[21] A court case ensued, and the Commercial won $1,700,000 worth of Detroit and Milwaukee seven per cent bonds in settlement.[22] Instead of selling them at a substantial loss, the bank decided to hold them, and when the Bank of Montreal's credit squeeze began the Commercial found itself in a liquidity crisis.[23] Under the terms of the agreement (whereby the Bank of Montreal became the government's agent, leading to the collapse of the Bank of Upper Canada), the government could not extend aid to any rival without the prior permission of the Bank of Montreal. This was granted once; then subsequently refused.[24] The Commercial failed shortly after.

Confederation approached with the Bank of Montreal's dominance within Canada virtually unchallenged, while the Canadian banks continued to extend their role in the U.S. even after the end of the Civil War. The American banks only rarely tried to enter the field of foreign banking, and the Canadian ones very quickly got the upper hand. The new Bank of Commerce, Toronto's attempt to fill the void left by the collapse of the two big Ontario banks, quickly moved into buying bills of exchange drawn in the U.S. on cotton and other merchandise, and selling bills drawn on its London correspondents.[25]

Post-Confederation Commercial Patterns

In the post-Confederation period and beyond, Canada remained essentially a resource hinterland for Britain and, to a lesser extent, the U.S., with its payments position showing a new triangulation in reverse of the earlier one. While its balance of trade was in deficit with both Britain and the U.S. until 1890, it thereafter showed a rising deficit with the U.S. coupled with a substantial and increasing surplus with Britain. Even during the 1895 to 1901 period when its balance of trade was in surplus over-all, it was only its large surplus with Britain that offset the continuing growth in its deficit with the United States.

Despite the dominance of primary exports and manufactured imports, there were exports of manufactured goods during the period. It was part of the pay-off from the "industrialization by invitation" strategy based on patent laws so restrictive and tariff walls so high that American firms were forced to establish Canadian affiliates and branches, and much of Canadian-manufactured exports to the Empire and other areas came from these branch plants and licensed ventures. It was part of the commercial strategy of shifting the locus of production northward. Isaac Buchanan's pre-Confederation northern vision looked forward to free trade with the U.S., on the assumption it would force British firms to migrate to Canada to export to the U.S. Instead, American firms moved to Canada to export to the Empire, for, as the CMA put it:

> Canada belongs industrially to the American continental system, though not perhaps in the sense implied by Mr. Goldwyn Smith. The force of material circumstances is upon us, and we cannot escape from it. We must manufacture and manage our manufactures as the Americans do.[26]

These manufactured exports are important not only because the American firms often let their Canadian offspring handle the Empire trade, but also because they dispute the usual presumption that protected industry, by definition, cannot export.[27]

Canadian transportation projects too were part of an imperial design, the CPR being the integral link in Lord Strathcona's "all-red-route," which included steamships and cables on both the Atlantic and the Pacific. To the west the CPR followed the route of the fur trade — to Honolulu — and the Hawaiian Islands came close to becoming a Canadian colony. To cover its deficit in the wilderness stretches, the CPR strenuously developed long distance Pacific trade, planning as well an all-British cable from Vancouver to Japan and China with connections to Australia via Honolulu. The stumbling block to Canadian ambitions was the already existing American presence on the islands. A Hawaii-U.S. commercial treaty had been concluded in 1876, under which the U.S. secured fully 90% of the islands' trade, and which led to a rapid development of sugar production. Renewal was scheduled for 1886, but before it was effected opposition developed in the U.S. from the eastern sugar cartel and the domestic cane and beet growers.

In the interim, pressure grew from B.C. for a reciprocity treaty between Canada and Hawaii. Before 1876, B.C. had conducted a large exchange of its fish, lumber, and coal for the islands' tropical fruits and sugar, but the Hawaii-U.S. treaty had cut it off. With the progress of the CPR towards the coast, the Canada-Hawaii linkage had a new urgency.[28] In 1883, rumours became rampant in Ottawa that a commercial treaty was to be signed between Canada and Hawaii.[29] Although the American treaty was renewed, the Hawaiian officials continued to press for some sort of Reciprocity agreement with Canada.[30] By 1890, opposition from certain sectors in the U.S. led to cancellations of the island's special position in the American sugar markets.[31] American influence on the islands consisted mainly of a group of rabidly annexationist small planters, and a group of large planters who wanted only association with the U.S. for fear annexation would spell the end of their indentured labour system. No such fears of loss of the system existed in the possibility of Canadian relations, for in Canada there was considerable use of indentured labour, especially Chinese, for such projects as railway construction. But an abortive independence bid by the Hawaiians led to American takeover.[32] It also ended Canada's hopes for a Pacific empire there. The B.C. refiners switched their attention to Fiji, where they began to make direct investments in sugar plantations.[33]

But Fiji was a rather poor substitute. Its trade with Canada developed as an off-shoot of the establishment of a subsidized steamship service between Canada and Australia, to which the Fiji government began to contribute in 1892. The next year, the first shipment of tropical fruit from Fiji reached Vancouver.[34] In 1894, the Toronto Industrial Fair displayed a wide range of tropical goods,[35] and that year Fiji, along with Hawaii, was invited to join Canada and Australia in putting into effect an imperial Pacific cable,[36] a project that Strathcona had been promoting for some time.[37] But by 1898 the Fiji government lost interest in its Canadian connections in favour of American, withdrawing the steamship subsidy and with it putting an end to the Canada-Australia line's Fiji stop.[38] The investments in sugar did remain, however.

Canada-CPR interests spread much further east. As early as 1884, plans were afoot for a steamship line run jointly by the CPR and a Japanese company,[39] and the CPR's incursion into the Pacific steamer business followed closely the completion of its main line. Canada had a number of interests in China apart from a potential market for Canadian manufactured goods. Indentured Chinese labour was used in the gold mines during the B.C. rush, for coal mines, and for CPR construction. These de facto slaves were another of Lord Elgin's gifts to the country that had helped him retrieve his Scottish estates from the mortgage company. For upon leaving Canada Elgin proceeded to China as special emissary of the British government and imposed on the Emperor by force of arms the treaty stipulation that Britain could extract supplies of Chinese labour for its colonies.[40]

The CPR's expansion into the Atlantic was much slower; two Canadian-British lines, Cunard and the Allan Steamship Line already existed. In addition in 1880 the Elder-Dempster Line established the Beaver Line from Montreal to Liverpool.[41] In 1899, Van Horne ventured his opinion that "if the people of Canada knew what they were paying for ocean transportation they would rise up in rebellion,"[42] and the CPR's subsequent actions seemed to be geared toward testing that hypothesis. In 1902, J. P. Morgan had fathered a big, waterlogged merger of North Atlantic steamship lines, and the CPR threatened to break his hold.[43] In 1903 the Elder-Dempster's fifteen steamers comprising its entire Atlantic fleet, the Beaver line, were absorbed by the CPR,[44] which then proceeded to carry out its "threat" to the Morgan empire. Strathcona negotiated a combine arrangement with Morgan and all the other North Atlantic carriers to raise passenger rates to North America during the great wave of migration. Steerage rates went up immediately from £3/0/0 to £5/0/0. Since the passages were subsidized by the federal government, in part this represented simply another transfer payment from Canadian taxpayers to the CPR.

The arrangement broke down in 1904 when Cunard pulled out, followed by three other lines, and rate cutting began.[45] Order was soon restored, however, and combine arrangements for freight charges added to the passenger rate agreement. This arrangement permitted Canadian railways and shipping lines to appropriate the benefit of Imperial Preference in the form of higher freight charges rather than have it accrue to consumers in the form of cheaper commodities.[46] By 1911 the freight cartel was complete, while the combine controlled 90% of the steerage traffic.[47] The U.S. government that year prosecuted thirteen members of the combine including the CPR and the Allan Line for conspiracy in restraint of trade.[48] The Canadian Northern, which had just joined the cozy circle at a time when on land its hostility to the CPR was at a maximum, escaped prosecution.

Both the CP Atlantic and Pacific fleets received large federal subsidies directly as well, and even imperial mail subsidies. Their federal subsidies were raised substantially by both Sir Richard Cartwright, the Liberal Minister of Trade and Commerce, and Sir George Foster, his Tory successor, the increases showing a curious correlation to the timing of large gifts of CPR stock by Strathcona to the honourable ministers.[49] In addition, the Canadian lines were rewarded with a rule whereby only goods travelling to Canada on direct steamships would be eligible for the 33⅓% British preference. A similar ruling for immigrants existed whereby they had to come to Canada directly from their place of origin on a single ticket. This last directive was the work of Laurier's Minister of Labour, Mackenzie King, who used it to ensure that Indian immigrants would be effectively blocked without the need for an explicit White Canada policy.[50]

The Caribbean and South America were the areas most favoured by Canadian attentions. As early as 1874, witnesses before a Select Committee investigating manufacturing urged the development of trade channels with the Caribbean and South America to relieve surplus production.[51] But it was after the National Policy that the most active promotion of communication and transportation links occurred. The objectives were two-fold. First was to secure a source of tropical products, especially sugar for the new Canadian sugar refining industry in the Maritimes and Montreal. The main point of the National Policy strategy was effectively summed up by the fact that the first load of ordinary merchandise sent over the CPR to B.C. was a cargo of Jamaica sugar that had been refined in Halifax.[52] The second objective was to secure a vent for the surplus productive capacity resulting from over-investment in industry behind the National Policy tariff. For the first time in Canada's history it was haunted by the spectre of general over-production and resultant industrial crisis, rather than just the commercial crises or problems of periodic collapse of primary product prices as of old.[53] From the excess capacity of the National Policy investments came pressure for Canadian autonomy to make its own commercial treaties,[54] and by 1886 Canada was no longer automatically bound by British treaties.[55]

The Caribbean and South America

For the British West Indies, despite the perpetual interest of Nova Scotia merchants and refiners, and the growing interest of Montreal sugar refiners as well as Canadian manufacturers, the

Canadian relation took second priority to cultivating ties with the U.S. And in fact for Canada the Spanish Caribbean for some time seemed the preferable commercial objective.

During the early 1880's, Canadian manufacturers pressed for increased ties to the British islands. The non-competitive structure of the economies concerned was stressed: the Caribbean would produce raw tropical produce, Canada would export manufactures. And the fact that the area was under the British crown was an additional drawing card.[56] The years 1884 and 1885 saw profound depression in the sugar islands. The growth of bounty-fed beet sugar refineries in Europe and North America tended to depress demand. In Jamaica and in Canada, followed by Trinidad, Demerara, and the Leeward Islands, annexationist sentiment emerged in some quarters.[57] While the bulk of the mercantile opinion in the islands preferred the idea of union with the U.S., the Colonial Office pushed for a Canadian association.[58] The absentee proprietors in England pushed for Confederation,[59] undoubtedly influenced in no small measure by the success the P.E.I. absentees had in using the federal government to defend their claims against popular reform agitation on the island. And for planters in the islands, the indentured labour issue, as in Hawaii, was a factor favouring the Canadian association.

Except for Barbados, which argued its case through its former governor, Francis Hincks,[60] the bulk of island business opinion favoured only a commercial treaty and not outright annexation. Such sentiments went back at least as far as 1855 when Hincks served as go-between in Reciprocity discussion between the Windward Islands and the Quebec Board of Trade which wanted a new trade outlet to make the canals and shipping investments profitable.[61] But it was the sugar crisis that brought the issue strongly to the fore.

Inside Canada some pressure for outright annexation existed, especially after Britain announced it had no objection to Canada annexing Jamaica.[62] But opposition emerged from some circles, including Maritime boards of trade who avidly pushed for Reciprocity with the area, on political grounds — especially the possibility of Canada thereby acquiring a large black population in addition to mere Chinese "coolies." As the *Monetary Times* quaintly put it, "annexation would bring us a population which it is not desirable to have, the representatives of which would scarcely improve the general character of the House of Commons."[63]

At the same time, Canadians' attentions were focussed on

Spanish Caribbean possessions. In 1884 Tupper tried to negotiate a treaty with Spain to give Canada a preference in Puerto
Rico and Cuba. Canadian opinion felt that if it got access to
Cuban sugar under a Spanish treaty there would be no need to
annex Jamaica.[64] Although the U.S. secured a preferential
treaty, Canadian efforts continued. The debate over whether a
reciprocity arrangement with Spain would permit countries having most-favoured-nation agreements with Britain to demand
the same from the Canada-Spain treaty[65] led directly to Canadian commercial autonomy. In 1886, a commercial treaty was
signed between Britain and Spain giving Canada a substantial
preference.[66] Under the treaty, raw sugar moved to Canada and
the Maritimes exported timber and temperate foodstuffs to
Cuba and fish to Puerto Rico.[67]

For the British West Indies, though Canadian relations with
Cuba helped avert annexation, they also deepened the crisis in
sugar. Furthermore in 1888 came the first European sugar
bounty treaty prohibiting beet refinery subsidies in return for
Britain's agreement not to discriminate in favour of cane. The
islands lost their last chance to secure an advantage in Britain for
their cane.[68] Canadian interest in the British possessions certainly
remained, but it was tempered by its new resource hinterlands,
among them Brazil and Mexico.

Reflecting Canada's growing interest in these areas were the
efforts to establish transportation and communication links. In
1881, a line of steamers run by French and Brazilian capitalists
received subsidies from the Dominion Government and Brazil to
ply between Halifax and Rio de Janeiro. The first cargo to arrive
in Canada on the first of the line's steamers carried sugar for the
Halifax refinery as well as some coffee and other products. Its
return cargo was fish, grain, and timber.[69] A second Canada-
Brazil line was organized in Montreal by Canadian and British
capital, heavily loaded with Grand Trunk magnates, but never
became operational.[70] Later the establishment of a subsidized line
to Buenos Aires led to some interest in Mexico in negotiating a
future Canadian reciprocity treaty.[71]

Subsidies for other lines were also voted, those to the British
islands tending however to lag behind. Until 1886 the Cunard
Line maintained a direct link between Canada and the West
Indies, but thereafter it ceased. The maritime fish trade then
went in wooden sailing ships while exports in steamships all travelled via New York.[72] St. John and other cities with sizeable
commercial interest in the West Indies trade pressed for re-estab-
lishment of direct links.[73] Canada indicated its willingness to subsidize a Jamaican line in 1888 if Jamaica did likewise, but the

island refused unless it was also given exclusive control of the Canadian raw sugar market.[74] The next year a series of subsidies did begin, however, giving Maritime ports direct connections to the various Caribbean islands, subsidies which by 1912 totalled $1,399,128.[75] And by 1898 the cable line between Halifax and Bermuda had extended to Jamaica.[76]

The reciprocity issue did not die out. Canadian manufacturers agitated for improved commercial relations with the British Caribbean. In 1890, George Foster attempted to negotiate a reciprocity arrangement, but the islands preferred to try to break into the American market.[77] In 1893, Jamaica abolished wharfage charges for all goods sent via Halifax on Pickford and Black steamers,[78] but no further moves towards closer relations followed for some time, in spite of the fact that the Pickford and Black line received ample Dominion subsidies as well.[79]

War accomplished what negotiation could not, war being simply an extension of commerce by other means. With the Spanish American war, the U.S. annexed Cuba, Puerto Rico, and the Philippines, and became independent of the British West Indies for its tropical product needs. During the war, the Bank of Commerce, through its Manila agent, carried out a great deal of business on behalf of the American government, including paying the troops and financing food shipments, functions that American banks were not equipped to handle.[80] In the aftermath of the war, lingering Philippines resistance to the takeover caused some consternation in the upper echelons of power in the U.S. government. The Secretary of War called on Sir William Van Horne, who in 1885 had masterminded a plan to transport troops by rail to the Canadian Northwest to suppress the Métis independence movement, and asked him to apply his skills to designing pacification railroads in the Philippines.[81]

The seizure of the Spanish islands by the U.S. opened up the British ones to Canada, for it spelled the end of their American markets. Immediately after the war, the U.S. began admitting Puerto Rican sugar free, and extended a preference to the products of the Philippines and Cuba. Canada replied by extending a preference to Jamaican sugar, the island having been hit hard by the U.S. seizure of the Spanish islands.[82] Moreover, the Maritime export trade in fish to Puerto Rico, which provided most of that island's consumption, was immediately threatened[83] and new markets were sought. In 1899, the situation in the American market improved somewhat for the British sugar colonies with the U.S. imposition of heavy duties against the new round of beet root sugar bounties then the craze in Europe. But the 1903 Brussels convention abolished these bounties, leading to the removal of the American duties, and the loss of the market again for the British islands. Moreover, a Canada-Germany trade war led to the imposition of a surtax on German goods including beet sugar, and opened up more space in the Canadian market for the islands.[84] Prospects of political union between Canada and Jamaica, which had gained more favour in the island after the Spanish-American war,[85] improved even more after the sugar convention. Transportation links were improved, and Canadian exports promoted by CMA and boards of trade of major cities.[86]

Elsewhere in the Caribbean, Canadian ambitions also grew. In 1900 Trinidad and Canada tried without success to negotiate a reciprocity arrangement under which Trinidad would supply Canada with cocoa, asphalt, and sugar.[87] And in 1911 Canadian financiers led by the managing director of Sun Life began a campaign for the annexation of the Bahamas which could provide Canada with a new market, a coaling base for ships using the Panama route for Canadian trade and a naval station which would help Canada's increasingly important interests in the area.[88] In 1912, a trade treaty between Canada and ten West Indian colonies was signed, under which Canadian-manufactured exports got a 20% preference, while some natural products from the Indies entered Canada free, others at a 20% preference.

Further plans for the development of Canada-West Indian economic ties were made at a conference of trade officials in Ottawa in 1913. The Minister of Trade and Commerce, Sir George Foster, pointed out that with rapid growth of Canadian population and income, the demand for Caribbean products would grow. The area's role as a resource hinterland and field for investment was clearly spelled out by Sir George.

> The United States now has within her own territory or affiliated to her by special treaties, a tropical area which goes far towards satisfying her wants. . . . I have always been of the opinion that the West Indies is an underdeveloped country. . . . Development can best be assured by a certain and interchangeable market of such size and such quality, that it will call upon you, for your present protection and your future benefit to meet the more extended needs of Canada. . . . There ought to be a larger investment of capital and a greater cooperation between Canada and the West Indies. You know what power there is in invested capital to draw countries together and develop them. If we can in any way induce Canadian capital to invest in the West Indies, and if we can induce the businessmen of the West Indies, to co-operate with us in the development of their country, there will be common bonds between us that will be mutually advantageous.[89]

The conference went on to call for a new "all red cable" to link Canada and the Caribbean. The only skepticism registered by the Caribbean delegates to the schemes came from one delegate of Guyana:

> One thing we are nervous about in Demarara with regard to sending goods direct to Canada. . . . The railway people may appropriate a certain-amount of the preference by raising the freight on the goods and thus nullifying to a great extent the advantages we would get from the preference.[90]

In light of the domestic experiences of Canadian farmers and manufacturers with the railroad magnates, he had just cause for his apprehensions.

Elsewhere in the Caribbean, Canadian business was far from absent. Despite its being de facto an American colony, Mexico continued to attract the attention of Canadian capital, and steamship routes were established with Dominion subsidies to run from Vancouver to the Pacific coast of Mexico in 1906. One effect of the new line was to establish an entrepot trade between Britain and Mexico via B.C.[91] The next year a line along the Atlantic route began operating from Montreal to Cuba to Mexico, providing a great stimulus to trade.[92]

Export Development

The long-distance imperial and far eastern trade was the whole *raison d'être* of transcontinental railway building in Canada. The purchase of the Hudson's Bay Company in 1863 by the International Financial Society, a London investment banking firm, had as its objective the reorganization of the Grand Trunk Railway on a transcontinental basis. The rationale could only have been the far eastern trade, for in the absence of settlement of the Canadian West this was the only source of earnings to salvage the fortunes of the GTR security holders. The Interoceanic Company competing for the Pacific charter stressed that the Canadian route from Britain to the Orient was shorter than any American line. In 1873, the Tory *Mail* greeted the Allan contract with the words:

> We have the means in our possession of bringing the trade of India, China, and Japan to Montreal by the shortest route and at the cheapest rate possible.[93]

In 1878, Tupper justified his choice of possible routes through the Pacific province by stressing that it made the distance from New York to Japan 650 miles shorter than any route the United States can afford. So far as European traffic is concerned, the citizens of London, the citizens of Great Britain, will find that they can reach China and Japan by the line of the Canadian Pacific, and over Canadian soil from Halifax, instead of the line now existing to San Francisco, and effect a saving of over 1200 miles.[94]

And the CPR through the prairies followed a more southerly route than that originally planned, a route that avoided some established settlements and the more fertile regions in favour of rapid development of international trade along the shortest possible route. It was no accident that the year 1887, which saw the establishment of the CPR's Pacific fleet, also witnessed the first bottlenecks in the carriage of grain from Manitoba, as the long-distance trade took precedence over domestic in the allocation of the company's resources and energies.

The export of manufactured goods proceeded in a limited, but nonetheless significant way along the commercial arteries created, and in some cases preceded them. Once the National Policy was up and the CPR complete to the Pacific, the heavily protected cotton industry insisted on defying every principle of international trade theory and exported to China in active competition with British and American firms.[95] The cotton exports were not simply short-run dumping, for as late as 1890 a new cotton mill was built for the express purpose of serving the Chinese market. In 1892, four of the Canadian mills were concerned chiefly with exporting to China.[96] While the early shipments of cotton often went via New York firms, the CPR's expansion into the Pacific trade led to direct exports. For the CPR the China trade was crucial to its early profit position, based on long-distance and entrepot trade before the Canadian West developed. Exports of such commodities as Canadian cotton through China's conveniently opened doors were balanced by imports of such commodities as opium to be smuggled into the U.S., and the early monopolization of the tea trade from the Pacific to the Atlantic.[97] By 1891 it was established that the Canadian route to the Far East was twelve days faster than the Suez route, and it was expected that Canada was certain to become at least the chief imperial mail and military route.[98] Another of the CPR's early export developments was the carriage of Standard Oil's products from Ohio to the Pacific coast of the U.S. over the Canadian route,[99] the beginnings of the CPR's long, friendly relations with Standard to the dismay of the Canadian oil refining industry.

A fair degree of export activity occurred among some industries before the National Policy. Boot and shoe exports around the world were reported in 1874.[100] The organs so assiduously copied from American patterns by Bell and engine works built up by émigré Americans like Waterous also reported export activity.[101] The agricultural implements industry was an early leader. Massey, Cossitt, and John Watson exported to the West Indies, France, Russia, Australia, and South Africa by 1876.[102] Even very small semi-handicraft implement firms found export markets.[103]

After the high tariff, very little seemed to change, at least in the short run. The organ and piano industry continued to find foreign markets.[104] American émigrés like Wanzer or Raymond sent sewing machines around the globe, joined by new licensed ventures.[105] The Canadian secondary iron and steel industry in general staggered under its 30-35% *ad valorem* and exported widely. The Canada Tool Works at Dundas had the audacity in 1882 to reverse normal procedure and export lathes to Cuba via a New York wholesale dealer. The Hamilton Screw Company, American-owned but not a branch plant, at the same time announced it was exporting "to all parts of the world."[106] The agricultural implements industry gained more foreign markets after the tariff. Belgium, New Zealand, the Argentine, and the U.S. were added to the list by the late 1880's.[107] In 1888 the Masseys went on a world tour to show off their goods and establish export agencies;[108] the same year, W. E. Massey testified as to his conversion to protectionism. He admitted, nonetheless, that while the tariff was necessary for them to maintain their control of the home market, and while some loss would occur domestically without it, their export business would be unaffected.[109]

After the mid-1890's while Canadian-manufactured exports declined relatively, certain industries remained strong. The great surge in bicycle production and exports occurred to a number of European, South American, and Empire outlets, and even the U.S.[110] At the same time, by 1899, over half of the Dominion consumption of bicycles was imported, over 75% if one included complete sets of parts simply assembled in Canada.[111] Yet so successful were Canadian firms in securing American patents that an English firm was set up with the express purpose of dealing in "Canadian" bicycle patents.[112]

Also very successful during the period were furniture exports to various Empire markets, and even to the U.S.[113] This was especially disconcerting to American producers, and in 1896 the American consul in Belfast wrote to his government that Canadian furniture manufacturers had largely displaced American home and office furniture from United Kingdom markets.[114] In carriages, a similar pattern occurred.[115]

In secondary iron and steel, a fair degree of export activity was reported by leading firms.[116] Some of the large machine and tool firms such as Bertram or the Robb Engineering Works had secured wide markets. One firm actually exported textile machinery to Britain.[117] Just to prove how badly it needed the federal iron and steel bounties, DISCO, as early as 1902, began exporting to New England. It later secured markets with the American railroad companies, who received rails at rates considerably below Canadian prices.[118]

Branch plants and licensed ventures played a significant role as well in the new export markets. Quaker Oats and Heinz were among the food processors established in Canada to serve the Empire market, and most of their output was exported.[119] In automobiles, the typical pattern was to give the Canadian affiliate the Empire trade. Canadian General Electric did not do so well, and its extension rights were restricted to Newfoundland. But Sherwin-Williams allocated to its Canadian affiliate control of the English subsidiary, which in turn controlled those in India, South Africa, Shanghai and even France.[120]

Two points stand out from these export patterns. First, of course, is the prominence of licensed concerns, and to a lesser degree of branch plants. Without the existence of an Empire market, there would be little rationale for such a division of activity between parent and affiliate. Second, in those fields where independent Canadian firms were strong, they were for the most part traditional, mechanical industries. Apart from a few spectacular and short-lived machine works, Canadian presence in modern high-technology industry, except by licensing, was conspicuously absent. Even the bicycle boom was based on American patents. And the two industries that ranked highest in terms of the share of Canadian manufactured exports after 1900, excluding food, were agricultural implements — built by American émigrés on U.S. patents — and iron and steel — largely the creation of American bonus hunters or émigré master-craftsmen of an earlier era.

Manufactured exports were not, however, the core of the Canadian commercial strategy. Agricultural products, both field and animal, were the main object of government attention in efforts to find markets abroad. In the early post-Confederation period, the entrepot trade between the U.S. and Britain remained large. In 1878, some $10 million of Canada's total of $46 million of exports to the U.K. were re-exports. Of this entrepot trade, 95% was in agricultural products, accounting for nearly half of the Dominion's total agricultural exports to Britain. In 1881 again, $11 million of $42 million sent to Britain went as re-exports, overwhelmingly agricultural, and by this date they exceeded the value of native agricultural products sent there.

With the opening of the West, of course, native products — first mainly animal, later chiefly grain — quickly dwarfed the re-export business. The Dominion Government instituted a series of measures over and above shipping subsidies to key markets to facilitate this trade. Cold storage warehouses for dairy and animal products began to spread across Canada in the mid-1890's, supported by federal and provincial bond guarantees. Among the latter was a guarantee from New Brunswick to Sir Frederick Borden's firm, a firm which also subsequently secured a federal guarantee while Borden himself sat in the Cabinet. Cold storage arrangements were also worked out with leading shipping companies and with the creameries that began to spread across the prairies.

The creameries were an object of special attention both in Manitoba and in the Northwest, beginning in 1895 when both the Manitoba and the federal governments began to make loans to keep up or or improve the butter and cheese factories in their respective spheres of authority. The federal Department of Agriculture took over the operation of sixteen creameries, nine of which had been in financial difficulty. Lack of capital, incompetent management, and other causes led to losses to the owners. The farmers began to feel that the proceeds of the operations would be channelled off to reimburse the owners rather than going back to the farmers as a return on their butter and cheese, and stopped supporting the local factories. The Dominion then set up a $15,000 revolving fund to bail them out by making loans, the creamery itself to be operated by the Department of Agriculture until the loans were repaid. After 1905 the burden of maintaining the creameries devolved upon the new provincial governments of Alberta and Saskatchewan.[121]

There were other steps taken by the federal government to promote agricultural exports. Systems of government inspection were established to maintain or improve standards of dairy products for export: at the same time, the Canadian canning industry had a remarkable record of poisoning domestic consumers without any system of workable inspection being imposed.[122] And the Dominion made advances of funds to exporters — an ill comment on the Canadian banking system's performance in even that most orthodox of commercial banking functions, financing Canadian commodity trade, however useful the banks may have been to American commodity movements.

Canadian Banks in the United States

After Illinois' experiences with the Canadian banks' agencies, it relaxed its laws to permit foreign banks to enter, and between 1875 and 1881 the Commerce, the Merchants' and the Bank of British North America followed the Bank of Montreal into Chicago. These banks collectively took most of the grain moving business away from the local banks, which began to model themselves on their Canadian counterparts.[123] In 1886 panic and depression led to all but the Bank of Montreal closing their doors and returning to Canada.[124] But the exodus soon reversed itself, and by 1892 the Bank of Nova Scotia had entered Chicago, followed by others.[125]

Many other American cities received branches of Canadian banks. The grain trade in Minneapolis attracted the Bank of Nova Scotia in 1885. It closed down its Winnipeg branch, which had lost heavily in the collapse of the land boom, and shifted it to Minneapolis.[126] Pacific trade took the Bank of British Columbia to San Francisco and Portland, Oregon, even before Confederation. Its business in Hawaiian sugar grew steadily until it was absorbed by Bank of Commerce, which in turn became active in sugar movements.[127] The Commerce held control of the National Bank of New Orleans from 1900 to 1915. By 1912 the Nova Scotia had eight branches throughout the U.S.[128] That year one Canadian bank alone, probably the Commerce, was financing between 25 and 50% of the total American cotton exports.[129]

New York had a veritable deluge of branches and agencies, attracted by the profits in call money and currency speculation, rather than commodity movements as in the other American centres. These profits on currency speculation were sufficient that in 1870 the Bank of Montreal managed to get itself sued for breaking New York States's usury laws — loans were reported bearing interest rates up to 150-200% per annum. At the same time, until 1913, American national banks were forbidden from entering foreign banking, and for the most part lacked the resources to do so.[130] Canadian bank loans abroad, virtually all in the U.S., net of deposits abroad were $23 million in 1900; by 1909 the net export of funds reached nearly $90 million; thereafter it declined somewhat.

The result of these extensions was to further twist the structure of the Canadian capital market towards north-south flows at the expense of east-west integration. In 1891 it was noted that a virtual currency union of a lopsided nature had been effected. American notes passed at par in Ontario, while those of the remote provinces were at par only by special arrangement. Not until after the creation of the central redemption fund — over the objections of some of the major Canadian banks, coupled with the extinction of Maritime and local banking and centralization of monetary control in Toronto and Montreal—was the anomaly partly rectified. Although Dominion notes then became exchangeable at par, American and British currency remained legal tender in Canada while Canadian was not legal tender in the U.S.[131] At the same time within Canada, Dominion notes, though payable in gold, were for a long time only partially convertible: Canadian banks preferred to deal in American gold.[132] In 1914, the *Monetary Times* remarked on the fact that notwithstanding the large deposits of Canadian banks in New York (nearly $150 million), "Canadian industrial development seems to attach more naturally to Philadelphia and Boston."[133] Financial capital moved from Canada to the U.S., industrial capital back to Canada. Canadian funds went to support American stock exchanges or into corporate bonds. Hence, as a result of financial integration with the U.S., Canada in effect ended up "borrowing" back its own money in the form of direct investments by American firms. The result of the export of funds from Canada to the U.S. was the same in the post-Confederation period as in 1857 and 1866: financial stringency within Canada followed the export of short-term funds, and increasingly of long-term funds as well.

In B.C. the chief circulating medium was gold, in the form of dust or ore certificates, prior to the entry of the Canadian banks to the area. The Bank of British Columbia, the Bank of British North America, and the private banks exported the mineral to the U.S. as fast as it could be dug.[134] When the gold rushes ended, B.C. was left with holes in the ground and debts. The same pattern was repeated in the Klondike rush. Of the $72 million of gold imported into New York in 1896, $10 million was handled by the Canadian banks.[135] Gold dealing during the second rush became centered in Seattle, for the banks operating in B.C. refused to pay as much as those in Seattle. The result was a drain of trade of such an order of magnitude that Vancouver merchants met to organize a fund to subsidize the local purchase of gold and thereby secure the trade of the Klondike.[136] The result of the banks' policies, which facilitated the export of gold and successfully blocked its minting inside Canada until 1912, was reflected in the Dominion reserve position. Of $98.5 million in gold reserves held in 1913, $93.2 million were in U.S. coin, $4.3 million in British coin, only $800,000 in Canadian coin, and about $220,000 in bullion.[137]

In the East, the drainage of funds via the Canadian banks to New York in 1888-9 drove up interest rates and led to complaints from Canadian business over the lack of accommodation.[138] That these drains were possible could be blamed on the tightly cartelized structure of the Canadian banking system, according to one businessman:

> I am informed by leading bankers in New York City that our banks, whenever money becomes tight, appear on the scene and make enormous loans on the most insecure and speculative stocks such as local institutions would not dare do. The result is that they drain every dollar from customers here and many perfectly solvent concerns go to the wall. This has been admitted to me by bank managers here of local offices and the effects upon their customers lamented.[139]

Canadian funds continued to pour into Wall Street stock or gold speculations after the Bank of Montreal's successes in the 1860's. One private bank failed in 1869 because of its gold deals. The Merchants' came close to failing because of unwise gold speculations in 1877.[140] Call loans to New York brokers were a factor in the Ontario Bank failure in 1906. But without the Canadian call money, Wall Street would have been hard pressed to function.[141]

The exports of gold to New York for speculation gradually put Canadian exchanges on a system unusual for the period. Neither gold nor sterling balances served as the banks' first line of reserves. Instead of gold or the key currency of the period, the Canadian banks' reserves took the form of call and short-term loans in New York.[142] This system, the outgrowth of the banks' greed for gold speculation, was defended on the grounds that there was no adequate call loan market in Canada, and that it imparted elasticity to the banking system, permitting the banks to call loans in New York whenever money became tight in Canada.[143] But the record shows very little cushioning of Canadian monetary conditions against the effects of crises from abroad.[144] The effect of the system was to stifle the creation of a short-term money market in Canada, which had to wait until 1953, while treasury bill auctions did not commence until the creation of the Bank of Canada in 1934.[145] Over the period 1900 to 1913, call loans in the U.S. by Canadian banks rose five-fold, while those in Canada little more than doubled. As a percentage of total assets, call loans in Canada in 1900 were 6.2%, while by 1913 they had fallen to 4.4%; over the same period those abroad rose from 5.3% to 8.0%.

Even more doubt is cast upon the supposed rationale of the system by the fact that while in theory the call loans should have been used to impart a seasonal elasticity to Canadian credit, the facts are otherwise. Call loans abroad should have expanded in the summer, as the banks prepared for crop movement, and contracted in the autumn and early winter. No significant seasonal variation in fact existed. And for a system of reserves supposedly so important for Canadian monetary stability, very few banks seemed inclined to participate. Of 36 chartered banks in 1900, only six made call loans abroad, 70% of the total of which was accounted for by the Bank of Montreal, a full eighteen per cent of that institution's assets being involved there.[146] In 1913 of 25 chartered banks, only eight lent any money on call in New York. The Bank of Montreal accounted for over $51 million of the total of $93 million.[147] At the same time, the Bank of Montreal refused to lend on call in Canada.[148]

Even more important was the outflow of long-term funds. In 1876, the Bank of Montreal proved its loyalty to the Crown by purchasing American government and Cincinnati gold bonds.[149] One major reason for the failure of the Federal Bank in 1889 was the long-term credits it extended to American lumber firms.[150] The Ontario Bank's collapse was assisted by its losses on Minneapolis and St. Louis Railway stocks.[151] Railway bonds were especially popular. The Bank of Montreal between 1886 and 1896 bought and sold 111 different American railway bonds of sums from $50,000 to $500,000, of which 35 transactions incurred losses. Its dealings in Government of India bonds exceeded those in Canadian government; it invested in St. Louis debentures more than it had in Toronto, and it even managed to lose $10,000 in an American government bond transactions.[152] These investment dealings were never published. Similarly, the Sovereign Bank's virtual ownership of the Chicago and Milwaukee and Central Alaska railroads was not disclosed until the bank failed.[153] American railroad and tramway bonds, too, attracted the attentions of the Home Bank from an early period, and were a major factor in its ultimate failure.[154]

For a period of four years, from 1906 to 1909, the general manager of the Bank of Nova Scotia, H. C. McLeod, insisted on publishing the bank's investment portfolio — a move which, like his campaign for outside inspection, met with the stern opposition of the banking establishment.[155] In 1910 he was replaced, and no further publication occurred. But from the data provided for those years and some supplementary figures, the bank's investment portfolio can be constructed. A few points stand out. In all years, foreign holdings were about 50% of the total, sometimes more. Included in these were a number of foreign utility bond issues — the Havana Electric Railway, and Rio and Sao Paulo utilities. The American industrial bonds included $150,000 in United Fruit Company Bonds. And of the "Canadian" total, a fair amount was accounted for by items like Bell Telephone bonds.

TABLE XVI (2)

Bank of Nova Scotia Investments, 1906-1909

	1906	1907	1908	1909
Government Bonds			*($1,000's)*	
Provincial	605	598	600	728
Municipal	1,342	1,544	1,647	2,017
Foreign & American	74	196	214	255
Railway Bonds				
American	1,908	1,999	3,093	2,606
Canadian	486	356	405	351
Foreign	129	33	165	—
Industrials and Misc.				
American	311	462	567	711
"Canadian"	250	250	365	804
Foreign	—	—	—	—
*Totals**				
American	2,219	2,462	3,660	3,317
Canadian	2,682	2,749	3,900	3,900
Foreign	129	228	214	255
	4,965	5,439	7,774	7,471

Sources: Bank of Nova Scotia, *Annual Reports,* 1906 - 1909; *CBC,* p. 497.

*Totals not exact due to rounding errors.

Insurance Company Activities in the United States

For most of the pre-war period, fire insurance companies did not establish branches in the United States, nor did their holdings of securities appear to be major. Their importance to the export of funds appears to lie in their role in driving Canadian business into purchasing American fire insurance policies, the policy funds then being available to the American companies to make long-term investment in the U.S.

There were, however, some exceptions. The Royal Canadian, on being barred from New York business after the impairment of its capital in the St. John fire of 1877, had that year well over two-thirds of its total investments in U.S. securities, some $680,000 out of $970,000. By 1900, while four of Canada's nine Canadian-owned fire insurance firms did some premium business abroad, two of them accounted for the overwhelmingly large share — the British American and the Western Assurance, both part of the George Cox empire — and for both of these their American business was far more important than their Canadian premium sources.

TABLE XVI (3)

Premiums Received by Canadian Fire Insurance Companies Operating Abroad, 1900

Company	In Canada	Abroad
British-American	235,868	1,058,215
Quebec	87,494	32,655
Victoria-Montreal	37,474	58,537
Western	329,120	1,655,489
	689,956	2,804,896

Source: Superintendent of Insurance, *Report,* 1900, p. xi.

Moreover, for all but the Quebec Fire Assurance Company, which lost money in both domestic and foreign operations, losses paid as a percentage of premiums received were lower abroad than at home. Perhaps for this reason other companies followed, and by 1913 fifteen of Canada's 29 Canadian-owned fire insurance firms were active abroad, chiefly in the U.S., but not on the scale of the two established leaders, which by 1913 were doing abroad three times the amount of premium business they did in Canada.

In terms of investments, British-American and Western again were in the forefront. As early as 1900, a third of Western's portfolio consisted of American federal, state, municipal, and utility bonds and debentures, while British-American held about 15%. By 1913, British-American foreign investments were over one-third its total, while Western's exceeded 50%.

Life companies had followed the banks in establishing American branches. The first seems to have been Sun Life, which opened its Michigan branch in 1889. The purpose of the branch was to solicit policies among the large émigré Canadian population in the Michigan timber areas.[156] By 1914 every major Canadian life company had U.S. branches. The Independent Order of Foresters led with 24, followed by Canada Life, Sun Life, and others.[157] The life companies, while soliciting local business, were actively engaged in the export of long-term capital to the U.S. In addition to stock and bond investments, they provided interim financing to American promoters. Yet in 1906 they complained that legislative restrictions on their investment portfolio were hampering their competitive position vis-à-vis U.S. life companies.[158]

The long-term investments in the U.S. were based on a deliberate misreading of the law regarding their investment portfolios. Canadian life companies were permitted to hold investments in foreign countries in which they had branches to the extent that they were required by law in those countries to deposit securities as a reserve. But the Canadian companies had put what Sun Life euphemistically described as a "liberal construction" on the regulatory legislation,[159] and had engaged in a wide variety of speculative ventures in the U.S. incompatible with their position as trustees of policy holders' funds.[160] The lead in U.S. investments was taken by Sun Life, but almost all of the companies were involved. North American, a relatively small company, managed to illegally hold $800,000 in Chicago and Milwaukee bonds.

In 1906 Sun Life openly admitted that the best utility investments it felt it could make were those in Ohio, Michigan, Illinois, and Indiana. The threat of public ownership then so rampant in Canada with respect to utilities, with the possible consequence that all the water would be squeezed out on expropriation and the value of its equity holdings considerably reduced, did not perturb the company. For it felt that in the U.S. public ownership of utilities would be unconstitutional.[161] In fact, Sun Life generally preferred American investments to Canadian ones.[162] By 1906 it held $7,900,000 in the bonds of the sprawling Illinois Traction and its sundry subsidiaries, out of a total issued of $18,760,000, and it held $6,975,297 in American equity in its contingent account while not a single Canadian stock appeared there.[163] Sun Life's activities were so successful that it inspired all manner of imitators, even the Sulpician Order came close to bankrupting itself in Detroit tramway speculations.

The Supreme Court of the Independent Order of Foresters pursued a vigorous investment policy that left in its wake a trail of graft that touched the Hon. Rodmond Roblin, Premier of Manitoba, and Sir George Foster. Thus when Foster publicly declared "political corruption is abroad everywhere, in our local, provincial, and Dominion elections"[164] it is hard to tell whether he was condemning or bragging. Of $1,360,614 worth of securities held in 1906, $729,109 were American.[165]

Industrial, Railroad and Other Investments in the U.S.

Canadian industrial investments in the U.S. were a variety of types and motivations; they included branch plants, individual investments, and even an occasional licensed venture. There was relatively little investment in mining, reflecting the conservative structure of the Canadian capital markets, and the ready availability of mineral resources within Canada.[166] There were a few exceptions. In 1887 the private banker, Loftus Cuddy, in conjunction with another Canadian, established a coal mining, transportation, and dealing firm with docks at Erie, fueling wharves in Detroit, car dumpers, steam derricks, and wharves at a number of lakeports. In 1900 they sold out to an American coal trust.[167] There was also an iron mine tributary to one of Canada's railway investments in the U.S., and two later additions, one in coal in 1910 and another iron mine in 1914.[168]

There was also at least one instance of a wholesale migration of a Canadian firm to the U.S. In the early 1870's a woollen firm left Hespeler, Ontario, and shifted its entire plant to the U.S. because Canadian retailers preferred foreign to domestic goods![169]

One of the earliest branch plants was that of E. B. Eddy, the émigré American, who set up a match factory at Ogdensburg, New York, in 1881. But his machinery and equipment were so advanced and so frightened the American match manufacturers that he was given $100,000 for his $15,000 investment and asked to confine himself to Canada.[170] Equally short-lived was a pharmaceutical company in Toronto which took over a Detroit firm in 1880. It then discovered that it was the victim of a fraud, the former owner having flooded the market before the sale, and the company quickly failed.[171]

There were few cases of pulp and paper firms in the U.S. under Canadian control,[172] of which the largest was the Carter-Crume Co. It had a curious history. Initially it seems to have been established as a branch plant in Toronto of an American cheque book firm in 1882. But the company came in part at least under Canadian control, though the patents in which it was based remained American. By 1899 it became incorporated, with participation in the equity by A. E. Ames, Joseph Flavelle, and Hart Massey,[173] by which time it had a branch plant in Niagara Falls, New York, affiliates using its patents in London (England), Berlin (Germany), and Melbourne, as well as another in California with which it divided the American market. When it offered shares in Canada through A. E. Ames and Co., the chief selling point in its advertisements was a reproduced letter from an American patent attorney attesting to the validity of its patents.[174] In 1911 it absorbed a series of other sales book manufacturing companies in New York, but its headquarters remained in Toronto.[175]

There were a few other cases of industrial direct investments in the U.S.: a hemlock bark extract company (1882); textile investments (1885 and 1912); a Toronto soap company with a Rochester branch plant (1885) followed by a Brantford one with a Buffalo joint venture (1887);[176] a carriage factory with a Michigan branch plant (1891);[177] an Alaska tannery (1896); a New York branch of a Toronto paint factory (1897); a mica mining and processing firm, headquartered in Montreal, with a branch factory in New York (1911).[178]

What stands out most in the pattern of Canadian industrial investments in the U.S. is the number of firms in secondary iron and steel. The engine works branch of the American émigré C. H. Waterous was closed down in Winnipeg in 1886 and shifted to St. Paul.[179] Edward Gurney, Jr., the son of another U.S. émigré, added a Boston branch plant to his Canadian holdings in 1890.[180] In 1899 T. J. Drummond, who was involved in a joint venture in Montreal to manufacture railway car wheels, joined in the promotion of a New Jersey car wheel company.[181] In 1902 the Robb Engineering Co. of Amherst, Nova Scotia, established a joint venture in New Jersey, the Robb-Mumford Boiler Works, in partnership with the American patentee of some of the engines Robb made in Canada.[182] Similarly the Canada-U.S. joint venture, Page-Hersey Tubes, absorbed a rolling mill in Cohoes in 1914. Canadian Car and Foundries and several others too had their American branches.[183]

There were a number of cases of individual investments. Canadian money went into iron and steel in Birmingham, Alabama.[184] And by 1907 a group of Montreal financiers held over two million dollars in U.S. steel stocks.[185] By 1914, Montreal holdings of U.S. steel stock reached $7,892,000[186] — nearly eight million good reasons why J. P. Morgan never established a full-fledged branch plant in Canada to compete with the CPR's affiliate, Stelco.

Agricultural implements also saw a chain of American investments. In 1889, the Mann Manufacturing Co. of Brockville arranged for production of its patents under licence in the U.S.[187] In 1910, Massey-Harris took over a New York harvester plant, and when it decided to move into production of gasoline-powered implements it bought up a New York manufacturer of gasoline engines in 1913.[188] In 1911 the Cockshutt Plow Co. opened an Illinois branch.[189]

Just as Canada had manipulated its commercial policy to force the movement of American firms across the border, so too did the United States to cause a return flow. In the U.S. in the 1880s insufficient malt was produced to meet the demands of the breweries; large amounts of Canadian malt were imported. Canadian barley produced a malt that made a longer-lasting beer than the U.S. product.[190] The U.S. tariff on malt was raised, and by 1890 the Canadian industry was all but gone. Plants in Hamilton, Chatham, Galt, London, Guelph, Palmerston, and Toronto closed down. And many malt plants led by the firm of W. D. Matthews, grain speculator and president of the Toronto Board of Trade, migrated to the U.S. and imported barley from Canada — with serious effects on the cost structures of Canadian breweries.[191]

The most ludicrous case of commercial-policy-induced transborder migrations came in lumbering. Canadian forests were supposedly being denuded in the 1880s by American lumbermen who exported the logs to the U.S. for sawing. Agitation for export duties mounted, and after the duty was imposed, many saw mills, most of them American, sprang up in Canada. (How this prevented the depletion of Canadian forests is unclear.) But the U.S. government retaliated with an import duty on sawn lumber to retransfer the saw mills back to the U.S. The Canadian government capitulated and removed the export duty. This led to a migration of Canadian lumbermen to Michigan pursued by Sun Life, and by 1890 many towns in the lumbering districts of northern Ontario were badly depopulated.[192] By the turn of the century, when pulp duties were imposed by Canada, the flow reversed itself again, and pulp and saw mills moved north.

In addition to bond investments by financial institutions, American railways and utilities attracted direct investment by Canadian firms and individuals. Sun Life's protégé, Illinois Traction, showed net earnings of $1,361,952 in 1906, and $1,-498,689 in the first eleven months of 1907.[193] The results of the earlier investments tempted others. There was considerable Canadian equity investment in border city utilities; for example,

Montreal finance was involved in the Detroit and Adrian Electric Railway and the Detroit United Railway.[194] As well, Toronto investors held equity in the Twin City Railway Co. and the St. Paul and Minneapolis Street Railway.[195] The Alabama Traction, Light and Power Co. grew out of the Birmingham, Alabama, street railway built by William Mackenzie's contracting firm in 1899. By 1902 James Ross of Montreal was the sole owner, and sold control to British investors, though the headquarters remained in Montreal.[196] These were the major investments, though Canadian capital was involved in a string of other utilities as well.

One early case involved the Ontario private bank of McGregor and Bros., which was established in 1863 and got rich speculating in greenbacks during the Civil War. It invested heavily in Great Lakes transportation operations run by a Detroit firm, prospered for a time, then began losing money on the investments. A depositors' run began, but was weathered. Unfortunately Molson's Bank took a dim view of the proceedings, and another Canadian private bank was added to the scrapheap in 1877.[197]

One last utility case of interest involved one of the few instances of the migration of a Canadian entrepreneur to the U.S., namely Erastus Wiman, of mercantile agency fame. Among Wiman's activities was the establishment of a tramway system on Staten Island, followed by an electric light and power operation and a series of real estate deals.[198] These operations were not financed directly by Canadian capital but rather by embezzling funds from the mercantile agency. The 1893 bankruptcy of the power operations led to Wiman's arrest on a charge of forgery; he was found guilty but won an appeal.[199] Pushed out of the mercantile agency business by his former partner, R. G. Dun, who had preferred the charges, Wiman eventually established a rival Canada-U.S. agency but, like many of his schemes, it failed very quickly.[200]

In steam railways, apart from Grand Trunk and Great Western extensions, the first major post-Confederation investment was the financial coup of Lord Strathcona, Lord Mount Stephen and company in the St. Paul and Pacific railroad job. In the swindle their excellencies, along with J. J. Hill and J. S. Kennedy, conspired with the receiver of a bankrupt American road to steal the line from its Dutch bondholders for a fraction of its real value, the funds for the purchase in turn being taken illegally from the Bank of Montreal.[201] By 1906, the return from the investment of not one penny of their own money reached $416 million worth of interest-bearing securities over and above the interest and dividends obtained. The returns included those from a huge area of high-grade ore in Minnesota, partly secured by purchase out of the earnings of the road, and partly included in the railroad's land grant. The mine had a perpetual contract with U.S. Steel for all the ore it could produce. [202]

After Confederation, the Grand Trunk undertook extensions into Portland, Maine, into Michigan and to Chicago. Part of the funds for these extensions came from the illegal diversion of the money paid it by the federal government for the Rivière du Loup branch. In 1882, the GTR at the request of Chicago built the Grand Trunk and Chicago line.[203] By 1893 there were 1,000 miles of GTR track forming the chief through road for Maine, Michigan, Iowa, and Indiana.[204] The takeover of the Portland line required an outlay of one-and-one-half million dollars to put it into operating order, and it never earned more than two-thirds of its total rental cost. The Michigan line also ran a steady deficit, part of which took the form of state taxes. In effect, Canadian taxpayers paid a subsidy to the Michigan treasury through Canadian government aid to the Grand Trunk.[205] In 1911 the GTR strove to extend through Vermont and Rhode Island to Providence to reach water there, but this line was impeded by the American companies, who opposed its construction. [206]

The CPR and the Canadian Northern also undertook a series of American extensions, by takeover, by lease, or by new construction. These roads were virtually all designed to facilitate long-distance traffic rather than local business. By 1914, the Grand Trunk held $18.6 million in the equity of its American lines, mainly the Grand Trunk Western and the St. Lawrence and Atlantic, plus four-and-one-half million in bonds. The CPR held $55.2 million in stock and $26.8 million in bonds, while the CNR held $5.5 million in stock and $200,000 in bonds.[207] In terms of mileage controlled, too, the CPR had a substantial lead.

TABLE XVI (4)

Canadian Railways' U.S. Holdings: 1916

Company	Proprietory	Leased	Controlled	Total
C.P.R.	145	32	4,771	4,948
G.T.R.	—	—	1,868	1,868
C.N.R.	44	181	—	225
Total	189	231	6,639	7,041

Source: *RCRTC*, p. xxi.

In addition there were substantial portfolio holdings by individuals in American railroads. In 1907, two wealthy Montrealers were reported to hold $30 million worth of securities in J. J. Hill's American lines: others held $2.5 million in the Chicago and Milwaukee.[208] On his death in 1914 Strathcona's holdings still included (despite substantial sales and giveaways) $6,606,000 in equity of the Great Northern, the line J. J. Hill had fashioned from the St. Paul railroad, and $3,380,000 in the Northern Pacific, then also part of Hill's system. [209]

There were substantial holdings of American equities by small-scale Canadian investors as well. The fact that Canadian brokers dealt more heavily in American than in Canadian stocks was in part attributable to the thinness of stock markets in Canada, in turn due in no small measure to the underdevelopment of the call money market for domestic as opposed to New York dealers. In part, too, it was due to the backwardness of Canadian industrial organization, to the fact that the shortage of long-term outside capital for most industries delayed the transition to the incorporated form. In addition to the dealings of brokers, the highly-paid American branch plant managers and corporate executives resident in Canada, whose salaries were drawn from the Canadian earnings of their firms invested heavily in American securities.[210]

Canadian Banking Abroad

Canadian capital became very actively involved in commerce, finance, and public utilites in the Caribbean and South America, and in a few cases even further afield. There were also some resource and agricultural investments in the tropical areas, though not on anything like the same scale as the others. There were a few cases of individual direct investments in the area as well. One of the more short-lived involved a bank clerk who stole $50,000 from the Crown Bank and ran off to the Caribbean with a girl he married en route. He was caught, and a judge lacking all romantic impulses sentenced him to five years in 1906.[211] This was the same year that Senator George Cox revealed his enormous system of financial racketeering before the Royal Commission of Life Insurance: Cox was sternly rebuked.

The Canadian banks led the way for the post-Confederation investments following earlier commercial routes. In the 1860's, the Bank of British Columbia contemplated a Hawaiian branch. Further efforts were made after 1876, when the treaty with the

U.S. sparked off a sugar boom. The bank's proposal was supported by the Hawaiian Minister of Finance, who was a partner in a San Francisco sugar jobbing firm, but the move was never made — undoubtedly because of the failure of Canadian commercial ambitions in the area.

In the Atlantic, the Newfoundland financial crisis of 1894 created the conditions for Canadian expansion. The collapse of several large fish merchant houses led to the failure of both of the island's commercial banks, one of which was headed by the Premier, and which were interlocked with the fish firms. The larger of the two banks, the Commercial of Newfoundland, had been bled white by the depredations of its directors before failure.[212] The crisis also led directly to the suspension of the government savings bank, which had loaned half of its deposits to the commercial banks. The crisis reduced Newfoundland to a state of barter and led to widespread distress among the fishermen.[213] Members of the Newfoundland government went to Canada to try to get the Canadian banks to move onto the island to alleviate the crisis.[214] The Bank of Nova Scotia, the Merchants' Bank of Halifax (the Royal), and the Bank of Montreal responded to the invitation in 1895,[215] with the Montreal becoming the government's financial agent.[216] Negotiations for Newfoundland's entry into Confederation ensued with the enthusiastic support of the Montreal commercial and financial community,[217] the British government, and leading Newfoundland politicians including the Premier. At that time the island was on the verge of completing a railway, the result of which would be a public debt per capita double the Canadian level. The Canadian government asked the British government to share the burden of assuming the debt of the bankrupt island but this was refused, much to the disappointment of the railway contractors who had received Newfoundland bonds, now much depreciated, in payment. The debt question led to the breakdown of negotiations for annexation.[218]

With the growth of the Canadian sugar refining industry and the failure of the banks' Hawaiian ambitions came a quickening of interest in the sugar plantations of the West Indies. In 1882, a group of wealthy Jamaican planters visited Canada with an unsuccessful proposal for a Planter's Bank capitalized at two-and-a-half million dollars to be floated in Canada.[219] In Canada A. W. Ogilvie and M. H. Gault promoted the bank.[220] A charter was granted, but the bank was never established. Other banks were more successful. By 1882 both the Halifax Banking Company and the Merchants' Bank of Halifax (the Royal) had Bermuda branches.[221] In 1889 the Bank of Nova Scotia followed the rum trade to the islands, establishing a Kingston, Jamaica, branch and from there spreading to other British possessions as well as to Puerto Rico and Cuba.

The Union Bank of Halifax established a series of Caribbean branches in Trinidad and Puerto Rico before being absorbed by the Merchants' of Halifax (The Royal) in 1910. The Royal itself quickly took the lead, especially in Cuba. The establishment of its first Cuba branch coincided with the American victory in 1899, and it thereafter began taking over a series of local banks from their Spanish owners, buying the Banco de Oriente, Santiago de Cuba in 1903 and the Banco del Commercia in Havana in 1904. Its activities were by no means restricted to Cuba. In 1912 it bought out the British-owned Bank of British Honduras. By 1910 it had nineteen branches in the Caribbean.[222]

It expanded rapidly under the Reciprocity Treaty of 1913,[223] that year bringing its total branches to 32.[224] Cuba in particular was covered with branches, and by 1914 it reached Venezuela.

In contrast to the Halifax banks, those of central Canada did not move into the Caribbean area, apart from the Bank of Commerce and the Bank of Montreal, each of whom established a Mexico City branch. The Bank of Montreal's Mexican involvement began in 1900, when the United States Banking Company was established there by an émigré Canadian. Because of political entanglements the private bank got into difficulty; the Bank of Montreal, which stood behind it, came to its rescue. In the final analysis the Bank of Montreal lost several million in covering bad debts. The crisis even had repercussions in Montreal, where a few runs started.[225] In 1906 the private bank was displaced by the Bank of Montreal's establishment of a full-fledged branch in Mexico City.

TABLE XVI (5)

Canadian Banks in Latin America, 1914

Bank	Cuba	Puerto Rico & Dominica	Mexico	British West Indies	Central & South America
Nova Scotia		1		6	
Commerce			1		
Montreal			1		
Royal	22	5		6	3

Source: Deputy Minister of Trade and Commerce, *Report,* 1919.

The year 1906 was a bad one for the Royal as well, for a revolution against American rule in Cuba interfered with its operations there. Its involvement on the island was sufficiently heavy that fears of a lockup of its Cuban assets forced it to forego a large merger in Canada.[226] Alas, the bank it had planned to absorb was none other than the hapless Ontario Bank, which promptly collapsed when the Royal's takeover bid was withdrawn. The directors must have bemoaned the travesty of justice that permitted a Cuban revolution to bring down a bank whose real foreign interests lay in fraudulent manipulations of New York reserves.

The banks in the southern climes did a considerable local business in deposits, and less so in loans. For the West Indies were regarded as a "surplus" area for the banks, the volume of deposits exceeding the volume of loans and investments in the area much after the fashion of the Maritime provinces of Canada, and Newfoundland after 1895. Like the Maritimes, the West Indies suffered a net drain of funds that helped perpetuate their underdevelopment. As the Chairman of the Committee on Banking and Currency in Canada succinctly summarized, "How does it concern us if Jamaica complains?"[227] Deposits in the Royal's Havana branch in 1913 equalled more than double the amount of loans withstanding.[228] The Union of Halifax reported of its Trinidad and Puerto Rico branches that the deposits came to "quite an amount." Notes of the Canadian banks also circulated there,[229] and the importance of local deposits were increased by the fact that they were generally made to current accounts, and did not bear interest. The Royal took its large, free surplus from the West Indies and loaned it on call in New York at two-and-one-half to three percent, none of the surplus ever reaching Canada.[230]

As to the loan business, the Nova Scotia reported in 1910 that it restricted its loans to merchants and that its involvement lay in moving sugar, rum, cocoa, and coffee,[231] that is, in accommodating staple trade and not in local development. The long term investments of the banks in the area were negligible. The Royal and the Nova Scotia held a few Havana municipal debentures. But the Bank of Nova Scotia's holdings of United Fruit Company bonds illustrated well the real interests of the Canadian institutions as far as any long-term investments in the area were concerned, and defined very nicely the relations of Canadian and American capital in the area. Foreign exchange business as well as deposits attracted the Canadian banks, and by 1908 the Bank of Montreal reported capturing two-thirds of the exchange business in Mexico.[232]

Canadian Insurance Companies Abroad

Insurance company overseas branches also proliferated. Sun Life
was the pioneer again, establishing its first West Indian branch
in 1879, pushed out of Canada into seeking outlets abroad by the
pressure of competition for a then-limited business potential
inside Canada. It expanded so rapidly that its foreign and American business soon outstripped its Canadian.[233] By 1913, two-
thirds of its policy business was done abroad. By 1914 it was
present in Honolulu, Japan, China, the Philippines, Hong Kong,
Burma, Egypt, France, Belgium, Holland, Britain, Newfoundland, Chile, Peru, Ireland, Thailand, in addition to its Mexican,
West Indian, and American branches. Virtually all of the big life
companies followed, and by 1914 Canada Life, Confederation
Life, Mutual Life, North American Life, National Life, Imperial
Life, and Manufacturers' Life had branches in the Caribbean as
well as some in continental Europe and the Far East.[234]

Fire insurance companies also spread abroad. Many of the
Canadian fire insurance firms established branches in
Newfoundland, while the two leaders in the foreign field, George
Cox's creations, British-American and Western, spread across the
Caribbean, Latin America, and the Far East.

TABLE XVI (6)

Life Companies' Policy Business, 1913

Company	% Canada	% Abroad	Total ($1,000)
Sun	34	66	11,419
Canada	57	43	5,590
Manufacturers	59	41	3,150
Confederation	67	33	2,667
Imperial	88	12	1,591
North American	88	12	1,851
Federal	91	9	1,001
Great West	98	2	3,234
National	99	1	692

Source: Superintendent of Insurance, *Report,* II, 1914, p. lxxv.

Parallelling the banks' deposit business, the insurance companies actively sought local policy subscriptions. This was sufficiently attractive a business to occasionally provoke opposition
from established local insurance companies. The Independent
Order of Foresters, for example, met determined opposition to its

expansion in Australia. This was partly circumvented by bribing the Prime Minister to ask questions prepared by the IOF local representative during parliamentary question periods, the answers to which, also prepared by the IOF representative, were given by yet another M.P. in the company's pay. The only Australian long-term investment made by the IOF consisted of contributions to party election funds.[235]

Other companies made a few investments in locally issued securities. Of the four major insurance companies operating in Japan in 1913, two were Canadian,[236] holding some Japanese government bonds as mandatory deposits. In addition they had some minor holdings of locally issued securities. Confederation Life held a few Mexican and Cuban government debentures, more in fact than was legally permitted. But a slight ambiguity in the legislation regulating insurance companies' foreign investments permitted the companies to ignore the restriction.[237] But the most important role these institutions played in the area was their financing of utility promotions.

TABLE XVI (7)

Canadian Life Companies' Non-U.S. Foreign Investments

	(total at year's end)
1900	$ 110,312
1901	319,603
1902	1,032,472
1903	943,188
1904	1,125,313
1905	1,352,362
1906	921,680
1907	963,831
1908	1,085,955
1909	1,329,558
1910	1,555,829
1911	1,578,108
1912	2,266,161
1913	2,377,339

Source: Superintendent of Insurance, *Annual Reports,* 1900-1914.

The sudden increase in foreign investments from 1901 to 1902 was largely due to two factors. First, the Bank of Montreal's ally Sun Life made a major foray into foreign bond holdings with a number of small investments, raising its total from $135,103 to

$429,811 in a year. Second, Manufacturers' Life showed a similar surge connected with interim financing for Sao Paulo Tramways. The decline in 1903 was due in large measure to the ending of this interim finance operation. The decline from 1905 to 1906 was due to a substantial reduction in the holdings of Sao Paulo bonds by both Manufacturers' Life and Sun Life. The increase in 1909 was largely the result of Sun Life's promotion of the Mexican Northern Power Co. Ltd.

The two firms, Sun Life and Manufacturers', dominated these activities abroad. Sun Life alone accounted for often as much as 75%, Manufacturers' for most of the remainder. The residuals were Confederation Life's Mexican and Cuban government bonds and the few Japanese holdings. While the Sao Paulo utility initially attracted several other insurance companies, Canada Life, Imperial, North American, and the Federal, after 1904 their investments ceased, and the two leaders were left undisputedly in charge of utility promotions.

In addition, Sun Life's investments included debentures of two Chilean mortgage loan firms, and bonds in a Shanghai land company. But they were negligible by comparison to its utility investments.

Canadian Investment in the Caribbean

Utility and railway promotions in Latin America parallelled those in Canada and were undertaken by the same groups of Montreal and Toronto financiers in the same alliances. While Canadian investments abroad were not restricted to the activities of the CPR and CNR magnates and their associates, the great bulk of the activity was accounted for by those two groups.

The flow of investment was a slow process until after the Spanish American war led to a redivision of the Caribbean. Thereafter, Canadian capital flowed with increasing ease into both British and American possessions. Cuba was the first prize to be secured. By 1906 the U.S. and Canada together had some $160 million invested there.[238] While most of the funds in the production of staples like sugar, tobacco, and cotton were American, Canadian capital was heavily involved in utilities and railroads as well as banking, and even to a lesser degree directly in agriculture too.

"Patriotic sentiments have never in the history of the world stood long against the pocket book,"[239] thundered the same William Van Horne who had earlier denounced as "annexationists" those Manitobans who had objected to the CPR's monopoly clause. It was only natural that this American's Canadian-nationalist vision should encompass the export of capital at a time when Canada found it necessary to borrow huge sums abroad to give to railroad promoters and their colleagues. When in July, 1898, Spain signed articles of capitulation, Van Horne's agent "was on the first passenger boat to leave New York for Havana."[240]

Canadian capital had been reluctant to move in, but Van Horne regaled the Montreal commercial and financial community with tales of the Caribbean cornucopia. Another stumbling block was the reluctance of the American occupying authorities to let the Canadians share in the island's fruits. The *Monetary Times* rebuked them, saying that "one of the most disappointing results of American rule is that it has not done more to encourage the speedy in-coming to the island of capital."[241] But Van Horne rectified that by securing the personal assent of President McKinley to set up shop, much assisted by McKinley's Secretary of War, General Alger, who had earlier collaborated with Van Horne in the Grand'Mère, Quebec, pulp and paper works.[242]

A final difficulty was the presence of rival claimants to the utility monopoly. One group forming the Havana Traction Co. consisted of Van Horne with a Toronto syndicate — George Cox, Fred Nicholls, William Mackenzie, A.E. Ames, Edmund Walker et al. On the other hand, New York's F.S. Pearson, who was involved as the consulting engineer in the Cuban Electric Co., in conjunction with an international group including Halifax interests and the Hanson Brothers brokerage firm in Montreal, had a claim on all existing railway properties in Havana. After litigation ensued, the solution was found in a merger under the presidency of Montreal's A.F. Gault. David Morrice, B.F. Pearson of Halifax, W.D. Matthews, and E.B. Osler also joined the adventure.[243] In early 1900, A.F. Gault, William Hanson, and other Montreal notables, each suitably decked out in their Sunday finest and accompanied by their daughters, arrived in Cuba to attend the opening ceremonies of the new tramway system. In addition to the Havana line, the electric railroad system connected Regle and Guanabacoa "a high and healthy city with an ante-bellum population of over 30,000 souls, now considerably reduced."[244] By 1907 a proxy fight gave control of the system to an American group led by the American consul in Havana, whose investigations revealed a rather large shortage in the accounts of the transactions of the former Canadian directorate.[245]

In addition to the electric tramway Van Horne established a

steam railway system on the island in 1902. On the board were two American generals.[246] The land for the railroad was not purchased, but seized by the American military authorities and given to Van Horne's syndicate. It was a resource road designed to open sugar lands, and by 1904 Van Horne's company had a sugar refinery in operation.

Though the funds for the railway and refinery were chiefly American,[247] there were several instances of Canadian direct involvement in staple production. In 1899, the Halifax promoters of the Havana Street Railway formed a tobacco company to operate in Cuba.[248] In 1901, two Toronto capitalists established a colony on the island called "New Toronto." Their lands were sold off in small lots for orange groves and other fruit plantations and Canadian planters began to move in.[249] By 1907 the Canada-Cuba Land and Fruit Company was advertising itself as "Cuba's largest Canadian colony," boasting 100 tobacco plantations in operation as well as many thousands of other acres of tobacco and fruit lands open to potential Canadian planters.[250] Montreal capital also moved into fruit plantations, and Cuba soon became a more important source for Canadian fruit importers than the British West Indies.[251]

The 1906 upheaval which frightened the Royal Bank had repercussions as well on the value in London of the securities issued by the various utilities and railroads, and posed some threat to the Canadian claims. While political agitation on the island continued, American intervention restored the Canadian investors' confidence, and the securities were but little affected by subsequent disturbances.[252]

Compared to ventures in Cuba, Canadian interest in Puerto Rico was very restricted. The major investment was the Puerto Rico Railway Co., largely under the supervision of Max Aitken, who developed a substantial promotional career in the Caribbean before his main burst of Canadian activities.[253] It was during his Caribbean sorties that he developed into an ardent imperial federationist, seeking to actuate the idea of the British West Indian colonies being attached to Britain just as Cuba and Puerto Rico were to the U.S.[254] Aitken's Puerto Rico concern acquired a utility monopoly in San Juan and several other towns, controlling electric light and power plants, tramways, and water. In addition, resource extensions to the steam railway were made to develop traffic in sugar and tobacco.[255]

Aitken and Van Horne were both active in the British colonies as well, along with Montreal, Toronto, and Halifax associates. Trinidad had Canadian capital in its telephone system, courtesy of Aitken, and in its electric light and tramway company. Van Horne, George Drummond, A.F. Gault, T.G. Shaughnessy, Strathcona, and James Ross were all on the board of the electric company. The same syndicate was responsible for utilities in Demerara and Kingston.[256]

Van Horne was active in the informal American possessions as well. He established a system of Guatemala railroads in conjunction with an American general and the president of the United Fruit Company. Nicaragua, while not benefiting from Van Horne's attentions, did attract the attention of Montreal investors in its fruit potential in 1911.[257] In fact, so highly regarded in Canada were the possible returns from tropical fruits that in 1912 a Winnipeg securities firm began a big advertising campaign to sell banana lands in central America for $20 an acre. The *Monetary Times* could not restrain itself from pointing out that the typical Canadian investor knew "as much about banana cultivation in central America as he did canal construction on Mars."[258]

Canals on Mars were actually about the only type of utility that Canadian adventurers of the period declined to invest in, as their activities brimmed over the confines of the Caribbean and moved deep into Mexico and South America.

Canadian Investment in Mexico and South America

Mexico's importance to Canadian investors was at least as great as Cuba's, if not more so, though the movement into the country was a little slower. But by 1904 there were enough resident Canadian businessmen in Mexico City to form a Canadian commercial club.[259] The Mexican investment, too, brought to the fore the CNR twins, Mackenzie and Mann, much more than the Caribbean. Donald Mann in fact appears to have been the pioneer of Canadian railway and utility ventures abroad. As early as 1888, while still part of the CPR contracting firm with James Ross, Herbert Holt, and William Mackenzie, he travelled to Panama, Ecuador, Peru, Chile, and even Imperial China at the invitation of their government with a view to building railways there. Only political instability prevented them from beginning.[260]

Mexican Light and Power established in 1902 featured the two promoters along with Van Horne, Cox, E.R. Wood, J.H.

Plummer, James Ross, Clouston and F.S. Pearson. Despite the presence of Plummer and Cox, the Bank of Commerce had no direct interest at all in the new utility;[261] it was completely the Bank of Montreal's affair.[262] Much the same groups were involved in the promotion of Mexican Tramways and both companies prospered for sometime, undertaking a series of extensions and mergers.[263] But by 1908 Mexican Light was in trouble. A tour of inspection by E.S. Clouston led the Bank of Montreal and the English bondholders to force a merger over the protests of the directors of the Light and Power Company.[264]

A long list of other utility and railroad promotions followed Mexican Light. Mexico's Pueblo Light and Power was the creation of roughly the same groups as the tramway and light companies. Mackenzie and Mann joined Herbert Holt in a Monterey sewerage project in 1907.[265] A group of Montreal bankers and brokers secured water concessions and a power franchise for a large mining district, and organized the Mexican Northern Power Company in 1909. It also got the franchise to supply light to Chihuahua.[266] The Mexican Midland Light and Power Co. followed in 1911. Though it was essentially a British company which headquartered in Canada to avoid paying British taxes, there was some Toronto investment in it as well. Its objectives were to secure power, lighting, telegraph, and telephone concessions.[267]

Canadian participation in Mexican business went far beyond utilities. The Canada-Mexico Steamship Co., operating under Dominion subsidy, erected grain elevators in 1909.[268] Victoria money was involved in a Pacific coast resource railroad.[269] Canadian money was tempted into the Kansas City, Mexico, and Orient Railway, which drained timber and mineral resources out of northern Mexico to the U.S.[270] And most important of all was F.S. Pearson's Mexico and North West Railway and Timber Co., a resource road into Chihuahua — one of the towns it serviced modestly adopting the name "Pearson."

As with Cuba, fruit lands attracted Canadian planters, colonists, and investors. The establishment of the subsidized steamship run between B.C. and the Mexican Pacific coast brought Victoria interest in fruits lands, and a concession of 400,000 acres was secured in 1907, followed by the building of the resource road to move the products out of the area.[271] A stream of Canadian colonists from B.C. followed. [272] In addition, Pearson's resource railroad opened up its own saw mills.[273] The Canadian meat packing firm of Gordon, Ironsides and Fare established cattle ranches in the country.[274] And the Montreal real estate broker,

D.W. Ogilvie, son of one of the flour milling magnates, was involved in a mining operation there in 1913.

The secret of Canada's success could be summed up in a word: "Diaz." In 1908 Sir Edward Clouston, General Manager of the Bank Of Montreal, returned from a reconnaissance mission to Mexico and announced that he was "particularly struck with the stability of the present Mexican government and the powerful character of the ministry."[275] He even declared Mexican investment to be safer than Canadian, for socialist ideas — which were then deemed rife in Canada as the Ontario industrial capitalists forced public ownership of privately owned utilities — had not disturbed the investors' peace in Porfirio Diaz's Mexico. Clouston's sentiments were shared by A.E. Stillwell, president of the Kansas City, Mexico and Orient Railway, who addressed the Canadian Club of Toronto in 1908. The *Monetary Times* reported that

> his description of Mexico's attractions for the capitalist would make it appear quite a corporate Mecca. As a result of Mexican fair dealing, Mr. Stillwell pointed out, there was invested in the Southern Republic $1,400,000,000 of foreign capital.
>
> The personal element of prosperity of, and faith of the foreign investor in Mexico is vested in President Diaz. He is gifted with a keen judgement and a fine business ability. Mr. Stillwell labelled him as the most marvellous man in the world today.[276]

Unfortunately for the Canadian investors, the Mexican people did not seem to share Stillwell's assessment of their leader. The outbreak of insurrection led to serious declines in London of the value of some of the securities issued by the railroad and utility firms[277] which, because of their monopoly concessions, were all the more vulnerable to political unrest, and the result was the invasion of Mexico City late in 1910 by the Canadian directors of a number of these firms.[278] One of their number, Sir Edmund Walker, proceeded to give advice to the military authorities on how to deal with Emiliano Zapata, whose activities were taking their toll of Canadian profits.[279]

Especially hard hit was the Chihuahua area, where Pancho Villa's rebels were busy requesting "loans" from the banks and blowing up bridges over which F.S. Pearson's Mexico Northwest ran.[280] It was thus given the distinction of being the only foreign promotion of the venerable Dr. Pearson that lost money.[281]

While the two Chihuahua-based operations, Mexico Northwest and the Mexican Northwest Power Co., were hardest hit, by 1913 the spreading insurrection had begun to interfere seriously with Mexican Light and Mexican Tramway as well.[282] Canadian investors began calling for the intervention of British troops to defend their property,[283] and for a change in the political structure. As the manager of the Mexico City Branch of the Bank of Commerce put it, "Democracy has not proved an unqualified success anywhere, and here it is an absurdity."[284] However, Diaz stopped off in Montreal on his way to Europe to reassure the Canadian companies that their Mexican interests would "be safeguarded to the utmost ability" of the new military dictatorship under General Huerta.[285]

Elsewhere the tale of Canadian long-term investments was much more sedate. There were a variety, ranging from the Spanish utility operation, Barcelona Traction, Light and Power, in which Sun Life held nearly a million dollars of bonds (1913) to a Manila tramway which sold bonds in Toronto (1906),[286] to a Venezuelan oil company (1913).[287] But the most important were the series of Brazilian utilities which Mackenzie and Mann began with George Cox, Fred Nicholls, E.R. Wood, B.F. Pearson, and F.S. Pearson in 1899.

That year an old mule-drawn tramway in Sao Paulo was taken over and reorganized as the Sao Paulo Tramway, Light, Heat and Power, including the city tramway, the suburban tramway, and an electric power supply monopoly for the city. It expanded its power plants and its monopoly control to include other cities. Soon the Sao Paulo utility was joined by Rio de Janeiro Tramways, Light and Power, with a monopoly as well of the tramway operations and the generation and distribution of hydroelectric power.[288]

The Rio operation's concessions dwarfed even the considerable ones granted to the Sao Paulo firm: water rights on several rivers, perpetual ownership as absolute private property of a long stretch of the banks of one major river, a huge tramway system, gas and electric lighting monopoly, and a couple of short steam railway routes thrown in for good measure. In addition, the syndicate incorporated a subsidiary, Rio de Janeiro Telephone Company, under Maine law, which in turn bought up a German firm, Brasilianische Elektricitats-Gesellschaft with its monopoly of Rio's telephone system. Like the Mexican operations, those in Brazil were politically vulnerable, and any political unrest caused their securities to fall.[289] However, no serious disturbances were felt. In 1912 the two were merged under E. R. Wood's direction in Brazilian Traction, Light and Power, the stock climbing after the consolidation was effected.[290]

Financing Canadian Investment Abroad

Canadian banks and insurance companies abroad played an indispensable role in the promotion of these enterprises. According to Sir Edmund Walker, the banks did not underwrite, but simply provided interim financing on the security of the underwriting and functioned as bankers for the various operations. The Commerce, for example, serviced the Rio and Sao Paulo utilities. The Bank of Montreal served as banker for some of the principal Mexican operations, while Herbert Holt's Royal Bank backed Van Horne's Caribbean escapades. Walker claimed in 1913 that "Canada hasn't a dollar in the South American enterprises that cost us anything." The funds were raised in Britain, and to a lesser degree in continental capital markets.[291]

While Sir Edmund's contention that there was no direct flow of funds abroad from the banks may have been technically correct for the most part, but this did not mean no money moved out from Canada. It was standard practice for the banks to form alliances with life and trust companies or establish security and loans firms as appendages and slough off the promotion business on them. Senator Cox's Canada Life network linked to the Commerce was the most spectacular, but it was by no means unique. Royal Trust did a great deal of promotional business and interim financing of merger activity in Canada with or without the Bank of Montreal. [292] Mackenzie and Mann, in addition to their links to Cox and Walker, controlled the resources of Manufacturers' Life along with Lloyd Harris and Sir Henry Pellatt.[293]

In fact there were many cases of bondholding by Canadian financial institutions which did cost something in the short run, for although the water that constituted the equity of the utility adventures was unpolluted by any trace of hard cash, the bonds did constitute a genuine flow of funds. In 1905, a $20 million lease of Rio de Janeiro Tramway bonds was floated publicly in Canada.[294] Part of the issue seems to have been taken up by the Bank of Montreal, for in 1906 that institution had over a million dollars in securities of Rio Tramway, and of Mexican Tramway and Electric,[295] providing at least one example of the inaccuracy of Sir Edmund's appraisal. In 1907, of eighteen millions of bonds of Mexican Light outstanding, six million were held in Canada.[296] But it was Canadian insurance companies, rather than banks, that provided the greatest amount of Canadian money flowing into these firms. Most of the attraction lay in the rates of return. In the early period, the bonds of the various utilities were yielding nominal rates of 5 to 5.5%: since most were bought at a

discount, the real rates were in fact higher; at the same time
Canada bond yields were averaging only about 3.5%. The return
to investors in the Sao Paulo utility in 1905 was running at the
rate of about one million dollars a year.[297] Nonetheless, most of
the long-term capital was raised in Britain, especially in the later
years. In 1911, the various Latin American utilities marketed
$26,820,000 in senior securities, of which only $320,000 was
placed in Canada, the rest in Britain.[298] In 1912, out of a total
issue of $42,155,000, 89.5% was placed in Britain, 8.3% in the
U.S., and only 3.3% in Canada.[299] The high rate of return on
these monopolies — Sir William Mackenzie alone boasted a
return of a million dollars from his Sao Paulo investment from
1902 to 1905 — together with the drain of funds from the Caribbean through the banks and insurance companies' deposit and
policy business, must have had a favourable impact on the Canadian payments position from the start. These operations provided a flow of earnings into Canada that helped to sustain the
heavy burden of interest payments to Britain, and the outflow of
long-term capital to the U.S.

The transfer of long-term capital out of Canada met with
some hostile reaction, for at the same time enormous loans from
Britain were necessary to construct infrastructure or finance government activity in industrial mergers, and American direct
investment was accelerating. In 1907, the Royal Commission on
Insurance called for regulation of the foreign investments of the
life companies. Organized farmers too protested the anomaly.
But Sir George Foster made clear in his address to the Caribbean delegates in 1913 that it was government policy to
encourage the investment of Canadian capital abroad. It is difficult to see how he could have done otherwise in light of the character of the investment portfolio of the Independent Order of
Foresters, in which he was a leading figure.

To them that have shall be given, the federal government
seemed to decree, and like true Christians, the honourable ministers piled high the government largesse on the plates of the CPR
and CNR magnates and their associates. The same groups that
received an overwhelming share of federal handouts in land
grants, cash, bond guarantees, iron and steel bounties, shipping
subsidies, and the like — much of it paid for with funds borrowed in Britain — were those same groups most actively
exporting capital abroad. At the same time that the federal subsidies to the development of agriculture (which employed directly
or indirectly three million people) were niggardly and closely
supervised, the railway kings were given carte blanche to spend
their subsidies. In 1913 alone, Mackenzie and Mann were given

a subsidy of $15,640,000 which was, in the words of the *Grain Growers' Guide*,

> thirty-one times greater than the entire grant to agricultural development, and they may spend it in buying coffee plantations in Brazil, wheat lands in the Argentine, or on a picnic excursion to the Fiji Islands.[300]

The literally golden age of Canadian promotions ended with World War I and the drying-up of British loans to Canada. New ventures occurred, but no longer in great waves as in the past, and without the same verve. Most of the growth of Canadian investments would now be limited to expansion of established firms.

Notes to Chapter XVI

1.   H. M. P. Eckhardt, "The Growth of Our Foreign Investments," pp. 343-4.
2.   Sir Charles Tupper, *Recollections of His Public Life,* p. 6.
3.   *Globe,* Jan. 5. 1911.
4.   W. Sutton, "National Decadence or Imperial Prosperity."
5.   Address Before the Canadian Club of Montreal, Jan. 29, 1912, *Walker Papers,* p. 7.
6.   *Globe,* Oct. 11, 1873; J. A. Hobson, *Imperialism,* p. 214.
7.   Macdonald to Tupper, March 12, 1885, *Macdonald Papers*; A. Nutting, *The Arabs,* pp. 237, 242-4.
8.   *MT,* Sept. 24, 1884, p. 288.
9.   *MT,* Sept. 24, 1884, p. 228.
10. N. Miller, *The Enterprise of a Free People.*
11. D. Creighton, *Empire of the St. Lawrence,* p. 192 *et passim.*
12. B. Hammond, *Banks and Politics in America from the Revolution To the Civil War,* pp. 319-20.
13. F. C. James, *The Growth of Chicago Banks,* I, pp. 267-8.
14. O. J. McDiarmid, *Commercial Policy,* p. 86.
15. Bank of Montreal, *The Centenary of the Bank of Montreal,* p. 45.
16. G. Hague, "The Late Mr. E. H. King," pp. 22-3.
17. G. Hague, *Banking and Commerce,* p. 351.
18. V. Ross, *Bank of Commerce,* II, p. 17.
19. W. A. Williams, *The Roots of the Modern American Empire,* p. 11.
20. R. M. Breckenridge, *History of Banking in Canada,* pp. 77-82.
21. G. Myers, *History of Canadian Wealth,* p. 189.
22. R. M. Breckenridge, *The Canadian Banking System,* p. 143.
23. Senate Select Committee on the Causes of the Recent Financial Crisis in the Province of Canada, *Report,* 1867, *passim.*
24. A. Shortt, "The Passing of the Upper Canada and Commercial Banks," p. 215.
25. V. Ross, *Bank of Commerce,* II, p. 63.
26. *CM,* Jan. 6, 1882, p. 2.
27. See for example J. H. Dales, *The Protective Tariff in Canada's Development,* p. 81.
28. *HCD,* May 1, 1882 p. 1249; MT May 18, 1882 p. 1291.

29. M. Tate, "Canada's Interest in the Trade and Sovereignty of Hawaii," pp. 20-1.
30. *MT*, June 10, 1887, p. 1473.
31. W. A. Williams, *Roots of the Modern American Empire,* p. 34.
32. R. Van Alstyne, *The Rising American Empire,* p. 178.
33. "Canada-West Indies Conference," p. 63.
34. *MT*, Dec. 29, 1893, p. 793.
35. *MT*, Oct. 5, 1894, p. 449.
36. *MT*, Feb. 23, 1894, p. 1053.
37. *MT*, Dec. 7, 1888, p. 645.
38. *MT*, Nov. 11, 1898, p. 626.
39. Macdonald to George Stephen, July 28, 1884, *Macdonald Papers.*
40. Royal Commission on Chinese Labour, *Report of the Hon. Mr. Gray,* 1885, p. xcvi.
41. *MT*, July 2, 1880, p. 8.
42. *MT*, Jan. 20, 1899, p. 960.
43. *MT*, May 14, 1902, p. 1486, 1493; May 20, 1902, p. 1549.
44. *Ec*, March 7, 1903, p. 420; *CPR Annual Report,* 1903, pp. 6-7.
45. *Ec*, Oct. 1, 1904, p. 1571; May 13, 1905, p. 797.
46. *Globe,* March 3, 1910.
47. *MT*, Jan. 24, 1911, p. 213; April 29, 1911, p. 1709.
48. *Globe,* Jan. 5, 1911.
49. W. T. R. Preston, *Strathcona,* pp. 279-80; *RCLI Evidence* p. 2536.
50. H. S. Ferns and B. Ostry, *The Age of Mackenzie King,* p. 78.
51. *SCM* (1874), p. 3.
52. *Report of the Commercial Agent of the Government of Canada to the West Indies,* 1886-7, p. 9.
53. *MT*, April 28, 1882, p. 1329.
54. *MT*, April 28, 1882, p. 1325.
55. *MT*, Nov. 5, 1886, p. 525.
56. *CM*, March 3, 1882, p. 117.
57. Macdonald to Tupper, June 4, 1884, *Macdonald Papers; MT,* Sept. 5, 1884, p. 264; Nov. 14, 1884, p. 545.
58. *MT,* Sept. 12, 1884, p. 291.
59. Macdonald to Hincks, Sept. 18, 1884, *Macdonald Papers.*
60. Tupper to Macdonald, June 4, 1884, *Macdonald Papers.*
61. A. Borrowman to F. Hincks, Nov. 14, 1855, F. Hincks, *Reminiscences,* p. 368.
62. *MT,* Oct. 24, 1884, p. 462.
63. *MT,* Nov. 7, 1884, p. 264; Sept. 19, 1884 p. 320.
64. *MT,* Nov. 7, 1884, p. 516.
65. Macdonald to Tupper, Jan. 24, 1885, *Macdonald Papers.*
66. *MT,* Oct. 22, 1886, p. 467.
67. *MT,* June 21, 1887, p. 834.
68. *MT,* Sept. 7, 1888, p. 267.
69. *MT,* Feb. 18, 1881, p. 957; July 22, 1881, p. 236, p. 94; Aug. 26, 1881, p. 236; April 28, 1882, p. 1330; Jan. 13, 1882, p. 848; Dec. 16, 1882, p. 724.
70. *MT,* March 18, 1881, p. 1086.
71. *MT,* Sept. 7, 1888, p. 273.
72. *Report of the Commercial Agent,* pp. 7-8.
73. *MT,* Oct. 28, 1887.
74. Macdonald to J. F. Stairs, Jan. 21, 1889, *Macdonald Papers.*
75. "Canada-West Indies Conference," p. 57; *MT,* Jan. 17, 1890, p. 866; May 25, 1907, p. 1841.

76. U.K. Royal Commission on Trade Relations Between Canada and the West Indies, *Report*, p. 43, *(RCTR); MT,* Feb. 4, 1898, pp. 1015, 1017.
77. *RCTR*, p. 3.
78. *MT,* July 23, 1893.
79. *MT,* May 17, 1895, p. 1478.
80. V. Ross, *Bank of Commerce,* II, p. 64.
81. W. Vaughn, *Sir William Van Horne,* p. 331.
82. *MT,* Oct. 14, 1898, p. 499.
83. *MT,* Sept. 23, 1898, p. 407.
84. *Ec,* Oct. 1, 1910, p. 655.
85. *MT,* Oct. 17, 1902, p. 496.
86. *RCTR*, p. 40; *MT,* Jan. 17, 1902, p. 908.
87. *HCD,* March 23, 1900, pp. 2589-94; *MT,* May 23, 1902, p. 1581; May 30, 1902, p. 1552.
88. *MT,* April 1, 1911, p. 1318.
89. "Canada-West Indies Conference," pp. 4-5.
90. "Canada-West Indies Conference," p. 40.
91. *MT,* Dec. 1, 1906, p. 792; May 4, 1907, p. 1732; June 13, 1908, p. 2082.
92. *MT,* May 11, 1907, p. 1770.
93. *Mail,* Oct. 7, 1873.
94. *HCD,* May 10, 1878, p. 1892.
95. *RCT,* p. 35.
96. *MT,* Sept. 19, 1890; *MT,* Sept. 9, 1892, p. 277; *MT,* March 16, 1888, p. 1159.
97. *MT,* Nov. 18, 1887, p. 637; Aug. 10, 1888, p. 154.
98. *MT,* Sept. 11, 1891, p. 309.
99. *MT,* Oct. 29, 1886, p. 490.
100. *SCM* (1874) p. 8; *HCD,* March 8, 1878, p. 882.
101. *MT,* July 12, 1878, p. 65; *SCCD,* p. 36.
102. *MT,* April 21, 1876, p. 1209; *SCCD,* pp. xiii, 121.
103. *MT,* March 9, 1877, p. 1023.
104. *CM,* March 17, 1882, p. 100; *MT,* March 1, 1881, p. 1056.
105. *CM,* May 15, 1885, p. 1185; *MT,* Aug. 31, 1883, p. 233; Sept. 26, 1890, p. 369.
106. *CM,* March 17, 1882, p. 100.
107. *MT,* June 7, 1889, p. 1419.
108. *CM,* July 6, 1888, p. 19.
109. *SCC, Evidence,* p. 356.
110. *CE,* April 1896, p. 341; Nov. 1896, p. 210; March 1898, p. 334; Jan. 1898, p. 276; April 1899, p. 352.
111. *MT,* Aug 25, 1899, p. 239.
112. *CE,* Jan. 1897, p. 273.
113. *CE,* Sept. 1895, p. 129; Jan. 1899, p. 263, Jan. 1898, p. 275.
114. *CE,* Sept. 1896, p. 151.
115. *CE,* Dec. 1896, p. 240; May, 1896, p. 23.
116. *CE,* June, 1895, p. 48; May, 1896, p. 23.
117. *CE,* March, 1898, p. 334; Jan. 1899, p. 263; Aug. 1895, p. 100.
118. *CE,* Oct. 1901, p. 424; W.J. Donald, *The Canadian Iron and Steel Industry,* p. 180.
119. *HCD,* Feb. 28, 1911, p. 4391; *CE,* Feb. 1900, p. 282.
120. *MT,* April 8, 1908, p. 1756; M. Wilkins, *Multinational Enterprise,* pp. 145-6.
121. Canada, Department of Agriculture, *Annual Reports,* 1895, 1897; A.S. Morton, *History of Prairie Settlement, et passim.*
122. *MT,* Aug. 23, 1901, p. 244.

123. *CBC*, p. 316; *MT*, April 23, 1880, p. 1254; F.W. James, *Chicago Banks*, pp. 495-96, 521.
124. *MT*, March 26, 1886, p. 1099.
125. H. Marshall *et al*, *Canadian-American Industry*, p. 16.
126. *CBC*, p. 324.
127. *CFC*, Dec. 15, 1900, p. 1199; V. Ross, *Bank of Commerce*, II, p. 213.
128. Bank of Nova Scotia, *Annual Report*, 1912.
129. *MT*, April 6, 1912, p. 1435.
130. M. Wilkins, *Mutinational Enterprise*, p. 107; *MT*, Nov. 4, 1870, p. 226.
131. Goldwyn Smith, *Canada and the Canadian Question*, p. 47.
132. *CBC*, p. 520.
133. *MT*, *Annual*, Jan. 1914, p. 28.
134. V. Ross, *Bank of Commerce*, I, p. 251 *et passim;* E.O.S. Scholefield, *British Columbia*, I, pp. 641, 644-5; R. C. McIvor *Canadian Monetary, Banking and Fiscal Development*, p. 90.
135. *MT*, Dec. 18, 1896, p. 811.
136. *MT*, May 31, 1901, p. 1602.
137. *Public Accounts* (1913), p. xiii.
138. *RCRLC*, *Ontario Evidence*, p. 86-7.
139. *SCC*, *Evidence*, p. 555.
140. *MT*, July 6, 1878, pp. 40-1; July 13, 1878, p. 75.
141. *Brad*, Feb. 14, 1903, p. 100.
142. H.M.P. Eckhardt, "Modes of Carrying Cash Reserves."
143. *CBC*, p. 534, testimony of Sir Edmund Walker.
144. *CBC*, pp. 467-8.
145. B. Land, "Canada's Money Market."
146. *Canada Gazette*, 1900 monthly.
147. *Canada Gazette*, 1913 monthly.
148. *FP*, April 6, 1907.
149. M. Denison, *Canada's First Bank*, II, p. 184.
150. *MT*, July 4, 1884, p. 11; Nov. 21, 1884, pp. 471-2.
151. *MT*, Oct. 20, 1906, p. 597.
152. Bank of Montreal, *Investment Operations*, 1886-1896.
153. *MT*, May 13, 1911, p. 1918.
154. *MT*, Oct. 5, 1923, pp. 3-5; Dec. 14, 1923, p. 10.
155. *CBC*, p. 567, testimony of Sir Edmund Walker.
156. *MT*, Nov. 3, 1906, p. 621.
157. Superintendent of Insurance, *Report, II*, 1916, p. xxi.
158. *MT*, Nov. 3, 1906, p. 621.
159. *RCLI*, *Evidence*, p. 2799.
160. *RCLI*, *Report*, pp. 167, 185.
161. *RCLI*, *Evidence*, p. 2883.
162. *RCLI*, *Evidence*, pp. 2930-1.
163. *RCLI*, *Report*, p. 26.
164. *MT*, Dec. 2, 1898, p. 731.
165. *RCLI*, *Report*, pp. 134-5.
166. H. Marshall *et al*, *Canadian-American Industry*, p. 182.
167. *MT*, Dec. 18, 1891, p. 719; May 28, 1898, p. 1560; March 9, 1900, p. 1177.
168. C. Lewis, *America's Stake in International Investments*, p. 564.
169. *SCM* (1874), p. 9.
170. *JC*, June 3, 1881, p. 490.
171. *MT*, Nov. 19, 1880, p. 580.
172. C. Lewis, *America's Stake*, p. 566.
173. *CE*, Sept. 1899, p. 141.
174. *MT*, Sept. 15, 1899, pp. 339, 350.

175. *MT,* June 10, 1911, p. 2324.
176. *MT,* March 24, 1882, p. 1177; March 13, 1885, p. 1026; Oct. 16, 1885, p. 428; May 6, 1887.
177. *Globe,* Jan. 9, 1891.
178. *CE,* April, 1896, p. 340; Oct. 1897, p. 174; A. G. Brown and P. H. Morres, *Twentieth Century Impressions,* p. 454.
179. *MT,* Aug. 6, 1886, p. 146; Dec. 10, 1886, p. 660.
180. *Globe,* Nov. 17, 1890.
181. *MT,* June 9, 1899, p. 1603.
182. *CE,* Dec., 1902, p. 339.
183. H. Marshall *et al, Canadian-American Industry; MT,* March 22, 1901, p. 1240.
184. *Brad,* Feb. 14, 1903, p. 100.
185. *CAR,* 1907, p. 50.
186. *MT,* Jan. 3, 1919, p. 153.
187. *MT,* June 14, 1889, p. 1442.
188. *MT,* Dec. 17, 1910, p. 2519; March 22, 1913, p. 595.
189. *Globe,* Sept. 6, 1911.
190. *SCC, Evidence,* p. 312.
191. *Globe,* Dec. 26, 1890.
192. *CM,* Oct. 16, 1891, p. 244.
193. *CAR,* 1907, p. 50.
194. *Ec,* April 18, 1908, p. 843; *MT,* July 27, 1907, p. 132; Feb. 8, 1908, p. 1316.
195. *Brad,* Feb. 14, 1903, p. 100; *MT,* June 21, 1910, p. 1702.
196. *MT,* Jan. 22, 1898, p. 967; June 13, 1902, p. 1610; Jan. 20, 1912, p. 312.
197. *FP,* March 2, 1907; *MT,* June 22, 1877, p. 1476; Jan. 4, 1913, p. 112.
198. *MT,* April 30, 1880, p. 1286; May 5, 1893, p. 1323; Sept. 1, 1893, p. 252.
199. *MT,* Feb. 23, 1894, p. 1051; June 22, 1894, p. 1605.
200. *MT,* Dec. 8, 1899, p. 738; Aug. 30, 1901, p. 268.
201. G. Myers, *History of Canadian Wealth,* pp. 250-4.
202. W. T. R. Preston, *Strathcona,* pp. 147-8.
203. *CFC,* Jan. 21, 1882, p. 86.
204. *MT,* Jan. 6, 1893, p. 788.
205. E. B. Biggar, *The Canadian Railway Problem,* pp. 78-80.
206. *Globe,* Jan. 12, 1911.
207. C. Lewis, *America's Stake,* p. 547.
208. *CAR,* 1907, p. 50.
209. W. T. R. Preston, *Strathcona,* p. 273.
210. *MT,* May 3, 1918, p. 9.
211. *MT,* April 6, 1906, p. 1350.
212. *MT,* Dec. 21, 1894, p. 797.
213. *MT,* Dec. 28, 1894, p. 837.
214. *MT,* Dec. 14, 1894, p. 766.
215. Bank of Nova Scotia, *The Bank of Nova Scotia,* p. 73.
216. Bank of Montreal, *The Centenary of the Bank of Montreal,* p. 47.
217. Montreal Board of Trade, *Annual Report 1895,* pp. 34-5.
218. *MT,* Jan. 25, 1895, p. 965; May 17, 1895, p. 1287; May 24, 1895; April 5, 1895, p. 1287.
219. *CM,* March 31, 1882, p. 117; *MT,* Sept. 6, 1881, p. 334.
220. House of Commons, *Journals,* 1882, p. 74, 83.
221. *MT,* May 2, 1882, p. 1390.
222. *CAR,* 1911, *Historical Supplements,* p. 70.
223. Royal Bank of Canada, *Fifteenth Anniversary of the Royal Bank of Canada,* p. 26.
224. *CBC,* p. 535.

225. M. Denison, *Canada's First Bank,* p. 300.
226. *MT,* Oct. 20, 1906, p. 565-6.
227. *CBC,* p. 161, 531.
228. *CBC,* p. 262.
229. *RCTR, Canada Evidence,* p. 55.
230. *CBC,* p. 535-7.
231. *RCTR, Canada Evidence,* p. 53.
232. *MT,* March 21, 1908, p. 1597.
233. *RCLI, Evidence,* p. 2797.
234. Superintendent of Insurance, *Report,* II, 1915, p. xxii.
235. *RCLI,* Report, p. 122; *Evidence,* p. 2271-9.
236. *MT,* April 12, 1913, p. 699.
237. *RCLI, Evidence,* p. 843.
238. *MT,* Oct. 5, 1906, p. 456.
239. W. Vaughn, *Van Horne* p. 377.
240. *Ibid.,* p. 300.
241. *MT,* Oct. 19, 1900, p. 501.
242. W. Vaughn, *Van Horne,* p. 287.
243. *MT,* May 19, 1899, p. 1507; Oct. 20, 1899, p. 510; Dec. 28, 1899, p. 860; Jan. 5, 1900, p. 884.
244. *MT,* Jan. 19, 1900, p. 950; Oct. 19, 1900, p. 501.
245. *MT,* March 2, 1907, pp. 1373-4.
246. *MT,* Dec. 19, 1902, p. 784.
247. *MT,* July 7, 1905, p. 1.
248. *MT,* March 17, 1899, p. 1218.
249. *MT,* March 22, 1901, p. 1244.
250. *Globe,* Jan. 12, 1907.
251. *RCTR, Canadian Evidence,* p. 100.
252. *Ec,* June 1, 1912, p. 1245; *MT,* Jan. 27, 1912, p. 410.
253. A. Wood, *The True History of Lord Beaverbrook,* p. 26; E. Middleton, *Beaverbrook,* p. 22.
254. F. Mackenzie, *Beaverbrook,* p. 32.
255. *MT,* July 20, 1907, p. 99; Jan. 4, 1908, p. 1077.
256. *RCTR, Canada Evidence,* p. 55; *MT,* Sept. 10, 1897, p. 335; March 22, 1901, p. 1245; May 24, 1901, p. 1583; July 5, 1901, p. 7.
257. *MT,* July 22, 1911, p. 460.
258. *MT,* Feb. 10, 1912, p. 610.
259. *MT,* July 22, 1904, p. 100.
260. C. G. D. Roberts and A. L. Tunnell (ed.) *Standard Dictionary of Canadian Biography,* II, p. 265.
261. B. E. Walker to F. H. Mathewson, Jan. 26, 1903, *Walker Papers.*
262. *FP,* March 21, 1908.
263. *Globe,* April 7, 1906; *MT,* April 11, 1908, p. 1707.
264. *MT,* March 21, 1908, p. 1597; Oct. 10, 1908, p. 595; Oct. 17, 1908, p. 638; Oct. 31, 1908, p. 711; Nov. 7, 1908, p. 762; Feb. 20, 1909, p. 1459; May 24, 1913, p. 892; Feb. 22, 1913, p. 429.
265. *MT,* May 25, 1907, p. 1841.
266. *MT,* Feb. 13, 1909, p. 1427; Dec. 3, 1910, p. 2331.
267. *MT,* Sept. 23, 1911, p. 1313; Nov. 11, 1911, p. 2108; Feb. 10, 1912, p. 615.
268. *MT,* April 17, 1909, p. 1863.
269. *MT,* Oct. 24, 1908, p. 688.
270. *FP,* March 21, 1908; *MT,* Oct. 19, 1907, p. 624.
271. *MT,* Nov. 9, 1907, p. 759; April 18, 1908, p. 1770, 1777; Oct. 24, 1908, p. 688.
272. *MT,* Jan. 30, 1909, p. 1322.
273. *Ec,* Sept. 18, 1909, p. 1322.

274. Manitoba Beef Commission, *Report,* p. 371, 377; A.G. Brown and P.H. Morres, *Twentieth Century Impressions,* p. 447.
275. *MT,* March 21, 1908, p. 1597.
276. *MT,* Jan. 18, 1908, p. 1165.
277. *Ec,* March 18, 1911, p. 559.
278. *MT,* Dec. 3, 1910, p. 2331.
279. L.R. Wilfley to B.E. Walker, May 20, 1912; B.E. Walker to J.P. Bell, Dec. 28, 1911, *Walker Papers.*
280. *MT,* April 6, 1912, p. 1419; Feb. 1, p. 291.
281. Walker to B. Mohr, Jan. 30, 1913, *Walker Papers.*
282. *MT,* March 22, 1913, p. 603; Jan. 30, 1914, p. 250.
283. *MT,* Jan. 18, 1913, p. 192.
284. J.P. Bell to B.E. Walker, June 4, 1912, *Walker Papers.*
285. *MT,* Aug. 23, 1913, p. 377.
286. *MT,* Feb. 2, 1906, p. 1007.
287. *MT,* March 8, 1913, p. 520; June 21, 1913, p. 1035.
288. *FP,* April 20, 1907; *MT,* June 23, 1899, p. 1671; Jan. 24, 1902, p. 952; Dec. 14, 1907, p. 949; J. Wileman (ed.), *The Brazilian Yearbook,* p. 750.
289. *MT,* Aug. 31, 1906, p. 287.
290. *MT,* June 29, 1912, p. 2619; May 31, 1913, p. 928.
291. *CBC,* pp. 562-3.
292. *MT,* Jan. 8, 1910, pp. 223-5.
293. *RCLI, Report,* pp. 52-3.
294. E.R. Wood, *Review of the Bond Markets of Canada,* 1906, p. 6.
295. M. Denison, *Canada's First Bank,* pp. 222-3.
296. *FP,* March 2, 1907.
297. *MT,* July 7, 1905, p. 1; July 20, 1907, p. 93; *et passim.*
298. *CLRII,* pp. 901-2; *MT,* June 29, 1912, p. 2619.
299. *MT,* Feb. 1, 1913, p. 291.
300. *GGG,* June 25, 1913, p. 10.

Where capitalism followed the more rigid channels of surviving commercialism, or where it arrived later in a highly centralized state, it was part of governmental machinery. In Germany, Italy, and Japan, and in the British Dominions, the state became capital equipment.

Harold Innis

CHAPTER XVII
Conclusion: The Lessons of Development

Canada undoubtedly represents the outstanding case of "industrialization by invitation" as a conscious development strategy, and the lessons to be drawn from Canada's "success" and the resulting structures are important ones. The Canadian strategy in effecting the transition from a mercantile-agrarian economy to a partially industrialized one involved drawing heavily on the resources of two metropolitan economies, from Britain for financial and commercial development and from the United States for industrial. In many respects it was an incompatible mixture.

In terms of industrial development, patent regulations and tariffs both aimed at keeping the border open to the flow of factors of production, while closing it to the movement of goods, thus forcing a northward shift in the locus of American production. Canadian dependence on American industrial capital was deep-rooted. First came an inflow of American entrepreneurs and pirated patents, followed by licensing, and increasingly by direct investment — precisely the opposite sequence to that which would lead to independent industrial development. The tariff, to the extent that it led to capital inflow, solved part of the problem of industrial capital supply.[1] To a certain degree the patent laws did likewise. The risks of invention, and the initial costs, were borne by the foreigner. Thus, by using imported patents, Canadian industry was automatically cast in a non-innovative role and the stage set for the replication in Canada of traditional industrial patterns. This strategy also meant there was less need for the local development of technical skills. To the extent skilled labour was required, it too could be imported.

The adoption of a high tariff strategy in 1879 was due to a number of transformations in the Canadian economy of the period. The end of the American Civil War left a new Canadian industrial capacity that had grown up as a result of the temporary protection of the war but was now threatened by an American industrial resurgence. The problem was accentuated by a number of factors. The discount on greenbacks until 1879 partly offset the protective incidence of the Canadian tariff. The advent of recession in 1873 signalled the beginning of nearly a quarter-century of secular deflation resulting in a squeeze on profit margins, to which increasing numbers of industrialists responded by demands for tariff protection and subsequently by strenuous cartelization efforts. The 1879 tariff schedule contained a range of specific duties whose *ad valorem* incidence grew over time until 1896. Thereafter, *ad valorem* rates replaced the specific duties as secular inflation began to undermine their specific incidence.

The initial demand for the high tariff came from several sources. Manufacturers were by no means unanimous. For many the high tariff was in fact anathema — at least in the short run. But as the effects of the secular deflation were felt more strongly over time, more manufacturers moved into the protectionist camp. With the progress of merger activity, high tariffs became essential for the maintenance of the industrial system.

The traditional manufacturing sector, then, was initially split into pro- and anti-protectionists. To carry a program of high tariffs the Tory strategists effected a coalition of the protectionist camp with the Montreal commercial capitalists. Montreal capital's shift to protection resulted from the movement of leading wholesale drygoods merchants into manufacturing. It also meant that the Conservative Party could weld the split in its Nova Scotia ranks by bringing the Nova Scotia West Indies merchants back into the fold. Sugar refineries built up behind tariff walls stabilized Canadian demand for raw sugar and restored the fortunes of the mercantile houses of the leading Maritime ports who had been threatened with annihilation during the crisis of the 1870's. The breach between the coal, iron and steel, and railway men of Nova Scotia on the one hand, firmly Tory, pro-Confederation, and protectionist, and the old seafaring economy, Tory by ideological persuasion, but anti-Confederate and anti-protectionist on the other hand, was mended.

The tariff had other major objectives. Perhaps most important of all were its revenue goals: the customs were hoped to be sufficient to pay for the main works of commercial infrastructure, along with the yield from government savings banks. Then, too, it was designed to protect foreign capital, both by restoring the public revenues and therefore easing the anxieties of British holders of Dominion public debt, and by protecting certain industries in which substantial amounts of British capital had been invested. It also helped force a northward and to a much lesser extent a trans-Atlantic migration of industrial plant and equipment by stimulating foreign direct investment.

The Canadian tariff of 1879, then, cannot be analysed with the tools of economic orthodoxy, for these are designed to consider the impact of a tariff on an existing industrial structure and resource endowment, rather than its effects in augmenting the economy's over-all supply of capital and labour.[2] Why the influx of American capital was necessary becomes explicable in light of the structure of the Canadian capital market and its inability to channel domestic or British funds into industrial capital formation.

The Canadian financial system was largely a British branch plant. Many of its institutions were designed specifically with a view to attracting British investment. The commercial banking system in particular showed a pattern of British domination very similar to that of American in the industrial sphere. British entrepreneurs abounded at the helm of Canadian financial intermediaries, along with British direct investment in joint ventures in Canadian banks or the wholly owned imperially chartered banks operating in Canada. Insurance companies too were often British-led or British branches. However, with life companies, Canadian control grew over time, unlike the industrial pattern.

The development of the chartered banking system falls into two distinct phases. In the first period, lasting until the 1890's, the economy was in the deflationary phase of the long cycle and the chartered banks lost ground relative to other intermediaries. Note issue tended to shrink, and a great deal of effort was made to keep up the circulation, notably by promoting the formation and proliferation of private banks as circulation agents. Gradually their priorities changed. In the 1890's the savings deposit business became of primary importance, and the chartered banks undertook systematic campaigns to swallow up their offspring in the private banking sector to take over the savings business, subsequently engaging in a major amalgamation effort to absorb the smaller chartered banks as well and to therefore redirect the flow of savings.

In terms of operations, the Canadian intermediaries were completely inappropriate to the needs of an economy bent on industrializing. The commercial banks grew up in the field of international commodity movements, and their adherence to the "real bills" doctrine never wavered. Apart from the Maritime non-Halifax banks and a few others, the banking system, chartered and private, was of little value to industry. In fact it was a positive hindrance, for the system was exceedingly effective in moving savings geographically after the demise of Maritime banking. The savings which had formerly been used to promote local industry in the Maritimes and other areas now deemed "surplus" were moved to the Canadian West to support grain dealers, and otherwise to contribute to the over development of a single cash crop. Similarly, Québécois industry and Ontario mixed farms were drained of the surplus needed to sustain them.

Insurance companies too were involved in staple production for, especially after the wheat boom really commenced, they shifted increasingly into mortgage lending. Not all of their mortgage loans were agricultural. A great deal of money went into sterile speculations in urban real estate. In this activity mortgage loan companies were also very prominent, and made heavy use of debentures sold in Britain to secure funds for their Canadian operations.

The orientation of the intermediaries towards staple movement left a gap in the market for long-term capital which was in part filled by governments. The federal and provincial governments gave direct cash subsidies to the construction of commercial infrastructure and to the primary iron and steel industry associated with the railroad building. The municipalities sold debentures at home and abroad and used tax receipts to engage in industrial fixed capital formation by the bonusing system. New industries sprang up, amply assisted by the municipal subsidies; old industries marched across Canada in search of handouts; municipalities actively competed; and many industries were clogged with new entrants as a result. While the bonusing system and its attendant horrors clearly played a role in fostering industrial capital formation, the wastes were enormous, and the burden fell on municipal taxpayers and established industry: the benefits accrued to the newcomers who were often wealthy foreign firms.

British loans to Canada, to the extent they went into municipal debentures, thus helped support industrial capital formation but via the municipality as intermediary, rather than through the organized capital market. Most British loans, however, went to federal or provincial government bonds or railroad bonds. The federal and provincial loans in turn tended to be spent on the construction of infrastructure, especially railroads.

The railroad loans helped promote an extreme overextension of trunk lines. The railways, through their structure of non-price competition, engaged in a process of building of competitive feeder lines to tap resources traffic for their long-distance trade.

Quick development of staple traffic reinforced the primary exports orientation of the economy and was forced by the need of the railways to generate immediate revenue to cover their fixed interest debt. The result was that local lines and secondary processing alike were underdeveloped. This pattern of commercial infrastructure geared to staple exports, as well as the direct impact of the vast expenditure on the construction of the railroads, contributed to the rapid inflation in the Canadian economy after 1900. Moreover, the railroads discriminated in favour of long-distance as opposed to local traffic. And they tended to keep their rate structures aligned to tariff changes. In effect, the Canadian tariff protected the British railway bondholders by assuring them a flow of earnings to pay the interest.

The industrial structure in Canada until the 1890's was fairly traditional. Small firms, often with a local orientation, typified most industries. Many of the consumers' goods industries in particular were badly overcrowded. During the deflation phase of the long cycle, the result was a squeeze on profit margins and vigorous, often unsuccessful efforts at cartelization. Cartels and profit pools were difficult to maintain during a period of secular deflation, for falling costs encouraged firms to break ranks and begin price cutting. Mergers were occasionally attempted as a method of curbing competition during this period, but they were relatively few and far between, partly because of the effects of the deflation and partly because the Canadian capital market provided no scope for dealing in industrial equities. After the inflation phase began, monopolization accelerated. From 1896 to 1907 many new mergers were created, mainly by the participating firms. For secular inflation meant that the former potential for getting one step ahead of competitors by price cutting was restricted due to the prospect of increasing costs over time. After 1907, when tariff stability was assumed, and capital market conditions improved greatly, the potential existed for a great merger wave. The expectation of continued inflation encouraged enormous stock watering operations, and the inflated prices at which the components of the mergers were purchased would be recovered in part automatically through inflation, in part through the exploitation of the monopoly created, which monopoly price increases in turn fed the inflation. Supported by British industrial bond purchases, the merger wave created an industrial structure totally dependent on the tariff to permit the mergers earnings levels sufficient to pay interest and dividends on their waterlogged capital.

While not completely accurate for all of the time-period under consideration, for the era of the great expansion the following model of the interregional and international flow of funds is of some value in illuminating the geographic and sectoral distribution involved.

The inflow of foreign direct investment into Canada located largely in southern Ontario and the Montreal area. The inflow of portfolio investment came via the capital markets of Montreal and Toronto, and financed either central Canadian industrial mergers or infrastructural spending, largely in the West. Mortgage company debenture funds also flowed via Montreal and Toronto to the west. In B.C., northern Ontario, and Quebec, there occurred substantial amounts of direct investment in resources industries, the bulk of whose products were exported unprocessed. From B.C. the American lumber investments also serviced prairie needs during the "wheat boom." After 1900 a large amount of direct investment in pulp and paper was added in Ontario, Quebec, and B.C.

Central Canada ran a steady balance of trade surplus with the rest of the country, exporting manufactures and importing raw materials. It therefore exported large amounts of capital to the prairies in the form of bank loans, mortgage funds, and sales credit through implement dealerships, for the building of infrastructure. Central Canadian as well as American direct investment flowed into B.C. But the funds exported from central Canada were not to the detriment of its own development. Although small towns in Ontario were drained of their savings deposits, Ontario and Montreal exhibited faster growth over-all than their own savings would have sustained, due to the influx of foreign capital. The funds for export to the West were derived in part from the imports of portfolio capital, and in part from the Maritimes.

The Maritimes provided primary iron and steel and staple exports for Canadian markets. But unlike the West, it ran a balance of trade surplus and the area became a net exporter of capital through the intermediary structure.

Simultaneously with these interregional movements of funds, Montreal and Toronto capitalists undertook substantial exports of long-term capital to the U.S., to the Caribbean, and to South America. The export of capital to the U.S. helped in the formation of industrial capital there through the investments of banks, insurance companies, and individuals. The Caribbean area, by contrast, was a surplus area for the banks and suffered a drain of funds through bank deposit and insurance company policy business. South American investments were largely utilities financed in the main with British capital and therefore provided a net inflow of funds to Canada in the shape of dividends on the water

that constituted their stock. The flow of funds into Canada from
Latin America helped to pay the costs of servicing the British
and American capital invested in Canada.

The obvious question that arises in light of the simultaneous
export and import of capital is whether Canada really "needed"
to borrow so extensively abroad. Assuming that the funds
diverted abroad had been retained inside Canada, it would
appear on the surface that the need for external funds would be
thereby lessened. In fact no such conclusion can be drawn. The
export and import of capital were opposite sides of the same
coin, both reflecting something more basic, namely the pattern of
dependent development of Canada within the broad confines of
the British empire. It was its hinterland status that led to unbal-
anced development, to a staple orientation of the economy, and
therefore to the flow of funds that occurred. Huge imports of
capital were required to finance the construction of trunk
railway lines and other works. Enormous sums were diverted
into land speculations. At the same time, funds moved abroad
into railway extensions or financing commodity flows.

One ingredient often held to be indispensable for development is the enigmatic quality of "entrepreneurship"[3] and the
"lack of entrepreneurship" is often regarded as the primary
reason for Canadian dependence on the U.S in the industrial
sphere.[4] While in a modern context the concept of an entrepreneur is largely a polite fiction,[5] in the late nineteenth and early
twentieth centuries the issue of the availability of entrepreneurial
ability must be given some consideration. "Lack of entrepreneurship" as a cause of industrial underdevelopment and reliance on
American patterns and capital is either true but trite, or patently
false, depending upon how it is interpreted. It is false in the sense
that entrepreneurship can be either industrial or commercial, and
Canadian business history shows no lack of commercial capitalists of undisputed ability. In railways, utilities, commercial
banking, and finance, "Canadian" entrepreneurs (often domiciled British ones) were strong, and their hold on those sectors of
the economy increased over time. The vigour of Canadian
finance, utility, and railroad promotions at home was matched
by those abroad. British support in the form of portfolio loans
was available to these sectors, and with this assistance Canadian
entrepreneurs clung to, and replicated, the familiar patterns of
development.

This strength was not matched by industrial efforts. Rather,
the strength of the commercial sector went hand-in-hand with
industrial weakness, by virtue of the absence of funds due to the
twisting of the capital market so that funds flowed freely into

commerce and staple movements, and away from industry, and because of the absence of independent innovative capacity. Yet here again the phrase "lack of entrepreneurship" is sheer obfuscation. For entrepreneurs are the product of their social context. If by deficiency of indigenous entrepreneurship it is meant that American industrial capitalism possessed some special attributes permitting it to take advantage of productive opportunities which Canadian capitalism in the particular period did not, then the explanation is tautological, and thus trivial insofar as it fails to make specific reference to the objective social conditions of the period, especially the pattern of dependence. For the existence of domination by itself precludes innovation. It creates the social conditions for the replication of existing patterns.

The strength of commercial capitalism in Canada was the result of the British colonial connection, and together they served to lock the Canadian economy into the staple trap. The domination of the Montreal commercial community in the colonial economic and political structure was the outgrowth of the pattern of dependence, and the stultification of industrial entrepreneurship followed from their control of the state and state policy, most notably with regard to the structure of the federally controlled banking system. The resulting vacuum led directly to the reliance on American industrialism, in the form of entrepreneurs, patents, or direct investment.

What are normally regarded as the two great Canadian industrial success stories, agricultural implements and primary iron and steel, are the exceptions that prove the rule. The agricultural implements industry was largely the work of émigré American industrialists whose access to American patents assured them control of the Canadian market without any ownership ties with American parents. The primary iron and steel industry was the creation of American bonus hunters who migrated north, again without formal ownership ties with American firms. It was thus a relatively simple matter to "Canadianize" these two industries, which, too, bore a very direct relationship to the wheat boom through the expansion of farms and transcontinental railways.

Dependence, like protection, was addictive. The very ease of access to British portfolio investment and markets and to American direct investment and technology ensured a particular pattern of development culminating in the reinforcement of the principal structural weaknesses of the Canadian economy during the "wheat boom." This "golden age" of Canadian growth was in some respects an economic catastrophe. British funds were readily available to be misallocated into overextensions to commercial infrastructure or for floating huge mergers, both of which projects led to drastic liquidation after the war and bequeathed to the Canadian economy a huge burden of fixed interest debt owing to British investors. The capital market was shifted increasingly to servicing the production and movement of staples. And American direct investment in manufacturing and resource industries accelerated. As a result, the Canadian economy never fully made the vital transition form commercialism to industrialism. Funds moved internationally to service commerce more easily than they moved intranationally into industry. Lack of integration between commerce and industry reflected the ease of access to external sources, and this obviated any real pressure for the development of policies and financial institutions appropriate to domestic industrial development, or any desire or need on the part of the dominant strata of its capitalist class to change their colonial position.

Notes to Chapter XVII

1.   Nurkse, *Problems of Capital Formation,* p. 105. See also *JC,* Sept. 19, 1879, p. 145. Canadian opinion at the time was fully aware of the fact that the tariff by itself was inadequate.

2.   Cf. J. H. Dales, *The Protective Tariff in Canada's Development,* who accedes to the fact that the tariff did increase the scale of the Canadian economy, but claims its long-run effect was to reduce per capita income below the level it would have reached in the absence of the tariff. He arrives at this conclusion by utilizing the traditional static resource allocation theorems and in so doing contradicts his own initial premise. For to conclude that the allocation of resources that results from the tariff is less efficient than the allocation that would exist without it must assume that the same resources are available before and after the tariff, a premise explicitly contradicted from the outset. Furthermore, Dales's argument accepts the notion of under-full employment before the tariff to justify his theorems regarding immigration. Yet, according to the best principles of neoclassical welfare economics of which Dales is a dedicated follower, two second-best situations are incomparable in the welfare sense, and his conclusions are therefore meaningless in terms of their own inner logic. See especially R. Lipsey and K. Lancaster, "The General Theory of Second Best."

3.   Notably by Schumpeter in *The Theory of Economic Development* and his other writings.

4.   See especially K. Levitt, *Silent Surrender;* S. Hymer "Foreign Direct Investment," and M. H. Watkins, "A New National Policy."

5.   Cf. the argument of Schumpeter in *Capitalism, Socialism and Democracy* on the withering away of the entrepreneurial function.

Independence is a farce. Canada must belong either to the British system or the American system. . . . If we had to make the choice between independence and annexation, I would rather that we should have annexation and join with the United States at once.

John A. Macdonald, 1881

CHAPTER XVIII
Epilogue: Aftermath of the National Policy

Canadian development policy in the National Policy era was essentially a policy of mercantilism, of consolidation and expansion led by a commercial capitalist class in which the state structure in the hands of that class played a critically active role. Access to foreign capital and technology was the *sine qua non* of success. It was a strategy inextricably related to the state of the British Empire. The Empire provided markets and thereby the rationale for both the expansion of major staples and the influx of American manufacturing investment and technology. Britain supplied, as well, portfolio capital for financial and infrastructural purposes. In 1844 Frederick List had predicted,

> The United States and Canada, the more their populations increase and the more the protective system of the United States is developed, so much the more will they feel themselves drawn towards one another, and the less will it be possible for England to prevent a union between them.[1]

The Canadian strategists of the period felt otherwise. As long as the Empire existed, Canada was safe from the threat of absorption into the U.S. In addition to the "countervailing British influences," there was the anti-imperial sentiment in the U.S. to reckon with. As H.M.P. Eckhardt, hired eulogist of the Canadian Bankers' Association asked,

> If this sentiment is so strong upon the question of controlling inferior races like the Filipinos and the Cubans, what would it be upon the question of Washington interfering in Canadian affairs?[2]

World War I led to drastic reorganization. The beginning of the end of the British Empire, it was equally the beginning of the

TABLE XVII (1)

Government Investment in Railways, 1916

Railway	Subsidies	Proceeds From Land Sales	Loans Outstanding	Guarantees Outstanding	Total
Canadian Northern	$ 38,874,148	$ 34,379,809	$ 25,858,166	$199,141,140	$298,233,263
Canadian Pacific	104,690,801	123,810,124	—	—	228,500,925
Grand Trunk	13,003,060		15,142,633		28,145,693
Grand Trunk Pacific	726,320		70,311,716	43,432,848	114,470,884
National Transcontinental			159,881,197	13,469,004	173,350,201
Intercolonial			116,234,204		116,234,204
P.E.I.			9,496,567		9,496,567
Total	$157,294,329	$158,189,933	$396,924,483	$256,042,992	$968,431,737

Source: *RCRTC*, p. xix.

end of the National Policy. Cut off from the continued inflow of capital necessary to maintain the hothouse growth of the system, collapse began almost immediately.

By 1916 Canada had sunk into railways nearly a billion dollars in subsidies, value of lands sold, "loans," and guarantees outstanding, and much more if account is taken of foregone interest on interest-free loans, tax exemptions, value of unsold lands, and minerals acquired with land grants. But the two new transcontinentals were tottering on the brink of bankruptcy, unable to generate sufficient earnings to meet obligations on their funded debt. Under the terms of the 1914 Canadian Northern Railway Guarantee Act, the federal government had guaranteed a $45 million bond issue, and received in exchange $40 million of the $100 million common stock of the railroad which Mackenzie and Mann had scrupulously avoided tainting with a hint of hard cash. The government also received the power to foreclose and become sole owner in the event of default. The $45 million was quickly exhausted, war closed the London capital market, and Mackenzie and Mann went back to the federal government for more aid.[3] Of the remaining $60 million of equity, most had been pledged to the Bank of Commerce in return for advances. In 1917 a joint agreement of Mackenzie and Mann, the Commerce, and the federal government provided for nationalization, with the government to acquire the shares pledged to the Commerce at a sum to be decided by arbitration.[4] The Minister of Finance in the Tory government who introduced the bill for nationalization was Sir Thomas White, a Liberal who had deserted the party over Reciprocity, and vice president of the Bank of Commerce until he assumed the portfolio. He was also connected with Mackenzie and Mann, Walker, Wood, and the others of the Commerce-Northern alliance in a number of other ventures. The equity, which a Royal Commission deemed valueless,[5] was set at $10.8 million by the arbitration committee.[6]

The Grand Trunk followed its rival shortly. The National Transcontinental, which was to have served as the eastern half of the GTR's new transcontinental, was completed in 1915. The GTR, which was to have leased it for three per cent of its capital costs, promptly refused to carry out the bargain on the grounds that the costs were excessive. It was an astonishing piece of effrontery, given that the Grand Trunk as contractor had done all in its power to escalate those costs and derive the benefit in the form of middleman's profits. The railway then tried to have the government relieve it of all liabilities for the Grand Trunk Pacific as well, and to repay it for any expenditures it had made on that system.[7] During 1915, 1916, and 1917, when the London management was anxious to have the government take over the burden of the Grand Trunk Pacific, they understated the operating revenues of the road by eight million dollars per annum. Then in 1919 and 1920, when sale of the entire system to the Canadian government was being contemplated, they manipulated their accounts to show earnings larger than actually existed.[8]

During 1918, the Prime Minister announced that negotiations were underway for the acquisition of the Grand Trunk Pacific. As a result, "various members of the Government carpet bagged back and forth across the ocean . . . ," acquiring the bonds of the line, Clifford Sifton reportedly among them.[9]

Early in 1919 the government refused further aid, and the railway was called upon to pay up on its guarantee of interest of the Grand Trunk Pacific bonds. The line planned to shut down and create as much chaos as possible, but under the terms of the War Measures Act then in force the railway was put into receivership. [10] Prices of the railway's equity fell precipitously, a depreciation of four million pounds on its guaranteed stock alone, and another one-and-a-half million on its first preference issue. After a vehement anti-nationalization campaign conducted by the railway and by the CPR, the government agreed to assume all securities but the common and preferred stock at par, the value of these last to be determined by arbitration. The result was a substantial rise in the value of the stock.[11] The GTR directors could not resist indulging themselves in a last piece of systematic robbery, voting themselves five years of directors' fees plus large sums for officials in Canada and England. These sums were taken from the fire insurance fund, in violation of the takeover agreement. The directors were forced to refund them.[12]

The arbitration tribunal began its deliberations. On its tours of inspection of plant and buildings, it announced itself surprised at their high quality. Unfortunately for the railway, subsequent investigation showed that the condition was in fact the result of a lot of window-dressing done by the railway specifically to impress the tribunal, and that the railway was really in terrible condition. [13] The tribunal, which included Sir Thomas White, declared the common stock to be worthless, which made the CNR award doubly reprehensible. The Judicial Committee of the Privy Council, the ultimate trustee over the fortunes of British investors in the Empire much as the Royal Navy was for investments in the rest of the world, granted leave for an appeal. Fortunately for the Mackenzie King government, the appeal failed to bring a reversal of the verdict, and the mounting public pressure for abolition of appeals to the Judicial Committee was relieved.[14] The stockholders, supported by a number of British newspapers, began urging a boycott of Canadian borrowings in London. It was a suitably squalid ending to the sordid saga of the Grand Trunk Railway, which had thoroughly debased Canadian politics for three-quarters of a century.

While the Grand Trunk's demise was greatly assisted by the excessive duplications that followed the absorption of the Great Western, and by the rapacity of its English shareholders whose greed for dividends had been of such an order of magnitude that nothing was left for operating revenue,[15] overexpansion during the wheat boom was the ultimate cause of failure of both of the new systems. This pattern of overextension was the result of the logic of railway competition of the period, with the burden of waste falling on the Canadian lower-income taxpayer, who paid for the huge fixed interest debts that followed nationalization.

Bank behaviour once again parallelled that of the railways. During the war, farmers were virtually begged to borrow. The idea was foisted upon them that it was patriotic to borrow large sums to buy larger holdings from the land companies and railways and to grow more crops.[16] Then, too, the very nature of bank competition through branch proliferations while colluding on interest rates, thus raising the overhead costs of banking, led to vigorous efforts to increase the amount of debt contracted by farmers.[17] The end of the war brought recession and a big slump in primary product prices. Wheat had fallen to 67¢ a bushel by 1923, leaving the farmers with drastically curtailed money incomes to meet the heavy burden of fixed interest debt. It was a portent of the problems to face the Canadian economy on a grand scale a decade later. The banks too had begun to cut back on their overextensions after the war. The first banks in the West were absorbed by the more powerful ones, and branch closures occurred in many small communities. The withdrawal of branches increased the burden of the credit squeeze on farmers, for the branches, despite having frequently promised farmers renewal of debts, insisted on settlement of claims before closure.[18]

The drastic liquidation of the early 1920's brought with it a string of bank failures in spite of the enormous amounts of public money poured into the banking system to keep it afloat under the auspices of the Finance Act of 1914. Gold convertibility had been suspended, and the Department of Finance engaged in what it called "rediscounting," while in fact it was making direct loans to the banks. The manna of fiat money continued until 1923; Sir Thomas White having declared that under no circumstance would he let a bank fail. Apparently he did not make the declaration loudly enough for the directors of the Merchants' Bank of Canada to hear; for that institution, insolvent by 1921, failed in 1922. It was the greatest single bank disaster to date in North America. In 1921 in the U.S. 28 national banks out of 8,240 failed, or one in 290, while in Canada the Merchants' was one in eighteen. Moreover, the aggregate loss from the Merchants' alone was as great as the losses from all 28 American banks. The Canadian Bankers' Association propaganda had always insisted that large banks were stable; the Merchants' at the time of failure was the fourth largest in Canada.[19]

While an effort was made to disguise the failure as a merger with the Bank of Montreal, stockholder losses of over eleven million dollars suggest otherwise. The collapse of the bank followed the failure of a stock brokerage firm to which the bank had loaned no less than $3.6 million.[20] The trial of its officers was so blatant a farce that it even outraged the Canadian financial press. Sir Hugh Montagu Allan, in addition to being acquitted of the usual charges of fraud along with the general manager, was actually commended by the judge for his conduct of the bank's affairs during his presidency.[21]

The next year, the Home Bank came tumbling down. In 1922 it had paid a seven per cent dividend; by 1923 its losses were over five million dollars.[22] The dividends the year before were justified at the time by the fact that the president of the bank, who was also a director of Canada's newly formed Canadian National Railways, had stolen one million dollars of the railway's funds and deposited it with the bank to improve the annual statement to the shareholders and the monthly return to the federal government. Five days after its deposit, the fabricated return and report having been duly sent out, the money was removed from the bank and sent back to the railway.[23] The bank's losses resulted from a number of sources: from its American utility holdings, from B.C. timberland speculation, from some thinly disguised real estate deals, but especially from the excessive loans made to further Sir Henry Pellatt's mining stock speculations.[24] Creditors of the bank lost eleven million; shareholders another two-and-one-half million.

In the aftermath, runs began on the Dominion Bank and several others,[25] as the entire banking system verged on catastrophe with a total collapse of earnings due to bad debts. To disguise the extent of the crisis, the banks continued to pay out big dividends. The Union Bank was earning less than four per cent and paying out 9.35% dividends supported from government loans. The Bank of Hamilton earned 7.35% and paid out 12%. The Standard

lost money for five years but paid out dividends at 13.4%. La
Banque Nationale, whose liabilities had risen to 22 times the
level of its capital and reserves, managed to keep up its stock
quotations by paying dividends out of its deposits. It was saved
by a Quebec government loan of fifteen million dollars, and then
merged with another bank into La Banque Canadienne
Nationale. The Bank of Hamilton was absorbed by the Commerce. Other mergers followed.[26] The government in 1923
decided to maintain the supply of Dominion notes being loaned
to the chartered banks as a permanent part of the monetary
system. Under the terms of 1923 Finance Act, not only were
public securities of Canadian governments, plus those of the
U.K., colonial, or U.S. governments acceptable collateral for
advances of Dominion notes, but so too were the notes and bills
of the private sector.

In the immediate post-war period, too, were felt the consequences of the merger epidemic. Many of the mergers were in
trouble by 1913; the war provided a brief respite; then the
bottom fell out. During the commercial recession of 1920-21, a
series of drastic reorganizations and reductions of nominal capital occurred.[27] With prices of output falling, drastic liquidations
were really inevitable. The watering operations that had created
the mergers required a climate of secular inflation to justify
them. When the inflationary phase of the long cycle came to an
end, so did the economic life of many of the mergers. Some of
the mergers had been cursed by the greed of their directors, who
drained off their resources into dividends, running down the
plant in the process. Many firms suffered cutbacks, including
some in sugar and pulp and paper, but especially in the iron and
steel industry, which had badly overextended during the railway-
building frenzy. These cuts had repercussions in London: English investors, already made very wary by the pre-war debacles,
were frightened away from Canadian industrial bonds, which
thereafter began to be floated largely in the U.S.

The crisis reflected itself in the state of foreign exchange markets. Canadian exchange in late 1919 and early 1920 fell to a
nine per cent discount vis-à-vis American currency, while its
exchange rates with Europe moved in its favour. The result was
a great deal of liquidation of holdings of Canadian securities by
European investors, who sold them largely to Americans. Canadian Northern and Grand Trunk securities were among those
moving to North America in considerable numbers.[28]

Canadian municipal debentures were another security of
which an enormous volume had been placed in Britain just
before the war, and western Canadian municipalities tended to

follow the financial fate of the grain trade. In 1919 the city of Prince Arthur went into default.[29] Regina tried to avoid the same fate by taking advantage of the exchange rate changes, paying its interest in sterling which was at a discount with respect to Canadian funds. Bondholders and dealers were outraged, and the city was sued by Toronto General Trust on behalf of the British investors. The city lost the case, and Canadian municipalities were obliged to settle their debenture debt at the old exchange rates.[30]

Those gaining from the state of the exchanges were American investors, whose takeover of Canadian assets was greatly facilitated. The 1909 merger, Canadian Car and Foundry, was among the first to go, passing into Francis Clergue's hands early in 1920 and becoming closely affiliated with American Car and Foundry.[31]

The degree of foreign ownership of industrial securities (bonds and equity) including manufacturing, resource industries, construction, and some utilities declined slightly in relative terms in the immediate post-war period. In absolute terms, however, it continued to grow.

TABLE XVIII (2)

Ownership of Industrial Securities by Country

	% Total held by Residents of			
Year	Canada	U.K.	U.S.	Other
1918	56	9	34	1
1919	58	10	31	1
1921	61	8	27	3

Source: *FP,* Oct. 19, 1923.

By 1921, American direct investment in Canadian industry totalled nearly one billion dollars. Direct and portfolio investments by Americans reached $1,084 million, by British $310 million, by other foreign investors $131 millions. Thus a total of

TABLE XVIII (3)

Distribution of Security Ownership by Type, 1921

	Canada	U.K.	U.S.	Other
equity	61	7	29	3
bonds	57	15	18	10
other securities	55	9	32	4
average	61	8	27	4

Source: *FP,* Oct. 19, 1923.

nearly $1,567 million of foreign capital comprising nearly 40% of the total capital was invested in these industries.

The distribution of foreign ownership of securities (including bonds) by that early date already showed certain very critical patterns. American ownership was exceptionally high in automobiles and accessories, electrical apparatus, chemicals and drugs, copper smelting, and non-ferrous metal foundries even before the major takeover of key firms in the high growth-high technology industries began in the early 1920's. And of course even the remaining Canadian ownership was greatly circumscribed by patent control. In textiles and other light industries, the Canadian share was overwhelming. There were two especially revealing cases. In food products, the industries like meat packing and cereal milling most capable of organization on big agribusiness principles were almost half American-owned, while biscuit makers, fish canners, distillers and the like were largely Canadian-owned. In footwear industries, those producing from rubber were two-thirds under American control, reflecting American monopolization of the raw material and the degree of technology implicit in their manufacture, compared to the traditional industry based on leather, which was 98% Canadian-controlled.

Over and above the exchange rate changes and the impact of the loss of new British portfolio investment, the cessation of the growth of the Empire had important effects on Canadian industrial structure. Without an expanding imperial market, the joint ventures and licensed firms of old had no *raison d'être.* A series of takeovers by American parent firms in leading industries embodying advanced technology occurred. General Motors became wholly owned by the parent by 1918. Ford used part of its fabulous return in dividends from its equity of Ford Canada to raise its holdings to 85% by 1927. And by 1923 Canadian General Electric had become majority-owned by the American parent once more.[31]

The remaining Empire market was still an important commercial objective of American firms, though the Canadian industrial intermediaries were no longer required. American firms finished the war with surplus earnings available for export, while Canada sought to replace the loss of British portfolio capital with American direct investment. A steady influx of branch plants resulted. Even during the war, before American entry, informal discussions of a possible tariff arrangement between the Allies and the Dominions had triggered off a movement of American branch plants into Canada who insisted on their right to be reckoned as Canadian firms for commercial purposes.[32]

TABLE XVIII (4)

Distribution of Ownership of Securities
Selected Industries - 1921 (%)

	Canada	U.K.	U.S.	Other
lumber-mill	75	8	17	—
lumber-forest	68	1	25	6
pulp & paper	69	3	18	10
cotton	82	1	17	—
woollens	94	2	4	—
hosiery & knit goods	91	4	5	—
meat packing	52	—	46	2
flour & cereal mills	54	—	45	—
other food and beverages	81	5	13	1
steel furnace & rolling mills	71	1	28	—
copper smelting	17	32	46	5
foundry & machine shop	58	7	35	—
brass & copper foundry	38	—	63	—
agricultural implements	52	8	24	16
automobiles	22	—	78	—
auto accessories	20	—	80	—
car construction	66	—	34	—
ship building	47	45	8	—
paints, drugs, chemicals	35	9	55	1
artificial abrasives	—	—	100	—
rubber products	67	10	22	—
rubber footwear	33	—	67	—
leather footwear & tanning	98	—	2	—
electrical generation	68	6	15	11
electrical apparatus	42	14	42	2
petroleum refining	64	—	36	—
construction	83	16	1	—
minerals	54	13	31	2

Source: *FP,* Oct. 19, 1923.

After the war, municipalities were eagerly advertising themselves as attractive places for itinerant American plants to settle. Cheap power, the promise of docile labour, and good sites were all dangled before the eyes of American capitalists.[33] The appearance of American products on the Canadian market was the signal for cities, Chambers of Commerce, banks, and business publications to "campaign" the producer to build a factory in Canada.[34] By 1927, the level of American direct investment in Canada had reached $1.5 billion in book value, nearly six times its 1914 level.[35]

The declining importance of imperial trade, and the accompanying threat the decline posed to the momentum of American direct investment, were especially traumatic during the Great Depression. For with the collapse of world primary product prices came a great increase in the real burden of carrying the huge fixed interest debt with which the Dominion had been bequeathed by its railway promoters. Service charges rose to absorb up to 25% of total foreign exchange earnings.

The policy response was the predictable myopic one of trying to lessen the burden of the problem by increasing its extent, by soliciting more foreign investment especially in the form of American branch plants.[36] The Imperial Preference arrangements of 1931 were defended by the Dominion government on the grounds that they had caused 90 new branch plants to blast their way into Canadian markets.[37] The preceding year the negotiations had attracted 97; the succeeding year saw 92 new entrants; thereafter the new investment fell off.[38]

In the meantime, the banking situation had worsened. The Finance Act of 1923 was supplemented by a return of gold. It was an incompatible mixture. Gold drained out of the country while the reserves of Dominion notes remained constant. The result was a continued steady inflation of the circulation despite the external leakage of gold. At the end of 1928, Canada abandoned gold, well before the onset of the Great Depression, a depression which forced the complete re-organization of the Canadian banking system.

The Canadian dollar failed to depreciate during the early years of the Depression. A continued net inflow of foreign capital — mainly American in the form of a Dominion loan, private loans, and direct investment — kept the exchange rate high. The collapse of world primary product prices led to a severe deterioration in the balance of visible trade. However, the capital inflow not only offset it but was sufficient to cause a net import of some $30 million in 1930. In addition, the banking system's adherence to "sound money" kept the domestic circulation from undergoing a compensating expansion. A high level of the exchanges was actually welcomed as a means of helping to pay off the debt charges due foreigners, despite the fact that it was greatly exacerbating the deflationary pressures already active.

Pressure for the establishment of a central bank took two forms in Canada in the early period. One school argued for a bank which would loan money to the government for such things as public works and would compete with the chartered banks for savings. The second, advocated by some chartered bankers like the general managers of the Royal and the Imperial, though opposed by others, wanted a bank of rediscount. What the second proposal emphasized was a permanent mechanism, privately owned and effectively under direct control of the chartered banks, whereby the commercial paper lying dormant in the banks' portfolios could be liquified. It therefore involved the ceding of the note issue power completely to the central government, or its agent in the form of a central bank.

This last change was really a minor concession. Chartered bank note issue had been increasingly supplanted by government of Canada notes since 1914. The demands of war finance had led to a very marked expansion of the relative importance of government notes. Then the crisis of the early 1920's required loans of government notes to the "stable" banking system to ward off total collapse. A central bank of issue which would exchange the chartered banks' bills for notes was a logical outgrowth of these earlier changes. The existence of such a body on which to unload the worst bills in their portfolios was certainly no hardship to the chartered banks, and was worth far more than the loss entailed in the cession of their already badly eroded issue power.

The Great Depression brought the national policy, the wheat economy, and the British Empire that provided them with a *raison d'être,* equally down in ruins. Private investment in Canada virtually ceased. Incomes in the West fell precipitously as world grain prices plummeted. In B.C. and Manitoba, money incomes by 1933 were only about 50% of their 1928 level. In Alberta they were less than 40%. In Saskatchewan, money income was a mere quarter of its 1928 level and of every fifteen bushels of wheat produced, it was estimated that seven were required to discharge farm debts to mortgage loan companies, land companies, railways, grain dealers, banks, and implement firms. Organized farm parties threatened eastern big business and British finance capital with repudiation of debts and with nationalization of credit and commercial infrastructure. Organized labour, faced with measured unemployment rates of 20% and more, underwent a profound radicalization. But fortunately for the Canadian business class, just when things looked blackest, the Second World War brought respite, rejuvenation, and hope for the future.

Notes to Chapter XVIII

1.   F. List, *The National System of Political Economy,* p. 177.
2.   H.M.P. Eckhardt, "Americanizing Influences," p. 288.
3.   R. Graham, *Arthur Meighen,* p. 78.
4.   Department of Railways, *Annual Report,* 1920, p.xiii.
5.   *RCRTC,* p. xiii.
6.   L.T. Fournier, *Railway Nationalization in Canada,* pp. 68-9.
7.   *RCRTC,* p. xxvi.
8.   L. T. Fournier, *Railway Nationalization,* p. 107.
9.   *HCD,* March 20, 1919, p. 668.
10.   *Ec,* April 5, 1919.
11.   *Ec,* Oct. 18, 1919, p. 612.
12.   *Ec,* April 28, 1923, p. 894.
13.   *Ec,* March 5, 1921, p. 516.
14.   *Ec,* Aug. 26, 1922, p. 360.
15.   H. A. Lovett, *Canada and the Grand Trunk,* p. 232.
16.   W. Drummond, *Financing the Purchase of Land in Canada,* p. 378.
17.   *ACBCA,* p. 15.
18.   *ACBCA,* p. 33.
19.   H. C. McLeod to Sir John Aird, Jan. 19, 1924, *Peter McArthur Papers.*
20.   *Ec,* Jan. 7, 1922, p. 16; Jan. 21, 1922, p. 88; Feb. 4, 1922, p. 187.
21.   *Ec,* Oct. 14, 1922, p. 628; Dec. 2, 1922, p. 1035.
22.   *MT,* Oct. 5, 1923, pp. 3-5.
23.   *Ec,* Oct. 20, 1923, p. 601.
24.   *MT,* Dec. 14, 1923, p. 10; Dec. 21, 1923, pp. 12-17; Dec. 28, 1923, p. 10.
25.   *MT,* Aug. 24, 1923, p. 3; Oct. 19, 1923, p. 5.
26.   H. C. McLeod to Peter McArthur, March 2, 1923; H. C. McLeod to Peter McArthur, March 19, 1923, *Peter McArthur Papers.*
27.   W. Stapells, "The Recent Consolidation Movement," pp. 189, 211.
28.   *Ec,* March 6, 1920, p. 556.
29.   *Ec,* Aug. 23, 1919, p. 314.
30.   *Ec,* March 5, 1921, p. 516; Feb. 18, 1922, p. 280.
31.   *Ec,* Feb. 14, 1920, p. 321; Sept. 18, 1920, p. 440; H. Marshall *et al, Canadian-American Industry,* pp. 63-70.
32.   MT, Oct. 27, 1916, p. 6.
33.   FP, May 6, May 20, June 17, July 1, 1927; et passim.
34.   FP, Oct. 7, 1927.
35.   FP, May 6, 1927.
36.   H.A. Innis, *Problems of Staple Production in Canada,* p. 117.
37.   FP, Aug. 8, 1931.
38.   H. Marshall *et al, Canadian-American Industry,* p. 21.

Glossary of Financial Terminology

The exact meanings of many terms in commerce and finance change over time as financial practices change and as new institutions evolve. As a result, the following definitions are often not completely precise. Rather, they are intended to give the reader a general sense of the nature of the financial operation described, taking account of the historical context. Definitions are therefore cast in a descriptive and functional mould rather than a precise legal one.

Accommodation Paper: Refers to a line of credit extended by a bank to a customer. It can be a short-term loan that takes the form of an overdraft of the customers' account. It could also take the form of a banker's "acceptance" whereby the bank on behalf of a customer, for example an importer of merchandise, "accepts" the liability of paying off the foreign exporter when he demands payment, and in return secures a commitment from its customer to pay off the claim when it falls due. In effect the high credit rating of the bank is substituted for the lower credit of the particular importer by the bank's accepting the liability on behalf of the import merchant.

Ad Valorem Tariff: When a tax or tariff is levied *ad valorem,* it signifies that the tax is reckoned as a certain fixed percentage of the value of the item being taxed.

Assignment: A process whereby a debtor, unable to pay his obligations in cash on demand to his creditors, can avoid "bankruptcy" by assigning his assets in whole or in part to one of his major creditors, who thereafter administers or "liquidates" the assets to attempt to realize his claim.

Bankruptcy: In the case of a bona fide bankruptcy, as opposed to an assignment, the debtor unable to meet his debts submits to a court which appoints a receiver for the property. The receiver, who is not appointed from among the creditors, undertakes to administer and/or liquidate the property so as to meet the debts owed to various claimants to the extent possible out of the assets of the bankrupt person or company. The claims are settled in a certain legally fixed order. For example, the claims to the assets of an incorporated company begin with the bond holders, then the debenture holders, then general debtors, then preferred stock holders and finally, if there is anything left, the holders of ordinary equity or common stock.

Banking School: A philosophy of how banks should behave that emerged out of a protracted debate in England in the early nineteenth century. Among the central ideas that found their way into Canadian banking practice were the notion that the note issue and loans of a bank required no fixed amount of cash reserves in the bank's vaults, which would have tended to limit the extent of the bank's expansion of its liabilities. As long as the bank's discounts were restricted to simply loaning on the security of bills of exchange issued in conjunction with commodity movements, the bank's expansion would be automatically linked to the expansion of commodity trade in the economy as a whole. There would thus be no danger of excess or deficiency of bank notes or loans in relation to volume of trade. See also *real bills* below.

Bill of Exchange: An order to pay a certain sum on a certain date or on demand. It is a debt claim between parties in different countries or separated by a considerable distance in one country which is not perfectly integrated financially. It is an unconditional promise to pay. There are three parties involved, the one ordering payment, the one to whom payment is to be made, and the party who must make the payment, generally a bank. Sometimes there are but two parties, the first and the third being the same. Under some circumstances, when cash is in short supply, the bill of exchange can itself circulate as a means of payment. Each person receiving the bill in payment for a debt will endorse it and then use it in turn for settling his own debts.

Bond: A certificate of debt owed to the bearer, which debt bears a fixed rate of interest and falls due at a specific future date. A bond is generally secured against physical property and is then referred to as a mortgage bond. In the event of non-payment of interest or principal, the holders may seize the property against which the bond is issued and sell it at a public auction to satisfy their claims.

Bucket Shop: A term whose meaning has changed over time: in general it refers to a financial operation involving sales of securities to the public, the nature of which borders on or is overtly illegal. For example, a bucket shop could involve the sale of completely valueless stock certificates in an unabashed swindle. But in the context of late nineteenth-century Canada, many operations involving trading in securities on margin or dealing in commodity futures (see below) which are now accepted as perfectly legitimate were then outlawed in an effort to stamp out small-scale operations and to centralize trading in the hands of a few brokers in major centres.

Call Loan: A loan extended, generally by a bank, which, rather than falling due at a future date specified at the time of the loan, remains outstanding until recalled by the bank on very short notice. Call loans are especially important for brokers buying and selling securities. The broker buys securities from one institution or individual, sometimes the issuer of the securities, and sells them to other institutions or individuals, financing the transaction with call loans from the bank. Because the loan is callable on such short notice, the broker must always ensure as much as possible a quick resale market for the securities before undertaking the initial purchase.

Cartel: An association of merchants or industrialists formed to fix prices or to otherwise restrict competition and exercise control over markets. It may involve profit pooling and sharing arrangements too. However, it does not involve a formal integration of the business units concerned, each of which, therefore, retains its separate legal existence.

Chartered Bank: refers to a bank which is incorporated in Canada by the granting of a charter of operation by the federal government. All bank incorporations in Canada require Acts of the federal Parliament. However, unincorporated or private banks did exist which, while regulated by the federal government, did not require formal statute to permit their operation.

Chattel Mortgage: A debt backed by a pledge of the moveable property of the borrower, for example a farmer's livestock. A mortgage on real estate, by contrast, is secured against immoveable, landed property.

Conversion Loan: A borrowing body may wish to change the interest rates and due dates of its outstanding debts, in which event it might convince existing holders of its bonds to return their currently held bonds and accept in their place a new issue of bonds of different maturity, interest rates, etc. This exchange of one set of debt instruments for another is called a "conversion loan."

Currency School: The converse of the *Banking School* (above). Under the Currency School philosophy of banking, it was felt that the note issue of the banks should be regulated by a fixed "reserve ratio" (see below) to ensure that they be convertible into gold and not issued to excess, resulting in inflation. Furthermore it was held that the notes of a central bank (or the Bank of Montreal in nineteenth-century Canada) should be treated as being equivalent to gold for purposes of the reserves held by the individual banks.

Debenture: Also referred to as debenture stock or even debenture bond, this security is very close to a bond in terms of having a fixed due date and a fixed interest yield. Unlike a bond, however, it has no specific security, but rather is backed by the general credit of the issuer. It is a general charge against the assets of the issuer rather than being a mortgage on specified property.

Discount: Analogous to interest, but the discount on the loan is deducted in a lump sum at the beginning of the loan rather than being reckoned as a percentage of the principal during the term of the loan, as interest payments are. For example, a bank buying a *bill of exchange* (see above) might pay only 90% of its face value. The discount rate would be 10%, for the bill at maturity would yield the bank 100% of its face value while its cost was but 90%. Discounts and interest payments can coexist. A bond sold at a price below its face value, or par value, is said to be sold at a discount. Its yield to the owner then consists of the difference between its purchase price and its full par value at maturity, plus the interest payments calculated as a percentage of the par value. On the other hand, a bond could sell at a "premium," above its face value, in which case its net return to the holder would be less than the interest payments due on it.

Double Liability: Shareholders in an *incorporated company* (see below) generally stand to lose only the sums representing their investment. But, in the case of banks in Canada until the 1930's, all shareholders were liable to pay up to double the amount of their subscribed shares in the bank in the event of its *insolvency* (see below).

Fee Simple: A manner in which lands, especially Crown land, can be alienated. In the case of a transfer of the land "in fee simple," the land becomes to all intents and purposes the absolute private property of the party to whom it was transferred with no provision for reversion of title to the original owner.

Fiat: Translates literally as command or order. A fiat currency is acceptable as a means of payment because a governmental authority decrees that it must be accepted in exchange and for the settlement of debts.

Fiduciary: Means simply "trust." Thus, a fiduciary bank note is one based on public confidence in its ability to maintain its exchange value in terms of commodities or on its convertibility into precious metal or some other money form, the stability of whose exchange value seems assured. Fiduciary also refers to the type of financial operation performed by a trust company which administers funds on behalf of some other party.

Futures Market: An organized system of buying and selling commodities or currency for delivery at some future date. The price at which the exchange will take place is set at the time of trading, while the actual delivery of the traded items at the agreed price will not occur until some fixed date in the future. Futures trading thus functions as a means of guaranteeing supplies of a commodity in the future at known constant prices, thus protecting the purchaser or seller from variations in the prices that could prove detrimental. Clearly the seller hopes to sell forward in time at a price that will be higher than that which will actually prevail in the future, while the buyer hopes to buy for less than the price in the future by contracting to take commodities at currently negotiated prices.

Guarantee: The most important use of the "guarantee" principle in financial transactions is when one corporate body or government authority "guarantees" the payment of interest and/or principal on the securities issued by a lesser body, — for example, a subsidiary corporation in the case of a guarantee by a corporation, or a lower level of government in the case of a government guarantee. Then, too, a government might guarantee a railroad's bonds, or those of some other major corporate endeavour. In the event of the lesser body being unable to meet its debt obligations, the higher authority which guaranteed the debt becomes liable for them.

Incorporation: The process by which a company is organized as a limited liability venture, each shareholder being liable for the debts of the company only to the extent of his subscription to the shares of the company. By contrast, if the company is not incorporated and the liability is not therefore limited, each partner in the company can be called upon to put up all of his personal wealth to meet the obligations of the company, should such prove necessary to completely discharge all of the company's debts.

Inscribed Stock: A type of *debenture* (see above) issued especially by governments. In the normal case of a debenture, principal and interest are payable to the bearer of the security, which security is thus freely transferable and saleable at will to other investors. An inscribed stock, however, is legally registered in the name of a particular investor or investing body to whom alone it is payable. Transfers of title require a formal legal procedure. The debenture is thus protected against theft, fraud, etc.

Insolvency: Simply, the state of a debtor unable to meet his obligations in cash when they are due. It is a general term that does not carry a specific legal connotation as do assignment and bankruptcy.

Kiting: A rather complex financial arrangement which gives the participants use of funds they do not properly have claim to, yet is perfectly legitimate. If B gives A a cheque for e.g. $1,000 drawn on B's bank account, and assuming it takes two days for the cheque to clear the banking system, then for that two days B retains a bank balance of $1,000 while A can deposit the cheque in his account giving him a credit balance of $1,000 as well. Thus until the clearing process is finished, A and B collectively have secured access to an extra $1,000 of bank credit. Kiting is a game many participants can play at once.

Lien Note: A type of short-term debt certificate. It is a promissory note (i.e. a promise to pay) that is secured against certain specified property against which the lender is said to have a lien, (i.e. the ability to seize the property in event of non-payment of the debt.)

Lock-up (or lock-in): The state of a bank loan that cannot be readily liquified, i.e. repaid. If, for example, a bank lends to a manufacturer who uses the loan and all his other liquid assets to build plant and equipment, then the assets are frozen into the plant, and the bank cannot expect repayment until the plant begins to produce and sell its output. The converse case, and from the bank's point of view the desirable one, would involve a loan secured on actual existing commodities, the proceeds from the sale of which are immediately available to cover repayment of the loan when necessary. (See *Real Bills, Currency School, Banking School.*)

Note Issue: Prior to 1935, the great majority of the paper money in circulation in Canada was issued by the chartered banks rather than by the government. The federal government had a very restricted power to issue some notes, but in deference to the chartered banks tended to minimize its issue. Provincial governments after 1867 could not issue notes. The power of note issue was jealously guarded by the chartered banks, for the banks could issue paper at no cost to themselves and use it to buy income-earning assets. After the establishment of the Bank of Canada in 1935, all note issue was undertaken by that institution and the notes of the chartered banks were taken out of circulation.

Patent (of invention): A legal monopoly granted to the "inventor" of an industrial process, mechanical device, etc. The patentee, who might well have bought or stolen the invention from its actual creator, is given a monopoly on its use for a certain number of years. The notion was that, by protecting "inventors," investment in the actual manufacturing of the invention would be encouraged.

Patent (of land): The process of filing a claim to an area of unclaimed land, the certificate acknowledging the claim being a "patent" and the land being therefore "patented." To hold the patent does not mean ownership; ownership follows the issue of a patent only after certain conditions are met with respect to payment, development, etc.

Pre-emption Right: At the time a certain piece of land is transferred to the purchaser, he may also secure the right to purchase in the future another piece of land at a price fixed at the time of the purchase of the original piece. Pre-emption rights were included in land granted to settlers under the Homestead Act in Canada until 1904, but in fact the right was seldom exercised because of the difficulty of finding contiguous government land to claim. The pre-emption right was of little use if the only land available for pre-emption was considerably removed from the initial plot.

Preferred (preference) share: Unlike common stock in a corporation, preferred stock or preferred shares carry a fixed maximum rate of return. Furthermore, the obligations of the company to the preferred stockholders must be met before those to the common stockholders.

Promissory Note: Simply, an unconditional promise to pay made by one person to another for a fixed sum at a specified future date. It may or may not be secured against certain property, and the debt is generally transferable to a creditor other than the one involved in the original contract.

Real Bills: A type of bill of exchange arising out of financing goods-in-process. The "real bills doctrine" of banking was a British transplant. A legacy of the post-Napoleonic-Wars currency debates, the doctrine contended that banks should confine their loans and discounts to those secured on bills of exchange and other paper representing actual commodities in existence. As long as this was done, the supply of credit would always be in step with the supply of commodities whose movement the credit served to finance. Bank credit would automatically terminate when the commodity movement was finished: The whole orientation of "real bills" was thus towards very short-term loans for the movement, rather than the production, of commodities. The same considerations held for bank note issue as well as loans, since the note issue was simply another component of the general credit mechanism controlled by the banks.

Receivership: A company that becomes bankrupt has a court-appointed "receiver" administer the affairs of the company on behalf of the creditors, thus replacing the power of the board of directors elected by the common shareholders when the company was solvent.

Reserve Ratio: Banks are often required to hold a certain percentage of certain liabilities in the form of cash or highly liquid securities so as to be able to meet the demands of their creditors with cash. For example, a cash reserve ratio of, say, ten per cent might be held in the form of gold to meet all demands by noteholders for gold. The reserve ratio would be considerably less than 100% because it is clear that except under very extreme circumstances only a small percentage of noteholders would demand gold in exchange for their notes at the same time. Reserve ratios in modern banking are held similarly against deposits.

Roll-Over Operation: A process of refunding a debt. When a bond or debenture issue is about to fall due, the debtor gets the cash to meet the debt by a new bond issue, sometimes sold to the same group who held the old. The debt thus is said to have been "rolled over."

Scrip: Similar to a promissory note but applying to land. The certificate is transferable and entitles the bearer to a grant of public land. War veterans in Canada used to receive scrip entitling them either to select a piece of government land or to sell their claim to some other party.

Terminating Building Society: An early type of mortgage loan company, formed by a fixed group of individuals for mutual assistance in financing land purchases or building homes. The society was wound up automatically when all members of the group had finished their purchase from the collective funds, and the funds were then redistributed back to the members.

Trust: A term evolved in the U.S. to describe a variant of the cartelization process whereby a group of firms forming the "trust" selected "trustees" either from among themselves or generally acceptable outsiders to co-ordinate pricing, output, profit pooling and other aspects of the cartel's behaviour.

Trust Company: A financial institution whose primary role is the administration of estates or other operations on behalf of another party or company.

Trustee List: In Britain, government regulations were strict as to the type of investments a trust company could make with the funds entrusted to it for administration. The group of securities in which investment was permitted was known as the "trustee list." Because of the considerable volume of funds trust companies could mobilize in Britain, a land of much old landed wealth, admission of their securities to the list was a very desirable objective of corporations and governments seeking to borrow in Britain.

Underwriting: When a corporation or government seeks to sell a security issue, one or a group of financial institutions guarantee to the issuer that it will receive by a designated time a certain specific amount of money for the issue. The simplest way is for the financial institutions to simply buy up the issue at the agreed price and then try to resell it to the general public at a higher price. In effect they act as a type of wholesale security merchant, buying a large lot and then selling the securities retail in small lots to the public. If a buyer cannot be found for all or part of the issue, at the guarantee price, it is the underwriter who must bear the loss or else hold the securities itself.

Warehouse receipts: When goods are received at a warehouse, the receipt issued verifying their existence is often a negotiable instrument and can be used as collateral for bank loans, since the goods against which the loan is secured have been verified by the warehouse man.

Watered stock: Stock watering operations were a method by which financial promoters could earn large profits without the need for any actual cash investment. While a bond represents a bona fide investment of cash, stock need not. For example, a handful of stockholders controlling a company could authorize the issue of new stock and simply distribute it to the existing stockholders, i.e. themselves. They could then have the company which they control pay dividends not only in the initial stock, but also on all of the new paper capital they have created and drain the resources of the company off into their own pockets without any actual investment. The new stock issue not corresponding to any real investment is referred to as "water."

Bibliography

Newspapers and Private Periodicals

Bradstreets, New York, 1895-1914

The Canadian Annual Review, Toronto, 1903-1914

Canadian Engineer, Toronto and Montreal 1894-1903

Canadian Countryman, Toronto, 1913-1914

Canadian Finance, Winnipeg, 1911-1914

Canadian Manufacturer, Toronto, 1882-1897

Canadian Municipal Journal, Montreal, 1905-1909

Commercial and Financial Chronicle, New York, 1875-1911

Dun's Review, New York, 1893-1914

Dun, Wiman & Co., *Mercantile Agency Reference Book, Dominion of Canada,* 1880-1914

The Economist, London, 1860-1923

Farmers' Advocate, London, various numbers, 1879-1914

Farm and Dairy, Peterborough, 1912

Farming World, Toronto, 1904-1906

Financial Post, Toronto, 1907-1912, 1923-1927, 1930-1931

The Gazette, Montreal, *passim*

The Globe, Toronto, 1860-1866, 1878-1880, 1890-1891, 1906-1912

Grain Growers' Guide, Winnipeg, 1908-1914

Industrial Canada, Toronto, 1900-1914

Journal of Commerce, Montreal, 1878-1913

Journal of the Canadian Bankers' Association, Toronto, 1894-1914

The Mail, Toronto, *passim*

Monetary Times, Toronto, 1867-1923

The Pilot, Montreal, 1850

The Times, London (U.K.), *passim*
New York Times, passim

Company and Board of Trade Reports

Bank of Nova Scotia, *Annual Reports*, 1906-1912.
Calgary Board of Trade, *Annual Reports*, 1903, 1912.
Canada Life Assurance Co., *Sixty-Fifth Annual Report*, 1912.
Canadian Bank of Commerce, *Annual Reports*, 1900-1911.
Canadian Northern Railway, *Annual Reports*, 1903-1914.
Canadian Pacific Railway, *Annual Reports*, 1897-1913.
Dominion Board of Trade, *First Annual Meeting*, 1871.
——, *Eighth Annual Meeting*, 1878.
Dominion Iron and Steel Corporation, *Annual Report*, 1910.
Dominion Securities Corp. Ltd. (E. R. Wood), *Annual Review of the Bond Markets of Canada*, 1906-1910.
Eastern Townships Bank, *Annual Reports*, 1859-1912.
Montreal Board of Trade, *Annual Reports*, 1867, 1876, 1895.
——, Semi-Centennial Report, 1892.
State of New York Chamber of Commerce, *Report in Favour of Reciprocity with Canada*, 1909.
Toronto Board of Trade, *Annual Reports*, 1883, 1896, 1897, 1901, 1902.

Unpublished Theses and Manuscripts

Bank of Montreal, "Investment Operations 1886-1896," Bank of Montreal Archives, Montreal
Canada, Department of Finance, "Bank Liquidation Files," Public Archives, Ottawa
Canada, Department of Finance, "Tariff Enquiry Commission Minutes, 1906," Public Archives, Ottawa
Ontario, Legislative Assembly "Return Re Bonusing," Sessional Paper No. 69, 1906, Ontario Archives, Toronto
Sir Byron Edmund Walker, papers, University of Toronto Archives
Sir Herbert B. Ames, papers, financial notebooks, etc. McGill University Archives
Peter McArthur, papers, University of Western Ontario Library
Acheson, T. W., "The Social Origins of Canadian Industrialism," University of Toronto, Ph.D. thesis, 1971

Bellan, R. C., "The Development of Winnipeg as a Metropolitan Centre," Columbia University, Ph.D. thesis, 1958

Drummond, I. M., "Capital Markets in Canada and Australia 1895-1914," Yale University, Ph.D. thesis, 1959.

Drummond, W. M., "Financing of Land Purchases in Canada," University of Toronto, M.A. thesis, 1924.

Easterbrook, W. T., "Agricultural Credit in Canada 1867-1917," University of Toronto, M.A. thesis, 1935.

Goldberg, S., "The French Canadian and the Industrialization of Quebec," McGill University, M.A. thesis, 1940.

Hall, C. A., "Electric Utilities in Ontario Under Private Ownership, 1890-1914," University of Toronto, Ph.D. thesis, 1968

Hymer, S., "The International Operations of National Firms," M.I.T., Ph.D. thesis, 1960.

Lewis, K. G., "The Significance of the Yale Foundry and Steam Engine Manufacture," mimeo, Toronto, 1972.

Nelles, H. V., "The Politics of Development: Forests, Mines and Hydroelectric Power in Ontario 1890-1935," University of Toronto, Ph.D. thesis, 1969.

Pentland, H. C., "Labour and the Development of Industrial Capitalism in Canada," University of Toronto, Ph.D. thesis, 1968.

Stapells, H., "The Recent Consolidation Movement in Canadian Industry," University of Toronto, M.A. thesis, 1927.

Stevens, P. D., "Laurier and the Liberal Party In Ontario 1887-1911," University of Toronto, Ph.D. thesis, 1966.

Government Publications

(S.P. denotes Sessional Papers)
(H.C.J. denotes House of Commons Journals)

I Dominion of Canada

(a) Royal Commission Reports (Chronological)

Royal Commission . . . The Pacific Railway, *Report and Evidence,* H.C.J. 1873

Royal Commission on the Working of Mills and Factories of the Dominion and the Labour Employed Therein, *Report,* S.P. 1882.

Royal Commission on Chinese Labour, *Report and Evidence,* S.P. 1885

Royal Commission on Railways, *Report,* S.P. 1888

Royal Commission of the Relations of Labour and Capital, *Report and Evidence*, 6 Vols. 1889

Royal Commission Upon the Sweating System, *Report*, S.P. 1896

Royal Commission on the Shipment and Transportation of Grain, *Report*, S.P. 1899

Royal Commission on Railway Rates, Grievances etc., Report, S.P. 1902

Royal Commission in Re the Alleged Combination of Paper Manufacturers and Dealers, *Report*, S.P. 1902

Royal Commission in Re the Tobacco Trade of Canada, *Report*, S.P. 1903

Royal Commission on the Grain Trade of Canada, *Report*, S.P. 1906

Royal Commission of Life Insurance, *Report and Evidence*, 5 Vols. 1907.

Royal Commission on Industrial Disputes in the Cotton Factories of Quebec, *Report and Evidence*, S.P. 1909

Royal Commission...To Make Investigation...The Farmers' Bank, *Report*, S.P. 1913

Royal Commission on Industrial Training and Technical Education, *Report*, 2 Vols. 1913

Royal Commission to Investigate William Davis Co., *Report*, 1917

Royal commission to Inquire into Railways and Transportation in Canada, *Report*, 1917

Royal Commission on Price Spreads and Mass Buying, *Report*, 1932

Royal Commission on Banking and Currency in Canada, *Report*, 1937

Royal Commission on the Textile Industry, *Report*, 1938

Royal Grain Inquiry Commission, *Report*, S.P. 1938

(b) Select Committee Reports (chronological)

Select Committee Upon the Causes of the Recent Financial Crisis in the Province of Ontario, *Report*, Senate Journal, 1867-8

Select Committee on Bankruptcy and Insolvency, *Third Report*, H.C.J. 1869

Select Committee of Enquiry into the Manufacturing Interests of the Dominion, *Report*, H.C.J. 1874

Select Committee on the Causes of the Present Depression, *Report and Evidence*, H.C.J. 1876

Select Committee on the Salt Interest of Canada, *Report*, H.C.J. 1876

Select Committee to Inquire into the Operation of the Tariff on the Agricultural Interests of the Dominion, *Report,* H.C.J. 1882

Select Committee Relating to Manufacturing Industry in Existence in Canada, *Report,* S.P. 1885

Select Committee to Consider the Fraudulent Obtaining of Promissory Notes from Farmers etc., *Report,* H.C.J. 1888

Select Committee Appointed to Examine into Combinations, *Report and Evidence,* H.C.J. 1888

Select Committee on Prices Charged for Lumber in the Provinces of Manitoba, Saskatchewan, and Alberta, *Report and Minutes,* H.C.J. 1907

(c) Departmental Reports and Miscellaneous Committees etc.

Auditor General, *Annual Report,* S.P. various years.

Department of Agriculture, *Statistical Yearbook of Canada,* 1888-1903

Department of Agriculture, *Canada Yearbook,* various years

Department of Agriculture, *Annual Reports,* S.P. 1870-1914

Department of Justice, *Dominion-Provincial and Interprovincial Conferences 1887 to 1926,* 1951.

Department of Justice, *Memorandum on Dominion Power of Disallowance of Provincial Legislation,* 1937.

Department of Labour, *Labour Gazette,* 1902-1914

Department of Labour, *Report on Strikes and Lockouts in Canada 1901-1916,* 1918

Department of Railways and Canals, *Annual Report,* S.P. 1920

Department of Railways and Canals, *Return Re Pacific Railway,* S.P. 1873

Department of Trade and Navigation, *Annual Reports,* S.P. various years

Department of Trade and Commerce, *Reports,* S.P. various years

Department of Trade and commerce, *Deputy Minister's Report,* S.P. 1919

Department of Trade and Commerce, *Canada-West Indies Conference,* S.P. 1913

Department of Industry, Trade, and Commerce, *Foreign Owned Subsidiaries in Canada,* 1964-1967, 1968, 1969

Board of Inquiry into the Cost of Living, *Report,* 2 Vols., 1915

The Canada Gazette, various numbers

Colonial Conference, *Minutes,* S.P. 1907

Committee on Public Accounts, *Minutes,* H.C.J. 1906

Committee on Banking and Currency, *Minutes, Evidence Etc.,* 1913

Commercial Agent of the Government of Canada to the West Indies, *Report,* S.P. 1887

Commissioner, Combines Investigation Act, *Investigation into Alleged Combine in the Manufacture, Distribution, and Sale of Rubber Products,* 1952

Censuses of Canada, 1871, 1881, 1891, 1901, 1911

Dominion Bureau of Statistics, *Canada's International Investment Position 1926-1967*

House of Commons, *Debates,* 1869-1923

Investigating Committee, National Transcontinental Railway, *Report,* S.P. 1914

Senate, *Debates,* various years

Statutes of Canada, various years

Superintendant of Insurance, *Annual Reports,* 1870-1929

II Provincial

(a) Province of Canada

Committee on Public Accounts, *Seventh Report,* S.P. 1858

Railway Company Returns, S.P. 1861

Parliamentary Debates on the Subject of the Confederation of the British North American Provinces, 1865

(b) Alberta

Commission on Banking and Credit with Respect to the Industry of Agriculture in the Province of Alberta, *Report,* 1922

Commission to Investigate the Organization of the Alberta and Great Waterways Railway Company, *Report,* 1910

Statutes of Alberta, various years

(c) British Columbia

Legislative Council, *Confederation Debates,* 1870

Royal Commission of Inquiry into the Conduct of the Affairs of the Municipal Council of Victoria, *Report,* 1892, S.P.

Statutes of British Columbia, various years

(d) Manitoba

Royal Commission on the Financial Affairs of the Province, *Report,* S.P. 1900

Manitoba Beef Commission, *Report,* S.P. 1908

Statutes of Manitoba, various years

(e) New Brunswick

Submissions by the Province of New Brunswick to the Royal Commission on Dominion-Provincial Relations 1957

Journals of the Assembly, 1866

Statutes of New Brunswick, various years

(f) Nova Scotia

Submissions by the Province of Nova Scotia to the Royal Commission on Dominion Provincial Relations, 1937
Royal Commission, Provincial Economic Enquiry, *Report,* 1931
Statutes of Nova Scotia, various years

(g) Ontario
Commission on Railway Taxation, *Report,* S.P. 1905
Commission of Inquiry . . . Conspiracy to Corrupt and Attempt to Bribe Certain Members of the Legislature, *Evidence,* 1885, S.P. 1885
Journals of the Legislative Assembly, Vol. 22, 23, 1888, 1889
Bureau of Mines, *Reports,* S.P. various years
Statutes of Ontario, various years

(h) Prince Edward Island
Submissions by the Government of Prince Edward Island to the Royal Commission on Dominion Provincial Relations
Statutes of Prince Edward Island, various years

(i) Quebec
Assemblée Legislative, Comité Spécial, *Rapport Sur L'Emprunt de £800,000 Stg. . .et Le Crédit Foncier,* 1881
Commissioner of Crown Lands, *Report,* S.P. 1891
Commissioner of Colonization and Mines, *Report* 1897, S.P. 1898
"La Caisse Populaire de Levis," S.P. 1901
Correspondence . . . Relating to the Resignation of the Treasurer of Quebec, S.P. 1895
Statutes of Quebec, various years

(j) Saskatchewan
Commission on Agricultural Credit, *Report,* 1913
Statutes of Saskatchewan, various years

III United Kingdom

Colonial Office, *Hudson's Bay Company,* 6 May, 1857
Select Committee of the House of Commons on the Hudson's Bay Company, *Report,* 1857
Royal Commission on the Natural Resources etc. of Certain Parts of His Majesty's Dominions, *Report and Evidence,* 1916
Royal Commission on Shipping Rings, *Report and Evidence,* 1907
Royal Commission on the Trade Relations Between Canada and the West Indies, *Report and Evidence,* 1910

Books and Pamphlets

Aikman, C. H. *The Automobile Industry of Canada,* Macmillan, Montreal, 1926

Aitken, H. *American Capital and Canadian Resources,* Harvard University Press, Cambridge, Mass., 1961

Allin, C. D. & G. M. Jones, *Annexation, Preferential Trade and Reciprocity,* Musson Book Co., Toronto (n.d.)

Annett, D. R., British Preferences in Canadian Commercial Policy, Ryerson Press, Toronto, 1948

Anonymous, *Canada Under the National Policy, Arts and Manufactures, 1883,* Industrial Publishing Company, Montreal 1883

Ashton, T. S. *The Industrial Revolution,* Oxford University Press, London, 1948

Bagehot, W., *Lombard Street* New Ed., Smith, Elder, & Co., London, 1910

Bagehot, W., *Postulates of English Political Economy,* G. P. Putnam's, London, 1885

Bain, J. S., *Barriers to New Competition,* Harvard University Press, Cambridge, Mass., 1954

Bank of Montreal, *The Centenary of the Bank of Montreal 1817-1917,* Bank of Montreal, Montreal, 1917

Bank of Nova Scotia, *The Bank of Nova Scotia 1832-1932,* Bank of Nova Scotia, Montreal, 1932

Barber, C. L., *The Canadian Electrical Manufacturing Industry,* Queen's Printer, Ottawa, 1956

Baster, A., *The Imperial Banks,* P. S. King, London, 1929

Bates, S., *Financial History of Canadian Governments,* King's Printer, Ottawa, 1939

Beckhart, B. H., *The Banking System of Canada,* Holt & Co., New York, 1929

Behrman, J. N., *National Interests and the Multinational Enterprise,* Prentice-Hall, N.J., 1970

Bergithon, C., *The Stock Exchange,* Gazette Publishing Co., Montreal, 1940

Biggar, E. B., *The Canadian Railway Problem,* Macmillan, Toronto, 1917

Brebner, J. B., *The North Atlantic Triangle,* McClelland and Stewart, Toronto, 1966

Breckenridge, R. M., *The Canadian Banking System 1817-1890,* (n.p.), Toronto, 1894

Breckenridge, R. M., *History of Banking In Canada,* Government Printing Office, Washington, 1910

Brown, R. C., *Canada's National Policy 1883-1900,* Princeton University Press, Princeton, 1968

Buchanan, I., *The Relations of the Industry of Canada With the Mother Country,* John Lovell, Montreal, 1864

Buckley, K., *Capital Formation In Canada 1896-1930,* University of Toronto Press, Toronto, 1955

Cairncross, A. K., *Home and Foreign Investment 1870-1913,* Cambridge University Press, Cambridge, 1953

Cameron, R., *et al, Banking And Economic Development: Some Lessons of History,* Oxford University Press, New York, 1972

Cameron, R., *et al, Banking In the Early Stages of Industrialization,* Oxford University Press, Toronto, 1967

C. Campbell, *Nova Scotia In Its Historical, Mercantile and Industrial Relations,* John Lovell, Montreal, 1873

Cartwright, Sir Richard, *Reminiscences,* William Biggs, Toronto, 1912

Caves, R. E., and Holton, R. H., *The Canadian Economy, Prospect and Retrospect,* Harvard University Press, Cambridge, Mass., 1959

Caves, R. E., and Reuber, G. L., *Canadian Economic Policy and the Impact of International Capital Flows,* University of Toronto Press, Toronto, 1969

Chamberlin, R. H., *The Theory of Monopolistic Competition, 8th Ed.,* Harvard University Press, Cambridge, Mass., 1962

Chandler, A. D., *Strategy and Structure: Chapters in the Rise of the Industrial Enterprise,* M.I.T. Press, Cambridge, 1962

Clark, S. D., *The Canadian Manufacturers' Association,* University of Toronto Press, Toronto, 1939

Cockshutt, I., *Memoirs of Ignatius Cockshutt,* privately published, Brantford, 1904

Cole, A. H., *Business Enterprise In Its Social Setting,* Harvard University Press, Cambridge, Mass., 1959

Cole, C. W., *Colbert and a Century of French Mercantilism,* Vol. II, Archon Books, Connecticut, 1964

Cooper, J. I., *Montreal, A Brief History,* McGill-Queen's University Press, Montreal, 1969

Creighton, D., *British North America At Confederation,* King's Printer, Ottawa, 1939

Creighton, D., *Canada's First Century,* Macmillan, Toronto 1970

Creighton, D., *Dominion of the North,* Macmillan, Toronto, 1969

Creighton, D., *Empire of the St. Lawrence,* Macmillan, Toronto, 1970

Creighton, D., *Sir John A. Macdonald,* 2 Vols., Macmillan, Toronto, 1968

Cunningham, W., *The Growth of English Industry and Commerce In Modern Times*, Vol. II, Cambridge University Press, Cambridge, 1919

Curtis, C. A., *Statistical Contributions to Canadian Economic History*, Vol, I, Macmillan, Toronto, 1931

Dafoe, J. W., *Sir Clifford Sifton In Relation to His Times*, Macmillan, Toronto, 1931

Dales, J. H., *The Protective Tariff In Canada's Development*, University of Toronto Press, Toronto 1966

Dales, J. H., *Hydroelectricity and Industrial Development: Quebec 1898-1940*, Harvard University Press, Cambridge, 1957

Denison, M., *Canada's First Bank: A History of the Bank of Montreal*, Vol. 2, McClelland and Stewart, Toronto, 1967

Denison, M., *Harvest Triumphant: The Story of Massey-Harris*, McClelland and Stewart, Toronto, 1948

Denison, M., *The People's Power*, McClelland and Stewart, Toronto, 1960

Desjardins, A., *The Co-operative People's Bank: La Caisse Populaire*, Russell Sage Foundation, New York, 1914

Dicey, R. V., *et al*, *The Credit of Canada: How it is Affected by the Ontario Power Legislation*, R. G. McLean, Toronto, 1909

Donald, W. J. A., *The Canadian Iron and Steel Industry*, Houghton Mifflin, Boston, 1915

Driberg, T., *Beaverbrook*, Weidenfeld & Nicolson, London, 1956

Easterbrook, W. T., *Farm Credit In Canada*, University of Toronto Press, Toronto, 1938

Easterbrook, W. T., & H. Aitken, *Canadian Economic History*, Macmillan, Toronto, 1965

Eastman, H. and Stykolt, S., *The Tariff and Competition In Canada*, Macmillan, Toronto, 1967

Eckhardt, H. M. P., *Manual of Canadian Banking* 5th Ed., Monetary Times, Toronto, 1909

Feis, H., *Europe, The World's Banker*, 1870-1914, W.W. Norton, New York, 1965

Firestone, O. J., *Canada's Economic Development 1867-1953*, Bowes & Bowes, London, 1958

Field, F. W., *Capital Investments in Canada*, Monetary Times, Toronto, 1911, 1914

Forsey, E., *Economic and Social Aspects of the Nova Scotia Coal Industry*, Macmillan, Montreal, 1926

Fowke, V. C., *The National Policy and the Wheat Economy*, University of Toronto Press, Toronto, 1957

Friedman, M. and Schwartz, A., *A Monetary History of the United States*, Princeton University Press, Princeton, 1966

Galbraith, J. S., *The Hudson's Bay Company as an Imperial Factor,* University of Toronto Press, Toronto, 1957

Gershenkron A., *Economic Backwardness in Historical Perspective,* Harvard University Press, Cambridge, 1967

Gesner, A., *The Industrial Resources of Nova Scotia,* A. & W. McKinlay, Halifax, 1849

Gesner, A., *New Brunswick,* Simmonds & Ward, London, 1847

Gibbon, J. M., *Steel of Empire,* Tudor Publishing Co., New York, 1937

Gilbert, H., *Awakening Continent: The Story of Lord Mount-Stephen,* Aberdeen University Press, Aberdeen, 1965

Glazebrook, G. P., *Sir Edmund Walker,* Oxford Press, Toronto, 1935

Gordon, W. L., *A Choice for Canada, Independence or Colonial Status,* McClelland and Stewart, Toronto, 1965

Goschen, Viscount, *Essays and Addresses on Economic Questions,* Edward Arnold, London, 1905

Graham, R., *Arthur Meighen,* Clarke, Irwin & Co., Toronto 1960

Grenfell, W. T. *et al, Labrador, the Country and the People,* Macmillan, New York, 1909

Hague, G., *Banking and Commerce,* Bankers Publishing Co., New York, 1908

Hague, G., *Some Practical Considerations on the Subject of Labour and Capital,* Witness Publishing House, Montreal, 1874

Hambro, C. J., *Newspaper Lords in British Politics,* Macdonald & Co., London, 1958

Hammond, B., *Banks and Politics in the United States from the Revolution to the Civil War,* Princeton University Press, Princeton, 1957

Hamon, E., *Les Canadiens Francais de la Nouvelle Angleterre,* N. S. Hardy, Quebec, 1891

Hanney, J., *Sir Leonard Tilley,* Oxford University Press, Toronto, 1926

Hanney, J., *History of New Brunswick,* II, John A. Bowes, St. John, 1909

Hartz, L., *The Founding of New Societies,* Harcourt, Brace & World, New York, 1964

Hawtrey, R. G., *The Economic Problem,* Longmans, Green & Co., London, 1926

Heckscher, E., *Mercantilism,* Revised Ed., 2 Vols., Allan & Unwin, London, 1962

Henderson, D. McLaughlin, *Robert McLaughlin — Carriage Builder,* Alger Press, Toronto, 1965

Hidy, R., *The House of Baring in American Trade and Finance,* Harvard University Press, Cambridge, Mass, 1949

Hill, C., *Reformation to Industrial Revolution,* Penguin, Harmondsworth, 1969

Hincks, Sir Francis, *Reminiscences of His Public Life,* William Drysdale & Co., Montreal, 1884

Hincks, Sir Francis, *Canada: Its Financial System and Resources,* James Ridgeway, London, 1849

Hincks, Sir Francis, *The Political History of Canada Between 1846 and 1859,* Dawson Brothers, Montreal, 1877

Hind, H. Y. *et al., Eighty Years of Progress in British North America,* L. Stebbins, Toronto, 1863

Hind, H. Y., *Manitoba and the North West Frauds,* Knowles & Co., Windsor, N.S., 1883

Hind, H. Y., *The Canadian Pacific Railway, and Sir Leonard Tilley's and Sir Charles Tupper's Fire Bricks and Clay Series,* Windsor, N.S., 1884

Hobsbaum, E., *Industry and Empire,* Penguin, Harmondsworth, 1969

Hobson, C. K., *The Export of Capital,* Constable & Co., London, 1963

Hobson, J. A., *Canada Today,* T. Fisher Unwin, London, 1906

Hobson, J. A., *Gold, Prices and Wages,* Methuen, London, 1913

Hobson, J. A., *Imperialism: A Study,* Allan & Unwin, London, 1936

Hobson, J. A., *The Industrial System,* P. S. King, London, 1927

Holt, W., *The Opium Wars,* New York, 1964

Hurlbert, J. C., *Field and Factory Side by Side,* John Lovell, Montreal, 1870

Hurlbert, J. C., *Protection and Free Trade,* A. S. Woodburn, Ottawa, 1882

Imlah, A. H., *Economic Elements in the Pax Brittannica,* Harvard University Press, Cambridge, 1958

Innis, H. A., *The Cod Fisheries,* Macmillan, Toronto, 1935

Innis, H. A., *Essays In Canadian Economic History,* University of Toronto Press, Toronto, 1967

Innis, H. A., *The Fur Trade In Canada,* Yale University Press, New Haven, 1930

Innis, H. A., *A History of the Canadian Pacific Railroad,* McClelland and Stewart, Toronto, 1923

Innis, H. A., *Political Economy in the Modern State,* Ryerson Press, Toronto, 1946

Innis, H. A., *Problems of Staple Production in Canada,* Ryerson Press, Toronto, 1933

Islam, N., *Foreign Capital and Economic Development,* Charles Tuttle, Tokyo, 1960

James, F. C., *The Growth of Chicago Banks,* 2 Vols., Harper, New York, 1938

James, R. W., *John Rae, Political Economist,* 2 Vols., University of Toronto Press, Toronto, 1965

Jamieson, A. B., *Chartered Banking in Canada,* Ryerson, Toronto, 1957

Jenks, L. H., *The Migration of British Capital to 1875,* Knopf, New York, 1927

Jenks, L. H., *Our Cuban Colony,* Vanguard Press, New York, 1928

Johnson, H. G., *The Canadian Quandary,* McGraw-Hill, Toronto, 1963

Johnson, H. G., et al., *Economic Nationalism in Old and New States,* Allan & Unwin, London, 1967

Johnson, W. W., *Sketches of the Late Depression,* J. T. Robinson, Montreal, 1882

Jones, R. L., *History of Agriculture in Ontario, 1613-1880,* University of Toronto Press, Toronto, 1949

Kilbourn, W., *The Elements Combined, A History of the Steel Company of Canada,* Clarke, Irwin, Toronto, 1960

Kindleberger, C. P., *American Business Abroad,* Yale University Press, New Haven, 1969

Kindleberger, C. P., *Power and Money,* Macmillan, London, 1970

Knowles, L. C. A., *The Economic Development of the British Overseas Empire,* Vol. I, Routledge, London, 1930

Knox, F. A., *Dominion Monetary Policy, 1929-1934,* King's Printer, Ottawa 1939

Landes, D., *Technological Change and Development in Western Europe 1750-1914, Cambridge Economic History of Europe* Vol. VI, Part I, Cambridge University Press, Cambridge, 1965

Lavington, F., *The English Capital Market,* Methuen & Co., London, 1921

Leacock, S., *Baldwin, Lafontaine and Hincks,* Oxford Press, Toronto 1926

Lenin, V. I., *The Development of Capitalism in Russia,* Foreign Languages Publishing House, Moscow, 1956

Levitt, J., *Henri Bourassa and the Golden Calf,* Macmillan, Toronto 1972

Levitt, K., *Silent Surrender: The Multinational Corporation in Canada,* Macmillan, Toronto, 1970

Levitt, K. and McIntyre, A., *Canada — West Indies Economic Relations,* McGill University, Montreal, 1967

Lewis, C., *America's Stake in International Investment*, Brookings Institution, Washington, 1938

Lindsey, C., *William Lyon Mackenzie*, Morang, Toronto, 1910

List, F., (trans. S.S. Lloyd), *The National System of Political Economy*, Longmans Green, London, 1885

Lipton, C., *The Trade Union Movement of Canada*, 2nd ed., Canadian Social Publications, Montreal, 1968

Liverpool Financial Reform Association, *The Hudson's Bay Company Versus the Magna Carta*, P. S. King, London, 1857

Longley Hon. J. W., *Sir Charles Tupper*, Oxford, Toronto, 1926

Longley, Hon. J. W., *Joseph Howe*, Oxford, Toronto, 1926

Longley, R. S., *Sir Francis Hincks*, University of Toronto, Toronto, 1943

Lovett, H. A., *Canada and the Grand Trunk 1829-1924*, Montreal (n.p.) 1926

Lower, A. R. M., Saunders, S. A. and Carrothers, W. A., *The North American Assault on the Canadian Forest*, Ryerson, Toronto, 1935

Luxembourg, R., *The Accumulation of Capital*, Routledge & Kegan Paul, London, 1963

Macdonald, N. *Canada, 1841-1903, Immigration and Colonization*, Aberdeen University Press, Aberdeen, 1966

McDiarmid, O. J., *Commercial Policy in the Canadian Economy*, Harvard University Press, Cambridge, 1949

MacGibbon, D. A., *The Canadian Grain Trade*, Macmillan, Toronto, 1932

McIvor, R. C., *Canadian Monetary Banking and Financial Development*, Macmillan, Toronto, 1958

Mackay, D., *The Honourable Company*, 2nd ed., McClelland and Stewart, Toronto, 1949

Mackenzie, Alexander *et al*, *Reform Government in the Dominion*, Toronto, 1878

Mackenzie, F. A., *Beaverbrook: An Authentic Biography*, Janolds, London, 1931

Mackintosh, W. A., *The Economic Background to Dominion Provincial Relations*, King's Printer, Ottawa, 1938

Macnaughton, J., *Lord Strathcona*, Oxford University Press, Toronto, 1926

MacNutt, W. S., *New Brunswick, A History 1784-1867*, Toronto, 1964

Macphail, A., *History of Prince Edward Island, Canada and Its Provinces*, Vol. XIII, Glasgow, Brooke & Co., Toronto, 1914

Macpherson, Hon. D. L., *A Letter to the Hon. John Rose*, E. T. Brumfield & Co., Toronto, 1869

Main, O. D., *The Nickel Industry of Canada,* University of Toronto Press, Toronto, 1935

Mantoux, P., *The Industrial Revolution in the Eighteenth Century,* Revised edn., trans. M. Vernon, Jonathan Cape, London, 1928

Marlio, L, *The Aluminum Cartel,* Brookings Institute, Washington, 1947

Marshall, H. F. Southard, & K. Taylor, *Canadian-American Industry,* Yale University Press, New Haven, 1936

Marx, K., *Capital,* 3 Vols., Foreign Languages Publishing House, Moscow, 1961

Marx, K., *Pre-Capitalist Economic Formation,* Lawrence & Wishart, London, 1964

Masters, D. C., *Reciprocity, 1846-1911,* Canadian Historical Association, Ottawa, 1961

Masters, D. C., *The Rise of Toronto 1850-1890,* University of Toronto Press, Toronto, 1947

Mendels, M. M., *Asbestos Industry of Canada,* Macmillan, Montreal, 1930

Middleton, E., *Beaverbrook: The Statesman and the Man,* Stanley Paul & Co., London, 1936

Mill, J. S., *Principles of Political Economy,* Ashley (ed.), Longmans, Green & Co., London, 1921

Miller, N., *The Enterprise of a Free People,* Cornell University Press, New York, 1962

Moore, E. S., *American Influence in Canadian Mining,* University of Toronto Press, Toronto, 1945

Morton, A. S., C. Martin, *History of Prairie Settlement/Dominion Lands Policy,* Macmillan, Toronto, 1938

Myers, G., *History of Canadian Wealth,* Charles Kerr & Co., Chicago, 1914

Myers, G., *History of the Great American Fortunes,* Modern Library, New York, 1936

Neufeld, E. P., *The Financial System of Canada,* Macmillan, Toronto, 1972

Nurkse, R., *Problems of Capital Formation in Underdeveloped Countries,* Oxford University Press, New York, 1967

Ohlin, B. *Interregional and International Trade,* Revised ed., Harvard University Press, Cambridge, Mass., 1967

Park, L. C., Park, F. W., *Anatomy of Big Business,* Progress Books, Toronto, 1962

Phillips, W. G., *The Agricultural Implements Industry in Canada,* University of Toronto Press, Toronto, 1956

Plewman, W., *Adam Beck and Ontario Hydro,* Ryerson Press, Toronto, 1947

Porritt, E. C., *The Revolt in Canada Against the New Feudalism,*
    Cassel & Co., London 1911

Porritt, E. C., *Sixty Years of Protection in Canada: 1846-1906,*
    Macmillan, London, 1917

Pressnell, L. S., *Country Banking in the Industrial Revolution,*
    Clarendon Press, Oxford, 1956

Preston, W. T. R., *The Life and Times of Lord Strathcona,*
    McClelland, Goodchild & Stewart, Toronto (n.d.)

Preston, W. T. R., *My Generation of Politics and Politicians,* D.
    A. Dice, Toronto, 1927

Rae, John, *Statement of Some New Principles on the Subject of
    Political Economy,* (1833) Reprint, University of Toronto
    Press, Toronto, 1965

Reich, N., *The Pulp and Paper Industry of Canada,* Macmillan,
    Montreal, 1926

Reuber, G. L. & Roseman, F., *The Takeover of Canadian Firms,
    1945-1961,* Queen's Printer, Ottawa, 1969

Ricardo, D., *Principles of Political Economy and Taxation,*
    Everyman, London, 1911

Rich, E. E., *The Hudson's Bay Co.,* 3 Vols., McClelland and
    Stewart, Toronto, 1960

Roberts, L., *Montreal: A Brief History,* Macmillan, Toronto, 1969

Robin, Martin, *The Company Province,* Vol. I, McClelland and
    Stewart, Toronto, 1973

Robinson, Sir John B., *Canada and the Canada Bill (1840),*
    Johnson Reprint Co., London, 1967

Ross, V., *A History of the Canadian Bank of Commerce,* Vols. I
    and II, Oxford University Press, Toronto, 1920, 1922

Rostow, W. W., *The Stages of Economic Growth,* Cambridge
    University Press, Cambridge, 1960

Rowthorn R. and Hymer, S., *International Big Business, 1957-
    1967,* Cambridge University Press, Cambridge, 1971

Royal Bank of Canada, *Fiftieth Anniversary of the Royal Bank of
    Canada,* Royal Bank, Montreal, 1920

Ryan, W. F., *The Clergy and Economic Growth in Quebec (1896-
    1914)* Laval University Press, Quebec, 1966

Safarian, A. E., *Foreign Ownership of Canadian Industry,*
    McGraw-Hill, Toronto, 1966

Saunders, E. M., *The Life and Letters of the Rt. Hon. Sir Charles
    Tupper,* Cassel, London, 1916

Saunders, S. A., *Economic History of the Maritime Provinces,*
    King's Printer, Ottawa, 1939

Sayers, R. S., *Modern Banking,* 7th edn., Clarendon Press,
    Oxford, 1967

Scholefield, E. O. S., *British Columbia,* Vol. I, S. J. Clarke, Montreal, 1913

Shortt, A., *The Banking System of Canada,* Canada and Its Provinces, Vol. X, Glasgow, Brook & Co., Toronto, 1914

Schull, J., *100 Years of Banking in Canada: A History of the Toronto Dominion Bank,* Copp Clark, Toronto, 1958

Schumpeter, J. A., *Business Cycles,* 2 Vols. McGraw-Hill, New York, 1939

Schumpeter, J. A., *Theory of Economic Development,* Oxford University Press, New York, 1961

Schumpeter, J. A. *Capitalism, Socialism and Democracy,* Allan & Unwin, London, 1970

Servan-Schreiber, J. J., *The American Challenge,* Penguin, Harmondsworth, 1968

Skelton, O. D., *Fifty Years of Banking Service 1871-1921,* Toronto, (n.p.) 1922

Skelton, O. D., *The Railway Builders,* Toronto, 1921

Skelton, O. D., *General Economic History, Canada and Its Provinces*, Vol. IX, Glasgow, Brook & Co., Toronto, 1914

Skelton, O. D., *The Life and Times of Sir Alexander Tilloch Galt,* McClelland & Stewart, Toronto, 1966

Smith, Goldwyn, *Canada and the Canadian Question,* University of Toronto Press, Toronto, 1971

Soule, G., and Carossa, U. P., *American Economic History,* Dryden Press, New York, 1957

Stanley, G. F. G., *The Birth of Western Canada,* University of Toronto Press, Toronto, 1970

Steindl, J., *Maturity and Stagnation in American Capitalism,* Basil Blackwell, Oxford, 1952

Stevens, G. R., *The Canada Permanent Story,* Toronto, 1960

Stevens, G. R., *Canada's National Railways,* 2 Vols., Macmillan, Toronto, 1965

Stokes, M., *The Bank of Canada,* Macmillan, Toronto, 1937

Stovel, J., *Canada in the World Economy,* Harvard University Press, Cambridge, 1959

Taggart Smith, T., *The First Hundred Years, A History of the Montreal and District Savings Bank 1846-1946, Montreal,* (n.p.) 1946

Taylor, K. and Mitchell, H., *Statistical Contributions to Canadian Economic History,* Vol. II, Macmillan, Toronto, 1931

Thompson, S., *Reminiscences of a Canadian Pioneer,* Reprint, McClelland & Stewart, Toronto, 1968

Trigge, A., *A History of the Canadian Bank of Commerce,* Vol. III, Bank of Commerce, Toronto, 1934

Tupper, Sir Charles, *Recollections of Sixty Years,* Cassel, London, 1914

Underhill, F., *In Search of Canadian Liberalism,* Macmillan, Toronto, 1960

Van Alstyne, R. W., *The Rising American Empire,* Quadrangle, Books, Chicago, 1965

Vaughn, W., *Sir William Van Horne,* Oxford University Press, Toronto, 1926

Viner, J., *Canada's Balance of International Indebtedness 1900-1913,* Harvard University Press, Cambridge, 1924

Viner, J., *Studies in the Theory of International Trade,* Harper, New York, 1930

Wade, M., *The French Canadians,* Revised edn., 2 Vols., Macmillan, Toronto, 1968

Walker, Sir. B. E., *A History of Banking in Canada,* Journal of Commerce, Toronto, 1909

Watkin, Sir E. W., *Canada and the States, Recollections 1851 to 1886,* Ward Lock & Co., London, 1887

Watkins, M. H. *et al., Foreign Ownership and the Structure of Canadian Industry,* Queen's Printer, Ottawa, 1968

Wileman, J. P., *The Brazilian Handbook 1907,* Rio de Janeiro, 1908

Wilkins, M., *The Emergence of Multinational Enterprise,* Harvard University Press, Cambridge, Mass, 1970

Williams, W. A., *The Contours of American History,* Quadrangle Books, Chicago, 1961

Williams, W. A., *The Roots of the Modern American Empire,* Vintage Books, New York, 1969

Willison, J. S., *The Railway Question in Canada,* Toronto, 1897

Willson, B., *The Great Company,* Copp Clark, Toronto, 1899

Willson, B., *The Life of Lord Strathcona and Mount Royal,* Cassel, London, 1915

Wood, A., *The True History of Lord Beaverbrook,* Heinemann, London, 1965

Young, J., *Canadian Commercial Policy,* Queen's Printer, Ottawa, 1957

Articles

Abramowitz, M., "The Nature and Significance of Kuznets Cycles," in R. A. Gordon and L. R. Klein (eds.), *Readings In Business Cycles*

Barber, C. L., "Canadian Tariff Policy," *CJEPS,* XXXI, No. 4, Nov. 1955

Baster, A. S., "A Note on the Colonial Stock Acts and Dominion Borrowing," *Economic History*, II, Jan. 1933

Bertram, G., "Economic Growth in Canadian Industry 1870-1915," *CJEPS*, XXIX, No. 2, May 1963

Bliss, M. "Canadianizing American Business: The Roots of the Branch Plant," in I. Lumsden (ed.), *Close the 49th Parallel*

Breckenridge, R. M., "Free Banking In Canada," *JCBA*, I. No. 3, March 1894

Calvert, J., "The Ontario Development Corporation," *Canadian Forum*, June 1971

Chambers, E. J., "Late Nineteenth Century Business Cycles in Canada," *CJEPS*, XXX, No. 3, August 1964

Clergue, F. H., "Address by Francis Clergue at a Banquet Given in His Honour By the Citizens of Sault Ste. Marie, on Feb. 19, 1901" (pamph., n.p., n.d.)

Currie, A. W., "The First Dominion Companies Act," *CJEPS*, XXVIII, No. 3, Aug. 1964

Davis. L. E., "Capital Immobilities and Finance Capital", *Explorations in Entrepreneurial History*, 2nd Series, Vol. 1, Fall, 1963

Dougall, H. E., "Some Comparisons of Canadian and American Railway Finance," in H. A. Innis (ed.) *Essays In Transportation*

Eastman, H. C. and Stykolt, S., "A Model for the Study of Protected Oligopolies," *Economic Journal*, LXX, No. 307, March 1960

Eckhardt, H. M. P., "Causes of Bank Failures," *JCBA*, XVII, No. 1, Oct. 1909

Eckhardt, H. M. P., "A Study of Bank Failures," *JCBA*, XVII, No. 3, April 1910

Eckhardt, H. M. P., "The Growth of our Foreign Investments," *JCBA*, VIII, No. 4, July 1901

Eckhardt, H. M. P., "Americanizing Influences," *JCBA*, XVII, No. 4, July 1910

Eckhardt, H. M. P., "Modes of Carrying Cash Reserves," *JCBA*, XVI, No. 2, Jan. 1909

Eckhardt, H. M. P., "The Immediately Available Reserve," *JCBA*, XX, No. 4, July 1913

Eckhardt, H. M. P., "Manufacturers and Bank Mergers," *IC*, Sept. 1912

Eckhardt, H. M. P., "The Use by the Manufacturer of His Own Capital and of Bank Loans," *IC*, Sept. 1913

Eckhardt, H. M. P., "Financing the Promotion of a New Industrial Company in Canada," *IC*, Aug. 1913

Eckhardt, H. M. P., "How the New Bank Act Deals with Manufacturers' Pledges of Raw Materials," *IC,* Oct. 1913

Fysche, T., "The Growth of Corporations," *JCBA,* II, No. 2, Dec. 1894

Galbraith, J. S., "The Land Policies of the Hudson's Bay Company 1870-1913," *CHR,* XXXII, No. 1, 1951

Galt, A. T., "Canada 1849 to 1859," in H. J. Morgan (ed.), *The Relations of the Industry of Canada to the Mother Country*

Galt, A. T., "Report to the Duke of Newcastle, 25 Oct. 1859," in H. J. Morgan (ed.), *op. cit.*

Galt, A. T., "Speech at the Chamber of Commerce, Manchester," in H. J. Morgan (ed.), *op. cit.*

Greening, W. E., "The Canadian Banks and the Financial Crisis of 1907," *Canadian Banker,* Vol. 72, No. 1, Spring 1965

Hague, G., "The Late Mr. E. H. King," *JCBA* IV, No. 1, Oct. 1896

Heaton, H. "Criteria of Periodization in Economic History," *Journal of Economic History,* XV, No. 3, 1955

Hedley, J., "Canada and Her Commerce," in J. Hedley (ed.), *Canada and Her Commerce*

Hymer, S., "Direct Foreign Investment and the National Economic Interest," in P. Russell (ed.), *Nationalism In Canada*

Jackson, G. E., "The Emigration of Canadians to the United States," *The Annals,* CVII, May 1923

Kondratieff, N., "Long Waves in Economic Life," in G. Harberler (ed.), *Readings In Business Cycle Theory*

Land, B., "How Canada's Money Market Keeps Idle Cash at Work," *Canadian Business,* Feb. 1958

Lehfeldt, R. A., "The Rate of Interest on British and Foreign Investments," *Journal of the Royal Statistical Society,* LXXVI, Jan. 1913

Lipsey, R. G. & K. Lancaster, "The General Theory of Second Best," *Review of Economic Studies,* XXIV (1), No. 63, 1956-1957

Lowe, P., "All Western Dollars," *Papers Read Before the Historical and Scientific Society of Manitoba,* Series 1944-1945, Winnipeg, 1945

Masters, D. C., "Toronto Versus Montreal, The struggle for Financial Hegemony," 1860-1875, *CHR,* XXII, No. 2, June 1941

McLeod, H. C., "The Necessity for External Examination," Fifth edn., 1909, reprinted in Bank of Nova Scotia Annual Report, 1909

Meier, G. M. "Economic Development and the Transfer Mechanism, Canada 1895-1913", CJEPS, XIX, No. 1, Feb. 1953

Mikesell, R., "Decisive Factors in the Flow of American Direct Investment to Europe," *Economia Internaziole,* Vol. 20, 1967

Morris, M., "The Land Mortgage Companies, Government Savings Banks and Private Banks of Canada," *JCBA* VIII, NO. 3, April 1896

Payne, A. M., "Life of Sir Samuel Cunard," *Nova Scotia Historical Society Collection,* Vol. 19, 1918

Perry, J. H., "Origins of the Canadian Bankers' Association," *The Canadian Banker,* Vol. 74, No. 1, Spring, 1967

Porritt, E. C., "Iron and Steel Bounties in Canada," *Political Science Quarterly,* Vol. 22, No. 2 June, 1907

Radosh, R., "American Manufacturers, Canadian Reciprocity, and the Origins of the Branch Plant System," *CAAS Bulletin,* Vol. III, No. 1, 1967

Reid, R. L., "The First Bank in Western Canada," *CHR* VII, No. 4, Dec. 1926

Robinson, J., "The New Mercantilism," Cambridge University Press, London, 1966

Ryan, Claude, "Alphonse Desjardins: Une Méthode et une Pensée Très Actuelle," *Le Devoir,* 13 Mars, 1975

Schumpeter, J. A. "The Analysis of Economic Change," in G. Harberler (ed.), *Readings in Business Cycle Theory*

Shortt, A., "The Early History of Canadian Banking," *JCBA,* III, No. 2, Jan. 1896

Shortt, A., "The Passing of the Upper Canada and Commercial Banks," *JCBA,* XII, No. 3, April 1907

Shortt, A., "Railroad Construction and National Prosperity, An Historic Parallel," Royal Society of Canada *Proceedings and Transactions,* Third Series, Vol. VIII, 1914

Sifton, Sir Clifford, "Reciprocity," *The Annals,* XLV, Jan. 1913

Smith, K. C. and Horne, G. F., "An Index Number of Securities, 1867-1914," *Royal Economic Society Memoranda,* No. 47, June 1934

Sutton, W., "National Decadence or Imperial Prosperity," *JCBA,* XVIII, No. 3, April 1911

Sutton, W., "Canada-At the Parting of the Ways," *JCBA,* XVIII, No. 1, Oct. 1910

Tate, M., "Canada's Interest in the Trade and Sovereignty of Hawaii," *CHR,* XLIV, No. 1, March 1963

Vernon, R., "International Investment and International Trade in the Product Cycle," *Quarterly Journal of Economics,* Vo. 80, 1966

Viner, J., "Political Aspects of International Finance," *Journal of Business,* I, No. 2, April 1928, No. 3, July 1928

Wadsworth, H.W., "The Dominion Commercial Travellers' Association," in J. Hedley (ed.), *Canada and Her Commerce*
Walker, B. E., "Banking in Canada," *JCBA* I, No. 1, Oct. 1893
Walker, B. E., " A Comparison of Banking Systems," *JCBA,* XII, No. 4, April 1905
Watkins, M. H., "A New National Policy," in T. Lloyd and J. T. McLeod (eds.), *Agenda,* 1970
Watkins, M. H., "A Staple Theory of Economic Growth," *CJEPS,* XXIX, N. 2, May 1963

Collections and Editions

Beck, J.M. (ed.), *Joseph Howe: Voice of Nova Scotia,* McClelland and Stewart, Toronto, 1964
Brown, A. G. and Morres, P. H. *Twentieth Century Impressions of Canada,* London, 1914
Gordon, R. A. and Klein, L. R. (eds.) *Readings In Business Cycles,* R. D. Irwin Homewood, 1965
Hall, A. R. (ed.), *The Export of Capital from Britain 1870 to 1914,* Methuen, London, 1968
Harberler, G. (ed.), *Readings in Business Cycle Theory,* Blakeston Co., Toronto, 1944
Hedley, J. (ed.), *Canada and Her Commerce,* Sabiston Co., Montreal, 1894
Innis, H. A. (ed.), *Essays in Transportation,* University of Toronto Press, Toronto, 1941
Innis, H. A. and Lower, A. R. M. (eds.), *Select Documents In Canadian Economic History,* University of Toronto Press, Toronto, 1933
Kindleberger, C. P. (ed.), *The International Corporation: A Symposium,* M.I.T. Press, Cambridge, 1970
Lloyd, T. and McLeod, J. T. (eds.), *Agenda 1970: Proposals For a Creative Politics,* University of Toronto Press, Toronto, 1968
Lumsden, I. (ed.), *Close The 49th Parallel,* University of Toronto Press, Toronto, 1969
Morgan, H. J. (ed.) *Canadian Men and Women of the Time,* (n.p.) Toronto, 1898
Morgan, H. J. (ed.), *Isaac Buchanan on the Relations of the Industry of Canada with the Mother Country and the United States,* John Lovell, Montreal, 1864
Norris, J. F. (ed.), *The Consolidated Bank: A Compilation,* Witness Publishing Co., Montreal, 1873
Pope, J. H. (ed.) *Correspondence of Sir John A. Macdonald,* Oxford University Press, Toronto, 1921

Roberts, C. G. D. & A. L. Tunnell (eds.) *Standard Dictionary of Canadian Biography,* 2 Vols., Toronto, 1934
Urquhart, M. C. and Buckley, K., (eds.), *Historical Statistics of Canada,* Macmillan, Toronto, 1965

Index

McInnis, D. I 50, 263, II 169
McIntyre, Duncan I 133, 220, 269;
    II 20, 21, 60, 89
McKinley, William II 82, 259
McLaren, James II 270
McLaughlin, Robert II 58, 147
McLeod, H. C. I 78, 118, 119, 144,
    243
Meaford, Ontario II 153
Meat packing industry II 131-132,
    166-167, 212
Mechanics Bank I 126, 127
Medicine Hat II 145
Megantic, Quebec II 141
Meighen, Frank II 10
Meighen, Robert II 10
Merchants' Bank of Canada I 79,
    80, 109, 168, 240, II 240
    in Winnipeg land bloom I 84
    in New York gold market I 89;
    II 242
    Western expansion I 86, 97
    relations with Commercial
    Bank of Manitoba I 148, 175
    John A. Macdonald's debts to I
    263
    failure of II 291
Merchant's Bank of Halifax (See
    Royal Bank)
Merchants' Bank of Prince
    Edward Island I 75, 99, 123
Merchants Cotton Company II 36
Mercier, Honoré I 240, 281; II 6, 8
Meredith, William I 141, 145, 146,
    201; II 5
Merritt, William Hamilton I 20,
    21.
Merritton, Ontario II 169, 170
Metropolitan Bank of Canada I
    126
Mexico, Canadian interests in II
    235, 254, 256, 261-264
Mexico City II 261, 263, 264
Mexico and Northwest Railway
    and Timber Company II 262,
    263
Mexican Light and Power II 261,
    262, 264, 265

Mexican Northern Power
    Company II 258, 262
Mexican Northwest Power
    Company II 263
Mexican Tramway and Electric
    Company II 262, 264, 265
Miall, Edward I 274-5
Miami, Manitoba II 131
Michigan Central Railway II 23,
    110
Midland Railway I 194, 272
Mildmay, Ontario I 173
Millbrook Banking Company I
    171
Millers' and Manufacturers' Fire
    Insurance Company I 190
Mining Stock Exchange I 214
Minneapolis I 108
Minneapolis and St. Paul Railway
    II 243
Minneapolis, Duluth, and Western
    Canada Land Company II 10
Miramachi, New Brunswick I 120
Mitchell Banking Company I 171
M. J. Sage and Company I 216
M. Lefebvre and Company I 136;
    II 122, 131
Moline Wagon Company II 50,
    171
Molson, J. H. I 132
Molson's Bank I 119, 126, 157,
    203, 240; II 250
Monarch Bank I 97
Moncton, New Brunswick I 46,
    162, 163, 164; II 114, 145, 146,
    153, 169
Moncton Sugar Refining
    Company I 46, 162, 179
Moncton Tramways, Electricity,
    and Gas Company II 98n
Mond Nickel II 90-2, 178
Monetary Times I 123, 130, 131,
    134, 138, 143, 232-233, 252; II
    71, 74, 147, 148, 154, 231, 241,
    259, 261
Montreal I 44, 45, 46, 50, 81, 98,
    102, 103, 118, 126, 127, 131,
    136, 140, 142, 210, 213, 215,

Errata

353

p. 5, line 7. There was never any evidence to implicate Meredith himself in the conspiracy that I am aware of.

p. 8, lines 25-28. George Stephen wanted the law repealed—probably because settlers could mortgage their government lands and divert the proceeds into the purchase of CPR land, if the $500 mortgage ceiling on government land were lifted. As a promoter of an insurance company making mortgage loans and as a promoter of the CPR selling lands, Stephen would thus be twice blessed. However, the ceiling was not in fact lifted. I am grateful to Michael Bliss for pointing out the original error.

p. 28, line 18ff. This should read " . . . no regulation of railway rates by an independent agency." Galt argued that recourse to Parliament, as before, was all that was necessary.

p. 40, lines 19-20. Gooderham and Worts were British, not American, immigrants.

p. 85, lines 22ff. "Mining" here referred to quartz mining of gold as distinct from working of placer deposits. The first placer deposits seem to have been worked in the Seigneurie of Rigaud—Vaudreuil in 1846. B.C. gold was collected from placers by Indians from the mid-1850's. And Nova Scotia's first *major* find was at Tangier River in 1858. Since Nova Scotia gold was almost all mined, it is likely the starting date should be adjusted back two years.

p. 108, lines 6-10. Nova Scotia does win the prize, but the date is wrong. The origins of Nova Scotia's system of corporate welfare can be traced back to its first bounty system—in 1751.

p. 191, line 13. A complex point stated too glibly. The 1874 Federal Act regulating standards covered alcoholic beverages with food regulation inserted as an "afterthought" (J. A. Corry, *The Growth of Government Activities in Canada*, pp. 21-3). Not until 1920 was adulteration defined to include "unreasonable" variation from standard qualities fixed by the Governor-in-Council.

p. 210, line 8. H. N. Whitney was actually out of Domco well before the 1911 elections. It was the coal mine interests, not Whitney himself, that seem to have been powerful in the election.

p. 218, line 4. For "balance of trade" read "balance of commodity trade." The outflow of service charges on previous borrowings was sufficient to keep the overall trade balance in deficit.

p. 223, lines 18-20. The Halifax Banking Company's links to the Colonial Bank were more likely just an agency system rather than a real partnership.

717202